Every Spy a Prince

Also by Yossi Melman and Dan Raviv

Behind the Uprising:
Israelis, Jordanians, and Palestinians

The Imperfect Spies

Also by Yossi Melman

The Master Terrorist:
The True Story Behind Abu Nidal

The CIA Report on the
Israeli Intelligence Community
(in Hebrew)

A Profile of a Terrorist Organization
(in Hebrew)

EVERY SPY A PRINCE

The Complete History of Israel's Intelligence Community

Dan Raviv *and*
Yossi Melman

A Marc Jaffe Book

HOUGHTON MIFFLIN COMPANY/BOSTON

Library of Congress Cataloging-in-Publication Data

Raviv, Daniel.
Every spy a prince : the complete history of Israel's intelligence community / Dan Raviv and Yossi Melman.
p. cm.
"A Marc Jaffe book."
Includes bibliographical references.
ISBN 0-395-47102-8
1. Intelligence service—Israel—History. 2. Secret service—Israel—History. I. Melman, Yossi. II. Title.
UB251.I78R38 1990 90-4353
327.1'25694—dc20 CIP

Printed in the United States of America

HAD 10 9 8 7 6 5 4 3

TO DORI, JONATHAN, AND EMMA

TO BILLIE AND YOTAM

CONTENTS

ACKNOWLEDGMENTS

We are deeply grateful to our many informants and advisers, almost all of whom demanded anonymity. We interviewed dozens of intelligence people, some still active and others discovering there can be a life after an undercover career. In addition to Israeli intelligence veterans, including heads of the various agencies, we met former directors of the CIA and other old hands at the clandestine game to see how Israel's spies are really perceived — not by the newspapers, but by professionals worldwide.

Our research took us to many countries where Israeli intelligence has made an impact. In Israel itself, we were handicapped by the refusal of the secret agencies to share their documents with the public and by the fact that they have no official spokesmen to field questions. In addition, Israel's military censor insisted on brief deletions from material originating in that country.

We thank our editor, Marc Jaffe; his assistant, Erika Mansourian; our manuscript editor, Natalie Bowen; our agent, Carol Mann; the library staffs at *Ha'aretz* and *Ma'ariv* newspapers; Rob Forman, Howard Arenstein, and others at CBS News who contributed understanding and encouragement; curator Bill Kovach and his staff at Harvard's Nieman Foundation for affording us the opportunity to add final touches; and above all our parents and families for their support. All errors and omissions, however, are ours alone.

The Lord spoke to Moses, saying, "Send men that they may spy out the land of Canaan, which I give to the children of Israel; of every tribe of their fathers shall you send a man, every one a prince among them."

NUMBERS 13:1–2

KEY FIGURES IN THE ISRAELI INTELLIGENCE COMMUNITY

The Directors of the Mossad

1951–1952 Reuven Shiloah
1952–1963 Isser Harel
1963–1968 Meir Amit
1968–1974 Zvi Zamir
1974–1982 Yitzhak Hofi
1982–1989 Nahum Admoni
1989– (disclosure forbidden by Israeli law)

The Commanders of Military Intelligence (Aman)

1948–1949 Isser Beeri
1949–1950 Chaim Herzog
1950–1955 Binyamin Gibli
1955–1959 Yehoshafat Harkabi
1959–1962 Chaim Herzog
1962–1963 Meir Amit
1964–1972 Aharon Yariv
1972–1974 Eli Zeira
1974–1978 Shlomo Gazit
1979–1983 Yehoshua Saguy
1983–1985 Ehud Barak
1986– Amnon Shahak

The Directors of Shin Bet

1948–1952 Isser Harel
1952–1953 Izzy Dorot
1953–1963 Amos Manor
1964–1974 Yosef Harmelin
1974–1981 Avraham Ahituv
1981–1986 Avraham Shalom

The Directors of Shin Bet (continued)

1986–1988 Yosef Harmelin
1988– (disclosure forbidden by Israeli law)

The Directors of Lakam

1957–1981 Binyamin Blumberg
1981–1986* Rafi Eitan

The Heads of the Liaison Bureau (for Jewish Immigration)

1953–1970 Shaul Avigur
1970–1981 Nehemiah Levanon
1981–1986 Yehuda Lapidot
1986– David Bartov

The Prime Minister's Advisers on Counterterrorism

1972–1973 Aharon Yariv
1974–1977 Rehavam Ze'evi
1977–1978 Amichai Paglin
1978–1984 Rafi Eitan
1985–1988 Amiram Nir
1988– Yigal Carmon

The Political Department of the Foreign Ministry

1948–1951* Boris Guriel

*Agency disbanded

STRUCTURE OF THE ISRAELI INTELLIGENCE COMMUNITY

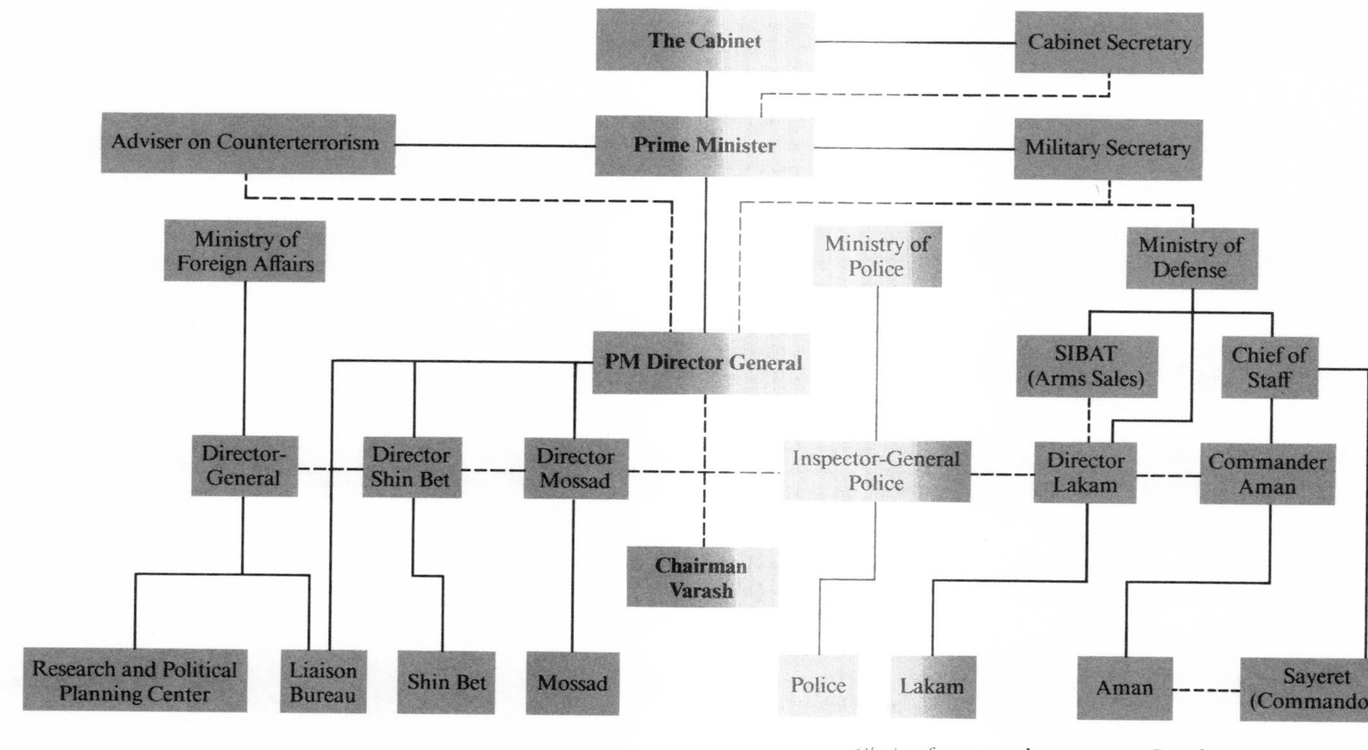

PROLOGUE

THE STATE OF ISRAEL employs more than ten thousand citizens in its intelligence community, and obviously not every one can be a prince among men or a princess among women. But they can try, and that is what the state's founding fathers wanted.

Prime Minister David Ben-Gurion and his colleagues, who declared Israel's independence in May 1948, knew from the start that they needed excellent intelligence to aid their fight for survival. Their country was among the tiniest on earth but would have to develop the finest secret services in the world.

The latter-day leader Ben-Gurion was creating a modern Jewish state, thirty-two centuries after Moses heeded God's command and picked twelve outstanding Israelites to infiltrate the Promised Land. Similarly searching for the "princes" of the Jewish people, the Ben-Gurion team made stringent demands of its first secret agents: that they be motivated by patriotism, not personal gain; that they represent the best aspects of Israeli society, not the worst; that they obey the unique tenet of self-restraint, which Israel's army calls "purity of arms," rather than be triggermen who would glory in bloodshed; and that they remember they are defending a democracy, not a monolithic state which ruthlessly crushes its enemies both at home and abroad.

"The human factor is the biggest and most crucial for our society and our security services," said Meir Amit,[1] a former head of the Mossad foreign espionage agency.

In asking whether Israel's spies have met the test, we may well be similarly concerned about the intelligence communities of the United States and other democratic countries. Hidden from our sight are the spies and counterspies in our midst. The Secret Service that protects the President is tiny, compared with the secret services that surround us all. There certainly are foreign espionage agents in America, whose activities are considered inevitable and even acceptable so long as they do not go too far. American security agencies are working in the United States and abroad to detect Soviet espionage rings, to combat international terrorism, and in more general terms to promote America's national interests.

When one's employer is a democratic state, the game is supposed to have some rules. The Central Intelligence Agency and its British, French, West German, and Italian counterparts have to protect their own national security against enemies who do not share their values, but they are not supposed to violate the human and civil rights they defend.

There does seem to be an inherent contradiction between democracy and clandestine defense. The United States and most of its major allies have demonstrated that an open society dedicated to freedom and civil liberties can be protected from its enemies by a secret subculture — an intelligence community. But the cohabitation has been far from smooth.

When abuses of civil rights by the CIA, the FBI, the Watergate burglars, and other clandestine civil servants were discovered in America, the courts, Congress, and the media were strong enough to reassert control. Covert operations conducted for the good of the mightiest democracy on earth continue to be controversial, and they have been scaled down in the face of increased Congressional oversight and public distrust of the CIA.

The American and British intelligence communities have even had trouble attracting new recruits. Hardly anyone wants to work for a government agency that is barely understood but widely detested. It is difficult, in the United States and other nations, to overcome the damage done by past scandals. In any event, people accustomed to working in the shadows of secrecy rarely display a flair for public relations.

Israel is unique in many ways, one of which has been the overwhelming support by its citizens for the secret services about which they know so little. Despite a constant state of war Israelis have usually slept well at night, confident that they are being defended both by an army and by clandestine agencies who are considered second to none.

A secret CIA study, discovered and released by the Islamic militants who seized the U.S. embassy in Teheran in 1979, concluded: "Israel's intelligence and security services are among the best in the world. Their expert personnel and sophisticated techniques have made them highly effective, and they have demonstrated outstanding ability to organize, screen and evaluate information obtained from recruited agents, Jewish communities, and other sources throughout the world."

The pinnacle of success came in 1967, with Israel's stunning triumph in the Six-Day War as the product of top-notch intelligence. The failure to foresee the Yom Kippur War in 1973, with Egypt and Syria catching the Israelis by surprise on Judaism's holiest day, was seen as an aberration. The secret services regained their almost mythic reputation in 1976, when they planned the astounding rescue by army commandos of hijacked passengers from Entebbe airport in distant Uganda.

The 1980s, however, brought major changes in both opinions and facts. Israel had new leaders, who issued bold orders to the secret services but without tightening the reins of bureaucratic control. Personal rivalries and ambitions clashed within the intelligence community and among many who left the clandestine brotherhood to seek their own fortunes.

It was a decade of challenges for Israel, and the intelligence agencies were called upon to help the state survive and thrive. The 1982 invasion of Lebanon managed to force the departure of Palestinian guerrillas but then went sour. Security men who were almost legendary in their ability to combat terrorism were caught killing hijackers during interrogation and then lying about it. The United States and Iran were drawn into arms-for-hostages trading that seemingly would help Israel, but the Mossad was locked out and simply watched the initiative go down in flames. A technician in the ultrasecret nuclear facility at Dimona defied security by photographing the compound and selling his story to the foreign press, leaving the embarrassed intelligence community to take the risk of kidnapping him from Europe.

By the end of the 1980s, a recently retired Israeli operative confessed, "We have caught the CIA disease. No one seems to love the Mossad and Shin Bet anymore, and we always felt more secure and effective with the whole nation behind us." Unlike the CIA, Israel's secret agencies are treated as so shadowy and unapproachable that they do not even have any official spokesmen to wage a public relations counterattack.

Politicians and the press, following the pattern set in the United States after the Watergate scandal more than a decade earlier, clamored in Israel for greater disclosure and discussion of the secret services' activities. Many in the government and the so-called defense establishment were extremely reluctant to reveal anything, but others said that answering at least some questions could help restore the public's confidence in its hidden defenders.

Only recently has a specially assigned Mossad team prepared a multivolume official history of the agency. But it is classified top secret and has been stored in the Mossad archives, to be leafed through by recruits as part of their two-year training course, and by intelligence veterans when they gather for morale boosting. It is never to be published.

Unveiling the full history of the Israeli intelligence community must, therefore, be an unofficial mission by civilians probing from the outside. The process touches many raw nerves, reopens painful wounds, and highlights the negative as well as the positive of the past forty-two years. The complete story, with many episodes revealed for the first time and others never before told in detail, proves one fact beyond doubt: Israel's spies are only human.

It might seem a simple assertion, but the extreme publicity given to Israel's successful and supposedly secret exploits gave rise to a myth of invincibility and omniscience. The intelligence community, primarily made up of the Mossad for foreign operations, Shin Bet for domestic security, and Aman as the army's intelligence agency, made mistakes but also made sure that the public never found out about them. There have even been other agencies whose existence or precise names have been kept under wraps.

Accepting that Israeli secret agents are human beings, while learning about their personal backgrounds and careers, we may still ask the black-or-white question of whether they are heroes or villains. Forced into a choice between those two blunt labels, we would have to say that most have been heroes.

That is not the whole truth, however. Ignoring the exceptions — the immoral, the ineffectual — would not help anyone understand how such men and women were mistakenly recruited or how they were handled once discovered. When the search for the courageous and capable instead produced the corrupt and conceited, Israel's intelligence chiefs were deeply disappointed.

Harsh punishment was imposed on secret agents who violated the high standards set by the founders of the clandestine community. The standards were established from the very beginning in 1948, when the first head of military intelligence was found within months to be unsuitable for the job. He was removed by Ben-Gurion, who emphatically ruled out the torture and extrajudicial killings of which the man had been accused.

When secret agents are operating in the field, often outside Israel's borders, it is difficult to control and monitor everything they do. It is nearly impossible for the "king" and his "court" back home to ensure that all the spies are behaving as princes. Perhaps worse, even after some misdeed is committed there has repeatedly been trouble finding who was responsible. "Who gave the order?" and "Not I" have been recurrent refrains throughout the history of Israeli intelligence.

No one wanted to admit responsibility for the failure of an espionage network in Iraq in 1951. Anonymous and bitter finger-pointing followed the collapse in 1954 of a sabotage campaign in Egypt which became known in the censorship-muzzled Israeli press simply as Esek Bish, Hebrew for "rotten business." The outside world came to know the political fallout in Israel as "the Lavon Affair," because Pinhas Lavon lost his job as defense minister after the Israeli-trained saboteurs were caught. But Lavon never accepted the blame, and the charges and countercharges continue to blight the record of the Israeli intelligence community.

A murder in 1965 was more successfully covered up, but again none of the princes or other members of the royal family of Israeli defense wanted to take responsibility for the Mossad's involvement in the killing of a famous Moroccan dissident. Morocco's own security service committed the deed in France, but Israel's spies helped. No one cares to talk about it now, but it left bitterness among intelligence chiefs and senior politicians.

Questions of responsibility again came to the fore when the intelligence community failed to predict the Yom Kippur War in 1973. Stunned by the Arabs and forced to retreat, the Israel Defense Forces nearly lost their first war. After the armies stopped fighting, the battle continued in committee rooms in Jerusalem. An investigatory commission protected Prime Minister Golda Meir and other politicians by primarily blaming Aman for inefficiency. For the Israeli public, however, it was not sufficient to be angry at an invisible intelligence community. Meir and her defense minister, Moshe Dayan, had to resign.

In the 1980s the crisis of responsibility became even more acute. Chains of command had supposedly been tightened, but successive scandals rocked the intelligence agencies. Instead of the public accountability generally expected in a democracy, there were redoubled efforts to leave questions of who was in charge blurry and unanswered.

Systematic perjury and brutality on the part of Shin Bet were exposed after Palestinian gunmen who had hijacked an Israeli bus were captured alive but died shortly thereafter. An attempted coverup was chronicled in detail by an inquiry commission, yet no one admitted giving the orders. The head of Shin Bet resigned, but the politicians got away scot-free.

An intelligence agency named Lakam, the existence of which had itself been a closely guarded secret, was exposed after Jonathan Pollard was arrested as an American spying for Israel within the U.S. intelligence community. Just after the exposure, Lakam was disbanded. The clandestine history of the agency's activities since the 1950s — primarily guarding Israel's hidden nuclear program — remained a mystery. Until now.

Again, no one was willing to take the blame for the decision to recruit an American Jew as a spy. Pollard envisioned himself as a prince among the people of Israel, but his actions spoiled the relationships of trust between U.S. Jewry and the Jewish state, and between the intelligence fraternities of the two nations.

When Irangate blew up in the Reagan administration's face in 1986, there was a concerted effort by U.S. officials to blame Israel. The secret services, it was alleged, manipulated both the Iranians and the Americans for Israel's own ends. The previously undisclosed truth is that the Mossad did not like the arms-for-hostages swap at all, but the agency chief who was supposedly responsible for all clandestine operations abroad was so low in bureaucratic prestige that he could not stop Israel's participation in the scandal.

By the end of the decade, an intelligence community that had been highly secretive and equally respected was becoming better known but widely disparaged. The Yom Kippur War had been the first public disgrace, but there were so many others in the 1980s that Israeli citizens lost much of their confidence in their secret services. Instead of assuming that they could sleep safely at night because the Mossad, Shin Bet, and Aman were protecting them, Israelis tossed and turned because of profound doubts about the intelligence community.

It was anything but reassuring to hear defense and intelligence leaders confirm that compared with "the good old days," the spies of today are not princes at all. "There is less professionalism in both the advisory and operational levels of the security services," said former chief of military intelligence General Shlomo Gazit. "There is less caution and less thought in the decision-making process. No doubt something has happened in the Israeli community."[2]

In parallel with the development of Israel, the history of its intelligence community can be broken into four major periods.

From 1948 to 1962, as in the rest of Israeli society, the pioneer spirit was dominant and the human factor was by far the most important in the fledgling intelligence community. After the early scandal that forced the departure of military intelligence chief Isser Beeri, domestic security chief Isser Harel emerged as the man at the center of the secret world for over a decade. He was the one and only Memuneh, a unique title meaning "the one in charge" of both Shin Bet and Mossad. It was Harel more than anyone else who determined the nature of the secret services. Under the guidance of his boss, Ben-Gurion, the Memuneh certainly wanted his spies to be princes.

Described as a kind of monk, Harel believed that the agency chief's job was to set an example. All Shin Bet and Mossad men and women were to be as patriotic and selfless as he. They were expected to share his enthusiasm about everything Israeli. In the country's early years, in any event, everything seemed new and exciting.

Perhaps the first spies of Israel did not know how to do certain things, lacking the experience and traditions of long-established secret services in other nations, but the Israelis found a way to do it. "If you are thrown out the door," they were told, "then reenter through a window." No one took no for an answer. Everything was possible, and the spy-princes would find a way.

Almost all of them came from the same background: European-born Jews who spoke many languages and prided themselves on their education and culture. They formed a British-style "old-boy network," turning social cohesion at home into an impressive unity of purpose in the field. They saw themselves as miles, even light-years, ahead of their Arab opponents. Some Israeli field operatives went too far, however, living out their espionage fantasies in expensive hotel suites and elegant restaurants. They clashed with Harel's puritanism and austerity, and the Memuneh invariably won.

Some of today's complaints about the intelligence community focus on alleged corruption or at best unnecessary expenditures, summarized simply as waste. The desire to accomplish the maximum at a minimum cost has survived from Harel's day.

Another Harel characteristic, although with less longevity, was his absolute commitment to the Mossad and Shin Bet agents in the field. The Memuneh tried to make them all feel that they were Israel's best and brightest, and that the intelligence community and society as a whole stood behind them in every way. If some were captured, Israel tried to plot raids to rescue them from foreign captivity. Alternatively, Arab prisoners would be taken so as to offer an exchange. International dignitaries ranging from the Pope to the President of the United States were approached for help. As in all matters, however, there were exceptions — including Israeli spies captured in Egypt who felt abandoned for years.

There was a period of transition from 1963 to 1967 in which Meir Amit dominated the secret services as director of Aman military intelligence and later of the Mossad. He introduced more professional methods of recruitment and training, shifting slightly away from what analysts call *humint* methods — "human intelligence." Computers and other technological aids were brought in, although Amit has always stressed the need for talented people as well.

Intelligence, Amit says, "is the battle of minds and brains, and the role of the gadgets and improvements is to assist the human being in his conceptual challenge." Israel uses "the integration of man and machine, and in that integration the human factor is the decisive one — even more so in intelligence."[3]

Amit wished to eliminate reliance on the "old boys" who fought together in the Haganah and other prestate underground movements. Rather than hiring people on instinct, as Harel had done, the new Mossad chief recruited them as American big business might do. He used more systematic methods to look for people, usually in élite military units, who displayed "aggressiveness, cunning, initiative, eagerness for engagement with the enemy, and determination."

Seeking to run Israel's foreign intelligence arm more like a major corporation, Amit moved the Mossad away from the defense ministry compound in Tel Aviv into new offices. They were too plush for the old-timers, and the first accusations of waste and even corruption emerged.

The third period, from 1967 to 1977, began with the Six-Day War and the huge changes caused by the lightning victory in many aspects of Israeli society. The spy-princes thought they were all invincible. Amit was the Mossad chief until 1969, and he admits: "After the war we succumbed to the disease of arrogance, of 'We know better, we are the best, far above the others.' It caused a loss of values and contempt for democracy."

The capture of the Sinai, the West Bank, the Golan Heights, and the Gaza Strip added to the intelligence community's burden. Instead of protecting democracy and domestic tranquillity within the borders of Israel, Shin Bet suddenly found itself defending the state from potential enemies in the occupied territories. Shin Bet officers were in daily contact with Arabs who had no democratic rights in Israel. More than ever, part of the intelligence community had to behave as a secret police. The one-time princes were now not even knights. They were more like feudal landlords in the "Shin Bet country" of the West Bank and Gaza.

At the same time, the continuing responsibility to monitor the neighboring Arab countries for any sign of a military threat was somewhat neglected. Brigadier General Yoel Ben-Porat, who was commander of the electronic eavesdropping units of Aman, recalls: "There was a general acceptance of the inherent inferiority of the Arabs. A single Israeli tank platoon [believed it] could hold back a battalion, three times as large. Of course it was nonsense. Aman was ignorant regarding the Arabs, their histories, culture, religion, and literature. Aman people did not speak Arabic, and they were contemptuous of the need to learn the language. If you want to be an intelligence analyst, however, you need to touch and understand things in their own language."[4]

Arrogance got its comeuppance in the surprise attack by Egypt and Syria on Yom Kippur in 1973. The intelligence community was torn apart with dissenting views of who was responsible for the failure in foresight, and there was a tremendous loss of faith on the part of the Israeli public. Once treated as princes by the defense and political establishment, Israel's spies became mere peasants.

The fourth period of development began in 1977 with the election of Menachem Begin, the first non–Labor party prime minister of Israel. He was fascinated by the intelligence community's cloak and dagger operations, and he rejuvenated the secret agencies by urging them to come up with exciting missions that could help rewrite history in Israel's favor.

Begin's appetite for action deteriorated, notably after the disgraced invasion of Lebanon in 1982, into a general era of adventurism. Analyses prepared by the Mossad and Aman were ignored by the prime minister and other top politicians. Agents were appreciated more for their brute force than for their brains.

Some of the spies who thought they could be princes by acting patriotically and courageously reached the conclusion that in modern times they would have to buy their own principalities. The quest for personal riches took the form of a rush into private business. A host of former intelligence operatives transformed themselves into self-employed security advisers and arms merchants willing to engage in commerce with the highest bidder. Around the world, they were giving Israel a bad name.

Almost anything that Israeli privateers did on their own was blamed on their government, and often more particularly on the Mossad. When reports emerged in 1989 that Israeli mercenaries had helped drug barons in Colombia and Panama, all the authorities in Jerusalem could do to prove their lack of complicity was to order an investigation.

Israel's spies were not alone in being linked with shady businesses abroad. British army veterans were especially active as mercenaries in obscure corners of the globe. Commenting on allegations that the CIA helped drug smugglers who agreed to transport arms to anti-Communist militias in Latin America, Senator Alfonse D'Amato of New York said, "The intelligence agencies of this country, by God, should be involved in this battle [against drugs] instead of working with the scum of the earth, which they have been doing."[5]

Even if it meant cooperating with scum, some of the Israeli arms dealers and consultants were so-called espionage formers who often found themselves in fascinating and strategically vital places. They offered Israel tempting opportunities which even the official intelligence community could not match.

There was only loose control of Israeli "agents" scattered around the globe. Many were not on the official payroll and thus would not follow orders even if any were given. Even those who were definitely employed by intelligence agencies — such as Pollard in America and a Palestinian used as a double agent in Britain — were ignominiously dumped by Israel after they were captured. In a major break from earlier tradition, there was no effort to prevent their imprisonment in the two friendly countries.

At home as well, bizarre escapades involving Shin Bet and other agencies became public knowledge. The prestige of the intelligence community sank again, and the quality of its chiefs was questionable. One of the oddest events was the wild birthday party thrown for the director of Shin Bet by his socialite girlfriend, and the fact that except for naming names the Israeli press reported this most unaustere affair as if the princes of intelligence were fit subjects for the gossip columns.

A senior Shin Bet operative, speaking after the coverup and perjury scandal involving the bus hijackers killed during interrogation, used a pungent Hebrew saying: "We let the urine rise to our heads." In other words, they were arrogant. Having to engage in deception and double cross to fight Arab terrorism, the fallen princes of Shin Bet also began to play tricks with the Israeli legal system. They forgot their royal heritage, and they were caught.

Israel's intelligence community, just like those of other nations, is a mirror of the society it serves and from which it draws its power and inspiration. Every country has an intelligence structure shaped in its own image. In parallel with the covert work itself, a certain folklore and mythology develop that reflect the individual nation's temperament and the character of its culture.

The British, as in other areas of human activity, consider intelligence to be a game. The stress is on the contest, which is more a struggle of the human mind and less the use of guns and muscle. British intelligence prefers to be depicted as elegant, brainy, sophisticated, and brimming with schemes. It is based on fine human qualities: understanding and intellect. It may be characterized as British gentility, with an added air of romanticism and adventure.

The French play a sport in which governments say one thing, but intend something entirely different. Their secret services bridle at having to follow orders, and they try to undermine the decisions of their political masters. For French spies, nothing is final: a deal is not a deal, and there is always an official willing to look the other way.

The Americans have made intelligence into big business. Their stress is on quantity. United States espionage is a massive conglomerate based not on the virtuosity of the individual, but primarily on the efficiency and methodology of the entire system. The emphasis is on teamwork, supported by the best equipment and the latest technology. U.S. secret agents have a reputation for occasional cruelty, bombing civilians when deemed necessary, toppling regimes, and even plotting to liquidate heads of state. The American agent always presents the justification that he is acting for the free world and democracy, not simply in the selfish interests of the United States.

The Soviets, before the era of glasnost, regarded intelligence primarily as a tool for preserving their own regime and the survival of the Communist system. The individual within the organization was a small cog who was only a part of the collective. He was an obedient instrument of a rigid bureaucracy that was, by nature, hierarchical.

The influence of all four models can be found in the Israeli intelligence community. The experiences of Britain, France, the United States, and the Soviet Union have, wittingly or unwittingly, left their mark on Israel's secret services since 1948.

The Israeli community is a synthesis of various traditions that were learned, adopted, inherited, or copied from other countries that have had longer histories as states and more deeply ingrained intelligence customs.

The little-known founder of the community, Reuven Shiloah, was one of the British-style patricians who oversaw the birth of Israeli intelligence. He loved secret schemes, diplomatic intrigues, and broad strategic concepts. He romanticized the role of the spy, while also paying little attention to efficiency.

Isser Harel improved the efficiency, largely on Soviet-style lines. Russian characteristics colored Israeli intelligence, perhaps subconsciously, as an inherent part of the Bolshevik spirit brought by the Jewish state's founding fathers from Russia and Eastern Europe. The Russian input included socialism, pioneering, centralization, and the notion that the state's interests should be placed above those of the individual. Harel was influenced by these traits, although his own instincts and force of mind outweighed the Russian contribution.

Meir Amit also injected much of himself into an American-style management of intelligence. Great efforts were made to incorporate efficient use of both personnel and gadgets. The latest computers and technology were essential tools in Amit's self-shaped community.

Israel's top two political rivals in the late 1980s, Shimon Peres and Yitzhak Shamir, had much in common as they uncomfortably shared the reins of government and of the intelligence community. Both gained their early experience in French-style clandestine dealings. Peres practically commuted to Paris from 1956 to 1963 on hush-hush defense projects, and Shamir was there as a senior Mossad operative. They inherited the deceptive practices of the labyrinthine French secret service and introduced them in Israel. The now traditional wink of the eye, as a surrogate for formal permission and bureaucratic approvals, means that Israelis feel they can always get away with it — whatever "it" may be.[6]

Indeed, it is the Israeli character that dominates the history of the nation's intelligence community. Above all, regardless of rockets in orbit, electronic eavesdropping, or other space-age inventions added to its arsenal, Israel has always relied on *humint*. Its human intelligence resources — its people — have given it the decisive edge.

Humanity itself stands at the center of one of the principal tasks of Israeli intelligence, differentiating it from any other country's secret services: immigration. From the beginning, the community has engaged in "Jewish intelligence" — covert campaigns to protect Jews throughout the world and help them come to their biblical homeland in Israel. Zvi Zamir, Amit's successor as Mossad chief, recalls: "Of all the operations and activities that I was responsible for, the strongest and most exciting experiences were saving our Jewish brethren from countries of oppression and bringing them over here. It was a great humane deed."[7]

Who can imagine the CIA assigned to protect every American passport holder throughout the world? Or Britain's MI6 intelligence agency using its resources to bring Englishmen home to their island nation? The mission of the Mossad and other secret agencies to defend both the state and the entire "people of Israel" makes Israeli intelligence truly unique.

Large sums of money and manpower continue to be spent on being a "Jewish intelligence" community, as in Israel's early days, but time and personnel are increasingly devoted to the difficult fight against Arab terrorism. By the end of the 1980s, in addition, intelligence analysts and Shin Bet officers in the field were having trouble coping with the Palestinian uprising, which they had failed to predict. The challenges of the 1990s may alter slightly, but they will surely include bolstering morale and recruiting consistently excellent personnel.

It is difficult to gauge the community's success rate in preparing itself for the twenty-first century. Whenever an Israeli intelligence officer resigns or retires, he invariably claims that things are not as they used to be. The "formers" contend that everything that was wonderful is collapsing, and that little excellence survives.

The truth, often, is that the nostalgic complainers are having trouble with the mind-boggling adjustment to life as civilians. To reassure themselves that they were great in their heyday, they go public — usually for the first time in their lives — to criticize the way things are run now.

Mossad veteran David Kimche claims that the secret agency is in decline, insisting that the men and women working there now are not the same kind of operatives who were there when he joined in 1953. "The main difference was in the great motivation of our people," Kimche says. "It was a matter of mission and readiness to work day and night with unlimited dedication."[8]

Graveyards, however, are filled with people who believed they were irreplaceable. The "formers" who leave are constantly replaced by newcomers, who with proper control and inspiration can overcome the shattering scandals and failures of the 1980s.

With apparent envy, the secret CIA study of Israel's covert community noted in 1979 that most Israeli operatives "realize that their very national existence depends on an effective and smoothly functioning intelligence and security community." The CIA analyst added that senior Israeli intelligence officers "all have known each other personally for a long period of time. These relationships have been forged during troubled times seldom experienced by any other nation and now provide a framework for cooperative teamwork and coordination among the services."[9]

Compared with foreign rivals in the espionage game, Israel's spies have unique advantages as well as singular challenges. Shared backgrounds and experiences inspire both veterans and new recruits to work exceedingly hard, night and day, to build on the successes of the past and lead the intelligence community into the future.

When the princes — the dignitaries — chosen by Moses returned from their espionage mission in the Promised Land, they delivered contradictory reports and argued about what they had seen. The history that follows here is an effort to provide a balanced report on what has happened beneath the surface of war, peace, and politics in Israel — through the eyes and experiences of its modern spies.

They are not always right, and the elected leadership does not always listen to them. But most do strive to be princes and princesses among the people, conducting themselves in accordance with the goals and requirements set forth when Israel was born.

ONE

First Steps

HALF A DOZEN MEN dressed in khaki arrived — prudently, in separate cars and taxis — at 85 Ben Yehudah Street on a typical summer day in Tel Aviv: a hot and humid June 30, 1948. They disappeared, individually, into the whitewashed apartment building that was identical to the others in the ordinary residential neighborhood. Up one flight of stairs, however, behind a door with a sign saying CONSULTANCY SERVICES, was the headquarters of Shai.

Shai was the acronym for Sherut Yediot, Hebrew for "Information Service," the intelligence arm of the underground, pre-independence army of Palestine's Jews known as the Haganah, which means "Defense." The Haganah had been swallowed up by the nation's new army, the Israel Defense Forces, with the birth of the State of Israel on May 15. Six weeks later, this was to be the end of Shai and the beginning of the Israeli intelligence community.

It was a unique group, in a unique situation. In the midst of its first war, the newborn Israel had to find a way to satisfy its security and defense requirements while constructing durable democracy. The men who gathered in Tel Aviv on that last day of June were the founding fathers of the secret agencies that would become the Israeli intelligence community.

They had vast experience in covert operations: spying, smuggling, and gathering information by all means however ruthless — all in the name of the struggle for Zionist independence. But when it came to democracy, they had only been observers and never full participants. They had seen the British at work, as intelligence operatives combating the Jewish underground movements in Palestine and as politicians in the Mother of Democracy back in London. And they liked both.

Their problem, however, was how to copy what they had seen. There was no instant recipe for defending a nation at war without stamping on its democratic values, especially in the Middle East, where Western notions had no natural constituency.

Shai's forty-seven-year-old commander, Lieutenant Colonel Isser Beeri, chaired the last meeting of his highly effective force, his small eyes darting from man to man as they took their seats around an old wooden dining table. The underground veterans chatted as they skimmed the headlines of that day's newspapers — filled, as usual, with reports from the various fronts of Israel's War of Independence. The battle for the state's existence had begun on the day of its birth, when the armies of all the surrounding Arab countries had attacked.

Beeri cleared his throat for attention: "I have just come from a meeting with *ha-Zaken*" — "the Old Man" — a reference to David Ben-Gurion, the charismatic first prime minister of Israel, who was also directing the war as his own defense minister.

The Shai officers unconsciously sat a bit more erect, as an announcement from the white-haired oracle of Israel appeared forthcoming. At sixty-two, Ben-Gurion was the nation's elder statesman and guiding light, bar none.

Beeri kept his men waiting a moment longer. "Before we turn to the agenda which brought you here," he said, "here is the latest information on the fighting." He told his colleagues that while Israel's army had halted the far more numerous enemy, the Egyptians continued their buildup only twenty miles from Tel Aviv while the Syrians threatened kibbutz farms near the Sea of Galilee. The picture was far from bright in Jerusalem, besieged by the Arab Legion of Transjordan.

"However," Beeri added, "the prime minister is looking beyond the present situation." In the long run, Ben-Gurion had just finished telling the Shai chief, Israel's defense would have to include intelligence. Not good intelligence; great intelligence.

The immediate "agenda," as Beeri put it, was how to carry out the prime minister's instructions: to disband Shai and use its people as the basis for a newly organized community.[1]

It was not to be simply a new name for Shai. Instead, the Haganah's intelligence arm would digest itself and other prestate Zionist underground groups to produce four agencies in a community:

Military intelligence: Beeri announced that he would henceforth head the dominant agency in the new community, then called the Intelligence Department of the army. Known later as Aman, the acronym for *Agaf ha-Modi'in* or "Intelligence Wing," the unit was assigned widespread functions ranging from collecting information on Arab armies, through censoring Israeli newspapers, to maintaining security within Israel's army, and on to a bit of counterespionage. Beeri was recognizable by his dark eyebrows, his deeply cleft chin, and white hair — not nearly as exuberantly scattered as Ben-Gurion's ghostly fringe — flanking his bald scalp. Above all, literally, he was so tall that his nickname was Isser ha-Gadol, "Isser the Big." He was Isser Birentzweig when born in 1901, but like most of Israel's pioneers he chose a Hebrew family name as a break from Jewish roots of oppression and prejudice in Europe. In the Haganah and Shai since 1938, he had proved himself a fanatic on one subject: corruption. He could not stand it. To him, Israel could, should, and would be a perfect society.

A domestic secret service: Beeri told Shai veteran Isser Harel that he would be director of the agency now known as Shin Bet — the first two Hebrew initials of *Sherut ha-Bitachon ha-Klali,* or "General Security Service." Harel was just in the process of changing his name from Isser Halperin, his name when he was born in Russia in 1912. His specialty in Shai had been surveillance on right-wing Jews who rejected the authority of Ben-Gurion and the Haganah. Harel's new post suited him well, because in his view enemies within Israel's borders could be just as dangerous as those outside; he believed in a strict code of conduct for Israel's defenders. He resembled Beeri except for darker hair and complexion, bigger ears, and short stature, which led to his contrasting nickname: Isser ha-Katan, "Isser the Little."

A foreign intelligence service: Beeri informed Boris Guriel that as the new chief of the foreign ministry's Political Department, he would be part of the intelligence community with responsibility for collecting information outside Israel. Born in Latvia some fifty years earlier as Boris Gurvitch, Guriel already had plenty of experience with foreigners: as a British soldier in World War II, he was captured by the Germans, and after surviving that ordeal his job in Shai was to spy on the British mandate authorities in Palestine.

The Institute for Aliyah B: Beeri added that *ha-Mossad le-Aliyah Bet,* "the Institute for Aliyah B,"* would continue to do its secret

*Despite the similarity in name, this organization should not be confused with today's espionage agency, the Mossad.

work under the direction of Shaul Avigur, although its original mission of smuggling Jews into Palestine would be modified now that immigration into Israel was perfectly legal. When the agency was set up by the Haganah in 1937, its name distinguished it from the legal *aliyah,* or "immigration," by the lucky few Jews who received entry permits from the British.

Born in 1899 in Latvia as Saul Meyeroff, the Aliyah B chief had helped set up Shai in 1934 and in 1948 was busy as Ben-Gurion's deputy defense minister, buying weapons abroad for the War of Independence. He took the name Avigur — "Father of Gur" — in memory of his son, Gur Meyeroff, who died in Israel's first war.

Avigur did not attend the intelligence community's birth in Tel Aviv, and neither did the other founder of Shai, Reuven Shiloah. But as a special adviser to the prime minister on foreign affairs and broad strategy, it was Shiloah who conceived the reorganization. Shiloah's name never found its way onto the list of national heroes revered by Jewish students around the world — from biblical warriors to the soldiers of modern Israel. The men and women who work in the secret world of espionage rarely receive the recognition they deserve. Shiloah, however, should be remembered as Israel's "Mr. Intelligence."

A short man with blue-gray eyes behind professorial glasses, Shiloah focused his penetrating gaze on whomever he spoke with, making them feel as if under interrogation, and radiated a blend of secrecy and strength. He was insatiably curious, delving into the tiniest details of any subject that caught his attention.

Colleagues who talked to Shiloah invariably noticed the scar on his right cheek, a lasting reminder of the hot shrapnel that hit him when an Arab car bomb exploded in March 1947 near the Jerusalem offices of the Jewish Agency, which was the unofficial government for the Jews of Palestine before their independence.

Shiloah was good at asking questions but volunteered very little information. He was a lone wolf, keeping to himself and doing his best work behind the scenes. He was a methodical planner, an analytical thinker who delivered his recommendations free of emotional coloring or additives. His projects were always anchored in the firm ground of reality, but in his personal life he preferred the mystique of mystery.

"Shiloah used to give different and contradictory details in interviews and questionnaires that he filled in about his life, even where the facts were of no special significance, as if in order to surround himself with total secrecy," his biographer, Hagai Eshed, wrote.[2]

"When Reuven Shiloah took a taxicab," his friend Abba Eban, the extraordinary Israeli diplomat, reminisced, "he would never tell the driver his destination. Only a short and laconic order: 'Move.' And when the driver lost patience and asked, 'But where to?' Shiloah would direct his penetrating and distrustful gaze at the man, as if he were facing a dangerous spy."[3]

He was a born secret agent, although there was no indication of that in December 1909, when he entered the world with the name Reuven Zaslanski. The family lived in an Orthodox Jewish neighborhood of Jerusalem, then ruled by Turkey's Ottoman Empire. Reuven's father, Yitzhak Zaslanski, was a rabbi who gave his four children — two sons and two daughters — a craving for general knowledge, rather than stopping with the religious education that dominated community life.

Reuven's teachers noted that he was a serious and talented student. He rarely had much to say, but occasionally he displayed a sense of humor. He excelled in drama, displaying an acting skill which he would later employ in his intelligence work. He was also an independent thinker, and by high school he had abandoned kosher food and the rest of his family's religious lifestyle.

He could be charming when he cared to be, and while teaching Hebrew to new immigrants from America he began to court Betty Borden, a social worker from New York. They were married in 1936.

His other great love was the Haganah, where Ben-Gurion and the other commanders quickly took note of his talents. They pushed him up the ladder of leadership, and he repaid them with unswerving devotion.

As part of his enlistment in the ranks of top Zionist activists, he shortened his name from Zaslanski to Zaslani, and later he adopted his codename in the underground, "Shiloah." No name could have suited him better, because it is derived from the Hebrew word *shaliah,* "emissary," and he was repeatedly used as a high-level envoy on various secret missions for Ben-Gurion.

This was not yet real intelligence work, but Shiloah's hush-hush travels contained the first seeds that would later sprout into his view of intelligence: clear identification of enemies, the comprehensive collection of information about them, and the perpetual search for allies. Heavily outnumbered in the Middle East, the Jews had to know, quickly and with certainty, how to distinguish between friends and foes.

Shiloah's first foreign assignment came in August 1931, before he had reached his twenty-second birthday. The Jewish Agency planted him deep in the Arab world: in Baghdad, capital of Iraq. His cover was a job as a schoolteacher. He also presented himself as a part-time journalist, which made his trips around the country appear quite natural. In three years of supposed interviews for his newspaper articles, Shiloah assembled an impressive network of information sources.

The most memorable lessons Shiloah learned came while trekking in the mountains of Kurdistan in northern Iraq, where he forged contacts with the stateless, non-Arab mountain dwellers. He never forgot the Kurds, and as he developed his personal vision of the future Israeli espionage community he focused on the need for clandestine alliances with all the non-Arab minorities of the Middle East. The Jews, he felt, could have friends dotted around the periphery of the Arab world. Shiloah's "peripheral philosophy" became a lasting tenet of Israeli intelligence.

When he returned to Jerusalem in 1934, the Haganah assigned him to the job of forming a professional intelligence department to protect the long-range interests of the Jewish community in Palestine. Shiloah worked on the project with Meyeroff/Avigur, and in a short while they created Shai. Shiloah's on-the-record job was as a liaison officer between Ben-Gurion's Jewish Agency and Palestine's British governors.[4]

When World War II broke out in Europe, Shiloah seized the opportunity to deepen the relationship. Nazi Germany was the common enemy of both the Jews and the British. Shiloah helped set up a Jewish brigade within the British armed forces — a move that showed great vision, because the brigade later was part of the foundation of the Israeli army.

The war was frustrating for the Palestinian Jews, who could save only a few of their European brethren from the Nazi extermination camps, but it was also a learning experience for Shiloah and his men. Fighting in every available way, they picked up priceless skills of infiltration, reconnaissance, and outright masquerade when sending Jewish agents behind enemy lines: those of Aryan appearance into German-held territory in Europe, and those who looked and spoke like

Arabs into Syria and Lebanon, then ruled by pro-Nazi Vichy France.

Twenty-six Jewish paratroopers, recruited by Shiloah for British intelligence, were dropped behind Nazi lines in the Balkan countries. Some, such as Hannah Senesh and Enzio Sereni, were taken prisoner and executed as spies — entering a heavenly hall of fame as Jewish heroes. Others, such as Yeshayahu (Shaike) Trachtenberg-Dan, survived to perform further exploits in Israeli intelligence.

Shiloah was not only learning during the war. He was making powerful friends who later could help the Jews in their widening struggle against the Arabs for control of Palestine. He had the opportunity to forge strong relationships with British army intelligence officers in Jerusalem and Cairo. In similar and more significant fashion, World War II saw the beginning of contacts between the Zionist movement and American intelligence. Shiloah shared drinks and ideas with agents of the Office of Strategic Services, which in 1947 became the nucleus of the Central Intelligence Agency.[5]

These ties were strengthened after the war and were the platform for building vital links between the CIA and Israeli intelligence. Shiloah's wartime activities are clear evidence of his wisdom and his ability to take a long-term, strategic view of the importance of intelligence in modern times.

Lecturing his fellow founders of the Jewish state, who were teaching themselves how to run a modern country in their people's ancient homeland, Shiloah called intelligence a "most essential political tool."[6] In a world with few public declarations or statements of intent, it is Shiloah who defined the secret side of Israeli diplomacy and foreign policy:

Enemy number one of the Jewish community was the Arab people, and Arab society had to be penetrated by professional agents.

Israeli intelligence also had to think beyond Palestine, as a "Jewish-Zionist" protector of Jews throughout the world.

Clandestine work should be based on modern technology, keeping up with the latest in espionage methods by maintaining ties with friendly agencies in Europe and the United States.[7]

Although he did not attend the Ben Yehudah Street meeting, which disbanded Shai and introduced the new state's intelligence structure — considering it a purely technical session — Shiloah watched over the fledgling community like a guardian angel. And he found much to worry about in Isser Beeri.

On the afternoon of June 30, 1948, only a few hours after assuming the mantle of military intelligence director, Beeri carried his sense of duty to an extreme never repeated in Israel's history. He convened a kangaroo court, which hurriedly convicted an Israeli army officer of treason and immediately had him executed.

The accused man was Captain Meir Tubianski, who had served in the Haganah and after independence was in charge of setting up the first permanent Israel Defense Forces base in Jerusalem. He also held a civilian job with the Jerusalem Electricity Company, and Tubianski's Israeli colleagues were suspicious about his relationship with the company's British managers.

Early in the 1948 war, Jordanian artillery was scoring devastatingly accurate hits on Israeli bases. Shai's Jerusalem commander, Major Binyamin Gibli, had concluded that there must be a spy in the Israeli ranks, and it seemed logical that Tubianski could be feeding information to his electricity company bosses. They, in turn, would advise the British officers who led Transjordan's Arab Legion. Tubianski had, after all, been a major in Britain's Royal Engineers during World War II and was known to be an anglophile.

The circumstantial evidence was enough to sentence him to death. The judges who convened in a derelict house near the main Jerusalem–Tel Aviv road were Beeri, Gibli, and two other Shai officers.

No detailed notes of the brief trial were kept. All the judges except Beeri claimed later that they were merely interrogating the suspect, that they did not know they were imposing any sentence to be enforced. But that very afternoon, Tubianski was shot by an impromptu firing squad, watched by other soldiers who could hardly believe that Israelis were killing one of their own.

One witness recalls hearing the shouts of fellow infantrymen: "'A traitor! They are going to execute a traitor!' We sat down on the rocky hill and watched. A young man dressed in khaki was being moved along by a group of seven young soldiers. They were just kids, dressed sloppily. They sat him on a chair. They didn't even cover his face with a kerchief. Then they moved away a bit. We heard the cocking of the Czech rifles. It was all quiet. The sun shone. Only a short volley disturbed the peace. The man fell from his chair."[8]

A few hours later, Beeri informed the prime minister that after "a field court-martial" an army unit had shot a traitor. Ben-Gurion reopened the case, however, after receiving an emotional letter from Tubianski's widow. He commissioned an official inquiry, which cleared the captain's name and paid compensation to his family.

On that same final day of June 1948, Beeri's Shai men in Haifa, the northern port city with a mixed Jewish-Arab population, were torturing a friend of the Jewish mayor, who was considered too liberal. The Shai agents were pressing for evidence that Mayor Abba Khoushy had gone beyond being "soft" on Arabs — that Khoushy was a traitor to the Zionist cause.

Their victim was Jules (Yehudah) Amster, and Beeri had ordered his arrest on May 15, 1948, the very day that Israel's independence was declared. Amster was a taxi owner and, behind the scenes, he was Mayor Khoushy's right-hand man. Amster was charged with espionage, and his nightmare lasted for two and a half months in a secret detention camp. Amster's property was confiscated, and his investigators — first from Shai and then from Beeri's new military intelligence agency — tortured him mercilessly. They pointed pistols at him, as though about to blow his brains out. They beat him, dripped water on his head, pulled his teeth out, burned the soles of his feet, and injected drugs into his bloodstream. He was released, without any charges being pressed, on August 1.

The unwarranted arrest and the torture that followed it were kept secret for many years. Only in 1964 did the defense ministry agree to pay financial compensation to Amster. It was clear, all along, that Beeri had been trying to wring a confession out of Amster that would implicate his friend Khoushy. Beeri even fabricated evidence that the mayor had spied on the Haganah for the British. Ben-Gurion learned of the forgery, and Beeri was on his way out.[9]

The last straw was the killing of a wealthy Arab in the summer of 1948. The victim was Ali Qassem, a double agent employed by military intelligence to penetrate Palestinian Arab militias. Suspecting, due to several mishaps, that Qassem was in fact a triple agent — working, above all, for the Arabs — Beeri's agents shot him.

Ben-Gurion, in his dual capacity as minister of defense as well as prime minister, ordered a comprehensive investigation of the Qassem case. Beeri was suspended from the army in November, and then a military court convicted him of manslaughter. He was demoted to private, and then put on trial again for the illegal killing of Tubianski and the torture of Amster. Beeri denied the charges, but he was again found guilty and was sentenced to a symbolic one-day jail term.[10]

The man who was the first commander of military intelligence and the most active force in the new espionage community had lasted only six months in that position. Beeri was brought down by his own narrow-minded view of national security. He had no time for political gamesmanship — or even human rights, for that matter. The state had to be protected, and Beeri's world was as simple as that.

He learned bitterly that he was wrong. Behavior which the authorities of a totalitarian state might get away with would not be tolerated for long in Israel — a nation determined, from its beginning, to be a democracy. Beeri continued to claim, until his death of a heart attack in January 1958, that he was innocent. His son, Itai Beeri, insisted years later that Isser the Big had only been following Ben-Gurion's orders.[11]

Beeri's downfall was the sort of shock that could have crippled the intelligence community for many years. Ben-Gurion, however, wisely chose Colonel Chaim Herzog as the new military intelligence chief, and the fact that he had been Beeri's deputy provided vital continuity. In addition, Herzog's friendship with Reuven Shiloah — who avoided all the domestic misdeeds and concentrated on strategic planning and foreign affairs — helped heal the wounds that cut deep into the community's young flesh.

During Herzog's short tenure at military intelligence, he introduced computers. To be more precise, they were collections of bulky calculators rather than compact computing systems. But they worked quite well and helped Israel to break, with little effort, the simple codes used by the armies of Egypt, Syria, and other neighboring Arab states. Herzog and his team of young visionaries made Israel one of the first nations to bring the advantages of new and sophisticated technologies to the world of espionage. Herzog went on to a long and distinguished career, culminating in his installation as Israel's president in 1983.

Deciding to take a more active, hands-on role in administering the community, Shiloah established a coordinating body which he himself chaired. He called it *Va'adat Rashei ha-Sherutim,* "the Committee of Service Chiefs," and it first convened in April 1949 after Israel's victory over its Arab enemies. Shiloah and Herzog were joined by

Isser Harel for Shin Bet and Boris Guriel for the foreign ministry's Political Department. Israeli intelligence chiefs refer to the committee by its Hebrew acronym, Varash, although this has never been declared publicly.

Varash's agenda and the timing and location of its meetings are closely guarded secrets. Its purpose is clear, however: to make cooperation between the various security agencies easy and immediate, and to minimize the possibilities of error caused by misunderstandings or by wasted duplication of effort.

When the panel first met, Shiloah merely called it the Coordination Committee. Yehezkel Sahar, chief of the national police, was invited to take part, because while the police were not ordinarily privy to all state secrets they did constitute the country's largest security force.[12]

Shaul Avigur of Aliyah B, mainly concerned with gathering immigrants rather than intelligence, did not take part. The other service chiefs, newly grouped and meeting frequently as Varash, soon faced an unusual challenge remembered as "the revolt of the spies."

The revolt was led by Asher Ben-Natan, who was known as Arthur — his codename in the prestate Jewish underground. His good looks brought him the nickname "Arthur the Handsome," and he earned a reputation for success with women. More generally, in the small family of Israeli intelligence, everyone knew that Ben-Natan believed in enjoying life.

Born in Austria in 1921, he escaped the Nazis by moving to Israel in 1938. To help even more Jews find a way to their historic homeland, he joined Avigur's Aliyah B and served as intelligence coordinator in postwar Vienna while posing as a journalist with the name Arthur Pier. Later, he joined the foreign ministry as operations chief in Guriel's Political Department.

The department, despite its innocuous title, was the overseas arm of Israeli intelligence. Guriel's operatives were in charge of planting agents in Arab countries and forming ties with foreign security services. A rare written record of Ben-Natan's work in France, Italy, and other nations can be found in a report he sent to Prime Minister Ben-Gurion: "We are gathering information on Arab property and the economic relations between Europe and the Arabs."[13] This was in the early days of the state, when every small detail seemed new and exciting to Israel's first spies.

The Political Department's operatives had diplomatic cover in the Israeli consulates and embassies in London, Rome, Paris, Vienna, Bonn, and Geneva — potentially advantageous, because diplomats enjoyed immunity from prosecution, but less useful operationally, because the agent was openly connected with his government, and many host countries act under the assumption that foreign diplomats are spies.

Until 1950, Israel's agents in Europe reported to Ben-Natan's headquarters in Paris, which had remarkable autonomy from Guriel. Later, Ben-Natan was generally in Tel Aviv, receiving reports and issuing operational orders. Each branch in the various European capitals had its own network of agents — mostly non-Israelis who sold information. Some of the leads they provided helped operatives in Europe sabotage military shipments on their way to Arab countries.

There was also, however, some smuggling by the Israelis in their "off hours": not for personal gain, but to finance various clandestine activities after the foreign ministry refused to pay all the bills and expense accounts submitted by Ben-Natan's team.

The Political Department's greatest achievement was obtaining the order of battle — the war plans — of the Syrian army, from an agent planted in Damascus. Such information was considered vital to the Jewish state, still facing a strong threat from its neighbors.

In general, however, the material obtained by Ben-Natan and his men was not highly regarded by their political bosses. Perhaps it was because of Ben-Natan's style.

He and his senior operatives, including Gershon Peres — brother of the future prime minister — behaved as they imagined spies ought to behave. They dined at elegant restaurants in Paris and Geneva, drank at the most fashionable watering holes, and used the lobbies of Europe's finest hotels as meeting places. Their extravagance was diametrically opposed to the puritanical, socialist spirit then prevalent in Israel. This provoked much anger, especially on the part of Avigur and Shiloah — the two founders of Israeli intelligence.

Guriel was not bothered, however, and shrugged off charges that his men in Europe lined their own pockets with unauthorized, phony expenses. There were even rumors that Political Department personnel had laid their hands on secret Swiss bank accounts belonging to Jews who were gassed in the Holocaust.[14]

Beyond the complaints about style and finances, the rest of the intelligence community was upset about the work performance of the

Political Department. Its rivals — in Aman, Shin Bet, and Aliyah B — cursed Guriel's men as mere amateurs masquerading as professionals and rarely contributing to Israel's vital defense.

Shiloah, as chairman of the Varash committee, was under great pressure from Ben-Gurion and military chiefs to produce precise information on the capabilities of the Arab armies. There was a growing fear in 1950 that with the Korean War raging and the Cold War chilling relations between the United States and the Soviet Union, the Arab states might feel inspired by international tension to launch their own second round against Israel to reverse the defeat they suffered in 1948–49.

The Jewish state's leaders were less interested in Guriel and Ben-Natan's specialty: the Arabs' political plans, their economic projects, and what was happening in their leaders' bedrooms.

Binyamin Gibli, promoted to lieutenant colonel, was the Political Department's most bitter opponent. He was a young and enthusiastic military intelligence officer who served as deputy to Chaim Herzog and then replaced him as Aman director when Herzog moved to Washington as military attaché in April 1950.

A major mark against Gibli was the fact that he had been one of the judges who sentenced Meir Tubianski to death. Ben-Gurion appointed Gibli to the top post in military intelligence primarily to ensure the continuity still needed after Beeri's downfall. The prime minister was sending a dangerous signal, however: that he was willing to sacrifice ethical considerations upon the altar of efficiency.

In any event, unprecedented inefficiency was the result. Gibli decided to launch an all-out campaign against the Political Department, and he found an ally in Shin Bet chief Isser Harel. As ascetic as he was professional, Harel had complete disdain for the Political Department's lavish style and its low productivity.

In the disarray that followed, both Gibli and Harel sent their own operatives abroad. Guriel simply rolled up his sleeves for a fistfight, and his Political Department encroached on Shin Bet's territory by sending burglars to break into Soviet-bloc embassies in Tel Aviv. Harel was furious.[15]

Guriel's European operatives considered themselves members of an exclusive club as intelligence agents posted overseas, and they scorned the coarseness and lack of civility of "Gibli's military men and Harel's policemen." Ben-Natan sneered that the new arrivals could never blend into the cultured and refined society of Europe. Needless to say, the various Israeli spies were not working in concert.

The security services of France and Italy, which were especially friendly toward Israel, could not believe what was happening. They were confused by a huge number of conflicting requests from Israeli liaison officers. This was a classic case of a power struggle, and the intelligence community's foreign friends did not know how to react. They did know that Israel, surrounded by hostile nations, could not afford the luxury of infighting.

Ben-Gurion was outraged, and he ordered Reuven Shiloah to put an end to the chaos. "Mr. Intelligence" would be given the opportunity to bump some heads together and reorganize the community. Shiloah declared that the Political Department would be disbanded and forced Boris Guriel to resign. Guriel's European network was told to expect new orders from new commanders.

Ben-Natan, however, refused to give in. A few days after Shiloah's coup, he assembled his senior operatives at Lake Geneva on March 2, 1951. "Arthur the Handsome" and his equally comely collection of wine connoisseurs and gourmets were in a huff, and in a final burst of pique they collectively submitted their resignations. They would not work for any of the other intelligence agencies. They would just pack up their toys and go home.

Ben-Natan enrolled in an international relations course in Switzerland, and his men refused to hand over their records to Shiloah. They would not give him guidance on ongoing operations. In some European stations, they even burned secret files. Israel's European spies simply declared a strike.[16]

The revolt never stood a chance. Shiloah, armed with the prime minister's full backing, carried out a thorough reorganization of the intelligence community, right over the heads of the men who refused to play the game. All responsibility for special assignments was transferred to Aman, the military intelligence agency, under Gibli. He quickly established a top secret "Unit 131" to plant agents in Arab countries.

On the ruins of the Political Department arose ha-Mossad le-Modiin ule-Tafkidim Meyuhadim, "the Institute for Intelligence and Special Tasks" — better known as the Mossad. For a short while, the new agency had other names: first "the Central Institute for Coordination," then "the Central Institute for Intelligence and Security." However, the day of Shiloah's strike-breaking reorganization, April 1, 1951, is considered the Mossad's date of birth.

Ben-Gurion appointed Shiloah to be the first director of the Mossad, which was directly subservient to the Prime Minister's Office. This was the first time that American influence was felt in the Israeli intelligence community. The previous model of overseas espionage, answerable to the foreign minister, like Britain's Secret Intelligence Service (MI6), was abolished. In the United States, the Central Intelligence Agency reports directly to the Oval Office, and in Israel the Mossad is responsible directly to the prime minister.

There was one clear difference. The CIA always had an operations department. When the Mossad was founded, however, it had to get along without one. All the agency did was take part in a joint committee with Aman, to oversee the use of the army's secret Unit 131. Otherwise, the Mossad's function was to collect facts, not to do anything about them.

Shiloah ended up serving as Mossad director for only a short while, but he managed to establish the basic principles guiding the agency for decades to come. Based on his own secret report to the Zionist leadership just after World War II, Shiloah made certain to establish working relationships with foreign security agencies — especially the CIA. He set up an economic intelligence unit, which looked for loopholes around and poked holes through the Arab embargo against trade with Israel. He also emphasized the need for the Jewish state to have a close and trusting relationship with Jews around the world.

Shiloah also launched an intensive review of the ongoing operations which he had inherited, for agents were still operating undercover despite the abortive strike staged by the case officers in Europe who "ran" them. It took Shiloah a year to spot a bad apple in the Political Department barrel. The spy who should never have been recruited was known in Israel as David Magen.

David Magen was Theodore Gross, however, when he was born in the early 1920s to a Hungarian Jewish family. The Gross family moved to South Africa, and Theodore later went to Italy to study music. An accomplished singer, he appeared in operas in Italy and Mexico. World War II brought him to the British army, where he changed his name to Ted Cross and became an intelligence officer on dangerous assignments in Italy and Germany.

When war broke out in Palestine in 1948, Gross/Cross felt obliged to move to Israel and join its army. Because of his experience and his knowledge of English, German, Italian, Spanish, and French, he was recruited into the Political Department by Arthur Ben-Natan. In Israel, the volunteer spy adopted the name Magen, Hebrew for "shield," and he was sent to Italy as Ted Cross to run a network of Arab agents who were gathering military and political information for Israel.

In 1950, Magen/Cross was sent to Egypt, where he operated a string of local informers. Shiloah and his new Mossad received reports from their Cairo operative, but they did not keep him for long. In 1952, he was ordered to leave Egypt, and after a transit stop in Rome he flew to Tel Aviv.

As David Magen, he was immediately arrested, tried, convicted, and sentenced to fifteen years' imprisonment. The astounding charge: spying for Egypt. Without authorization or reporting his actions, Magen/Cross had made contact with Egyptian intelligence personnel. In his defense, he claimed that his purpose had always been to deceive the Egyptians — to propose that he become a double agent, while in fact remaining loyal to Israel.

Magen's alibis were not accepted by the prosecution or by the court, in part because of evidence that he had been involved in illicit drug deals in Italy and had even been imprisoned for narcotics trafficking.

Many members of the disbanded Political Department continued to believe that Magen/Cross did not betray Israel. Boris Guriel testified on his behalf during the trial, claiming that Shiloah and the Mossad rigged a false case against Magen to ruin the reputation of the Political Department. A campaign for a parole led to his release in 1959, after seven years in prison. Gross/Magen/Cross changed identities one more time. Under yet another name, he married, raised a family, and lived in Israel with a deep sense of injustice until his death in 1973 — an anonymous man without his true identity or his life story known to the people of his adopted country.[17]

It was difficult to assess the long-term damage caused by Ben-Natan's revolt and by the Magen case, but deep distrust between the intelligence chiefs in Israel and operatives abroad also made it difficult for the community to function. Shiloah, now officially an agency chief as well as Varash chairman, was so preoccupied with internal matters of bureaucratic housekeeping that he paid insufficient attention to events overseas.

A big mistake was just waiting to happen. An embarrassing failure could practically be anticipated. But it was not. It came as a surprise, and it happened in Iraq, just as the reorganization took effect and the Mossad was born.

Two somewhat mysterious men dressed in nearly identical short-sleeved, open-necked shirts walked into the Tel Aviv factory of Techno-Kfitz, a manufacturer of springs. The men from the government — for their appearance and demeanor suggested nothing else but government men — asked to see one of the company managers, Yaakov Frank.

"Reuven Shiloah would like to talk to you," they told the solidly built thirty-year-old. It was January 1951, ten weeks before the Mossad's creation, and Shiloah's formal role in government was hazy to an Israeli public that had never been told about the Varash committee. Frank had heard of Shiloah, however, and agreed without hesitation to meet with the almost legendary spy.

Frank had been an enthusiastic member of the Haganah, and after fleeing a manhunt by the British in Palestine he worked for the Institute for Aliyah B in New York. He did his bit for the Allies in World War II as an American soldier, fighting the Japanese in the Pacific. Severely wounded in the Philippines in October 1944, Frank returned to Israel as it became independent in 1948, with U.S. citizenship and a monthly pension from the Pentagon.

Recovered to nearly perfect health, Frank fought in the War of Independence, and without prior warning he was about to be called into active service again in 1951. The two shadowy officials drove him from the springs factory to the Kirya, the "Town Center" — the name used for the military and defense-ministry compound so large that it comprised its own small neighborhood on the eastern edge of downtown Tel Aviv. They escorted Frank into one of the buildings, where there was no plaque or sign mentioning "intelligence," and up the stairs to Shiloah's private office.

The chief of Israel's intelligence community was looking down at the younger man's file. "I see, Frank, that you helped Aliyah B bring Jews to Israel, and then you were an army major," Shiloah said. "You have the kind of background we're looking for."

"What would you like me to do?" said the redheaded Frank, who had always agreed to any mission for Israel.

"I want you to go to Iraq," Shiloah replied. "Our man in Baghdad is about to end his tour of duty, and we want you to take over our station there."

"I agree under one condition," said Frank. "That I be given full authority there."

"Certainly," Shiloah agreed. "You will be responsible for the immigration of the Jews from there, as well as for the collection of information."

"But isn't Aliyah B responsible for getting the Jews out?" insisted Frank, a veteran of that agency but unsure who his next employer would be.

"Don't worry," Shiloah said. "Everything is being coordinated."

After a quick briefing by Shiloah's staff, Frank was invited for a chat with Foreign Minister Moshe Sharett, who stressed the importance of the Baghdad operation and assured Frank that the State of Israel stood behind him. Feeling fully confident, the new recruit left for Iraq a few days later — on what could be considered an unintended first mission for the Mossad.

Three weeks after he was first approached, Yaakov Frank was flying from Tel Aviv to Teheran, bearing a false Israeli passport in the name of Yitzhak Stein. In the Iranian capital, Frank/Stein was met by the Aliyah B station chief, Zion Cohen.

"Tell me, Zion," Frank asked. "Who am I working for?" Was he working for Shiloah? And what agency would that be? For Aliyah B? For Guriel's Political Department? For Gibli's Military Intelligence?

"I have no idea," Cohen replied. "I am completely in the dark. I have the feeling that Tel Aviv is busy with other things."

Frank waited in Teheran for over two months, doing absolutely nothing. But when Cohen, trying to help, gave him a false passport as the basis for a new cover identity, it only inflamed Frank's anger. The passport would force him to become Ismail Tashbakash, a rug merchant from Bahrain. He had thought his cover story would be that of a Canadian businessman. He spoke English well, had visited Canada a number of times, and believed that the years he spent in the United States would enable him to get away with it.

Now he was supposed to be an Arab from the Persian Gulf. "My facial features are European, not Arabian. It is true that I spoke a little

Arabic, but with a Palestinian accent. I found it hard to believe that, in the circumstances, I would be able to operate as required," he recalls. "I was boiling mad. For God's sake, I said to myself, how can they do this to me? Is this the way a secret agent is to operate?"[18]

He had no one to whom to complain. He considered returning to Israel, but his patriotism prevented his quitting the mission. Even without specific orders, he decided to carry on. First, he burned every document he had that linked him with the Jewish state. Frank/Stein/Tashbakash then bribed some smugglers to transport him from Iran into Iraq, no easy task because of the many police checkpoints, on April 20, 1951. His true torment was only now to begin.

Frank had believed Tel Aviv's promise that it would send a coded message to the Baghdad station to advise of his arrival. When his long and tiring journey was over, however, and he knocked on the door of a Jewish family he had been instructed to contact, he found that he was totally unexpected.

It was, ironically, the first night of Passover, the major Jewish springtime holiday, and the family — celebrating the traditional Seder banquet — refused to allow the newcomer to stay the night. Naturally, they feared he might be an agent for the Iraqi police. Frank's pathetic pleas fell on deaf ears, and even one of the Seder guests who should have known better, Mordecai Ben-Porat, refused to listen.

Ben-Porat was Aliyah B's principal operative in Baghdad. An Iraqi-born Jew who had emigrated to Palestine, he served in the Israeli army and was sent back to Iraq in the autumn of 1949 to organize the illegal departure of Jews. He borrowed the identities of two Jews who had already left Iraq, and he would alternate between two false names: Zaki Habi and Moshe Nissim. It was not a completely undercover existence, however, as far too many people knew his true identity.

In the disarray then reigning in the intelligence community, Ben-Porat was also in charge of other secret operations. A technique known in the espionage business as "compartmentalization" would have been far safer, but instead the immigration organizer also ran a network of agents, mainly Jews, who fed him military and political tidbits. They were linked to headquarters in Tel Aviv by two-way shortwave radio, and the Baghdad station used the coded call sign "Berman."[19]

Just inside the Jewish family's front door, and within earshot of the Seder table, Frank had the uncomfortable task of telling Ben-Porat that his mission was to take over Ben-Porat's station. The incumbent chief refused to yield, claiming that his team of agents and the heads of the Jewish community, who knew of his secret activities, would not agree to the change.

Frank, by now so tired that he could barely control his anger, was further enraged when Ben-Porat drove him to the large Hotel Semiramis. Frank knew that any foreigner who checked into a hotel would have to register his passport with the police, and the risk could undermine his mission.

Based more on emotion than rational logic, Frank decided to stick it out. He would remain in Baghdad, trying to carry out his assignment — at least until his life was clearly in danger. Not surprisingly, he found within days that he was being followed by Iraqi security men. He changed taxis a few times to shake off the tails, and then he approached Ben-Porat's operatives to ask for their aid in fleeing. They refused to help.

Frank remained calm and went into a travel agency, where he bribed an employee to arrange a flight and an exit visa. He had enough sense to fly to Beirut rather than to a European capital, as the Iraqi secret police kept a much tighter watch on flights to Europe than to Arab destinations.

Frank/Stein/Tashbakash had been in Baghdad for only a week, but even after leaving his troubles were not over. He transferred at Beirut and flew on to Turkey, intending to catch a flight to Tel Aviv. The Israeli consulate in Istanbul, however, refused to believe his story and would not grant a visa to a "rug merchant from Bahrain." That, after all, was the only identity Frank could prove with documents.

It took the consulate three days before it finally gave "Tashbakash" a visa for Israel. Even then, Frank was thinking as a patriotic agent and urged the consul not to stamp the visa into the Bahraini passport, which would render it useless in the future. No Israeli secret agent could use a travel document that had an obvious link to Israel. But the consul, a supreme bureaucrat, stamped the visa in anyway.

The flight to Tel Aviv was uneventful, and Frank arrived at Lod airport unmet by any intelligence official. Adding to Frank's puzzlement, when he went to Shiloah's office the next day — now part of the new Mossad — the espionage chief simply refused to meet him.

Nearly forty years later, Frank is as angry as ever at his intelligence handlers, charging them with "amateurism and dilettantism which almost cost me my life. The right hand knew nothing of what the left hand was doing. Disorganization ran rampant. We were fortunate that they, the Iraqis, are even worse than we."

Iraq's counterintelligence agents were not completely incompetent, however, because within a month of Frank's hurried departure they broke the Israeli undercover ring in Baghdad.

The collapse of the ring was inevitable, considering Ben-Porat's poorly maintained cover and his insistence on controlling both espionage and emigration matters. Exactly a year before his quarrel with Frank, Ben-Porat was in a dispute with a senior Aliyah B operative who arrived from Europe in April 1950 on a major mission. Shlomo Hillel was posing as "British businessman Richard Armstrong," representing Near East Air Transport Corporation of the United States in talks with the Iraqi government.

The obscure American airline covered its tracks carefully so as to disguise its close ties with the Israeli government. No one knew that in 1948 and 1949 the company had flown all fifty thousand Jews of Yemen and Aden to Israel in another secret Aliyah B operation, code-named "Operation Magic Carpet."

After two years of active anti-Semitic oppression, the Iraqi parliament passed a law in March 1950 that permitted every Jew who wished to do so to leave the country. They would simply have to give up their Iraqi citizenship. This seemed surprisingly lenient from a regime that had declared war on Israel and arrested hundreds of Jews for Zionist activities. The explanation lay in incentives offered to the prime minister who opened the emigration gates, Toufik al-Sawidi. He was also the chairman of Iraq Tours, which — by no coincidence — was appointed agent for Near East Air Transport Corporation. In other words and by a roundabout method, the head of Iraq's government received bribes and kickbacks from Israeli intelligence.

The prime minister was not unique. Hillel/Armstrong and his Aliyah B agents made sure that Sawidi's opponent and predecessor, veteran politician Nuri as-Said — who would later be prime minister again — would also benefit. The airline awarded a maintenance concession to Iraqi Airways, which was run by Colonel Sabah as-Said, Nuri's son.

This entire operation was endangered, however, because of Ben-

Porat. His involvement in the various clandestine contacts nearly blew their cover. Aliyah B headquarters in Tel Aviv had to tell him not to interfere, and from May 1950 to January 1952 Hillel's exit route managed to bring nearly one hundred and fifty thousand Iraqi Jews to Israel by air. The direct flights were known as "Operation Ezra and Nehemiah," named for the two Jewish leaders who led their people back to the Holy Land from exile in Iraq — then called Mesopotamia — some twenty-three centuries earlier. The Ezra and Nehemiah airlift supplanted Ben-Porat's much smaller operation, which smuggled Jews overland from Iraq to Iran and then flew them to Israel.[20]

Ben-Porat himself, moreover, ran into hard luck. Iraqi agents repeatedly arrested and brutally interrogated him. He finally escaped to Israel, on one of the flights that Hillel had arranged.

A second Israeli arrested with Ben-Porat, however, could not possibly maintain his cover story of being a Persian merchant. He could not even speak Farsi. His real name, he confessed to the Iraqis, was Yehudah Tajar. He was a veteran of the Palmach, the elite "Storming Forces" of the Haganah, sent to Baghdad by the Political Department — before it was disbanded — as case officer for a group of young Iraqi Jews and Arab hirelings who collected strategic information for Israel.

Ben-Porat and Tajar were supposed to have been working in parallel, but definitely not together. Ignoring all rules of compartmentalization, they met often, spoke to each other in Hebrew, and even sang Israeli songs when driving by car. Such elementary errors caused the network of Jewish spies to fall like dominoes.

The Iraqis arrested some one hundred Jews, one after another, and seized a huge cache of arms. Twenty Iraqi Jews were convicted in November 1951, and two were hanged. Tajar was sentenced to life imprisonment. He was deported nine years later, however, after Mossad agents established contact with the new Iraqi ruler, Colonel Abdel Karim Qassem, and secured Tajar's freedom in exchange for information on plots by Iraqi dissidents against Qassem.

Among other crimes, the defendants were convicted of four acts of sabotage. One was a bombing that caused minor damage to the U.S. embassy's public information center. The biggest and most surprising attack was a grenade explosion in the Masouda Shemtov Synagogue in Baghdad while hundreds of Jews were praying. Four congregants, including a twelve-year-old boy, were killed, and around twenty were injured.

The astounding accusation that an Israeli spy network had bombed a synagogue shocked Iraqi Jews. Rumors circulated among Iraqi immigrants to Israel, who suddenly suspected that their departures may have been hastened by Israeli agents waging terrorism. The Iraqis in Israel were already disgruntled, blaming the European-born leadership of the Jewish state for thrusting them into primitive tents and huts with little hope of decent housing or employment. The new Sephardic — "Oriental" — immigrants felt humiliated to be sprayed with insecticide and given no freedom of choice. The Ashkenazic, or European Jewish, politicians appeared too busy congratulating themselves on the good deed they had done by saving Iraqi Jewry to do anything concrete for them on the ground.

Annoyed that rumors about an undercover operation could add to the early divisions in Israeli society, Prime Minister Ben-Gurion ordered Harel in 1960 to set up an internal inquiry. The top secret report of a three-man committee said, "We could not find any factual evidence that Israelis or Jews were involved in throwing explosives."

Members of the intelligence community firmly denied using any terrorist tactics, but they were proud to say that they consistently came up with new and original methods to transport Jews to Israel. Disarray at home often required clever improvisation by agents in the field. They were, after all, battling for the survival of their new nation. Jewish immigration was vital for Israel in its first years as a tiny state in a huge sea of Arab nations. It was a matter of not only geography, but demography. Thanks to the secret agents of Aliyah B, the population of Israel nearly doubled, to over one million Jews, in the first four years after independence.[21]

What thanks did the men and women of Aliyah B receive, however? Their agency was disbanded in March 1952. Reuven Shiloah said it was no longer needed. As had Arthur Ben-Natan and his Political Department operatives the previous year, Aliyah B's staff members objected. They charged that Shiloah's Mossad was trying to grab their impressive assets.

Aliyah B was an economic empire and an operational masterpiece. The Jewish state has never had anything else like it: a huge organization involved in the global conveyance of Israel's most important asset, people. Built around a massive undercover travel agency,

Aliyah B owned over sixty ships and airplanes and countless cars and trucks. Their movements were well coordinated by a worldwide network of quasi-legal radio transmitters.

The agency helped hundreds of thousands of Jews make their way to their ancient Promised Land. Bribery and secret diplomacy were crafts learned early on by Aliyah B. Its agents concentrated on forming direct relationships with political leaders, often in nominally hostile nations: not only Iraqi prime ministers Sawidi and Nuri as-Said, but also Hungarian politicians, and both the shah of Iran and King Abdullah of Transjordan to explore possible arrangements for the safe passage of Iraq's Jews to Israel.

Aliyah B's budget was in the tens of millions of dollars, a sum so impressive that it had genuine economic impact in some of the port areas of war-ravaged Europe, so extensive was the system of bribes paid to policemen, port officials, government functionaries, and ship owners. Israel's agents distinguished themselves in the black markets of France, Greece, Italy, Austria, and other countries.

"Aliyah B's operations made it the largest organization of its kind in the annals of the state, and nothing since then has matched what we did," one veteran agent recalls.[22]

Some of its planes became the first El Al airliners. Its vessels helped form the core of Israel's national shipping company, Zim. The experience acquired by operatives worldwide helped Israel's new navy. Aliyah B also had some of Israel's finest forgers and field agents, whom the Mossad could put to good use.

To apply bureaucratic cement to the change in authority, Shiloah and his assistant, Akiva Levinsky, went to the trouble of signing a memorandum that put the Mossad in charge of immigration from the Arab countries — specifically, "underground activities in order to make contact with Jews and to bring them to Israel." The Jewish Agency promised to pay the bills. This became the pattern of operations in the future.[23]

Shiloah appeared to have amassed great power, dissolving both Aliyah B and the Political Department while creating a more efficient intelligence structure. But not all was well for Shiloah. His health was poor, after a head injury suffered in a car accident. He also felt that he was under pressure from an ambitious Isser Harel. Indeed, Prime Minister Ben-Gurion noted in his diary on May 24, 1952: "Isser came to me. In his opinion, Reuven has failed in his task."[24] A consensus built up that while Shiloah was brilliant, he was not much good at running an agency.

On September 20, 1952, after only eighteen months as first director of the Mossad, Shiloah submitted his resignation to Ben-Gurion. Asked to recommend possible successors, Shiloah named the obvious candidates: Levinsky, Gibli, and Harel.

Ben-Gurion chose Harel. After a dizzying first four years of hectic activity at home and abroad, the young intelligence community had been too busy to get its bearings. In perpetual motion, its orientation was unclear. Every mission had felt urgent in the covert side of Israel's fight for survival, as an influx of Jews from abroad was needed to strengthen the new state while spies were sent behind enemy lines and traitors and subversives were pursued. Yet it all seemed improvised and incoherent.

The first intelligence chiefs were still searching for the framework by which efficient security could live with true democracy. They looked to their political master, but even Ben-Gurion — who had found the answers to so many burning questions — did not know how to tackle this particular challenge.

Isser Harel's perseverance and rectitude had impressed the prime minister. Ben-Gurion thought that he was the man for a task still not fully understood. Given responsibility for both Shin Bet at home and the Mossad abroad, Harel became the supreme chief of Israeli intelligence.

TWO

Childhood Development

"ISSER, I NEED FIVE THOUSAND DOLLARS." Dan Pines, an editor of the Labor movement newspaper *Davar* had come to see Isser Harel on his first day as Mossad chief, September 20, 1952.

"Why do you need the money?" asked Harel.

"What, you don't know?" Pines tilted his head with astonishment as he launched into a long, complicated story about an espionage network he was running in the Soviet Union.

Harel listened patiently, but his suspicious instincts were twitching. "Dan, give me a few days to acclimatize, and I'll give you an answer."

The Mossad chief smelled embezzling. It was a sixth sense he had developed as head of Shin Bet. Instead of giving Pines any money, Harel formed a commission of inquiry to look into what seemed to be a crooked operation.

The investigation would not cause any public scandal, however, because it was customary in Israel's early years to appoint only members of the ruling Mapai party to a commission — rather than a mixed parliamentary committee. The practice guaranteed that anything embarrassing, especially if it touched on intelligence matters, would remain within the "family."

It took the inquiry commission only a short time to unravel the truth: Pines was lying and had been soaking easy money from a Mossad inattentively run by Reuven Shiloah. The Mossad's founder was guilty of nothing more than poor management mixed with naiveté, but both he and Foreign Minister Moshe Sharett had been convinced by Pines in December 1951 that he was working on setting up a "Zionist underground" inside Russia.

After the elimination of the clandestine immigration agency Aliyah B, Israel was especially concerned not to lose contact with Soviet Jews. This had made the Pines connection sound especially good.

The respected journalist had told of an unnamed Soviet official who was willing to help Israel secretly. He waved around letters, allegedly from potential agents, which he had received from abroad — actually, the investigators found, letters sent from overseas friends of Pines. The amateur spy continued to exploit Shiloah's lack of managerial control for nine months, claiming to have had secret meetings with clandestine Russian contacts in Paris, New York, and Copenhagen. Each time he returned to Tel Aviv, Pines received full reimbursement from the Mossad for his expenses.

The wandering newsman had cooked up the scheme because his daughter was very ill and needed expensive medication that was only available in Europe.[1] Because his motive was forgivable and they wanted to sweep the entire affair under the carpet, no criminal charges were filed against Pines.

The ease with which he deceived Shiloah was a product of the disarray then dominating Israel's intelligence community. The spy ring in Iraq had collapsed, secret agencies were being reorganized, and unexamined projects were consuming many thousands of dollars which the young Jewish state could barely afford.

By detecting the Pines scam, Harel proved his value on his very first day at the Mossad. Ben-Gurion had, after all, chosen Harel for his suspicious mind, among other attributes. The prime minister had gotten to know Harel as the Shin Bet chief, and the two men found that their concerns were identical. With Israel's independence won in the war of 1948, Ben-Gurion turned his attention to domestic issues: the absorption of hundreds of thousands of new immigrants, severe austerity measures, and bitter fights among political factions.

With less emphasis on foreign policy, it was only natural that Ben-Gurion was more interested in Shin Bet than in the Mossad or military intelligence. As the Shin Bet chief, Harel found the prime minister's door open to him, far wider than it had been to Shiloah and his assistants.

Similar to Ben-Gurion and Israel's other founders, Harel was of Eastern European stock — born in 1912 as Isser Halperin in Vitebsk, in the Volozhin region of czarist Russia. He was the youngest of four children of a wealthy businessman who was also a Talmudic scholar. Harel would grow up to be much as he was as a child: short and hyperactive.

Russia was in the throes of exciting turmoil, and Harel recalls the visit of Soviet revolutionary Leon Trotsky to Vitebsk. Little Isser might well have been swept along with the Communist current but for his thorough Jewish education. His father read to Isser and his brothers from Hebrew books and indoctrinated them in Zionism, not Marxism.

Isser the teenager did, however, join a left-wing Zionist group, Ha-Shomer ha-Tza'ir, the "Young Guard," which later developed into the Mapam political party — hated by Harel as a grownup in Israel. In January 1930, as one of the lucky few chosen by Ha-Shomer, Isser Halperin was sent to a kibbutz in Palestine. He was a socialist pioneer, but he rapidly lost any taste he had for socialism. After five years on the collective farm, Isser and his new wife, Rivka, left and started their own orange-packing business.

When World War II broke out, he joined the Haganah and in 1944 entered its intelligence branch, Shai. Eight years in the underground was excellent training. In the midst of the 1948 war, Ben-Gurion noted Harel's talents in intelligence, and at age thirty-six he became the first director of Shin Bet — appointed at the Ben Yehudah Street meeting in June that reorganized Israeli intelligence.

Four years later, when Shiloah fell from grace in September 1952, Harel was also appointed head of the Mossad. He was only forty years old, although it was generally agreed that he looked at least fifty. But Harel's tired, elderly appearance could be deceptive, for he had the limitless energy of a young boy.

He rapidly established his own intelligence empire: hundreds of operatives in two agencies reported directly to Harel, who was answerable only to the prime minister. Shin Bet did receive a new nominal chief, Isador Rot, a former Polish Jew who had earlier been Harel's deputy. He slightly altered his name to a more Hebrew-sounding Izzy Dorot, as he rejoined Shin Bet after a brief assignment helping Shiloah at the Mossad. In the first two decades of the Israeli intelligence community, transfers between Shin Bet and the Mossad were fairly common.

Dorot held the top job for only one year and was considered an unimpressive leader. In September 1953, he was asked to resign, and he lived in absolute obscurity in Israel until his death in 1979. Hardly anyone in Israeli intelligence remembers him.

Amos Manor was the next Shin Bet chief. He was born as Artur Mendelevici in Transylvania, in the Austro-Hungarian Empire's last days in October 1918. Mendelevici was in Hungary's army when World War II broke out in 1939, and he and other Jewish soldiers continued to serve even when the pro-Nazi Fascist government forced Jews to wear yellow stars on their clothing. Only in 1943 were they expelled from the army, and Mendelevici was in one of the first transport trains carrying Hungarian Jews to the Auschwitz extermination camp in Poland.

Millions of Jews were murdered at Auschwitz, but Mendelevici managed to survive the unspeakable horrors and returned to Transylvania — which had become part of Romania. A short while after the war ended, he realized that there was no future for a Jew in Eastern Europe and asked Zionist activists to help him move to British-ruled Palestine.

Instead of helping him leave Romania, Aliyah B operatives reviewed his application and decided that they could best use a tough survivor with military training just where he was. They persuaded Mendelevici to join Aliyah B, and he worked undercover in Bucharest for three years on projects that sent many thousands of Jews who had survived the Holocaust to their biblical homeland.

Mendelevici kept working for Israel after its independence in 1948, even though he had never even been there. He seized his own chance in 1949, however, when Romania's Communist government ordered that all Zionist institutions be closed. Clutching false passports, fearing they could be charged with illegal political activity or even with espionage, Mendelevici and his wife fled to the Jewish state.

Three days after their arrival in Israel in June 1949, Mendelevici went to see Foreign Minister Sharett and agreed to his suggestion that he shed his European Jewish name and choose a modern Hebrew one. Artur Mendelevici thus became Amos Manor.

He also resigned from Aliyah B. Having worked on clandestine immigration for so long, and now having traveled the Zionist "underground railway" himself, Manor came to the conclusion which Ben-Gurion and Shiloah would reach only three years later: that a legal state did not need an agency specializing in illegality.

Aliyah B's chief, Shaul Avigur, could see that Manor was still well suited for intelligence work, and that actually living in Israel in no way diminished his patriotism. Avigur sent him to see Isser Harel at Shin Bet. Harel was impressed and immediately signed Manor up. Starting near the bottom of the informal Shin Bet ladder, the new immigrant worked his way up extremely quickly to the post of counter-intelligence chief.

Manor believed from the start that the threat of foreign espionage was strongest from the Communist-bloc nations rather than from Israel's Arab neighbors. The Arabs had been defeated in their attempt to smother the newborn Israel, and there was absolutely no indication that Arab spies were any better than their armies had been in 1948–49.

When Harel replaced Shiloah at the Mossad, Manor was promoted to become deputy to the new Shin Bet chief, Izzy Dorot. When Dorot was shoved aside in 1953, Manor became the new director of Israel's domestic security.

Manor's rise was phenomenal, considering that he was only thirty-six and had been in Israel for barely four years. Also, he was not part of the state's élite clique of insiders who fought side by side in the Haganah underground or its Palmach strike force. He had not served in the British army or its famed Jewish legion. He had not even battled for Israel's independence in 1948–49. He spoke Hebrew with an unmistakable Hungarian accent and behaved more like a European than a "new Israeli" — admittedly a new and not easily describable nationality, but still one that had been created by the élite Manor was attempting to join.

At first, the formal hierarchy seemed to indicate that Manor had reached a level equal to Harel's. Both men were agency chiefs, Manor at Shin Bet and Harel at the Mossad. But it soon became apparent that Harel was first among equals. He had never surrendered the reins of domestic security, and with Prime Minister Ben-Gurion's assent Harel managed to run Israeli intelligence astride two horses at once: Shin Bet and the Mossad.

Harel called all the shots, and Ben-Gurion even created a special title for him in 1957. In the Knesset, Israel's parliament, the prime minister referred to the *Memuneh,* "the one in charge" of the secret services. Neither the cabinet nor the Knesset formally approved the title, but Ben-Gurion had no hesitation in announcing it. In a country where he was admired and almost worshiped as a father figure, he felt the freedom to act on instinct without bothering with some of the technicalities of democracy. Whereas the United States and other Western nations had established procedures assigning job descriptions to bureaucrats and announcing their official status, young Israel was run by "the Old Man" in a more personal style. Harel was also chairman of Varash, the committee that brought all the agency directors together.

Harel concentrated tremendous power within his grasp, more than any intelligence chief of any Western power had ever been able to obtain. One man had powers equivalent to those of the FBI's J. Edgar Hoover and the CIA's Allen Dulles combined. Isser the Little enjoyed this unprecedented clout and the unlimited trust and appreciation of Ben-Gurion.

In return, the Memuneh displayed boundless loyalty and agreed to undertake almost anything for the government. When requested to do so by Ben-Gurion, Harel happily transformed the intelligence community into a political tool for the ruling Mapai party. While Israel's founding fathers believed in democracy, they also had the unbreakable habit of identifying their own political interests with those of the state.

Loyalty to Ben-Gurion's party was perfectly natural. The full spectrum of political choice had not yet come into its own in Israel. No one had any experience in running a modern democracy, and there were few traditions and norms to give guidance. The nation was only beginning its long march away from the clandestine habits of a Jewish underground fighting for independence. Among the vast majority of Israelis, the Mapai party was practically synonymous with the state. Mapai certainly controlled most of its institutions: industrial factories, labor unions, the army hierarchy, and the intelligence community.

Harel sent agents, who were often reluctant, on what should have been police duties: fighting black marketeers and, together with Aman's military intelligence operatives, opening thousands of letters mailed abroad in a manhunt for currency smugglers and subversives.[2]

In the search for subversion, Ben-Gurion and his Mapai took a simple approach based on the belief that "those who are not with us are against us." Accordingly, Harel ordered Shin Bet operatives to infiltrate Israel's other political parties.

First, it was eyes to the Right. As a reflection of the gut hatred that Ben-Gurion felt for Menachem Begin, the former commander of the Irgun underground who now led the Herut party, Harel kept Begin and his colleagues under surveillance. Harel reported to the prime minister that Herut intended to establish "a mini-underground" in the army.[3] The suspicions were groundless because Begin had transformed himself into a true parliamentary democrat. But in the words of a Hebrew expression, Harel "saw even the shadows of mountains as mountains."

In the following months, Shin Bet broke up several small and insignificant dissident rings linked to religious zealots and the political Right. One of them, calling itself Brit ha-Kana'im, the "Covenant of the Zealots," vowed to renew the ancient kingdom of Israel under strict religious governance. Bearded and garbed in the dark clothing of the Orthodox, these Jews set fire to cars, a restaurant, and a butcher's shop that sold nonkosher meat.[4]

Shin Bet penetrated the group of zealots and arrested them. It was clear that they were naive amateurs, but Harel's report to Ben-Gurion portrayed them as mortal dangers to democracy. The Memuneh wanted his Shin Bet operatives to be known as efficient and sophisticated subversion-busters.

Harel also took credit for foiling the attempted assassination of Transport Minister Ben-Zion Pincus. Shaaltiel Ben-Yair and two other young veterans of the prestate Lehi underground, notorious as the Stern Gang, were arrested on charges of plotting antireligious violence. They allegedly plotted to plant a bomb near the minister's home, as a protest against his introduction of public-transport restrictions on the Sabbath. Buses were forbidden to travel on the Jewish day of rest, as part of a political deal between the Mapai party and religious politicians. Ben-Yair was tried, but acquitted for lack of evidence.[5] Ironically, he would later work in the intelligence community.

While liquidating right-wing subversion, the Memuneh increasingly turned his attention to the Left. Shin Bet mounted intensive surveillance of Israel's small Communist party, and this was in no way considered controversial because the general public thought of Communists as anti-Zionist outcasts in a patriotic, Zionist society.

Harel exceeded the wishes of most Israelis, however, when he turned his antisubversion searchlight on Mapam, a socialist party with unquestionable Zionist credentials. Although left-wing, Mapam was not beyond the political pale and was committed to the existence of an independent Jewish state. The party was more active than any other in building new Jewish settlements and kibbutzim. Its members served wholeheartedly in the army, and several rose to senior military ranks.

On the other hand, when Mapam leaders came to the conclusion that Ben-Gurion wanted to turn Israel away from socialism, they angrily ceased all political cooperation with him. When they went even further by worshiping Soviet dictator Joseph Stalin, Harel needed no stronger evidence to pounce on them.

The intelligence community's Memuneh decided that Mapam was acting as an agent for the Soviet bloc. He even suspected that because the party had many members in the officer corps of the army, Mapam could be planning a military coup to take over the country.

Shin Bet's secret assault on alleged subversives became public knowledge on January 29, 1953, when Mapam party secretary Natan Peled dramatically opened his hands at a Tel Aviv press conference to reveal a tiny radio transmitter. He told the journalists that the bugging device had been found under the table of Mapam leader Meir Ya'ari.

Peled said the party had long suspected that its private discussions were being leaked, somehow, to Ben-Gurion. The microphone and transmitter were found, he said, and then two burglars were caught attempting to break into Mapam headquarters with passkeys. They were caught by party members and turned over to the police. The judge, Peled noted, had been extremely lenient — imposing a minimal fine and two-week prison terms without ordering any investigation of the bizarre circumstances.[6]

Peled offered the assembled reporters an explanation. He said the two men were Shin Bet operatives sent by Harel, on orders from Ben-Gurion and Mapai. The ruling party denied the allegations, but Mapam had inside knowledge. The party had its own spies working inside Shin Bet — part of a Mapam security department that planted agents in other parties and inside the intelligence community.

Harel found one spy spying on Israel's spies as early as January 1951: senior Shin Bet operative Gershon Rabinovitz was fired for what were, at the least, strong pro-Mapam leanings. Other Mapam moles remained in place, however, providing the party with information for its self-defense.

Harel also exposed an informer who was working in the Arab-affairs section of the foreign ministry's research department. Fortunately for Israeli security, the spy was neither an Arab nor working for Arabs. He was Yaakov Bar'am, an Israeli who was well placed to get his hands on Mossad and military intelligence reports. In May 1955 he was caught passing secret documents to Mapam's security department. The party was obviously determined to develop its own ways of knowing what was going on everywhere in the Jewish state. Harel chose not to press criminal charges against Bar'am, so as not to deepen the Mapam-Mapai feud.[7]

Harel's watchful scanning of the foreign ministry produced even greater dividends with the capture of a spy who was an enemy agent even before he came to Israel. His original name was Wolff Goldstein, born in Switzerland to Jewish parents who had such strong Communist credentials that they gave refuge to Vladimir Ilyich Lenin before the Bolshevik Revolution of 1917. The hero-worshiping teenage Wolff became enchanted with Marxism-Leninism. Soviet spies hired him as one of their own, and he went to Moscow for a KGB intelligence course with the intention — from the start — of being planted in Israel's government.

He arrived during the battles of 1948 and managed to be hired by the foreign ministry with unbelievable ease. He joined the economics department, which was so small that it urgently needed staff. As was the custom, Wolff Goldstein changed his name to its Hebrew equivalent, Ze'ev Avni.

While Avni was a minor Israeli functionary, he had some important postings abroad. At the beginning of the 1950s, he was stationed in the Israeli embassy in Brussels as an economics counselor. Secret negotiations were being held with West German officials on the payment of reparations to Israeli Jews who had suffered in the Holocaust. Avni reported regularly to the KGB on all details of the negotiations.

He was later posted to Belgrade, where he inflicted his most severe damage on the Jewish state's national security. His responsibilities involved commercial relations between Israel and Yugoslavia, but because of a chronic shortage of manpower he was also allowed access to the embassy's top secret communications and codes room. Avni learned to operate the code machines that were used for all messages between the foreign ministry in Israel and its embassy in Yugoslavia.

His willingness to work overtime and to fill in for absent or ill communications clerks was accepted gratefully. Soon the Soviet spy had obtained the secret codes of the Israeli foreign ministry, making it possible for the KGB to decipher all messages transmitted to and from Israeli diplomats and intelligence operatives working under diplomatic cover.

Harel, constantly surveying the diplomatic lists with his good counterespionage instincts, found cause to doubt Avni and his enthusiasm. His somewhat odd behavior in Belgrade appeared linked with signs that Israeli agents had been compromised. Harel invented a reason to summon Avni to Tel Aviv in April 1956. Unaware that he was in trouble, Avni flew home and was arrested by Harel's Shin Bet. Under interrogation, Goldstein/Avni broke and confessed everything — a "debriefing" which the Israelis found most useful. He was so cooperative that after being sentenced to fifteen years in prison, he was planted in the jail cell of other suspected traitors as an informer for Shin Bet.

Goldstein/Avni was released after ten years. He went back to his childhood home in Switzerland, but astoundingly he returned to Israel a few years later. With the agreement of the intelligence chiefs in the Varash committee, Ze'ev Avni disappeared forever and adopted a new identity in a farming community north of Tel Aviv where he works as a psychologist.[8]

Harel often had to rely on his instinct, rather than on fast computers or fat budgets. For all of its first twenty years, Shin Bet was a very small organization with only a few hundred employees and financial restraints. A great many tasks, however, were entrusted to it.

The agency was divided into two divisions: Support and Operations. The Support branch had departments of administration, interrogation and legal counsel, technology, coordination and planning, and logistical supplies for operations.

The Operations division of Shin Bet had three departments:

Protective Security, responsible for guarding Israel's embassies and other representatives abroad, protecting the prime minister and other officials, and securing Israel's defense industry.

Arab Affairs, primarily responsible for monitoring subversion among the Arab minority within Israel's borders, who lived under military administration until 1965.

Non-Arab Affairs, the largest and most important of the departments, responsible for counterespionage, surveillance of foreign diplomats and delegations, and fighting subversion by Communists and other political extremists.[9]

Israel learned, long ago, to make do with little. Most security services in the world calculate that to keep a person under surveillance around the clock, thirty operatives are required to work in shifts. In the Israeli intelligence community, because of a chronic shortage of manpower, this job is usually assigned to no more than ten agents, who have to work overtime and are stretched to the utter limit. They are often helped by cadets, for whom this is training for the future when they will become full agents in the secret services.

It is generally assumed that anyone who is being followed and starts to use professional methods to shake off the tails is most likely a foreign espionage agent. Shin Bet quickly discovered, however, that the Communist countries cleverly trained many members of delegations they sent abroad to evade surveillance. Diplomats and visitors who were legitimate and were not spies thus appeared suspicious. The Israelis wasted time following them, and the many false leads could throw the scent off the trail of the true espionage agents.

Shin Bet, from its beginnings in 1948, has had the task of monitoring the activities of diplomats — not only those from the Eastern bloc, but also the envoys of friendly Western countries. Just a few months after the State of Israel's birth, the U.S. Army attaché in Tel Aviv, Colonel E. P. Archibald, discovered that his telephone was bugged.

A year later, an Israeli agent attempted to blackmail an official of the American consulate in Jerusalem, hoping to force him to leak secret documents to Shin Bet. The consular clerk had an Israeli lover, who was being pressured to extract information from the diplomat. The authorities even concocted a story that the young woman needed an abortion.

In 1954, security officers in the U.S. embassy in Tel Aviv found microphones concealed in the ambassador's office. In 1956, bugs were found attached to two telephones in the home of an American military attaché. Shin Bet also made crude attempts, decades before the KGB made it fashionable, to use women and money to seduce the U.S. Marines who guarded their embassy in Tel Aviv.[10]

Most of these efforts produced nothing of value, but Harel continued to use his imagination and refused to be bound by etiquette or tradition. Above all, he believed in recruiting the best. He ordered all members of the community to keep their eyes peeled for Israelis displaying potential, patriotism, and promise.

Harel persuaded Ben-Gurion in 1955 to recruit the most talented members of the former Lehi underground — despite the prime minister's distaste and dislike for them. In the strained and highly politicized atmosphere prevailing in Israel at that time, this was a move of unparalleled boldness. Right-wing former terrorists had been blocked from civil service jobs, even from teaching, on the grounds of being security risks. Harel had closely watched them and felt they had been neutralized, that they posed no real danger, and that their experience in conspiratorial and underground techniques should be exploited.

The new Shin Bet and Mossad men included Yitzhak Yezernitzki, who had been head of the *Lehi* or Stern Gang. He later changed his name to Yitzhak Shamir and would eventually become Israel's prime minister.

Other Lehi veterans were recruited by the intelligence community. Yaakov Eliav was sent to Spain. Yehoshua Cohen, who had been involved in the assassination in 1948 of United Nations mediator Count Folke Bernadotte of Sweden, was assigned to be Ben-Gurion's bodyguard. Shaaltiel Ben-Yair, who only four years earlier had been suspected of conspiring to bomb a cabinet minister, was sent under a false identity to Egypt, and he was one of Israel's most successful operatives abroad.[11] David Shomron was posted to the Mossad station in Paris, and Eliyahu Ben-Elissar became the case officer in Europe for agents in Arab lands. These right-wingers were eternally grateful to Harel for releasing them from quarantine and giving them the opportunity to prove their value to Israel.

Harel did his best to inspire a certain pride in belonging to an exclusive fraternity. "You are rare creatures in a game reserve," he remarked to his subordinates. Being all too human, they enjoyed the praise. They certainly were not in the espionage game for money. The salaries paid to employees of Shin Bet and the Mossad were in line with those paid to ordinary civil servants in Israel — low by Western standards — but approximately doubled for operatives on foreign assignment. The work was demanding and dangerous, and the hours unending. At the very least, Harel could ensure that his operatives saw themselves as a protected species.

His agents also knew that trips abroad, which were a rare commodity in those days and almost unavailable to the common Israeli, were among the fringe benefits of their work. Those who toiled in the Support division, not normally in the field, were also eligible to enjoy this benefit. From time to time, technicians, mechanics, or secretaries were sent abroad on missions that did not require any specific skill, such as acting as couriers or for guard duty.

In return, Harel demanded total loyalty and utter commitment to their assignments. Harel himself set the example: work, not waste. Rather than lodging himself in expensive hotels or eating at elegant restaurants, he would choose cheaper and more ascetic alternatives — even as he traveled frequently to Europe, the United States, and South America.

When in the 1950s there were severe restrictions in Israel on the amount of foreign currency an ordinary citizen could hold, members of the intelligence community were given special authorization to take far more than the usual one hundred dollars on a foreign journey. It was understood that the money was mainly meant to finance special operations, to pay informers, and to cover other unusual expenses such as bribery. Harel himself would return any money he had left over to the first bank he saw upon arriving at Lod airport near Tel Aviv.

Operatives did not have to supply receipts for their expenses, for who would sign a piece of paper for them to acknowledge having been bribed? The intelligence people's written reports, when they returned to Israel, were sufficient. Lurking beneath the honor system, however, was a strong hand regarding financial matters. The worst sin was to lie. "They train us to lie, to steal, and to cook up schemes against our enemies," a senior agent in the Mossad explained, "but we may not allow these things to corrupt us. We are duty-bound to see to it that our moral standards remain high."

If an agent was caught lying, even about a few measly dollars, or if he did not have a satisfactory explanation for his expenses, he would face a disciplinary hearing. A special internal court of the intelligence community was chaired by a judge selected from the civilian judicial service. The judge was, of course, sworn to secrecy. Any operatives found guilty of exploiting their clandestine profession by smuggling home appliances, television sets, or later, videocassette recorders into Israel were fined and warned. In severe cases, the corrupt few were dismissed immediately.

Such was the case with a Mossad operative who made contact in Europe with two informers normally reporting to him from an Arab country. He wined and dined them for a few days, and their entertainment included visits to brothels. When the case officer returned to Tel Aviv, he gave a detailed report of his expenses. He included the cost of the prostitutes. His superior at Mossad headquarters was not pleased:

"I certainly understand the need to spend money on your agents," he said, "but why the hell does the State of Israel have to pay for your whoring?"

The officer was formally rebuked, and the Mossad accountants also took a closer look at his previous expense reports. These, too, showed dubious entries, and the man was fired without the usual severance pay.[12]

A complaint was once received about a Shin Bet man who was having an affair and using his agency-provided car to drive his girlfriend around. While there certainly was a standing order not to use official cars on personal business, the man's Shin Bet bosses instead asked him to end the love affair and the ensuing gossip. Had this come to the attention of the puritanical and family-oriented Harel, his reaction would have been even sterner.

While the Memuneh had jurisdiction over the Mossad and Shin Bet, he was unable to prevent a huge and still confusing failure by military intelligence agents in Egypt in the mid-1950s. Still shrouded by official ambiguity but by far the most famous scandal in Israel's history, the entire series of mishaps and coverups is known as the Lavon Affair — named for Pinhas Lavon, the defense minister who lost his job because of it.

The vast expanses of Egypt were fertile espionage grounds for both the Mossad and Aman, the military intelligence agency. Under the traditional division of labor, Aman was predominant in collecting information on the armed forces of the hostile countries along Israel's borders, while the Mossad's responsibilities included secret operations in all foreign nations.

Egypt, as the largest of the neighboring Arab states, was always of prime interest and merited the double-teaming attention of Israeli intelligence. Aman's Unit 131, however, headed into serious difficulties with a poorly planned operation that began with the dispatch of Avraham Dar to Cairo in May 1951.

Dar did surprisingly well, considering the handicap he faced in traveling undercover as a Briton. He was the grandson of a Jew who had been born in Aden, and his dark skin made it difficult to appear British. But his English was excellent, and he had clandestine experience as an immigration operative for the Institute for Aliyah B.

As a Palmach officer in the 1948 war, Dar was reliable but had no outstanding reputation for either leadership or analytical abilities. In Egypt, he posed as John Darling, representative of a British electronics company. "The name Darling was not chosen purely by chance," Dar recalled years later. "The name of one of the British army officers in Egypt was Darling, and the family ties that I ostensibly had with him might be useful to me."[13]

After Dar had settled in under his cover — even the authentic Darling believing that they were related — he began working on the true goal for which he had been sent: to establish a network of "sleeper" agents who, when the time came, would be called upon to carry out secret assignments. Dar/Darling set up two cells of young, dedicated Jews who were supporters of the State of Israel. They were even brought secretly to Israel in 1952 for training.

Almost all of these Egyptian Zionists were rank amateurs. Unit 131 instructors had trouble making their lessons in tradecraft stick: invisible ink, coded radio broadcasts, and surveillance techniques were as strange to these second-rate agents as might be nuclear physics. No one in Israel's intelligence community seemed to protest, however. There were, after all, a few exceptions. Among the more talented espionage students was Eli Cohen, who a decade later would be considered the Jewish state's "best spy."

One of the female operatives, Marcelle Ninio, set up a travel agency in Egypt with secret Israeli funding. Popular for her vivacious personality and memorable beauty, Ninio was the link between the two Egyptian cells.

In early 1952, highly nationalistic officers in Egypt's army formed secret links with Kermit (Kim) Roosevelt and Miles Copeland, the top CIA agents in the Middle East, and plotted to overthrow King Farouk. In July, they succeeded. The coup leaders declared a republic and invited CIA operatives to train them, and eventually in 1954 their true leader, Lieutenant Colonel Gamal Abdel Nasser, surfaced as president. The CIA helped provide his personal security. Israeli intelligence was aware of the special, secret relationship and did not like it at all.

The Israeli recruits had "slept" for three years, but in June 1954 the prearranged codeword was transmitted from Tel Aviv to Cairo, activating Operation Susannah. Unit 131's secret cells were finally going into action, with the aim of discrediting the new Arab nationalist government. Dar/Darling, however, was no longer their case officer. He had been replaced by Avraham Seidenwerg.

Seidenwerg was the son of a Jewish politician in Austria who had died in a Nazi concentration camp. The younger Seidenwerg moved to Palestine, changed his name to Avri El-Ad, and excelled in the Palmach's battle for Jerusalem in 1948. He was a major at age twenty-two, but his army career ended when he looted a refrigerator in a captured Arab village and was court-martialed.

By the end of 1951, scorned, unemployed, and divorced, Seidenwerg/El-Ad met Avraham Dar and Mordecai Ben-Zur of Unit 131. They saw him as excellent material for a dangerous mission in enemy territory, because he had nothing to lose and would be grateful for the opportunity to rehabilitate himself.

Military intelligence borrowed the identity of a kibbutz member of German origin named Paul Frank and assigned it to its new recruit. Seidenwerg/El-Ad/Frank went to West Germany for nine months to close any gaps in his cover story, and he even underwent a uniquely painful operation to reverse his circumcision — so that he would not be identified, if naked, as a Jew. He told the German surgeon that he was a non-Jew who could not stand his sexual partners thinking he was Jewish. The doctor sympathized fully.[14]

The Israeli spy sailed to Cairo as wealthy businessman Paul Frank in December 1953. He was quickly accepted into the growing community of Germans in Egypt, many of whom had a Nazi past they wished to escape.

As case officer of the intelligence network in Cairo, Seidenwerg/El-Ad/Frank committed every mistake in the book. He knew all of his agents — not just a top few — and even visited them in their homes. They and their families could identify him, if the worst should happen, even though they called him "Robert."

On June 30, 1954, he went to Alexandria with the long-awaited codeword. Operation Susannah meant sabotage. The bombing targets were not Egyptian military facilities, however. They were movie theaters, post offices, and American and British institutions. The aim was to provoke the anger of Washington and London against the Egyptians, and to portray the new government in Cairo as unstable and unreliable.

The somewhat bizarre mission began with the bombing of a post office in Alexandria. Philip Nathanson, at age nineteen the youngest of the Zionist operatives, and Victor Levi carried the primitive incendiary devices in eyeglasses cases. There was only minor damage, and Egyptian military censorship forbade any publication of the event. As a result, Egypt's image did not suffer at all.

A week later, more ambitious instructions were given by codewords during an Israel Radio program. Seidenwerg/Frank ordered his team to place bombs in the Cairo and Alexandria libraries of the United States Information Center. This time, both the local and international press reported on the explosions. Unit 131, in Tel Aviv, was pleased.

On July 22, two bombs went off in Cairo. One of them, however, was still in the pocket of Philip Nathanson. A police officer helped extinguish the burning trousers and then arrested Nathanson. It was the end of Operation Susannah, which would haunt Israel's intelligence community for years.

Nathanson was the first to break under interrogation. As in Iraq, the Egyptian security police found it easy to round up an unprofessional espionage network made up mostly of local Jews who knew each other socially and did not protect each other with anonymity. Ninio, the travel agent and liaison, was soon arrested.

An Israeli operative who should have been operating under deep cover was caught, too. He was Meir (Max) Bennett, born in Hungary in 1917 to a family of Orthodox Jews from Germany. In 1935, his family arrived as illegal immigrants to Palestine. Out of gratitude, he became a secret agent for Aliyah B. Avraham Dar recruited him into Aman, where his command of six languages brought him to many nations on varied missions. By the time he was sent to Egypt in 1951, he had risen to the rank of major.

Similar to Seidenwerg/El-Ad, Bennett was given a German cover identity. Posing as a German was a favorite choice for the simple reasons that Israel had many German-speakers and that few people would expect a German to be working for the Jewish state. There was also a deeper reason: West Germany's intelligence service was helping the Israelis set up their cover stories, complete with passports and other documentation.

The engineer of the special relationship between the Jewish state and the "new" Germany was, ironically, a former Nazi sympathizer. General Reinhard Gehlen had been head of a special German intelligence force responsible for the Soviet front during World War II.

After the Third Reich's defeat, Gehlen was arrested by the Americans but instead of charging him as a war criminal they released both the general and his staff. American and British intelligence had learned of Gehlen's "blueprint" for German-American collaboration against Soviet Russia.[15] His captors put him in charge of the newly established West German intelligence apparatus, and the former general in Hitler's army established a deep professional relationship with Israel — the new homeland of the Jewish survivors of Nazi persecution.

Some Israeli intelligence operatives believed they were successfully exploiting German feelings of guilt after the extermination of six million Jews in the Holocaust. The CIA, however, took a more cynical view in assessing the actions of professional intelligence men such as Gehlen and his Israeli contacts. The Americans believed that the covert craft of intelligence required total separation of emotions from the logical calculation of interests.

The CIA concluded that Israeli intelligence must have had tangible assets, both positive and negative, in dealing with the West Germans. The carrot, in the American estimation, was a flow of espionage product obtained by the Israelis from the many thousands of immigrants who arrived from the Soviet Union and the rest of Eastern Europe. Israel's secret agencies were expert at utilizing every tidbit of information, even when it seemed of little direct value in the Middle East conflict. When it was of interest to the West Germans — for instance, when it shed light on Soviet-bloc military and diplomatic positions — the Israelis cut a deal.

America's spies also believed there was a stick: that Israeli intelligence must have collected compromising information about past Nazi activities of top West German politicians. The CIA believed Israel discreetly made it clear that the scandalous material would leak into the public domain unless the Germans were fully cooperative. The U.S. agents noted in their reports that such blackmail could succeed, especially with the West Germans, who were terrified of any skeletons in their closets, even if the Israelis did not in fact have much ammunition. The threat was always there.

Conscious or not of the extensive secret relationship and the mixed motives behind it, Max Bennett benefited from it on his way to Egypt.

According to his cover story, he was a former Nazi representing a German company that manufactured prosthetic devices. Later, he became the chief engineer in Egypt for Ford automobiles. Beneath the surface, Bennett was an exceptional intelligence man. Ford's most important client was the Egyptian army, and this gave the Israeli spy a great deal of access to military men and bases.

His wife, in Israel, was not supposed to know where he was, and he would first send his letters home to an address in London. Once, one of his operators erred and forgot to remove the Egyptian stamps. Jean Bennett suddenly knew where Max was. His widow believes such amateurism characterized the entire affair.[16]

Bennett, however, dutifully carried out his assignments. One was fatal. "It was a stupid error by his operators," Avraham Dar said years later. "There had been a break in their contacts with the Seidenwerg/Frank network, and they chose the easiest way to transfer money to them. The rules of compartmentalization in intelligence forbid any connection between two different networks, especially when their assignments are totally different. But the operators acted stupidly. Thus, Bennett met with Marcelle Ninio and with Frank, and gave them the money."[17]

Under interrogation, Ninio told what she knew about Bennett. The Egyptians broke into his home and stripped him, and when they saw that he had been circumcised they beat him cruelly. On December 21, 1954, Max Bennett slashed his wrists in a prison cell in Cairo and died the day before he was to stand trial. He must have realized that, as the highest-ranking Israeli spy, he was doomed. Bennett preferred not to be humiliated.[18]

Still, Israel stubbornly denied involvement. Bennett's body was sent to West Germany for burial, but in 1959 it was secretly disinterred and flown to Israel for reburial. His grave was unmarked, and the authorities told his widow about the reburial only a day before it took place. All of the family's requests for an explanation as to the circumstances of his death were turned down by the intelligence community. Only in 1988 did Israel admit officially that Bennett had been its agent, and, at a ceremony in the defense minister's office in Tel Aviv, he was posthumously awarded the rank of lieutenant colonel.

The Israeli authorities were similarly unhelpful to the other captured agents in the Lavon Affair. Two of the Egyptian Jews were hanged in 1955, and four others were sentenced to long prison terms. Israel even rejected an Egyptian offer to exchange them for Egyptian prisoners of war captured during the 1956 Suez campaign. Chief of staff Dayan was opposed to a deal, fearing it would embarrass Israel.[19] Only in 1968, after the Six-Day War, were Marcelle Ninio, Philip Nathanson, Robert Dassa, and Victor Levi exchanged for thousands of Egyptian POWs. More than twenty years later, the four were still complaining that they had been abandoned, and the debate flared publicly in the Israeli press, with contradictory accusations and counterclaims.

The only member of the network who escaped capture was the Israeli operator. Under the name Paul Frank, he even dared to remain in Egypt for two more weeks. Upon returning to Tel Aviv, Seidenwerg/Frank became Avri El-Ad again, and Aman sent him on another military intelligence mission to Europe. Only Isser Harel was opposed to this, as he suspected that El-Ad could have been a double agent — similar to David Magen a few years earlier. El-Ad's easy escape from Egypt seemed sinister. For the Memuneh the ability to detect disloyalty was almost a sense of smell, and something about El-Ad stank.

Gibli was forced to quit as Aman chief because of the Lavon Affair, but his replacement, Major General Yehoshafat Harkabi, continued to believe in El-Ad. Harel doggedly followed his own instincts. Without telling Harkabi, the Memuneh sent Shin Bet operatives to Europe to trail the suspect.

Shin Bet reported that El-Ad contacted an officer at the Egyptian military attaché's office in Bonn and gave him secret documents about Israeli intelligence. The Aman agent was a traitor, Harel understandably concluded. El-Ad was immediately flown back to Israel, interrogated for nine continuous months by Shin Bet, and then put on trial in July 1959. He was charged with spying for Egypt.

Hoping to save his skin, El-Ad reached a bit further back into the intelligence community's history. He confessed that he had helped cover up the truth about the Lavon Affair, saying that officers in Aman's Unit 131 had conspired to blame Defense Minister Lavon for the failure of Operation Susannah in Egypt.

Coming clean on unrelated matters did not help El-Ad in court. He was sentenced to ten years in prison after one of the most secret trials in Israeli history. Military censors forbade the press from printing details, and the names of the people involved were absolutely forbidden fruit. The newspapers referred to the entire affair as Esek Bish, the

"Rotten Business." Gibli was identified only as "the senior officer," Ben-Zur as "the reserves officer," and Avri El-Ad as "the third man" in a quirky homage to the cinematic thriller of that name.

All the same, Shin Bet interrogators were unable to break El-Ad and force him to confess that he had helped Egyptian intelligence, or to admit that he had betrayed his comrades in Cairo and Alexandria. After his release from prison, El-Ad moved to California and wrote a book which charged that Harel had framed him.[20]

The Lavon Affair had effects far beyond the mere failure of a single covert operation or the arrest of a hard-working espionage cell. For the first time, Israel's politicians realized that putting security at the top of the list of national priorities could be highly dangerous. After leaving security and democracy to find their own equilibrium, they found that no natural force would achieve a balance without their own positive action. As leaders of a democratic state, they would have to find the solution before the scales were tipped entirely in the direction of security.

The affair was a jarring signal that too much authority had been left in the hands of young, daring, but uncontrolled intelligence commanders. Decades later, the "Rotten Business" was still seen as a warning beacon.

The Israeli public was not told exactly what was "rotten" in their nation's intelligence community, but while the community and the government were in turmoil Isser Harel survived and thrived. He was the dependable force, through it all, rooting out subversion at home and protecting Israeli interests abroad.

At the same time, Israel was growing into a formidable regional power. Instead of a tiny fledgling nation barely surviving its tumultuous independence from Britain, the Jewish state became an active and important player in the game of international politics.

The attempted use of bizarre provocations, particularly in Egypt, to try to turn the Western powers against the Arabs, nearly backfired when Israeli involvement was revealed. Still, political facts spoke for themselves: Israel was the up-and-coming leader among Middle East states, in terms of strength, fortitude, and the kind of stability sought by the West. The United States, Britain, and most importantly France chose to befriend Israel.

Despite the humiliation of military intelligence in the Lavon Affair, the relationship with the French was of such an overwhelmingly military nature that Ben-Gurion put General Harkabi's Aman and the defense ministry in charge in 1956.

Harel protested that the Mossad should have sole jurisdiction over clandestine relations with foreign countries, but the prime minister trusted the military to handle cooperation with France. Ben-Gurion turned to General Dayan, top defense aide Shimon Peres, and even the man who had organized "the revolt of the spies" five years earlier, Asher Ben-Natan.

THREE

Nuclear Maturity and Lakam

"PACK YOUR BAGS AT ONCE," headquarters in Tel Aviv said by radio. It was September 1956 and the message was duly received by Asher Ben-Natan, former Israeli spy in Europe and now the general manager of a company his government owned in Africa.

The firm was Red Sea Incoda, located in Djibouti, a remote French colony in the Horn of Africa which was a mere rowboat's voyage across the Bab el-Mandeb strait to Yemen. Looking out over Arabia made Djibouti an ideal listening post for Israeli intelligence, but Ben-Natan's official job was to purchase Ethiopian meat and ship it the full length of the Red Sea to Israel's southern port of Eilat. Ritual slaughterers and rabbis were employed by Red Sea Incoda to ensure that the beef and lamb were kosher.

Clandestinely, Ben-Natan — assigned to Djibouti in 1953, his earlier rebelliousness forgiven by Prime Minister Ben-Gurion — was monitoring shipping movements and communications in the strategic Horn and the nearby Arab nations. The French authorities turned a blind eye to the espionage side of the meat company's activities.

The radio message to Ben-Natan signaled a further deepening of Israel's relationship with France. He flew to Tel Aviv, as instructed, and was driven straight to the defense ministry.

He was greeted by the young director general of the ministry, Shimon Peres. He was giving Ben-Natan a new assignment: "The Old Man wants you to leave for Paris immediately to renew your contacts from your Political Department days, and to serve as a special representative of the defense ministry for all of Europe. It is better that you not ask too many questions. Everything will be clarified in a very short time."

About a month later, on October 22, Ben-Natan believed that the smoke was finally clearing. He would soon learn why he was in

France. In a private villa in the Paris suburb of Sèvres, he was at a large and impressive wooden table with a group so varied that he literally pinched himself to believe what he was seeing.

Around the table sat more than a dozen men, including two famous Israelis: David Ben-Gurion, in his twin posts as prime minister and minister of defense, and the army chief of staff, Moshe Dayan, with his black eye patch a constant reminder of the loss of his left eye in 1942 while in action for British intelligence against the pro-Nazi Vichy French forces in Syria.

Ben-Natan focused primarily, however, on several men whom he knew only as faces in newsreel movies. Settling into their chairs were the French prime minister, Guy Mollet, Defense Minister Maurice Bourges-Maunoury, Foreign Minister Christian Pineau, and various assistants and advisers, some of them wearing army uniforms and others in civilian clothes. Facing them was Selwyn Lloyd, Great Britain's foreign secretary, surrounded by his advisers.[1]

The Sèvres Conference was no idle chat. These men were planning a war, which would be known in Israel as the Sinai campaign and worldwide simply as "Suez."

On October 29, 1956, Israeli paratroops and ground forces began moving into Egypt — across the Sinai and toward the Suez Canal. In accordance with the Sèvres plan, France and Britain then issued an ultimatum to the armies of Israel and Egypt, instructing them to freeze their forces in place, several miles from the canal. As prearranged, Israel accepted; but Egypt refused. The French and British used the excuse to drop paratroops into the Canal Zone on November 5, taking over the strategic waterway.

The Israeli army, meanwhile, had completed the conquest of the Sinai in only four days. It appeared that the Sèvres Conference's goal had been achieved, and the many months of planning by military men and intelligence services had borne fruit.

Israel's aims in the war were to destroy Egypt's Soviet-equipped army, while breaking President Nasser's declared blockade of the Red Sea route to Eilat. There was also the publicly stated aim of stopping Palestinian terrorist attacks from Egypt's Gaza Strip.

Britain's prime minister, Anthony Eden, motivated by his visceral hatred for Nasser, hoped to restore British control over the canal, which the Egyptian leader had nationalized. Eden expected that the humiliation would topple Nasser, who was riding a wave of Middle East radicalism directed against Western interests.

France was primarily concerned with stopping "Nasserism," because it provided inspiration to the FLN — the National Liberation Front in Algeria, which was fighting the French occupying forces.

Even before the Sèvres Conference, France had begun to arm Israel for the war to come. From April 1956, French cargo planes and ships arrived in the darkness of night and unloaded an abundance of weaponry: tanks, fighter planes, cannon, and ammunition.

The project required close intelligence cooperation. Aman's chief, General Harkabi, was frequently in Paris for talks with his counterparts in French military and civilian intelligence. To institutionalize the liaison, a permanent Aman representative was stationed in France. Even though Isser Harel tried to insist that his Mossad should at least have a monopoly over contacts with civilian intelligence agencies abroad, the Memuneh had to take a back seat while the blueprints for war were prepared.[2]

Israel and its partners also dabbled in some disinformation. Israeli intelligence operatives, just a few days before the Sinai attack, made a point of spreading false suggestions that Israel was planning to attack Jordan as retaliation for Palestinian guerrilla attacks from there.

As a military operation, the Sinai campaign — particularly Israel's part — was brilliantly executed. As a political maneuver, it was a failure. Israeli, French, and British intelligence believed that Nasser would succumb to widening international pressure, in part because their new tripartite alliance would naturally be extended to include the United States. Instead, the United States displayed total contempt for the invasion of Suez and forced the three aggressors to pull back, proving once and for all that the United States was a superpower, while France and Britain no longer qualified even for the old title of "great powers."

Israel, while still celebrating its army's triumph in the Sinai, began to withdraw its forces in November, and the final portions of captured land — Sharm esh-Sheikh and Gaza — were handed back to Egypt in March 1957. Severe damage had been done to Israel's image as a progressive, socialist nation seeking peace. The world concluded that Israel had taken part in an ill-judged imperialist plot.

But the Israelis knew precisely what they were doing. They joined the three-sided Suez conspiracy, above all, because of Ben-Gurion's burning desire to go nuclear. The public relations value was nil, but there was great value for the prime minister's strategic goals in cementing a strong alliance with France, dubbed "the bridge over the

Mediterranean."[3] The bridge brought the Israelis nearly everything they needed to build an atomic bomb.

Nuclear power was a goal fondly cherished by Ben-Gurion from the start of statehood. It would represent true independence in the modern world. Generating electricity without relying on imported coal and oil could be valuable, but developing a nuclear military potential was even more important: it would make Israel an unrivaled force in the Middle East. It could be the ultimate guarantee of the Jewish state's continued existence.

A mere seven months after independence, the prime minister summoned an expert from Paris, Maurice Surdin, described in Ben-Gurion's diary notation of December 20, 1948, as "the builder of the French atomic oven." A Jew born in the Russian Crimea in 1913, he moved to Palestine as Moshe Surdin but later settled in France, where he studied physics. He worked, after World War II, with the Commission for Atomic Energy in Paris, which was developing the French atomic bomb.

"Ben-Gurion was very interested in the topic, the atom," Surdin recalls. "He was very interested in the details."[4] Nothing came of the meeting, but Ben-Gurion and his cluster of young advisers refused to abandon the idea. Acquiring nuclear power, they felt, would compensate for Israel's tiny size and meager human resources.

As for the notion of an Israeli atomic bomb, General Dayan was certainly enthusiastic. He saw a nuclear arsenal as deterrence against an all-out Arab attack, without having to station "a tank in every Israeli courtyard." Maintaining a huge standing army would bankrupt the state, the chief of staff reasoned.

"We need to have a small army which is efficient, cheap, and professional, for ongoing security and for limited engagements — with nuclear weapons for a general confrontation," Dayan said. "Otherwise, we will regress to economic strangulation."[5]

Israel's cabinet formed the Israeli Atomic Energy Commission, the IAEC, in 1952. Its chairman was Ernst David Bergman, a brilliant chemist born in Germany in 1903, who moved to Palestine in the early 1930s and founded the science corps of Israel's army. While researching cancer and other matters, Bergman was director of the defense ministry's science department and a leading supporter of the nuclear option.

Almost at every opportunity, Ben-Gurion and his scientific, military, and political advisers considered the possibilities of purchasing a nuclear reactor. The chance presented itself in 1955, when President Dwight D. Eisenhower's "Atoms for Peace" program provided a small, 5-megawatt research reactor at Nahal Sorek, ten miles south of Tel Aviv. The facility was subject to American inspections, and in any event it was too small to produce anything of potential military use.[6]

That same year, Shimon Peres recognized an opportunity to obtain something bigger. It could come from France, where Guy Mollet's socialist government came to power in April. Mollet took a tough line on Algeria and thus had much in common with Israel's anti-Nasserist views. The fact that Israel had a socialist administration also helped.

Whenever Peres was in France, which was often, he raised the possibility of purchasing a reactor. He acted as a combination diplomat, intelligence officer, and arms buyer. Foreign Minister Golda Meir did not care for such hyperactivity, and her complaint against Peres was that he was turning the defense ministry into a second, independent foreign ministry. But there was more than that to the protest: Meir and the "old guard" of the ruling Mapai party did not want Israel to go nuclear.

Peres, however, had the total backing of Ben-Gurion, and the defense aide was therefore able to persist in his efforts. From April 1956 until the Sinai campaign in October, Peres's request for a reactor became an integral part of the secret collusion between the two countries.

The turning point came on September 21, 1956, in a country villa about a hundred miles south of Paris, set among bucolic French farms. Peres met there with Bourges-Maunoury, the defense minister who was busily planning the attack on Egypt. The French were beguiled by the notion that Israel would take part, hoping that Israel's troops would do the dirty work for them, sweeping the Egyptian army away from Suez.

On that autumn day, Bourges-Maunoury sought to ensure Israeli participation by acceding, finally, to Peres's repeated requests on the nuclear front. On behalf of the French government, the defense minister offered the Israeli a "sweetener" in the form of a reactor.[7] For the first time in human history, one state had agreed to supply nuclear know-how to another without requirements for safeguards and inspections.

Only now did Ben-Natan understand why he had been summoned

out of Africa and reassigned to the ministry of defense as European representative. He had not been sent to Paris to aid in the preparations for the Suez invasion, but to help acquire a second Israeli reactor. Reinforcing Peres's arguments, Ben-Natan lobbied various French ministries for a large reactor, not just the small installation the French may have had in mind.

Even the close cooperation of the Suez/Sinai campaign did not quite settle the nuclear matter. By the autumn of 1957, time was running out for the Israeli lobbyists because the French Fourth Republic was on the verge of collapse. The public was fed up with political instability, the Suez invasion had been embarrassing, and there were growing calls for the return to power of the hero of World War II, General Charles de Gaulle. Having won the socialist administration's assent in principle, Peres and Ben-Natan feared that the shaky government's successors would reject Israel's nuclear request.

Fortunately for the Israelis, Bourges-Maunoury had advanced to the post of prime minister and was determined to fulfill his commitment before leaving the scene. Still, it was far from easy for Peres, who shuttled between government ministries in Paris finding that many in the French bureaucracy were reluctant to give the Israelis what they wanted. Foreign Minister Pineau wrote to Peres, saying that there was no precedent in history for the aid he was demanding, that the Americans would cut off nuclear aid to France if they found out, and that the Russians might react by supplying atomic weapons to Egypt.

With the political hourglass running out on the socialist government, Peres argued passionately that Israel needed help to confront future, unforeseeable dangers. Pineau asked that Israel at least consult with France again when the reactor was ready to begin operating, and Peres agreed. The foreign minister had been persuaded.

Peres had to continue his dash over the bureaucratic hurdles, facing the energy minister, Pierre Guillaumat, who stubbornly insisted that the proposed agreement had diplomatic consequences beyond his purview. Prime Minister Bourges-Maunoury intervened, finally deciding the issue with a cabinet vote on October 2, 1957. On his last day in office, literally a few hours before losing an unrelated vote of no-confidence in the National Assembly, he granted Israel's wish. On October 3, Bourges-Maunoury and Foreign Minister Pineau signed two top secret documents with Peres and Ben-Natan: a political pact outlining the scientific cooperation between the two nations; and a technical agreement to supply a large, 24-megawatt reactor, with the necessary technicians and know-how.

Peres cabled the news to Ben-Gurion in a coded message from the Israeli embassy. The prime minister telexed back to Paris: "Congratulations on your important achievement."[8]

Even as the sizable nuclear reactor was obtained, there was growing concern among Israeli scientists and some senior politicians that a dangerous nuclear arms race could follow. When Ben-Gurion's cabinet discussed the issue, it was with great reluctance and with hardly any enthusiasm shown by the ministers, who felt the project would be too expensive and diplomatically risky. Seven of the eight members of the IAEC resigned in protest in late 1957. They claimed there was too much emphasis on the military side of Israel's budding nuclear potential, and they formed the Committee for the Denuclearization of the Middle East Conflict. There were heated debates behind closed doors, but the subject was shrouded in secrecy so deep that the arguments never burst into the open.

This did not seem to disturb Ben-Gurion and Peres. They still had Professor Bergman as a one-man IAEC and put him in charge of the reactor project. If anything, they were pleased that fewer people would now have the privilege of knowing what Israel was doing.[9] It was considered the ultimate secret of the Jewish state, and the nuclear program was subject to more security measures than anything in the history of a country where secrecy already abounded.

Peres, knowing that knowledge is power, insisted on keeping it out of the hands of others. This was his own, darling project. Therefore, he did not ask the existing intelligence community — as might be expected — to take care of the security and secrecy aspects of the reactor. Instead, he believed that Israel the nuclear power would need a nuclear intelligence agency.

Until then, the responsibility for obtaining technical and scientific information from abroad lay with Aman and the Mossad. Peres, however, established a new secret agency for nuclear matters in 1957, and he put a man called Binyamin Blumberg in charge.

Blumberg was an experienced officer, having left a kibbutz in northern Israel to serve in the preindependence Haganah underground army. After the 1948–49 war he joined Shin Bet, which assigned him to be chief security officer for the ministry of defense. Amos Manor, director of Shin Bet after 1953, suggested that for the sake of administrative tidiness Blumberg should draw his salary from the defense ministry. Blumberg preferred to remain on Shin Bet's payroll, obviously wishing to feel the glamour of belonging to the secret services rather than the relative ordinariness of a ministry job.

His duties, in any event, were to maintain security inside the ministry of defense and at factories working on armaments projects. The new, large reactor was just that: a defense facility. Blumberg seemed the appropriate man to ensure that it remained clandestine and to oversee the trustworthiness of its employees. Always on the lookout for loose lips, Blumberg never needed any lectures or guidelines on how to maintain silence. He himself was the high priest of secrecy.

When he started his new job, on Peres's invitation, he moved to a modest office in the defense ministry. To conceal his work, he named his new unit the "Office of Special Assignments."

A few years later, the name would be changed to *Lishka le-Kishrei Mada,* the "Science Liaison Bureau" or SLB. The few insiders who knew about the agency called it Lakam, its Hebrew acronym. Lakam was then transferred from the defense ministry compound to an undercover location in midtown Tel Aviv: an office building on Carlebach Street.

Supported fully by Peres, Blumberg tried to conceal the existence of the agency even from the other branches of the intelligence community — even from Isser Harel, the Memuneh. "Lakam was established behind my back and without my knowledge," Harel recalls angrily. "I had my suspicions. I knew that someone was running around the ministry of defense dealing with various matters, and that when he saw anyone from the Mossad he would make a point of crossing to the other side of the street. It was a mysterious body, formed in a conspiratorial manner. Deceptively. Even Ben-Gurion did not know of the establishment of the experimental unit from which Lakam grew."[10]

Peres felt that he did not need Harel's permission, even if he was Ben-Gurion's trusted head of the security services, to set up the special agency for nuclear security. The new reactor from France was, after all, even more secret than any previous top secret topics. In any event, it is difficult to believe that the prime minister did not know about Lakam, because Ben-Gurion was the guiding force behind the nuclear project and took a personal interest in Israel's other defense-related industries. Lakam was eventually used to help them, too.

Blumberg was not bothered by the envy or complaints of others. His sole concern was to seal the reactor project from any information leaks. It was not an easy task, with hundreds of French technicians and construction advisers working in Israel to build the new facility. The chosen site was in the Negev Desert — in the middle of nowhere, midway between the Dead Sea and Beersheba, the Negev's "capital," mentioned in the Bible as an oasis enjoyed by the patriarch Abraham.

The French work contracts spoke of "a warm climate and desert conditions," which did little to mask the location of the nuclear project. It was not just Blumberg but also French intelligence that became concerned about security in the Negev. The French did not fully trust the Israelis, known for their talkative nature, and sent their own agents to preserve secrecy and hunt for leaks.

One spy from Paris posed as a priest and tested the mayor of Beersheba by asking how development was going in the Negev. Proud of how his desert was blooming, in more ways than one, the mayor told the visiting cleric about the French nuclear reactor being built nearby. The spy-priest sent a highly critical cable back to his headquarters.[11] To conceal the three years of heavy construction near the immigrants' town of Dimona, Israel used the cover story suggested by Blumberg: that a "textiles factory" was being built.

While the Lakam chief protected the secret on the ground, a gathering storm came in by air. On a high-flying reconnaissance mission in 1960, an American U-2 jet photographed the facility, and U.S. intelligence analysts had no trouble identifying its true purpose. From that moment, American spies sniffed around Dimona and U.S. political leaders became concerned.

Based on a tip from sources in Washington, the American and British press reported that Israel was developing an atomic bomb. The U.S. government demanded the whole truth from the Israelis.

There was also pressure from President de Gaulle in Paris. The French attitude toward the Middle East began to change just after he took office in 1958. De Gaulle aimed at reconciliation with the Arab world and even offered independence to Algeria — policy shifts that were at the expense of Israel. In addition, he suspected that the Dimona reactor was destined for military uses and this greatly annoyed the French president.

De Gaulle ordered his foreign minister, in May 1960, to inform the

Israeli ambassador in Paris that France would supply no more uranium to Dimona. The president did not want Israel to produce plutonium at its reactor, because this would be a step toward building an atomic bomb. Shimon Peres the francophile continued to be optimistic, for several weeks refusing to admit that the bridge over the Mediterranean had become very shaky.

The danger to Israel's most clandestine defense project was finally recognized, and Ben-Gurion flew to Paris on short notice to see de Gaulle on June 13, 1960. In his Elysée Palace, the French president asked bluntly, "Why does Israel need a nuclear reactor at all?"

Ben-Gurion promised it would only be for peaceful uses, and that no facility for removing weapons-grade plutonium would be added at Dimona. Returning home to find that the pressure from France, the United States, and the foreign press was still growing, the prime minister prepared the first public confirmation that Israel had joined the nuclear age. From the podium of the Knesset on December 21, 1960, he announced that Israel was building a second nuclear research reactor — for peaceful purposes only, he assured Israel's parliament.[12]

This was the declaration which de Gaulle had sought. The Israelis had eaten humble pie, so the French now agreed to send the final parts required to complete the construction.

To preserve the fragile relationship with France, the Israelis were even prepared to do what hardly any intelligence community would do: "burn" a secret source. On March 16, 1961, the military attaché at Israel's embassy in Paris, Colonel Uzi Narkiss, learned of a plot to kill President de Gaulle. The informant was Claude Arnaud, a Jesuit and former colonel in the French anti-Nazi resistance. After the war, he was an officer in France's foreign intelligence agency but became disenchanted with de Gaulle's policies in Algeria. Arnaud resigned from the secret service and joined a mysterious Catholic sect that provided espionage services to the Vatican. Known as "the man with a thousand faces," Arnaud befriended Colonel Narkiss and began exchanging information with the Israelis.

Arnaud's motive in giving Narkiss a tip about the conspiracy against de Gaulle was never fully clear to the Israelis. He betrayed fellow members of his covert Catholic sect when he reported that they were attempting to recruit an Arab gunman to kill the president. Arnaud and his right-wing colleagues were opposed to the withdrawal of French troops from Algeria, but he obviously considered assassination to be out of bounds. It was probably good enough for him that the would-be killer be caught so that the Algerians would be blamed.

The plot was foiled at a far earlier stage, however, and Arnaud could not even protect his own anonymity. Narkiss had been exceedingly quick in relaying the information by urgent, coded telex to the defense ministry in Tel Aviv, where it is Aman's task to analyze such reports. Intelligence chiefs and politicians argued over what to do. Isser Harel recalls that Shimon Peres and army chief of staff General Zvi Zur agreed with Narkiss's recommendation that Israel not warn de Gaulle because there was no certainty that the information was correct. In a strange twist, Narkiss sent a further telex message to urge that his colleagues not behave like Judas Iscariot betraying Jesus — an odd thought, considering that the would-be assassin would hardly be a friend of Israel.[13]

Harel had long been annoyed that Aman was dominating the entire relationship with France, and this was one reason that the Memuneh took the opposite stand to that of the military. Harel insisted that the French should be informed about the plot. Ben-Gurion decided the issue in his favor.

De Gaulle was told about the murder plan, albeit after a delay of two weeks, but then demanded to know the source of the information. For the sake of good relations, Israel agreed to tell all. The French arrested Colonel Arnaud and questioned him but were unable to prove any charges, so he was released. Arnaud was angry at the Israelis, and Aman lost a valuable tipster.

The secret relationship between the two governments was far more important. With the final materials needed to complete the Dimona reactor definitely pledged by the French, it was business as usual for Israel on the nuclear front — or almost as usual, because it would become even more clandestine.

The 24-megawatt heavy-water reactor at Dimona could produce enough plutonium for at least one Hiroshima-sized 20-kiloton bomb each year, but the crucial question was whether the French also helped Israel obtain a reprocessing plant capable of extracting the plutonium from the reactor's spent fuel rods. François Perrin, son of a Nobel laureate and the scientific head of the French atomic energy commission from 1951 to 1970, indicated that reprocessing was an indirect part of the original 1957 agreement. His commission, under de

Gaulle's new policy, refused to supply a reprocessing plant; but it did not obstruct Israel's attempts to obtain one elsewhere. Perrin's panel also permitted a private company named St. Gobain, which supplied these plants for the military reactors of France, to sell its technology and plans to the Dimona project.[14]

De Gaulle's presidency meant, in general, that Israel faced a more difficult task in obtaining what it needed for nuclear development. Blumberg's Lakam took up the challenge by expanding its activities. No longer concerned only with the security of the nuclear project, Lakam also became involved in locating and purchasing parts and materials for Dimona. The secrecy enveloping such transactions required stepped-up cooperation with Israel's other secret agencies. The old wounds in the intelligence community began to be healed.

Blumberg also introduced the work habits of a professional secret service: compartmentalization and the ability to work undercover in the field. He was not a member of Varash, the committee of the heads of the services, but his Lakam was certainly in the community.

Lakam's chosen cover was hardly a fiction. The agency's personnel were sent abroad as science attachés in the large Israeli embassies in Europe and the United States. Blumberg's people reported directly to his headquarters in Tel Aviv, rather than through the foreign ministry as is normal for diplomats. The scientific advisers were required to purchase every publication in the field, and to make social and professional connections with scientists in the countries where they were posted.

Israeli scientists who traveled abroad on sabbaticals or research projects were asked to do favors for Lakam, although they usually did not know who precisely was asking. For their government, however, they would keep their eyes open for the latest developments in their fields, and would obtain manuals, plans, and publications. There was no need to apply pressure to persuade most of the scientists. Their institutes belong to the Israeli government, and the universities are closely linked to the defense establishment or enjoy government financing. Just as most Israelis, scientists are brought up on patriotism.

In a few cases, Israelis conducting research abroad were even asked to steal scientific material. This was often done in an amateurish fashion, which was liable to endanger both the scientists and those who served as their "case officers" — generally the science attachés, who enjoyed diplomatic immunity from prosecution.

One senior Israeli scientist, who was studying at a prestigious Western European institute, tells of secretly photocopying various documents on a regular basis. He brought the copies home, and once a week the science attaché of the Israeli embassy would come to pick them up. The attaché, apparently a Lakam man, displayed an unconscionable lack of responsibility, however. He often arrived late for meetings and sometimes did not show up at all. The two Israelis were lucky that the host country suspected nothing.[15]

It was important that the broad scope of such espionage not be discovered, for Israel was focusing much of its energy on making friends abroad.

The Sinai campaign in 1956 had already made Israel an object of fear and respect. Even with conventional weapons alone, the Israelis had easily swept aside the Egyptians, who had the largest of the Arab armies.

Although the whispers of nuclear might and the invasion of Suez ruined Israel's good image among developing nations, the fact that the Jewish state rapidly became a regional superpower turned it into a force to be reckoned with, a partner to be courted, and a desirable friend in a strategic but notoriously unstable region.

Israel aimed at forming friendships in the open, wherever possible, but it quickly became clear that foreigners often preferred secret ties. Much of the diplomacy was considered so delicate that it could not be left to the overt work of the foreign ministry. The intelligence community was assigned the covert task of forming alliances to help guarantee national security.

FOUR

Strategic Alliances

"WE ARE VERY INTERESTED in having a cooperation agreement with you," David Ben-Gurion said to the director of the Central Intelligence Agency. This was in May 1951, in the old offices of the CIA opposite the Lincoln Memorial in Washington, D.C. The prime minister happened to be in the United States on a private visit, his first after Israel won its war of independence. Ben-Gurion was helping raise funds for his country by personally endorsing the first sales of Israel Bonds in the United States. He used the visit for diplomatic purposes, too.

"The Old Man" met with President Harry S. Truman, and a secret luncheon was arranged for him with the director of the CIA, General Walter Bedell Smith, and his assistant, Allen Dulles. Even before Ben-Gurion left Israel, Reuven Shiloah, then still head of the Mossad, suggested that the prime minister propose intelligence cooperation between the two countries.

It was a far-reaching notion. Israel, ruled by left-wing parties, was considered to be a socialist state. The kibbutz, the unique Israeli farm cooperative that enshrined the principle of sharing assets among members according to their needs, was regarded as the embodiment of the Communist dream. Israel's economy, too, was based on the principles of collectivism and public ownership of most of the means of production.

"Capitalism" and "free market" were considered to be dirty words in the national lexicon of Israel. But especially disturbing, from an American point of view, was the impression that Israeli sentiment was believed to favor the Soviets — largely owing to the important aid given by the Eastern bloc in the first days of the new nation.

Had it not been for a speech supporting a Jewish state by Andrei Gromyko, the Soviet ambassador to the United Nations, there might not have been a Resolution 181 — which decreed the partition of Palestine into two states, Jewish and Arab. At Moscow's behest, Czechoslovakia and Yugoslavia supplied armaments and played host to Israeli pilots for training. Furthermore, the readiness of Romania, Hungary, and Poland to permit their Jews to emigrate added to Israel's sparse manpower.

Shiloah bucked the beliefs of the rest of the establishment by urging that Israel abandon its pro-Soviet orientation, basing its foreign policy instead on strong ties with America. His ultimate aim was to arrange a defense treaty with Washington, and to have Israel join the American-led North Atlantic Treaty Organization (NATO). As a first step toward this, he suggested secret contacts between the CIA and the Mossad.

Ben-Gurion and senior government officials did not believe there was much chance that Shiloah's proposal would be accepted, but they felt that the effort was worth making. Ben-Gurion was surprised when Bedell Smith and Dulles gladly endorsed the idea.

This was not the first meeting of the American general and the Old Man. They had met immediately after World War II, when Ben-Gurion visited Holocaust survivors in the displaced persons camps of Germany. Bedell Smith, who was then chief of staff to General Eisenhower, commander of the Allied forces in Europe, accompanied the Zionist leader on his inspection tour.

The extermination of six million Jews in Auschwitz, Treblinka, Dachau, and other Nazi death camps and the sight of the hundreds of thousands of refugees who survived left an indelible impression on many American soldiers who served in Europe during the war. Israel, for its part, was well aware of how to wring the memory of the Holocaust, when emotional manipulation appeared necessary. The sympathy and guilt felt by some Western leaders could be useful when the Jewish state requested political and military aid.

Israeli diplomats stressed, time and again, the necessity of their country being strong, so that there would never be another Holocaust. This was slight exploitation of the unspeakable horrors of the war era, horrors that remained unique in human history, but it worked. Among the persuaded were Bedell Smith and Dulles. In Washington, Ben-Gurion reached an understanding with the CIA chiefs to have talks begin immediately on pressing ahead with cooperation.

A month later, in June 1951, Shiloah was sent to Washington to hammer out the final details of a formal but secret agreement. He held long meetings with Bedell Smith, Dulles, and especially James Jesus Angleton.[1]

Angleton had also been influenced profoundly by the Holocaust, and he was the sort of man who doggedly pursued any subject in which he had taken an interest. After an unhappy childhood in Arizona, where the climate was supposed to help counter his tuberculosis, Angleton moved to Italy in 1933, at the age of sixteen, when his father took a job in Milan. After a few years abroad Angleton returned to the United States to study at Yale, where he started a literary magazine with a remarkable set of contributors including Ezra Pound and Archibald MacLeish.

In 1943, one of his teachers at Yale recruited Angleton for the counterespionage department of the Office of Strategic Services, reputedly peopled by eccentrics and intellectuals. It was tailor-made for Angleton. He had a suspicious mind, which always searched for veiled meanings beyond those that met the naked eye.[2]

Angleton served in the OSS in Britain and Italy, where he recruited informers and uncovered Nazi and Fascist spy rings. Among his best sources of information were the Aliyah B agents in Italy, who were involved in smuggling Jews to Palestine.

Angleton was especially impressed by the ability of the Jewish underground and its representatives in Europe. One of them, Teddy Kollek, later recalled: "Jim saw in Israel a true ally at a time when belief in a mission had become a rare concept."[3] He knew that some early efforts to strengthen the ties between the Zionist underground and America's spies had been thwarted by the British, who were still ruling Palestine. When Shiloah and the CIA reached their cooperation agreement in 1951, Angleton was pleased.

The agreement laid the foundation for the exchange of strategic information between the CIA and the Mossad and committed them to report to each other on matters of mutual interest. Israel and the United States pledged not to spy on each other, and to exchange liaison officers who would be stationed at their respective embassies in Washington and Tel Aviv.

To add flesh to the skeleton agreement, however, they had to overcome one major obstacle. Angleton, promoted to be head of counterespionage of the CIA, was an obsessive opponent of communism. Despite his admiration for Jewish secret agents in Europe, he believed that Israel — with its socialist values and its links with the Soviet bloc — constituted a high security risk.

Angleton was concerned that the emigration of Jews from Eastern Europe would enable Soviet spies to penetrate Israel as a launching pad into the West. The Communist authorities could easily blackmail Jews who were leaving for Israel by threatening to harm their relatives who remained behind. "The admixture of European races in Palestine offers a unique opportunity for Soviet penetration into a highly strategic area," said a State Department memorandum which advised that U.S. military attachés in Israel should observe "Soviet activities and should be thoroughly familiar with Soviet tactics." Washington also believed that the Russians were infiltrating Israel's army.[4]

Shiloah was aware of the Americans' fears and did not merely make promises in response. He persuaded them that Israel's intelligence community was already on the same wavelength. While still Mossad chief in late 1951, Shiloah told the CIA that Israel's security agencies were vigilant. Aliyah B and Isser Harel's Shin Bet were already giving close scrutiny to the new Jewish arrivals from behind the Iron Curtain.

What finally persuaded Angleton and the CIA was Israel's contention that "from the bitter could come the sweet," in the words of the Bible — that the new immigrants should not be feared; they should be used. After all, the Jews had come from all walks of life and had intimate knowledge of the Soviet military, science, economics, and politics. Israel began feeding such data to the United States and even agreed to put some of its agents at risk in the Soviet bloc, by allowing the CIA to use them.[5]

Despite efforts made by Israel to placate the Americans with anti-Communist credentials as strong as anyone's, the habits of the U.S. intelligence community continued unbroken. The worst scenario in the minds of America's spy catchers was that Soviet moles had tunneled their way into key positions of power and influence in the West: prime ministers, presidents, and chiefs of secret services.

Amos Manor, head of Shin Bet, fit the frightening picture drawn by the suspicious Americans because of his Eastern European origins and meteoric rise after arriving in Israel. The FBI believed he was a likely Soviet plant and tried to prevent Manor from even visiting the United States on official business. The CIA, regarding the FBI as mere policemen and not a serious domestic security service, dismissed the allegations and sponsored Manor's visit for the sake of smooth liaison.

Angleton's counterintelligence department sent its own experts to

Israel to evaluate the danger of Soviet penetration, and each mission created problems — especially for the CIA station chief at the U.S. embassy in Tel Aviv. The station chief, who felt he was the expert on local events and personalities, found that visits from headquarters sowed confusion, suspicion, and rumors in all directions. On at least one occasion a visitor from the CIA, who meant to raise a concern about a particular senior Israeli intelligence operative, got the Mossad and Shin Bet mixed up and revealed his suspicions to the wrong agency.

This not only embarrassed the local CIA chief but confused and angered many members of the Israeli intelligence community — especially the proud Isser Harel. Here were the Americans intruding on his turf, questioning his own effectiveness, and going along a path that might even end up at his door.

In any event, Harel felt that the Americans were not truly interested in bilateral cooperation. They wanted the unilateral transfer of everything learned by Israeli intelligence, he said, without a genuine exchange. Harel even suspected that the CIA might organize a coup in Israel, along the lines of the Agency's covert operation in 1953 in Guatemala.

Shiloah, as usual, took a different view. Even after leaving the Mossad, he was a special adviser to Ben-Gurion on international and regional strategy. He persuaded the prime minister that for the sake of an alliance with the United States, it was worth paying a price — interrogating new immigrants and providing information to the Americans — until the CIA's trust was won.[6]

The Americans did supply Israel with special technological equipment for its intelligence needs, including listening devices and electronic means to break codes. Israeli officers were sent to the United States to learn how to use the equipment.[7] To oversee the cooperation, two excellent intelligence men who were Shiloah allies were posted in Washington: Colonel Chaim Herzog, the former Aman chief who became a "mere" military attaché, and Shiloah's close friend Teddy Kollek as counselor in the Israeli embassy. Kollek already had experience, before 1948, in buying weapons for the Zionists and organizing networks of American sympathizers.

In parallel with the effort to become an ally of the United States, Israeli intelligence was also creating strategic alliances closer to home.

Shiloah had learned in the first years of Israeli statehood that secret contacts could — astonishingly — be established with neighboring countries that were officially hostile.

As Ben-Gurion's top clandestine diplomat, Shiloah himself took part in meetings with Transjordan's King Abdullah, his prime minister, other senior officials, and military men. They even reached a tacit understanding whereby the Palestinian state envisioned by the UN vote of 1947 was aborted well before birth: Israel overran some of the Arab territory, and Abdullah's army seized the West Bank of the Jordan in 1948. There was no serious attempt by Transjordan, unlike Egypt and the other Arab countries, to destroy Israel. King Abdullah became not only an "agent of influence" for Israel in the Arab world — an intelligence catchphrase to describe a person in a foreign country whose political goals fit into your own country's — but a paid agent. His Jewish contacts paid him ten thousand U.S. dollars for his services. Only Abdullah's assassination in July 1951 prevented his signing a peace treaty with Israel.[8]

In Syria, army chief of staff Colonel Hosni Zaim seized power in March 1949 and offered peace to Israel. Events overtook his seemingly peaceful generosity, and no treaty was signed. Only decades later was it revealed that Zaim had been on the payroll of American, French, and even Israeli intelligence agencies. CIA agents actually helped him plot his coup.[9] Israel had other contacts, often built on bribery, within the Egyptian and Iraqi leadership.

Shiloah realized, however, that the ability of Israeli agents to gain access to Arab leaders could not change the basic political and strategic facts of Middle Eastern life: that the inner circle of Arab countries would continue to hate the State of Israel and to perpetuate a state of war.

Shiloah also knew there were other geographic and ethnic factors in the Middle East. The inner circle was surrounded by an outer circle, the periphery of non-Arab nations; and the Arab states themselves had religious and ethnic minorities. Friendships could be formed with the peripheral nations and with the minorities that suffered, as did Israel and the West, from the rise of Arab nationalism and radicalism. The idea behind this plan can be summarized in the dictum "The enemies of my enemy are my friends."

Any force that opposed or fought Arab nationalism was considered to be a potential ally of Israel: the Maronite minority in Lebanon, the

Druze in Syria, the Kurds in Iraq, and the Christians in southern Sudan, who all suffered under the yoke of the Moslem majorities in their countries. Iran's people, although Moslem, were always proud to note that they were Persians and not Arabs. The concept of maintaining contact with them all was known to Israeli decision makers as "the peripheral alliance," and the intelligence community was in charge of this covert side of the nation's foreign policy.

In pursuing ties with the Kurdish minority in southern Iraq, Israeli operatives were following in the footsteps of Shiloah himself, who had worked with the Kurds under his journalistic cover in the 1930s. These mountain people were constantly struggling to obtain autonomy from the central government in Baghdad, and their most active and direct aid from the Mossad came in the 1960s when Israeli military advisers trained Kurdish guerrillas. Israeli cabinet minister Aryeh (Lova) Eliav, an almost legendary former Aliyah B operative, personally rode a mule over mountaintops in 1966 to deliver a field hospital to his Kurdish friends.[10]

Across the border to the east, in Iran, Aliyah B's Zion Cohen was recognized by the authorities in Teheran as the de facto representative of the Israeli government. The Shah of Iran, as leader of a Moslem nation, never established formal diplomatic relations with Israel. But the Shah respected Israel's struggle against the larger Arab countries, and he instructed the Iranian national airline to fly Jewish refugees from Iraq directly from Teheran to Tel Aviv.

Israel's main goal in its ties with Iran was to encourage pro-Israeli and anti-Arab views among Iranian government officials. The relationship was deep and all-embracing. The Mossad and Shin Bet helped train Iranian military men and agents of Savak, the Farsi acronym for *Sazmani-Amniyat Va Kisvar,* the "State Intelligence and Security Organization." Savak men were frequently in Israel, and the Iranians helped transfer aid to the Kurdish rebellion against Iraq.

The Mossad often had help from or coordination with the CIA and Britain's overseas intelligence agency, MI6. The Americans had become disenchanted with Nasser and changed their minds about clandestine collusion after opposing the Suez invasion in 1956.[11]

American and British efforts to draw Israel into a secret pro-Western alliance were especially strong in 1958 when anti-Western, pro-Nasser nationalism was scoring impressive gains. Nasserists came close to gaining control of Lebanon. In Iraq, Colonel Abdel Karim

Qassem seized power after murdering Nuri as-Said and the Hashemite royal family. Similar perils faced the Hashemite royal rulers of Jordan.

Washington and London advised Israel to participate in two cooperative groupings: the "northern tier" of a peripheral alliance tying Israel to Turkey and Iran; and the "southern tier" linking Israel with Ethiopia. All these states were involved in border disputes with Arab countries and feared Soviet subversion. Turkey was high on the list.

In December 1957, the Turkish prime minister Adnan Menderes met a special emissary from Israel, Eliyahu Sassoon, and arranged a follow-up session in June 1958 for intelligence officials of the two nations. The Israeli team was headed by Shiloah, even though he had not held any official Mossad position for years. Prime Minister Ben-Gurion and Foreign Minister Meir believed that Shiloah was the most appropriate person for secret diplomatic missions.

Ben-Gurion himself flew to Ankara to see Menderes on August 28, 1958, accompanied by Meir, Shiloah, and the army chief of staff. The official excuse for the presence of an El Al airliner in the Moslem nation was "engine problems" that forced a landing.[12]

The concrete result of all the talks was a formal, but top secret agreement for comprehensive cooperation between the Mossad and the Turkish National Security Service, the TNSS. The Mossad agreed on a similar pact, around the same time, with Iran's Savak.

At the end of 1958, the three secret agencies established a formal cooperation network called Trident, which held semiannual gatherings of all three espionage chiefs. Among their common interests were reports on the activities of Soviet spies throughout the Middle East. Turkey helped the Mossad by sharing information that TNSS agents had collected in Syria, dealing with the radical Arab regime's intentions toward Israel. Similar to the lessons for Savak men was the training the Mossad gave to Turkish secret agents in counterintelligence techniques and the use of technical devices.[13]

Israel's clandestine, alternative diplomats attempted to mirror their successes in the northern tier with similar work in the southern tier of the peripheral alliances. Sudan was of great interest to the Mossad because the country was just to the south of Israel's nemesis, Egypt's President Nasser. Just as he took command in Cairo in 1954, Sudan was in transition to independence with joint British-Egyptian administration. Politicians in Khartoum, the Sudanese capital, were alarmed that Nasser was intervening in their election campaign with slogans calling for "the unity of the Nile valley" — seen as a threat that Egypt would swallow Sudan.

Members of the populist Umma party and the nationalist Mahdia movement rushed to London, hoping for guarantees of British support against Egypt. Nasser's plan to nationalize the Suez Canal and expel British troops from the Canal Zone was likely to help the Sudanese gain sympathy. They also were banking on Prime Minister Anthony Eden's hatred of Nasser.

The Sudanese delegation was not satisfied, however, with London's response. The intelligence men at MI6 sounded sympathetic, but the diplomats of the Foreign and Commonwealth Office attempted instead to appease Nasser. The Sudanese happened to mention to MI6 contacts that they were willing even "to join with the Devil" to halt Egypt's expansionism, and that led the British intelligence men to suggest that they should indeed deal with the Arab world's Satan — namely, Israel. The British referred the Sudanese to an Israeli diplomat named Mordecai Gazit.

Gazit, then the first secretary of the Israeli embassy in London, had earlier been an operative in the Political Department of the foreign ministry. He did not resign in "the revolt of the spies" and continued to work in the ministry even after the department was dissolved. He happily met Sidki el-Mahdi and other politicians from Sudan in the exclusive Savoy Hotel, and various schemes for anti-Nasser cooperation were hatched. As a benefit to the poverty-stricken Sudanese, they would be taught to develop their cotton fields by Israeli experts who had made their own desert bloom.

Various politicians and parties came and went in Khartoum, but secret contacts between Sudan and Israel continued. Their peak came at a clandestine meeting in August 1957 at the Plaza Athenée Hotel in Paris between Foreign Minister Golda Meir and Abdallah Khalil, the Sudanese prime minister. The contacts ended abruptly the following year, when Khalil was overthrown by his army.

Further east, the Israelis, Americans, and British found Ethiopia in the 1950s to be more stable, pro-Western, and obviously of prime strategic importance, overlooking the sea lanes leading into the Red Sea and on toward Suez and Eilat. Emperor Haile Selassie had already been in power for over two decades, proclaiming himself a descendant of the ancient Hebrew tribe of Judah and using its symbol, a majestic lion, as his emblem. Selassie admired the Jewish state.

After an Israeli consulate was opened in Ethiopia, the diplomats were followed by agricultural advisers, by professors who helped establish the University of Addis Ababa, and by the inevitable military advisers and intelligence personnel. The Israelis helped the emperor train his security forces, and Israel was permitted to build a powerful listening post, which monitored Arab radio traffic. The Mossad ran a large "station" of operatives in the Ethiopian capital. Their work was similar to, but more extensive than, Asher Ben-Natan's intelligence tasks as head of the Israeli meat company in neighboring Djibouti before he went to France to help plan the invasion of Suez.

The United States and Great Britain supported and valued Israel's strategic contributions in establishing peripheral alliances, but Israel's true breakthrough into the top echelons of Western intelligence came with a coup scored in Europe. The Israelis managed to outrun all the CIA, MI6, French, Dutch, Belgian, and other Western spies who were scurrying around Eastern Europe in search of a speech. It was the secret speech delivered by the new Soviet leader Nikita Khrushchev to a special Communist party congress in Moscow in February 1956.

The address put an end to the Stalin era by detailing its horrors for the first time: the gulag prison camps, the show trials, and the killings. Khrushchev, who had just emerged from a collective leadership to be the new Soviet dictator, had to be better understood. The specific damage done to the Soviet Union by the late Stalin had to be cataloged. The Soviet leader's words could be used by Western propagandists to weaken the East's faith in Stalinism and communism.

In the search for a text, Western intelligence agencies tried to bribe Communists from the Soviet-bloc satellite states who had attended the Moscow congress. Most foreign guests, however, had been locked out of the February 23 session at which Khrushchev made his dramatic denunciation of Stalin. Each delegation from abroad was permitted to send only its leader into the hall, and these were top Communists so fiercely loyal to the Kremlin that they would never betray secrets to capitalist spies.

No wonder, then, that Allen Dulles would later remember April 17 as the date of one of the greatest accomplishments in his career as CIA director. It was on that date that Dulles received a printed copy of the

Russian speech from his counterintelligence chief, James Angleton, who reported that the mammoth text had been provided by "the Israelis." The cooperation agreement signed by the CIA and the Mossad five years earlier had now paid off. And the Mossad's reputation, in a flash, was made forever.

The man who personifies the Mossad, Isser Harel, is the only official — former or present — to confirm, on the record, that young and tiny Israel had managed to do the CIA such a huge favor. In his Hebrew-language memoirs, Harel wrote: "We provided to our American counterparts a document that is considered one of the biggest achievements in the history of intelligence: the full, secret speech of the First Secretary of the Soviet Communist Party." While confirming Israel's role in obtaining the Khrushchev speech for the West and calling it a "giant success," Harel still did not reveal who precisely got his or her hands on the speech — or how.[14]

The astonishing story which later emerged suggested that Harel simply never knew the source. The trail was difficult to follow decades later, but there were indications that it led through Poland and a Communist named Stefan Staszewski. He was the party chief in Warsaw in the 1950s and surprisingly revealed in the 1980s that he had personally lifted the veil of secrecy from Khrushchev's startling speech.

According to Staszewski, the Soviet party hierarchy sent texts of the speech to a few, selected Communists in the Eastern European satellite countries. A single copy, running fifty-eight pages in Russian, was brought by courier to Eduard Ochab, the first secretary of Poland's ruling party. He had not attended the Moscow congress and was shocked by what he read: total confirmation of all the worst allegations ever made about Stalin. It was like persuading a devout Christian no longer to believe in Jesus.

Ochab, cautiously and surreptitiously, shared the blasphemy from Moscow — in effect, the new gospel — with a few senior Polish Communists. At first, they had to read the one and only copy locked in his safe. He later ordered that it be translated into Polish, and limited, numbered copies were sent to municipal party chiefs, including Staszewski.

The Warsaw party boss decided that the speech ought to be more widely read and thus ordered that thousands of copies be made and distributed. He said he gave the text to three Western news correspondents, among them a newspaperman named Philip Ben.[15]

A Polish Jew born in Lodz in 1913 as Norbert Niszewski, Ben became a journalist in his teenage years but a soldier when Hitler's army invaded Poland in 1939. Niszewski served in the Polish Free Army, fleeing with his combat unit to refuge in the Soviet Union and later sent to the Middle East to liaise with British forces. Instead, his Jewish identity asserted itself in 1943 and he settled in Palestine, writing for Hebrew newspapers and abandoning his Polish name in favor of one that fit in better with the newborn Israeli culture. *Ben* means "son," and Philip was his father's first name.

Through Israel's independence in 1948 and the exciting years that followed, Ben wrote more about the outside world than he did about the Middle East and crises nearer home. His columns on international affairs showed flashes of brilliance, and the French newspaper *Le Monde* hired this intelligent Israeli in 1952. Eastern Europe was his special beat.

Ben built up an extensive network of sources, and his reputation grew larger than that of the average newsman. Moshe Avidan, who was Israel's ambassador to Poland in the 1950s, recalls that other diplomats in Warsaw used to approach the embassy for information because "your Israeli journalist knows everything." They meant Ben.

His reports on the workers' strike in Poznan in October 1956, in *Le Monde* and in Israel's *Ma'ariv,* caused such a sensation that the Polish authorities expelled him from the country. There was an additional reason: his love affair with a young and attractive Polish woman named Franka Toroncik. Ben, who was then married, smuggled his mistress out of Poland. When they declared him persona non grata, the Poles labeled Ben "an agent of Israeli and American intelligence."

His sister Hanna Tikicinski recalls: "He was always a man of mystery." "That's right," agrees Franka Toroncik, who has remained in Israel after sharing the rest of Ben's life with him. "It is correct that he knew how to keep secrets, and he wouldn't even tell me everything." After reporting for many years from the United Nations in New York, Ben died in 1978; and even though he wrote many thousands of words for public consumption, countless untold stories were buried with him.

One of the stories Ben locked away, according to the former Warsaw Communist chief Staszewski, was his role in publicizing Khrushchev's secret speech. One of Ben's longtime colleagues at *Ma'ariv* says it is "not impossible" and perhaps "only natural" that Ben helped his country's security agencies with information from the various cities he visited. If Staszewski did give the Khrushchev text to Ben, it may well have gone to Israeli intelligence — and then on to the CIA — rather than to *Ma'ariv* and its Israeli readers.

However, Staszewski also claimed that he gave the text to *New York Times* journalists Flora Lewis and Sidney Gruson, her husband at the time. Thinking back to 1956 with her faultless memory, Lewis says she and Gruson heard rumors of an important Khrushchev speech but despite their best efforts could not obtain the contents. Staszewski still insists that he personally gave a Khrushchev text to Philip Ben.[16]

Was Ben the secret agent who provided the speech to Israel, thus elevating the Jewish state into the big leagues of international intelligence? Only one man knows the whole truth. He is the Israeli spymaster who has managed to remain all but invisible throughout his life: Amos Manor, titular head of Shin Bet during most of Harel's years as Memuneh.

After rising through the ranks of Israeli security, Manor served as head of Shin Bet for eleven years until his retirement from the secret world in 1964. A businessman and member of various corporate boards a quarter century later, Manor seldom speaks with journalists. "I have never discussed my work and I will not now deviate from my habit," he says.

His one act of greatness, heretofore unknown, was obtaining the secret Khrushchev speech. It may come as a shock to intelligence analysts that Shin Bet — supposedly the domestic security agency — accomplished this feat, rather than the famed Mossad with its worldwide network of spies. But Manor had excellent sources in Eastern Europe, and apparently in the Soviet Union itself, who reported to Shin Bet rather than the Mossad because their main task was to trace Soviet-bloc attempts to infiltrate agents into Israel.

It was one of Manor's agents in the Soviet bloc who sent the Khrushchev speech in its original Russian to Shin Bet headquarters in the Jaffa neighborhood of Tel Aviv during the second week of April 1956. While his or her main order of business was to be an extension of Shin Bet's counterespionage function, the agent happened to have access to a Khrushchev text and passed it along as a curiosity.

Manor did not know Russian and asked a senior aide, who had immigrated to Israel from Russia, to translate the fifty-eight pages into Hebrew. Manor also assigned Shin Bet's top experts on the Soviet Union to read the text and judge whether it was authentic. The KGB already had a solid reputation for disinformation through fabricating documents.

On Friday the thirteenth in that month of April, at the end of the usual pre-Sabbath half day in the office, the Shin Bet chief sat at his desk in Jaffa and read the Khrushchev speech. He had been hearing for weeks that it was important, that it was a prize sought after by the CIA and others. It was indeed a strong speech, revealing much about the seemingly impenetrable politics of the Soviet Union.

When he finished reading the text, Manor put the Hebrew version into his briefcase — alongside the consensus opinion of his Soviet-affairs analysts, who declared it was genuine. He drove directly to Prime Minister Ben-Gurion's home in Tel Aviv and gave him the Hebrew translation and the Shin Bet analysis.

Manor and Ben-Gurion met again on Saturday, and when the prime minister was fully convinced that the Khrushchev speech was authentic he directed that it be passed immediately to the Americans. Only then did Manor drive to Isser Harel's house, to tell him for the first time about the text and to show it to the Memuneh — without naming the source, however.

Israel was always anxious to impress the Americans, and so it was that a mere two days after Ben-Gurion's personal decision to share the Khrushchev speech an Israeli intelligence courier was flying the text to Jim Angleton in Washington. The prime minister instinctively felt that this could be the breakthrough needed to make Israel a respected strategic ally of the United States. Ben-Gurion also felt that if Israel were itself to publicize the secret speech, it would further damage the Jewish state's already strained relations with its former Soviet benefactors.

The Khrushchev text was not merely read with great interest at CIA headquarters. The Americans leaked it to the *New York Times* and then had all twenty thousand words broadcast in all the languages of the Communist countries over Radio Free Europe and Radio Liberty. Printed texts were even tied to balloons and flown over the Iron Curtain into the Eastern-bloc nations. In this way, thousands of copies made their way into Poland. Perhaps this was the massive distribution of the Khrushchev speech recalled by former Warsaw party boss Staszewski. On the other hand, Philip Ben may have been Manor's man in Eastern Europe: the eyes and ears of the anti-Communist Shin Bet in the heart of the Communist bloc.

Even in his seventies, Amos Manor has no intention of ever revealing the name of the hero at the other end of the information pipeline. Manor is known to be annoyed that Harel, the ex-Memuneh, has tried to claim credit on behalf of the Mossad. It was not the Mossad but Shin Bet that got the secret Kremlin speech, but who in Europe sent it to Shin Bet? In the world of espionage, answers always lead to more questions.[17]

The Americans were not told of the precise process by which Israel obtained the elusive text, and as far as CIA director Allen Dulles was concerned it was the Mossad that had just demonstrated greatness. He rewarded both the Mossad and Angleton by putting him in charge of the "Israel account," as the bilateral relationship was known in the Agency. In addition to his job as counterespionage chief, Angleton became Israel's great advocate in U.S. intelligence and defense circles. Given the pro-Arab bias of most of the State Department and Pentagon, and of some CIA personnel, his friendship was an oasis in the American desert for the Israelis.

Angleton was even able to counter or distort information from other sources that was liable to harm Israel. When the U.S. military attaché in Tel Aviv sent a report in October 1956 that Israel was planning to attack Egypt, Angleton claimed that the information was not accurate. Intentionally or not, Israel's great friend in Washington helped to maintain the smoke screen that cloaked the preparations for the Suez invasion.[18]

Admiration for the Jewish state became an obsession with Angleton, who fell captive to the magic of Israeli intelligence. He zealously insisted on being the sole handler of the account. "Angleton had one major responsibility other than counterintelligence — Israel — which he had traditionally handled in the same totally compartmented fashion as counterintelligence," according to a later CIA director.[19]

Angleton was furious when others in the agency tried to make contact with the Israelis without his knowledge. His jealousy reached its peak in 1971 when Peter Wright, his counterintelligence counterpart in MI5, Britain's domestic security service, visited Washington. Angleton filed an official complaint to MI5 director Sir Martin Furnival Jones, charging that Wright conducted secret negotiations behind his back, regarding Israel and the Middle East, with other CIA officials. The British did not bother responding to the letter.[20]

On other occasions Angleton did not conceal his suspicions of Lord Victor Rothschild, London-based scion of the famous Jewish banking family. Rothschild was a former British intelligence operative, dating back to World War II, who maintained close ties with his ex-employers in London while nurturing personal friendships with Israel's intelligence chiefs. Angleton resented Rothschild's contacts.[21]

Israelis who worked with Angleton admit he had an unusual or even "kooky" personality, but they appreciate him for shattering the American wall of suspicion about Israel while paving the way for vital strategic cooperation. In November 1987, a year after Angleton died, Israel dedicated a "memorial corner" to its valued American friend. Within sight of the luxurious King David Hotel, where he loved to stay during his dozens of visits to Jerusalem, an inscription on a large stone was carved in Hebrew, English, and Arabic: IN MEMORY OF A DEAR FRIEND, JAMES (JIM) ANGLETON. It was unveiled at a gathering attended by present and former heads of the Israeli intelligence community.

Sharing reminiscences at the ceremony, Teddy Kollek, now mayor of Jerusalem, told how he met Angleton for the first time while touring CIA headquarters in September 1950. Minutes later, Kollek said, he happened to bump into a Briton he knew named Harold (Kim) Philby. Quite amazed, he hurried back to Angleton's office and asked him, "What is Philby doing here?"

"Kim is a good friend of ours and is the British MI6 representative in liaison with the CIA," Angleton replied.

Kollek had never liked Philby, possibly in part because the Briton's father had converted to Islam and settled in Saudi Arabia as a special adviser to the royal family there. More relevantly, Kollek felt he had to tell Angleton that he had known Philby in Austria in the 1930s — and that Philby was then decidedly left wing. Kollek had even attended his wedding to a Jewish Communist in Vienna. This was a part of his past that Philby concealed when he joined British intelligence.[22]

Angleton noted what his new Israeli friend said, but took no action until senior British diplomats Guy Burgess and Donald Maclean defected to Moscow in 1951. The CIA informed MI6 that Philby had also acted suspiciously and would no longer be welcome as liaison in Washington. Angleton's visceral anticommunism became obsessional and he launched a search for other traitors in the Western secret services, but he would always regret not pursuing Philby more doggedly after the tip from Kollek.

Another unheeded clue came from a British woman on a visit to Israel in 1961. Flora Solomon was the daughter of a wealthy Jewish banker in czarist Russia who had moved to England. She worked for the Marks and Spencer chain of stores, and like her employers she was an ardent Zionist. At a cocktail party near Tel Aviv, she met her old friend Lord Victor Rothschild. Solomon spoke harshly of Kim Philby, by then a British newspaper correspondent in Beirut, condemning his anti-Israel and pro-Arab newspaper articles. But one tiny remark she made intrigued Rothschild: "As usual, Kim is doing what his operators in Russia tell him to," said Solomon.

Rothschild responded with surprise, and Solomon told him how Philby had tried to recruit her in 1940 to work for Soviet intelligence. Philby had described his work to her as "secret and dangerous," and when she had not consented he had asked her not to tell anyone about it.

Word got back to both the Mossad and to British intelligence, but MI6 did not confront the matter quickly enough. In Lebanon, Philby heard that he was under suspicion and he simply disappeared in January 1962 — surfacing in Moscow late that year as a bemedaled general in the KGB, the Kremlin's *Komitet Gosudarstvennoy Bezopasnosti,* or "Committee for State Security."[23]

The British, smarting from three embarrassing defections, were impressed that the Israelis had known so much. Like Angleton in the United States, senior British intelligence men, including MI6 deputy chief Maurice Oldfield and MI5 deputy Peter Wright, came to appreciate the Mossad's abilities. Britain's secret services were realizing that Israel was not simply another third-class third-world country but a superpower in the intelligence world. Mossad liaison officers in London signed a formal cooperation agreement with MI6, similar to the pact between the Mossad and the CIA.[24]

From Israel's point of view, Oldfield became a British version of Angleton. The eldest of eleven children in a poor English farming family, Oldfield displayed his flair for intelligence work while stationed at Suez during World War II. He knew the Middle East, and he also knew Teddy Kollek. They met in the late 1940s and became good friends. Oldfield told Kollek that he had always admired Zionism. Kollek was very taken with Oldfield's personality, and their friendship would yield significant dividends in the 1970s when Oldfield became director of MI6, codenamed "C." Novelists Ian Fleming and John le Carré were also impressed by Oldfield, as Fleming's M in the James Bond series and le Carré's George Smiley were modeled on the real-life MI6 chief.[25]

Oldfield always made sure to protect Israel's interests in the British establishment, where civil servants and diplomats displayed hostility that could be summed up as "Arabist." The intelligence director was able to point to concrete benefits reaped by Britain from the hidden ties with the Jewish state.

The Israelis displayed their talent for unearthing security lapses in the case of Roy Guindon, a security officer with the Royal Canadian Mounted Police. Despite its equine title, the RCMP is equivalent to Shin Bet or America's FBI. Some Mounties are posted abroad as intelligence operatives, and Guindon was sent to Canada's embassy in Moscow in 1959. Among diplomats in the Soviet capital, Guindon soon earned a reputation as a ladies' man. When the women in his own embassy spurned his advances, word of his frustration reached the KGB. The Russian secret police, famed for their efficiency, set a classic trap for the Canadian. As bait, they used a young and attractive operative who called herself Larissa Fedorovna Dubanova.

By arranged coincidence, Guindon found himself seated next to Dubanova at the Bolshoi Ballet. By another coincidence, she spoke excellent English. Guindon and the lovely lady carried on an affair for a number of months, until she informed him that she was pregnant. KGB officers hurriedly arranged a secret and illegal wedding and now had Guindon exactly where they wanted him. Under the threat of never seeing Dubanova again, Guindon supplied the Soviet secret service with Canada's diplomatic codes and even planted electronic bugs in the Canadian embassy.

He was later transferred from Moscow to his country's embassy in Washington. Guindon continued to work for the KGB. His wife never had a baby, telling him she had an abortion, and the Soviet authorities "permitted" her to visit him in America only infrequently —just enough to keep the Canadian sufficiently interested to continue spying.

Guindon's treachery came to light only when he was transferred to Canada's embassy in Tel Aviv in the early 1960s. His telephone, like that of most foreign diplomats in Israel, was tapped. Shin Bet learned of his actions because Guindon was careless and spoke with his Soviet handler by phone. Israeli intelligence informed MI6. The British then told the Canadian Mounties, who quickly used a pretext to lure Guindon to London. Security officers then took him to Ottawa, where he confessed his guilt. In return for his full cooperation, he was not tried.[26]

Establishing strong links with foreign secret services was one of the greatest early achievements of Israeli intelligence, along with forming technological, strategic, and peripheral alliances for the Jewish state. These were the key contributions made by the intelligence community under the guidance of Shiloah.

However, when Shiloah died suddenly of a heart attack in May 1959 — while preparing for yet another clandestine mission to Turkey and Iran — he was quickly and totally forgotten. He had few political allies, quite a few enemies, a tendency to work alone, and no taste for making headlines. In any event, Shiloah and his grandiose concepts were relics of the past.

With Israeli intelligence barely eleven years old but in many ways reaching the age of maturity, the time was ripe for Isser Harel to reenter the stage and shift the spotlight to the detailed daily tasks of silently defending the country.

While the Memuneh was on the lookout for traitors, hardly any were found in Israel's diplomatic services and hostile spies were never unearthed in the Israeli intelligence community. "It's no wonder in a country constantly at war," former CIA director William Colby commented. "In America's Wild West, you would not have expected any cowboys to defect to the Indians."[27]

Constant and suspicious vigilance was an element, too, and the credit for establishing an excellent counterintelligence record goes to Harel. Fully in charge at the Mossad while more loosely overseeing Shin Bet for over a decade, he developed a highly personal style for directing Israeli security. Based largely on his own obsessions, Harel spent much of his time waging crusades.

FIVE

Harel the Crusader

IN ADDITION TO all his other qualities, Isser Harel had one more that made him a complex figure sitting on the throne of Israeli intelligence. He could ignore slights and snubs and convince himself utterly that he was uniquely qualified for the task of defending Israel.

Petty disappointments such as being shunted aside from the preparations for the Suez campaign in 1956, the formation of the technological espionage agency Lakam behind his back, and his exclusion from Israel's strategic and peripheral alliances did not stop Harel. Instead of gazing back with anger, he preferred to look ahead with hope.

Harel was devoted to serving Israel's interests and to consolidating Ben-Gurion's political primacy. The Memuneh surveyed the landscape for threats and concluded that a popular Hebrew-language magazine, *Ha-Olam ha-Zeh,* "This World," posed a clear and present danger to the prime minister, the Mapai party, and the entire system. Harel declared war on the weekly.

A mixture of juicy gossip, sex scandals, and investigative journalism, the magazine advocated reconciliation with the Palestinian Arabs and a generally unorthodox view of Israeli life. Its editor, Uri Avneri, called on Ben-Gurion to show magnanimity by allowing creation of a Palestinian state, despite Israel's victory in the War of Independence. In the early 1950s, that was sheer heresy.

Ben-Gurion and his centrally controlled method of government were natural targets for the magazine's poisoned darts. With true reciprocity, the ruling party hated Avneri. The Mapai political establishment organized a boycott against *Ha-Olam ha-Zeh,* but the publication kept its loyal readers. Circulation rose even further in 1956 when the magazine's cover splashed corruption allegations against the Tel Aviv police chief. The scandalous headlines were more than Harel could tolerate as faithful servant to the prime minister. The police chief, after all, just happened to be the premier's son, Amos Ben-Gurion.

Avneri also aimed his verbal artillery at Shin Bet itself, enraging Harel because at that time no one was writing about the Israeli secret services. Instead of naming Shin Bet, *Ha-Olam ha-Zeh* often referred simply to "the apparatus of darkness."

The magazine depicted the agency as a monster that cruelly infringed on civil rights, and Shin Bet was blamed for almost everything bad in Israel. When Avneri was beaten up by a group of off-duty paratroops, angered by a personal dispute, he blamed the security service. When one of the magazine's writers went into hiding, because of a love affair gone disastrously wrong, *Ha-Olam ha-Zeh* claimed that the man had been abducted by "the apparatus of darkness."

Avneri's antics annoyed not only Harel, the Memuneh, but also the titular head of Shin Bet, Amos Manor. Complaining of "provocations and lies" by the magazine, Manor put its staffers under surveillance, hoping to unearth some dirt against them. *Ha-Olam ha-Zeh* responded with investigative journalism, although somewhat bizarrely because it would be illegal to name any employee of the intelligence community in print.

Isser Harel decided to unleash an unusual weapon: a rival publication. In an attempt to cut Avneri's circulation, Shin Bet began to publish a weekly entitled *Rimon,* "Pomegranate," on August 1, 1956. Harel tried in vain to disguise the ownership of the new magazine. It was the mirror image of Avneri's publication. Instead of *Ha-Olam ha-Zeh*'s irreverent view of current events, *Rimon* offered the official establishment line alongside juicy show-business gossip meant to boost sales. The imitation's energy and writing were never as enticing as the original's, however.

Rimon launched a war of words against *Ha-Olam ha-Zeh,* but that did not sell many magazines, either. Manor had always felt uncomfortable with his boss Harel's magazine project, but no one could talk the Memuneh out of it until the circulation figures told their tale.

After an ugly exchange of mudslinging between the two publications, the intelligence community lost the circulation war. Three years of poor sales made it impossible for Shin Bet to afford financing *Rimon* any longer, and it folded.[1]

Harel could swallow his pride as a would-be publisher because of the formidable reputation he earned as a spy catcher. He foiled attempts by Communists to penetrate Israel's ruling circles, while simultaneously stopping similar missions by Arab countries and their agents. Around the same time that Harel exposed Goldstein/Avni as a Soviet spy in the Israeli foreign ministry, the Memuneh also caught Mary Frances Hagen.

Hagen was an American journalist at the United Nations headquarters in New York who was fond of many Arab delegates and agreed to spy in Israel for her fiancé, Syrian diplomat Galab al-Khieli. In 1956, she went to Israel as a foreign correspondent and began sending reports to Syrian intelligence. She seemed unusually interested in Israel's borders, so Shin Bet began to watch her around the clock. Harel's operatives arrested Hagen, and she was tried behind closed doors with her fellow correspondents not permitted to attend. Convicted of espionage on August 27, 1956, she spent eight months in an Israeli prison. The naive Hagen returned to New York, where she was surprised to find that Khieli did not even want to see her.[2]

Arab efforts to penetrate Israel were not, however, serious. Both the Israelis and the CIA observed that the intelligence services of the Arab countries lacked the diligence and stamina needed for long-term operations, which are the bread and butter of good espionage work. Great patience and attention to detail are required, with cool logic and no emotional involvement. The Israeli and American analysts believed that Arab spyhandlers fell short of the required level of skills.

The Soviet Union, on the other hand, was considered to have a huge pool of natural spy talent: the ability to sit and wait, thoroughness in piecing together the tiny details that complete a puzzle, and total detachment of the emotions from the work. In short, the Russians were great chess players and theirs were the most threatening pieces on the international espionage board.

Harel, of Russian stock himself, appreciated the talents of his Soviet-bloc foes and knew that some of them had to be spying in Israel. No doubt the Americans were right, he felt, when they warned that many Communist agents were planted among the Jews coming from Eastern Europe. There was little he could do about the ones who were working in minor industrial jobs or on agricultural settlements, mailing reports on life in the Jewish state to KGB controllers overseas. Harel aimed for perfection and wished that he could catch them all, but he concentrated on rooting out spies who might have reached positions of importance in Israel.

His sixth sense as a hunter of moles buried in Israeli society, and his obsession with Mapam, assumed new dimensions when he found that two members of the left-wing party were spies for the Soviet Union.

In the first case Shin Bet's counterespionage department spotted Aharon Cohen, a Mapam Middle East expert, meeting regularly with a Soviet diplomat who was stationed in Tel Aviv and identified as a KGB officer. Cohen was arrested in 1958, but his party leaders were so outraged that they rushed to Cohen's support and accused Harel of framing their friend. The accused spy admitted in court that he had met with Russians but insisted that he did not give them any secrets. He was convicted and sentenced to five years in prison, but Israel's supreme court later cut the prison term in half.[3]

The second prominent Mapam man arrested for spying was shockingly close to the prime minister. Lieutenant Colonel Israel Beer had won Ben-Gurion's unquestioning trust but was revealed to be a turncoat.

Beer was born in Vienna in 1912 and was a socialist from an early age. The life story he told spoke of fighting Fascists in the streets before the Nazis marched into Austria in 1938. Beer said he studied at a military academy in Austria and volunteered for the "international brigade" fighting Generalissimo Franco in Spain. Beer moved to Palestine in 1938, and on the basis of his claimed combat experience he was welcomed into the Haganah. His socialist views, his liberal education, and his expertise in military matters helped him befriend the leaders of the embattled Jewish community.

After independence was won in 1948, Beer came close to winning a post as the army's deputy chief of staff. Apparently disappointed and angry, he resigned his commission and took up work as the military correspondent for an Israeli newspaper. Around that time, he transferred his political allegiance from Mapam, where he was in the party's own security department, to Ben-Gurion's more centrist Mapai. He befriended leading defense figures including Shaul Avigur, Shimon Peres, and even the prime minister.

Before long, Ben-Gurion handed his private diary to Beer and asked him to write the official history of the War of Independence. The part-time job served as an excellent observation post, allowing Beer to see the most sensitive and secret documents on the defense of Israel.

Suspicion began to fall on Beer in 1956. General Moshe Dayan was only half joking when he pointed to the military historian and asked,

"What is that spy doing here?" This was just before Ben-Gurion, Dayan, and their entourage went to France for the secret negotiations at Sèvres that sent Israeli, British, and French troops to Suez. Dayan was surprised to find that Beer was at the clandestine assembly point, even though he was not going to fly to Paris.[4]

Harel harbored his doubts and ordered surveillance of Beer, but the nominal head of Shin Bet, Amos Manor, hesitated before taking action against the prime minister's friend. As the Memuneh, Harel took charge and ordered Beer's arrest — if he could be caught red-handed — on March 31, 1961.

Beer was picked up that day by Shin Bet and police officers while delivering documents to Victor Sokolow, a KGB officer under cover as a Soviet diplomat in Tel Aviv. The file contained extracts from Ben-Gurion's diary and a secret report on an Israeli defense corporation.[5]

Beer had caught Harel's watchful eye by establishing unauthorized contacts with West German intelligence chief General Reinhard Gehlen of the BND, the *Bundesnachrichtendienst*, or "Federal Intelligence Service."

Gehlen and his agency had a special place in the NATO alliance's plans for the defense of Europe. Gehlen had worked in World War II for Hitler's military intelligence unit, Abwehr, running spies in the Soviet Union. Now that he was working with the CIA and MI6, Gehlen revived his sleeper agents in Russia. The Soviets were aware of the threat posed by the BND, and they wanted someone to find out what Gehlen was doing. Beer — a senior Israeli who would be trusted in Bonn — could probably find out for his true masters in the KGB.

The West Germans, brimming with their postwar willingness to please the Israelis, granted Beer a surprising degree of access to the German army, NATO installations, and American and other bases. Beer even obtained, for his Soviet handlers, details of the construction contracts for U.S. nuclear missile sites in Europe. As a by-product of his espionage ventures, he gave the Soviets information on Israel's purchases of arms, visits by Israeli officers to Europe, and the morale of Israel's army.

Harel suspected that Beer had been planted in Israel from the beginning by the Communists and was activated on the orders of a correspondent in Tel Aviv for the Soviet news agency Tass in 1956. The Russians paid Beer in cash, which he promptly squandered on women, bars, and fine restaurants.

His life story was remarkably similar to that of the British traitor Kim Philby. Both were Communist sympathizers, recruited by Soviet intelligence in the Spanish Civil War as "sleeper agents" to be activated later. Beer, like Philby, penetrated the heart of the security establishment of his own country, becoming a highly valuable asset of the Soviets before ending his career as a successful journalist.

Philby, however, was never caught by the West. Beer was. In court, he admitted that he had invented his past. He had never received a doctorate in history, as he boasted, nor had he ever set foot in Spain. Confusion over who he really was deepened when, in prison, he renounced his courtroom confession and claimed his original autobiography was true.

Even without knowing his real name and background, the Israeli judges found the evidence against Beer to be incontrovertible, and the Tel Aviv court had ample reason to sentence him to fifteen years in prison for espionage. Until his dying day in prison in 1966, he insisted that he was no spy but a genuine patriot seeking only to make Israel nonaligned rather than pro-Western.[6]

Even if Beer had never existed, the Americans still would have good reason to suspect the ability of the Israelis to prevent moles from penetrating their security establishment. Since its birth in 1948, little Israel was a big target for Soviet intelligence and a massive sieve when it came to leaking secrets. The Russians were interested in Israel's geographical location and its widespread contacts with the West. Soviet agents included Eastern European diplomats, journalists, and scientific and commercial delegations.

A vast network of agents was needed to support this intensive activity, and the Soviets had some sixty employees in their Tel Aviv embassy. Around half were agents of the KGB or GRU, the *Glavnoe Razvedyvatelnoe Upravlenie,* the military's "Chief Intelligence Directorate of the General Staff." They recruited Israeli agents but because local Communists were under suspicion and Shin Bet surveillance, the Soviets preferred non-Communists in the Israeli establishment.

Among the espionage targets were diplomatic spouses. In the summer of 1955, the wife of a senior Israeli diplomat in one of the Communist countries of Eastern Europe returned home for a visit. In Tel Aviv, of all places, she met and fell in love with a Soviet diplomat. Watching the Russian, Shin Bet was instantly aware of the affair.

Harel's people invited the woman to the agency's headquarters and told her to break off all contacts with her lover.

At the same time, to protect the husband from being blackmailed he was summoned, without explanation, to Austria. He was astonished to find Harel himself waiting in the diplomat's hotel room in Vienna. Without mincing words, the Memuneh told the cuckolded Israeli the facts of life: his wife was sleeping with a Soviet, and therefore he would be transferred out of the Eastern bloc. The diplomat understood what was necessary, but he was naturally shaken by both the adultery and his sudden career move.[7]

Israel's diplomats were warned, before leaving for Eastern Europe, not to become entangled in love affairs. In fact, the foreign ministry refused to send single men or women beyond the Iron Curtain, and Shin Bet security officers were posted in every embassy to watch for potential blackmailers. However, such precautions can never be foolproof when human lust, passion, and foolishness are at play.

In February 1959, a senior Israeli diplomat in an Eastern European capital received a letter that said:

> Dear Sir,
> Some time ago, a number of sensitive pictures came into my possession, which testify to your intimate relationship with Miss Dagmar Novotna. If I use these pictures for blackmail against you or against the woman involved in these pictures with you, it will no doubt be unpleasant for you and for Miss Dagmar Novotna. I have thought about it, and have reached the following conclusion. The matter can still be covered up — provided you come to Vienna in the near future to speak to my assistant. He is completely trustworthy. You must arrive in Vienna by the end of February. I suggest that you stay at the Hotel Sacher. I would request your reply within fourteen days from the receipt of this letter.[8]

The diplomat, braving the unpleasant risk of scandal, informed Israel's foreign ministry of the attempted blackmail. His superiors hurriedly removed him from the Eastern bloc.

Harel's relentless search for Israeli traitors was the product of an honest concern for the nation's security, combined with his personal hatred of communism. In addition, as Shiloah before him, Harel wanted to prove to the United States that Israel was a reliable partner. As he was uncompromising by nature, like a crusader on a constant quest for perfection, Harel tried to prove that he could be holier than the Pope. If Allen Dulles of the CIA and John Foster Dulles, his brother in the State Department, saw "a Red under every bed," Harel was out to demonstrate that even pink had to be eliminated from Israel's bedrooms.

The Memuneh was therefore disappointed when he discovered in 1960 that Professor Kurt Sitta had penetrated Israel's scientific community. Sitta was born in 1910 in the Sudetenland of Czechoslovakia to a non-Jewish German family. Sitta studied in Prague, where he was considered to be a genius in mathematics and physics. The Gestapo arrested him, and he was imprisoned in the Buchenwald concentration camp because his wife was Jewish. He shared harrowing experiences with prominent Communists who were imprisoned in the camp, and when some of them went to work for Czech intelligence after the war they recruited their friend Sitta to be a spy.

He studied nuclear physics in Britain and then taught the subject at Syracuse University in New York. The FBI, believing that he was a Communist agent, interrogated Sitta and offered to hire him as a double agent. It was thus under shady circumstances that he left the United States for Brazil in 1953. Two years later he was invited to lecture at the Technion in Haifa, Israel's equivalent of MIT, and he found that he liked the school, the country, and the people. Or so he said, as he gladly accepted the post of chairman of the physics department.

Sitta's rare success, as a non-Jewish foreigner in Israel, provided a golden opportunity for the Czechs and their ultimate Soviet masters. An intelligence officer working under diplomatic cover at the Czechoslovak embassy in Tel Aviv met frequently with the professor between 1955 and 1960, collecting a huge mountain of material. It took nearly five years, but Harel's Shin Bet finally detected the espionage operation.

On the clear and somewhat cool night of June 16, 1960, two men knocked on the door of Sitta's villa on Horeb Street in an exclusive suburb of Haifa, which faced the Mediterranean much as San Francisco overlooks its bay. One of the men was a Shin Bet operative, the other with the special branch of the national police. They drove Sitta away to arraign him on charges of spying.

His arrest shocked his friends, students, and colleagues in both the Technion and the political leadership of Israel. They could scarcely believe the accusations, but when some of them attended his trial they were shocked again to hear what a damaging spy he had been.

Sitta's focus had been on Professor Bergman's Israel Atomic Energy Commission. By coincidence or not, Sitta was arrested just two days before Israel's experimental nuclear reactor at Nahal Sorek was operational. Israeli analysts compare his activities with those of Julius and Ethel Rosenberg in the United States and Klaus Fuchs in Britain, who betrayed their countries' atomic secrets to the Soviet bloc.

Sitta was sentenced to five years in prison, but Israel — to end the embarrassment — quickly paroled him to start a new academic life in West Germany.

Harel and the Israeli secret services launched efforts to repair the damage done to their record as mole hunters, which was quite impeccable up until Sitta. They claimed that he was just a small fish who only dabbled in spying because of blackmail, as Czechoslovakia's secret police threatened to harm his elderly father still living there. Harel's version insisted that Sitta had provided the Communists with insignificant information that did not touch on nuclear matters. He also blamed the FBI for not telling Israel everything previously known about Sitta. Shin Bet, properly informed, could have caught him earlier.[9]

Harel could find solace and success in his tireless efforts to bring new citizens to Israel. Alongside his obsessions with mole hunting and pursuing spies, Jewish immigration was one of Harel's constant interests. The first Mossad chief, Reuven Shiloah, had initially brought the intelligence community into the business of immigration, but Harel developed it into a fine art.

After a few years of relative inactivity on the immigration front, in 1953 there was a reawakening of ethnic consciousness in the two great Jewish communities that were reservoirs of future Israeli citizens: in the Soviet bloc and in the Arab world.

Veteran Aliyah B chief Shaul Avigur found himself without a job when the clandestine immigration agency was abolished in 1952. He returned to Kinneret, his kibbutz by the Sea of Galilee, and felt frustrated after two decades of active and secret service to his people. Avigur got some help from his brother-in-law, Foreign Minister Moshe Sharett, who became prime minister in December 1953 when Ben-Gurion began a two-year absence from the job. Sharett telephoned Isser Harel and asked the Memuneh to do Avigur a favor. "Bring Shaul back into the business," the new prime minister said.[10]

Harel was reluctant, but because he wished to maintain cordial relations with Sharett he agreed to the silent establishment of a new organization that was called simply "the Liaison Bureau." Avigur was its head, but ambiguity surrounded details such as to whom the new unit was responsible. Avigur held the obfuscating title of "assistant for special matters" to the defense minister. But the unit's offices were in the foreign ministry, and administratively it was part of the prime minister's office.

The Liaison Bureau's initial duties were to direct the struggle, within and outside Israel, for Jews to be permitted to leave the Soviet Union. The new unit would ensure that all efforts toward that aim were housed under one roof.

There were no rivalries or real arguments among the various intelligence agencies to prevent or delay the birth of the specialized agency. Bringing Soviet Jews to their Zionist homeland was a consensus mission, a true product of unity and common purpose.

The timing was not a matter of mere chance or of doing favors for Avigur and his brother-in-law Sharett, but cold political calculation. As long as Israel had maintained good relations with Moscow and its satellite states, Jerusalem did not want to irritate the Soviet bloc and attempted to play down the Jewish question. After the Korean War, however, Israel's leaders decided to adopt a clearly pro-Western orientation and they felt that they had nothing to lose. This was especially true when immigration from Hungary, Rumania, and Poland ceased and disturbing reports of anti-Semitism under Stalin emerged.

To carry out its assignment — as evidenced by its title — of keeping in contact with Jews, the Liaison Bureau sent its own special diplomats to the Soviet Union, which had the world's second-largest Jewish community: three million strong, second only to the six million of the United States.

Avigur chose his representatives extremely carefully. First, they had to be volunteers who demonstrated "high Zionist motivation." They had to know Jewish traditions and customs, because much of their work consisted of meetings in synagogues with Jews and Israel could not be disgraced by having representatives who were not qualified for Orthodox prayer.

The diplomats of the Liaison Bureau had to be relatively young to withstand the physical and mental ordeals of their assignments. Being in Moscow could be uncomfortable enough, but these men and women had to travel to all corners of the Soviet Union by various exhausting, long-distance routes. Married couples with families were preferred. Israel did not want to have any singles in its embassies, for it felt that they would be more vulnerable to subversion by sexual temptation. The candidates had to speak Russian with at least elementary proficiency.[11]

One of Avigur's men in Moscow was Aryeh (Lova) Eliav, who had long experience with Aliyah B as a clandestine emissary. He was sent to Russia in the summer of 1958 as the Israeli embassy's second secretary. In addition to his duties as a member of the consular team, dealing with property and other bilateral issues, Eliav disclosed in his memoirs that his work included slipping pocket-sized Jewish calendars or miniature Hebrew-Russian dictionaries into the jackets of Jews in synagogues. The diplomats also distributed prayer books, Bibles, Israeli newspapers, and books in Hebrew, even though they knew that the Soviet authorities considered these to be "antistate propaganda."

The KGB knew what Eliav's job was, more or less, and in due course the secret police arranged to have him seduced. As he traveled from Moscow to the University of Leningrad one day, Eliav noticed a remarkably attractive young woman at the capital's train station. She had the kind of European style that was all too rare in Moscow, and it was hard to resist looking at her. He ran into her again that evening in the hotel in Leningrad. Although quite certain that the young woman had been sent to compromise him and thus put him into the blackmailing clutches of the KGB, Eliav decided that he could not be hurt if he merely flirted with her, and he trusted himself to withstand further temptation.

Eliav asked the mystery woman to dance, and she responded enthusiastically. The Israeli had never experienced the kind of tango he danced that night. He felt her warmth as she clung to him. Hot kisses on his lips were but an invitation to further pleasures.

At this point, Eliav decided that matters had gone far enough and that the game might become dangerous. He fled the woman's embrace and found solitary shelter in his own hotel room. He locked the door until morning. He knew that if he was caught with that lady, the theatrics to follow could involve a "deceived husband" threatening to kill him, the mediation of "hotel employees," and finally a happy "arrangement" that would require Eliav to become a KGB plant in his embassy.[12]

Another Soviet technique was to use hidden cameras to film espionage targets making love, and to use the film for blackmail. According to a story circulated among Israeli and other diplomats, President Sukarno of Indonesia had an affair with a KGB plant, but when Soviet agents came and showed him incriminating photographs Sukarno did not give a damn. He is said to have nonchalantly pointed at the snapshots, saying: "I would like six of this picture and a dozen of that one."[13]

The special attention paid by Soviet intelligence to the Liaison Bureau diplomats stemmed from the KGB's certainty that these Israelis were spies, and the Soviets thus tried to obtain information about them even before they left Israel on their missions.

In March 1958, Israel informed the Soviet embassy in Tel Aviv that Lieutenant Colonel Moshe Gat was being sent to serve as the second secretary at Israel's embassy in Moscow. The Liaison Bureau requested the visa. A Soviet diplomat who was a secret agent asked one of his Israeli informers to check on Gat's background. Unfortunately for the KGB man, the Israeli whom he asked was a double agent who immediately reported to his true case officer in Shin Bet's counterespionage department.[14]

When diplomats of the Liaison Bureau arrived in the Soviet Union, the authorities there imposed especially strict travel limitations and tried to prevent them from meeting with Jews. "KGB men followed us 24 hours a day, including when we came and left, even within our homes and rooms," Eliav recalls. "Open surveillance, hidden surveillance, electronic surveillance, optical surveillance. All of these were constantly available to the KGB. But in addition, there was almost no member of our staff who had not been subject to more drastic measures: starting with staged 'scandals' against us by 'enraged citizens,' and including attacks and threats of imprisonment." The Soviet authorities realized that synagogues, in the absence of any other Jewish institution, became much more than merely houses of prayer, and they attempted to keep the Israeli diplomats away from the few Jews who attended Sabbath and holiday services.[15]

In another case, the KGB devoted special attention to Eliyahu Hazan, yet another second secretary at the embassy in Moscow. The Israeli eventually realized that the maid who worked in his apartment was a KGB agent. That was not so unusual, but a bout of food poisoning suffered by Hazan's wife was odd indeed. Severe stomach trouble struck just after Eliyahu and Ruth Hazan arrived in Odessa, on the Black Sea, to meet a Jewish contact in September 1955. Ruth was rushed to a hospital just after her husband went off to his meeting.

When he returned to the Odessa hotel, Hazan was stopped by KGB men who asked him to accompany them. He protested his detention and claimed that he had diplomatic immunity, but the secret policemen ignored international niceties and accused him of engaging in anti-Soviet activity. Some books he had given to the Soviet Jew were forbidden propaganda, they told him. Hazan was interrogated for many hours, and the questioning concentrated on his meetings with Jews.

The Soviets stepped up the pressure and demanded that Hazan work for them. He was told that the maid in his house was pregnant with his child — physiologically impossible, from the Israeli's point of view — and the Soviets threatened to publicize the scandal unless he signed a statement that he had volunteered to spy for them. They tellingly added that if he did not cooperate, "Your wife will not recover from her stomach troubles." By then, it had become clear that she had been poisoned.

Hazan's loyal resistance broke and he agreed to be an agent for the Soviets. The KGB gave him three days of briefings, a first payment of fifteen hundred rubles for "expenses," and his freedom. Ruth was feeling better, and they returned to Moscow from Odessa. For two days, Hazan suffered terrible pangs of conscience. His colleagues in the embassy sensed that he was frightened and agitated. Ambassador Yosef Avidar invited him in for a chat, and Hazan nervously confessed what he had done.

Accompanied by a fellow diplomat, Hazan was placed on the first flight to Israel, where he was quickly dismissed from the foreign ministry. No disciplinary action was taken against him, however. By late 1955, serving only as foreign minister, Moshe Sharett noted in his private diary: "It is shameful that one of our men could not resist, but caved in to threats and was broken. This is a blot on us."[16]

On the other battlefield of clandestine immigration, the Middle East, Israel's alternative diplomats were looking for ways to re-create the electrifying operations that had brought out the Jews of Iraq and Yemen. The next major human wave from the Sephardic or "Oriental" part of the world was expected from Egypt in November 1956.

At the beginning of the Suez/Sinai campaign, Shaul Avigur sent a small team of operatives to Egypt. Their mission was to take advantage of the joint military operations with the British and French to establish contact with Egyptian Jews and arrange their clandestine departure for Israel. On November 9, Lova Eliav and Avraham Dar, who had been the handler of the 1951 Israeli espionage network, left for Egypt with an Aman radio operator — all wearing French uniforms and flying in a French military aircraft to Port Said, at the entry to the Suez Canal.

Operation Tushia, the word for "cunning," began with the hope that the intelligence operatives would be able to reach Egypt's Jews and persuade most of them to leave for Israel. The plan was for Eliav, Dar, and their radio man to advance alongside the British and French forces as they marched on Cairo and Alexandria, which had large Jewish communities numbering thousands. When the Anglo-French force halted its invasion, the three Israelis found themselves stuck, however, in Port Said — where there were only two hundred, mostly elderly, Jews.

Still, they would have to do. Eliav and Dar went to the local synagogue, where they thinly disguised their true identity and offered to arrange safe passage out of Egypt. The Port Said Jews realized that the two "Frenchmen" they had met were Israeli secret agents, and sixty-five Jews packed their bags. They were taken to the dock, where they boarded two French navy landing craft.

The two small vessels sailed a few miles into the Mediterranean, where they rendezvoused with two ships of the tiny Israeli navy, which — with the cooperation of French secret agents — were camouflaged as two Italian fishing vessels, the *Aphrodite* and the *Castello del Mare*. French sailors carried the old people and the women from the landing boats to the Israeli ships, where they were greeted by a veteran agent of Aliyah B immigration operations in Iraq, Shlomo Hillel. A day later, they docked in Haifa. Eliav, Dar, and the radio man returned to Israel two days later the same way they had gone to Egypt, with the aid of French intelligence.[17]

The mini-exodus from Port Said was only a small-scale venture and an easy one to execute, thanks to French assistance. The clandestine departure of Jews from other nations involved tens of thousands of people, and Morocco was a prime example.

On March 2, 1956, French colonial rule in Morocco ended. Until then, for eight years, its exit gates had been open and about a hundred thousand Moroccan Jews had moved to Israel. In the early days of Moroccan independence, however, the new government gave in to the pressures of fellow Arab states and forbade the departure of Jews. Egypt's President Nasser bitterly declared that Jewish immigrants instantly became Israeli soldiers who killed Arabs.

The fate of the remaining hundred thousand Jews in Morocco was naturally the subject of great concern in Israel. Isser Harel, Memuneh of the intelligence community, had foreseen this two years earlier, when Morocco was still under French rule. To prepare for unexpected disruptions of the immigration campaign, Harel had established a secret infrastructure for Zionist activity in Morocco. The Mossad recruited a team of kibbutz members and reserve officers of Moroccan origin who spoke Arabic and French. All had to have been in combat units, and preferably they had experience in clandestine activities.

The intelligence officer in charge of the Israeli network in Morocco was Shmuel Toledano. He was known to colleagues as "Amnon," a nom de guerre he took with him when he left the military ranks of Aman to become a Mossad operative in 1954. Toledano worked under diplomatic cover at the Israeli embassy in Paris, where he concentrated on protecting Jewish interests around the globe — a duty unlike that of any other intelligence agency in the world.

The original aim of Toledano's unit, codenamed "Framework," was to organize young Moroccan Jews to defend their community if, as they feared, their Arab neighbors launched pogroms or other disturbances. When the legal emigration under French auspices ended in 1956, however, Framework was assigned to find a way to renew it by illegal means.

This was, probably unconsciously on Harel's part, a repeat of the pattern that had worked in Iraq until the network there fell. This time, though, the Mossad agents were able to learn from the mistakes of the past, and they were better equipped for the venture. Along the pattern devised by Shiloah in 1952, the responsibility for operating Framework was shared between the Mossad and the Jewish Agency. When complaints were heard Harel cut them short — not wanting to fall into the Iraqi-style trap of dissension — by firing Toledano's deputy, Shlomo Havilio, in February 1960 and making Alex Gatmon the Framework commander working undercover in Morocco.

Up until that point, about eighteen thousand Jews had left Morocco for Israel. The Mossad operatives established headquarters in the large towns of the new North African state, and they started using forged documents and other deceptions to arrange the departure of Jews willing to leave for their ancient Promised Land.

To the religious North African Jews, the young Israeli agents seemed to be envoys from the Messiah. The Jews were instructed to gather at various meeting places in the large cities, and from there they were taken by taxi or truck to the border. To smooth the way, the Mossad paid half a million dollars in bribes to Moroccan officials. A favorite route out was through Tangier, which at the time was an international city, and from there on to Israel. Later, two towns in Spain were used as bases for the project, which had the full cooperation of Generalissimo Francisco Franco — acting, so the Mossad believed, out of guilt feelings for Spain's close ties with Hitler and Mussolini and even for the expulsion of Spanish Jews in 1492.

The Mossad also purchased a former army camp along the southern coast of Spain, but actually inside the British crown colony of Gibraltar. The grounds and barracks were converted into an absorption camp for Moroccan immigrants. The British authorities knew, of course, how their old military base was being used but agreeably looked the other way. From the time that the Jewish refugees arrived in the camp, the Jewish Agency had the responsibility for putting them up, sailing them to the French port of Marseilles, and then aboard larger ships to Israel.

Tragedy struck on January 10, 1961. A fishing boat called the *Pisces,* packed with clandestine Jewish refugees, capsized in a storm between the Moroccan coast and Gibraltar. Forty-three men, women, and children, together with a Mossad radio operator, drowned. The disaster aroused worldwide sympathy, but it also triggered a sharp response from the Moroccan authorities. They uncovered the underground network, arrested scores of Zionist activists, and jeopardized the entire operation.

Israel asked the governments of France and the United States, as well as international welfare organizations, to apply pressure on Morocco. Luckily, King Hassan II was crowned in early March and had a high interest in gaining Western support, coupled with no interest at all in being seen as the persecutor of a Jewish minority. The king cooperated. The sinking of the ship thus had the ironically positive effect of accelerating the Jewish emigration from Morocco and making the entire project better organized.

The renewed operation to relocate Moroccan Jewry was given a biblical code name, Yakhin, the name of one of the two central pillars that supported the Holy Temple built in Jerusalem by King Solomon. Israel regarded immigration as a major pillar that supported the existence of the Jewish state.

Operation Yakhin was a joint project of Morocco, Israel, and France. Mossad agents fanned out to almost every Jewish neighborhood in Morocco. They invited the people to come live in their ancient homeland and were overwhelmed by the positive responses. The Mossad men gave instructions for reaching the rendezvous points and then brought the Jews by bus and truck to Moroccan ports, where ships and planes picked them up. France helped coordinate the transport arrangements.

More than eighty thousand Jews left Morocco under Yakhin's aegis. The Israeli-Moroccan cooperation also yielded an unusual by-product in another Arab country — Tunisia, less than a thousand miles to the east. In the summer of 1961 the Tunisian government demanded that the former colonial ruler, France, shut down its naval base at Bizerte. In the crisis that followed, the Tunisians arrested some French citizens as well as a few dozen Jews in Bizerte.

The Mossad agents in Morocco began to fear for Tunisia's Jews and arranged for French warships — following the pattern of Port Said — to sail off the North African coast and take on one thousand Jews from the coast at Bizerte. They were transported first to France and then on to Israel.[18]

While the Moroccan operation was getting into full gear, Harel had to turn to other concerns, and among them was arresting and punishing the man remembered for the most severe deviation from the high personal standards set for Israeli intelligence operatives. His name was Mordecai (Motke) Kedar.

Kedar was recruited by military intelligence in the summer of 1956 for a mission in Egypt. Colonel Yuval Ne'eman, Aman's technological expert usually concerned with inventing and developing new espionage gadgets, gave Kedar his final briefing at the Ta'am Tov ("Good Taste") Café in Tel Aviv. The new operative would first be flying to Argentina, to spend many months building up a cover story, before penetrating Egypt on behalf of Aman's Unit 131 operations department.

Kedar was born in Poland in the early 1930s as Mordecai Kravitzki. He was abandoned by his mother, brought to Palestine by his grandfather, and lived in Hadera, an agricultural town along the coastal road from Tel Aviv to Haifa. In his youth, he showed signs of high intelligence, leadership qualities, and a strong physique, but also definite criminal tendencies.

In the 1948 war, Kravitzki/Kedar served in the small Israeli navy but went AWOL because of disciplinary problems. In the early 1950s, he was a leader of the small but violent underworld of Hadera, a town north of Tel Aviv. His gang of criminals stole cars and handled other stolen property, and the police linked his name to armed robbery and murder cases. Kedar was arrested, but the authorities did not have enough evidence to press a case against him. Residents of Hadera's gangland feared Kedar more than they did the police, and they refused to cooperate with the authorities.

He moved to Tel Aviv, became a regular at various Bohemian cafés, beguiled women, and lived a life of leisure and extravagance without anyone knowing where he got his money. In private, he was tense and irritable and he started to go to a psychiatrist, Dr. David Rudi.

What Kedar did not know was that the good doctor was on the payroll of the intelligence community. He was notorious in the secret services for bizarre preliminary interviews with potential recruits, where he would clench his pipe between his teeth and ask a first question such as "How many times a month do you engage in sexual intercourse?" or "How often did you masturbate before you lost your virginity?" The would-be agent's reaction was noted, as Dr. Rudi posed a more serious follow-up question such as "Would you please tell me why you're willing to take a mission you might not return from?"[19]

In short order, Dr. Rudi performed the miracle of declaring Kedar fit for human society. The psychiatrist then introduced him to General Yehoshafat Harkabi, head of Aman, who recruited Kedar for Unit 131. As far as his friends and family were concerned, Kedar vanished shortly after the 1956 Suez/Sinai campaign. His wife and young son, whom he abandoned, began to receive postcards from him in various places around the world.

In November 1957, Kedar was summoned back to Israel. He flew first class on El Al from Paris, was taken to a small room at Tel Aviv's Lod airport, and was asked to write a routine report of his activities.

Then, unexpectedly, three armed policemen entered the room and arrested him.

For eighteen months, until May 1959, hardly anyone — even in the intelligence community — knew what had happened to Motke Kedar. He had disappeared again, this time without any trail of postcards, as if swallowed up by the earth.

Even the guards in Ramle Prison did not know who their new inmate was or why he was kept in total isolation. Only after half a year of solitary confinement was he permitted to walk by himself in the exercise yard for half an hour a day. He was moved to another cell, which was larger, but he was unable to see any other prisoners. Rumors began to circulate, inside and outside Ramle, about a Prisoner X known by no other name.

Avri El-Ad/Frank, the former Unit 131 case officer in Egypt who survived the Lavon Affair but was then jailed in Ramle, says he was known there only as "X4." In the neighboring cell — in shackles and unable to be heard through the thick walls — was Motke Kedar. They played chess, mentally, by tapping out their moves by Morse code on the wall. "Don't let them drag you down!" Kedar once tapped. "If you let them demoralize you, you're a broken man."[20]

After several incomplete, censored references to him in the Israeli press, the government confirmed only that a still unnamed man — understood by the newspapers to be connected with the secret services — had been arrested for serious criminal offenses. His trial was held behind closed doors, and he was sentenced to twenty years in prison.

Kedar refused to confess to the crimes with which he had been charged. He was not broken. In prison, he maintained his physical fitness and became a disciple of Ayn Rand and her philosophy. After seventeen years in prison — seven years without a cellmate — Kedar was released in 1974 and demanded a new hearing. The police, prosecutors, and the intelligence community all rejected his request.[21]

The Israeli government has maintained its absolute silence about the Kedar case, which continues to be one of its best-kept secrets. What the authorities wish to conceal is the fact that Kedar was not sentenced for mere criminal acts, but for murder committed abroad while on assignment for the intelligence community.

In Argentina, Kedar killed a Jewish businessman in November 1957 and stole his money. The victim was brutally stabbed eighty times. He was Kedar's contact, the person who was meant to help construct his cover story before the mission in Egypt. Most of the stolen cash was found in Kedar's pockets when he flew into Tel Aviv.

The precise nature of the quarrel or other motive for the killing is impossible to determine because of the secrecy and embarrassment still surrounding Kedar and his crime. He was clearly a bad choice for a delicate intelligence mission but the Aman chief who selected him, now Professor Harkabi, the active peace campaigner in Jerusalem, says only that "people who are recruited for these operations are not uncomplicated people. There is always some type of story."[22]

Isser Harel, who was responsible for recalling Kedar and putting him on trial, has disclosed that serious consideration was given to simply killing him so as to cover up the crime. There would then be even less chance of a diplomatic clash with Argentina or any embarrassment to the intelligence community. "I was insistent from the beginning that we cannot take the law into our own hands," Harel wrote. "For this there are judges and courts. The British services may eliminate people. We do not."

Harel proudly added: "During my tenure as Memuneh, no traitor was ever executed."[23]

From Harel's viewpoint, the Kedar case supplied further proof for his old argument that running secret agents is too serious a business to be left to Aman. Harel wanted it all for the Mossad. Eventually, a deal was struck. Responsibility for operations in Arab countries remained in the hands of military intelligence, but Harel was permitted to extend his own tiny operations department to responsibility for the rest of the world.

Harel established the operations unit with his typically uncompromising vigor. As he was, in practice, in charge of both Shin Bet and the Mossad, he insisted that the new unit be available to both agencies and that it use the best human resources of both. Leading this department were Rafi Eitan and Avraham Shalom, previously named Bendor, who would both feature later in various operations both brilliant and scandalous.[24]

In the years to come, Harel enjoyed using his new plaything. When the operations department went into action, the Memuneh was often on the scene to examine maps and plans, to supervise last-minute changes, and to experience the excitement. His agents began running all over the world: London, Paris, Geneva, Rome, Antwerp, Johannesburg, and New York.

Now that he had Eitan, Shalom, and other field operators at his beck and call, Harel could pursue a goal that had been beyond his available resources. As a perfectionist, he had always been bothered by the fact that the worst enemies of the Jewish people were still at large. Although a few Nazi war criminals stood accused at the Nuremberg tribunals in 1946, thousands escaped justice. Some were tolerated by Western intelligence to aid in the fight against communism. Israel, Harel believed, should bring the worst of the Nazis to justice.

Two men in particular were known to have gotten away: Adolf Eichmann, the administrator of Hitler's "final solution," who made sure that six million Jews were murdered with the utmost efficiency, and Dr. Josef Mengele, notorious for his brutal medical experiments at the Auschwitz death camp. Harel had made it clear to his contacts in West German intelligence that any information on Eichmann and Mengele would be most welcome. In late 1957, a tip from Fritz Bauer, the Jewish attorney general of the state of Hesse, sounded convincing when it said that Eichmann was living in Argentina.

Harel sent members of his new operations department to Argentina on a slow and painstaking search for the architect of the Nazi mass murders. This was about as far as Israeli intelligence men ever traveled from home, and the teams of operatives in Buenos Aires and elsewhere in South America were extremely costly. But Harel had a budget for his operations unit and this is where he was spending it.

Around the beginning of 1960, acting on new information from Bauer in Germany, Harel's men found Eichmann. Living with his wife and four sons in Buenos Aires, the ex-Nazi had taken the name "Ricardo Klement." Harel informed Ben-Gurion, who was again prime minister, and immediately won approval to kidnap Eichmann so he could be put on trial in Israel.

Over twenty men and at least one woman from both the Mossad and Shin Bet were chosen for the kidnap team, including support and surveillance roles. No one would be compelled to take part; all would have to volunteer, and they all did. Almost all had lost relatives in the Holocaust and hated Eichmann. Harel cautioned them to control their emotions. Because of the operational, political, and even personal complexities, the Memuneh himself flew to Paris to set up a staging post for the abduction and then went on to Argentina to take complete and personal responsibility.

The Mossad's finest forger went to Europe, where he prepared false passports and other documents for all the operatives so they could make their way to Buenos Aires on separate flights under names that would never again be used. So as to leave no traces, the forger also went to Argentina with all his special pens and papers to provide fresh identities for all the Israelis and for Eichmann himself so he could be smuggled out.

At least half a dozen "safe houses" and even more cars were rented in Buenos Aires, in a potential logistical nightmare that was handled with impressive ease. A female operative was chosen for the traditional role of "housewife," to cook the food and tidy the residence where the Nazi prisoner would be held. Eitan, Shalom, and their colleague Zvi Malchin had the honor of physically grabbing Eichmann. On May 11, 1960, they tackled him near his home and tossed him into the back seat of a car. "Klement," to the Israelis' relief, did not put up a struggle and immediately admitted to being Eichmann.

The abduction had been timed to coincide with the official visit of an Israeli delegation to Argentina, where many foreign guests were taking part in celebrations of the country's 150th year of independence. An El Al airliner flew the delegates in on May 19 and would be returning to Tel Aviv late the next night. Harel and some of his men said later that their most difficult task was feeding and caring for Eichmann for more than nine days while waiting for a flight to Israel. They interrogated their prisoner and at times simply stared at him in wonderment over how ordinary the personification of evil could appear. The balding man who depended on eyeglasses for his reading meekly signed a statement agreeing to be tried in an Israeli court.

It was chilling, however, for the kidnappers to hear Eichmann switch from German to a prayer in Hebrew, the *Shema,* which had been recited by Jews as they walked to their deaths in the Nazi gas chambers: "Hear O Israel, the Lord is our God, the Lord is One."

According to Harel, Eichmann "told us he was a great friend of the Jews. We were furious. Some of my people started to forget their orders not to touch him. They wanted to kill him. But they didn't, and he started to beg for small favors." The captive also said he would reveal all of Hitler's secrets if the Israelis would spare his life. Harel responded with a promise that Eichmann would get the best lawyer available to defend him at his trial.[25]

Harel spent little time in the safe house where Eichmann was chained to a bed. The Memuneh instead perfected a secure spycraft technique that could be called the roving headquarters. He told his senior operatives where they could find him at certain hours of the day, and he walked from café to café in the Parisian-style Argentine capital. No stranger was likely to remember seeing him in any particular location.

Sacrificing caution for the sake of on-the-spot control, Harel set up his headquarters on May 20 in a cafeteria at Ezeiza airport. He sat at a table with his forger, checking and distributing the identity documents his operatives would need to make a safe and unimpeachable departure from Buenos Aires.

At the safe house, Eichmann and the men who would accompany him were dressed in El Al airline uniforms. A Mossad doctor who specialized in anesthesia injected a powerful sedative into the war criminal's arm, and the seemingly sleepy "relief crew" aroused no questions as they boarded the Israeli airliner that night — along with unsuspecting Israeli dignitaries who had attended the Argentine celebrations, including Abba Eban, who was then minister of education.

The genuine El Al pilot was not told about his infamous passenger until after the takeoff from Buenos Aires in the first minutes of May 21, and on Harel's recommendation a refueling stop was scheduled in the most out-of-the-way city imaginable. It took every last drop of aviation fuel to reach Dakar, Senegal, but no one in West Africa was making any inquiries about a missing German-Argentinian. The refueling there went well, and the special flight carrying the notorious Nazi to meet Jewish justice arrived in Tel Aviv at seven o'clock on the morning of May 22.

Prime Minister Ben-Gurion took the rare step of giving credit to the intelligence community the next day, when he told the Knesset that "the security services of Israel found Adolf Eichmann and . . . he will shortly be brought to trial in Israel." The parliament's applause was unanimous.[26]

The judicial proceedings began nearly a year later on April 11, 1961, and with worldwide press and television coverage "the man in the glass booth" listened to witnesses who heartrendingly described his crimes and those of the entire Nazi killing machine. Eichmann claimed he was only following orders, but he was convicted of crimes against humanity. He was hanged in Ramle Prison on May 31, 1962

— the only person executed in Israel, aside from Captain Meir Toubianski, who was shot on the orders of military intelligence chief Isser Beeri in 1948.

Eichmann's abduction and the most massive public acclaim ever enjoyed by Israel's intelligence community were surely Harel's finest hour. Nearly thirty years later, wherever he went, he was hailed as "the man who captured Eichmann." The Memuneh's boldest operation was also a pure example of *humint* — the human intelligence skills at which Israel excelled, in this case without any technological gadgets.

Only with the passage of decades has Harel told how close his team came to capturing Josef Mengele on the same night that Eichmann was grabbed. Zvi Malchin, who later became a writer under the pseudonym Peter Mann, says he pressed Eichmann for information by demanding, "Tell us where your friend Mengele is. You must know where he lives." But Eichmann insisted that he did not know. Malchin had to tell Harel, "I tried everything. I believe that he has no idea where Mengele is, or that he is not willing to say a thing."[27]

Harel says, however, that he suspected that Eichmann, who lived in a slum neighborhood, "was being supported by Mengele, whose family was very rich." In any event, the Israeli operatives even had an address to go on: a luxury apartment in Buenos Aires where Mengele had been living. The Israeli operatives checked the building, only to find that Mengele and his family had fled the apartment just two weeks before the Eichmann abduction. The sadistic doctor was apparently frightened by reports of a speech by a Nazi-hunter in New York which said that Mengele could be found in the Argentine capital. According to Harel, the medical war criminal moved to Paraguay and later to Brazil.[28]

The attempts to capture Mengele nevertheless continued. When the Brazilian authorities reported in 1985 that the Nazi doctor had died, after years of rumors, the Mossad secretly sent a pathologist to examine the skeleton and confirm that the quarry atop the manhunt list could be crossed off once and for all.[29]

Harel did not wish to rest on the laurels of the Eichmann case and continued to press for the capture of more Nazi war criminals. For him it was a sacred mission, the payment of a debt owed to the six million Jews who were murdered. It was a mission which made the Israelis unique among the Western intelligence fraternity.

The secret services of other nations try to capture someone only when that enemy poses an active, potent danger to the state the agencies are defending. Harel was willing to have his Mossad launch a massive, worldwide manhunt for criminals from other countries who had acted in third or fourth nations against a people — rather than against the defense or security interests of the State of Israel, which had not even existed when the crimes were committed.

Harel came up with a unique solution in a world that did nothing about Nazis except indict them in court. The Israelis intended to find them. Harel set up a special coordinating unit with the specific task of hunting for Nazis who had tortured and murdered Jews. The Mossad officer in charge was Shmuel Toledano, who had proved himself so ably in arranging the exodus of Moroccan Jews in the mid-1950s.

West German officials helped the Israelis compile a list of the ten most wanted Nazis. Among other targets, the Toledano unit searched for Dr. Mengele, for Hitler's deputy Martin Börmann, for Gestapo chief Heinrich Müller, and for Leon de Grelle, a Belgian who served enthusiastically as an officer in the Nazi storm troopers.

The hunt for de Grelle triggered a bizarre affair. A former Shin Bet operative, Zwy Aldouby, heard in early 1961 that the Mossad was searching for the Belgian Nazi, and Aldouby dreamed of somehow stealing the glory. He approached Yigal Mossensohn, a famous Israeli writer and former captain in the police force, and recruited him for a kidnap operation — giving him the impression that it was an official mission for the government.

Aldouby was then a part-time journalist and used his contacts to recruit old friends in the French security service, including President de Gaulle's personal bodyguard. Hoping eventually to sell the tale as a film script — and having received an advance payment from major magazines — the oddly concocted team went into action in Spain. They followed de Grelle to his villa near Seville, planning to abduct him, Eichmann-style, and hand him over to the Belgian authorities, who had already sentenced him to death in absentia. They even hoped that de Grelle would lead them eventually to Börmann, because they intercepted letters between the two Nazis.

After several reconnaissance trips, Aldouby and his French partner Jacques Finston were arrested while crossing from France into Spain on July 14, 1961, for the actual kidnap. A few days later, Spanish detectives detained Mossensohn aboard a yacht that was intended to take the abducted de Grelle away. Mossensohn recalls: "We were probably shadowed all the time, because Aldouby had a big mouth. He would speak about the operation by telephone. All his girlfriends knew about it, and he had a lot of them."[30]

Aldouby and Finston were locked up by the Spanish, who tortured them and sentenced them to seven years in prison. Mossensohn was far luckier — released after just a few hours. More than twenty years later, he still did not know why he had been set free. A Mossad agent then told him that his good fortune had stemmed from the intervention of Israel's prime minister. He was told that because Ben-Gurion liked his writing, "the Old Man" had phoned Generalissimo Franco and urged him, "Don't touch Mossensohn. Release him."[31]

These odd events had definite and negative effects on Israel's intelligence community. Several countries in Western Europe became wary of Israeli agents after the rogue operation aimed at de Grelle.

Harel continued to send his Mossad–Shin Bet joint operations unit on foreign adventures, personally adding himself to the personnel list when a case was especially interesting. The next big manhunt was actually a boyhunt. Israeli intelligence scoured the globe for a ten-year-old nicknamed Yossele.

Yosef Schumacher was only eight when he was abducted at the end of 1959 by his own grandfather, an ultra-Orthodox Jew who was concerned that Yossele's parents were giving him a secular education. The old man was assisted by fellow members of *Neturei Karta,* the "Guardians of the Citadel," who are violently opposed to Zionism because they do not believe that Jews deserve a state until the Messiah comes.

Yossele was smuggled abroad, disguised as a little girl, and moved from one safe house to another in Europe and then New York. The case was constantly making headlines in the Israeli press, although no one seemed to have any idea where he was. The simple refrain of a popular song, based on the case, was sung almost nonstop by the entire State of Israel: "Where is Yossele?" the ditty asked, and jokes circulated that ridiculed the authorities, who were unable to track down the child.

Having captured Eichmann, Harel became obsessed by the challenge of finding another human needle in a haystack. It annoyed him mightily to see the press and opposition politicians mock Ben-Gurion and his cabinet for their failure to find the child. Harel launched Operation Tiger, putting the joint operations team onto the search for Yossele Schumacher despite reluctance expressed by deputies in Shin Bet and the Mossad. Senior agents abroad were told to stop their other activities, including the search for Mengele, and find the boy. And they did.

At first, Harel relocated his own headquarters to Paris for a while to interrogate religious Jews who appeared to have helped conceal the missing boy. The Memuneh pleaded with them to consider how Yossele's parents were suffering. The argument worked on a tough Neturei Karta lady named Ruth Ben-David, who had brought the boy out of Israel by ship after putting a wig on him and calling him Claudine. She gave Mossad interrogators the address in New York where Yossele could be found.

Israel's most wanted boy was located in July 1962 in an apartment occupied by Jewish zealots in Brooklyn. Word was flashed to the FBI, and Yossele was returned triumphantly to his parents in Israel. It may seem silly, but the secret services were warmly thanked again and Israel's clandestine defenders basked in the praise.[32]

Around the time that little Yossele was found, Morocco veteran and Nazi-hunter Shmuel Toledano was given another assignment by Harel — again in South America, but something different. The capture of Eichmann in Buenos Aires in 1960 earned kudos for the Mossad around the world, but the exploit also gave a boost to anti-Semitism in Argentina and endangered the half million Jews there. Reports spoke of a marked increase in the number of attacks on Jews organized by Tacuara, "Reed," an Argentine Fascist group that had many sons and daughters of prominent police and military officers among its members.

On July 1, 1962, a Jewish student named Garcia Sirota was kidnaped by Tacuara members, and they tattooed a Nazi swastika on her breast. The incident sent shock waves through the Jewish communities of Argentina, and in Israel newspapers published editorials urging their government to send assistance to "our Jewish brethren" in South America. Harel hardly needed any encouragement. Toledano was ordered to bring young Jewish activists from Argentina and nearby countries to Israel to receive intensive training in self-defense. It was a secret Mossad project.

The new emphasis on Nazis and anti-Semitism became — like his hunt for Communist moles — another of Harel's obsessions, which in the end led to his downfall. He specifically began to focus, in the early 1960s, on the ominous arrival of German rocket scientists in Egypt.

President Nasser wanted the Germans to help him develop ground-to-ground missiles that could be used in a future war against Israel. Harel genuinely believed that Germans were again involved in a major effort to exterminate Jews. He responded with Operation Damocles, a sword hanging over the head of every German scientist working for the Egyptians.

Israeli agents sent booby-trapped letters to the German scientists involved in the missile project and to their families. Similar intimidation was being carried out throughout Europe. In this, Harel was reverting to a successful technique that had been used in 1956, when by the orders of Aman chief Harkabi letter bombs were sent to the Egyptian officers who had been responsible for infiltrating terrorists from the Gaza Strip into Israel. Two senior Egyptians were killed in those first counterterrorist assassinations by Israeli intelligence.

In the campaign against German scientists, there were a few injuries and much intimidation. Harel felt his campaign could succeed, but his relations with Ben-Gurion became extremely strained because the prime minister kept urging him not to annoy the West German government. In effect, Ben-Gurion was saying "Hands off the Germans."

Harel went to unusual lengths to force the scientists out of Egypt. In a move that caused disquiet among many Mossad men, Harel sent a team to Madrid to meet with ex-Nazi officer Otto Skorzeny, who was friendly with some of the Germans in Cairo. Playing the "false flag" game of posing as representatives of a NATO intelligence service, the Mossad operatives persuaded him to urge his friends to get out of Egypt — for the sake of Western interests.[33] Barely two years after the genocidal Adolf Eichmann was kidnapped from Argentina by the Mossad, it was surprising that the Israelis would use a Nazi in any way. But Harel judged, just as a postwar trial had, that Skorzeny was only a German army veteran and not a war criminal.

The use of another unusual agent led to the disastrous end of Operation Damocles. He was an Austrian named Dr. Otto Joklik. His recruitment was quite an achievement for the Memuneh, because Joklik — it can now be revealed — had actually been one of the rocket scientists working for Nasser in Egypt. More of an adventurer than a ballistics expert, Joklik persuaded the Egyptians that he could build a high-energy cobalt bomb for them. He happily accepted a generous salary from Egypt while working on the project with no real success.

Harel persuaded Joklik to work for him instead, mainly — so it is said by Israeli insiders — so he could add a heap of Israeli money to the pile he had already earned from Egypt. The Austrian was the Mossad's man on the inside, and after leaving Cairo he flew to Israel to deliver a complete briefing on the clandestine missile project. Joklik warned that Egypt was rushing toward the highly dangerous goal of developing what experts call an "ABC" strike force. The initials stand for atomic-biological-chemical, and such weapons of mass destruction could be in warheads atop German-designed missiles. The Austrian's tale dovetailed neatly with Harel's concerns.

Largely because of his habit of compartmentalization, laudable among intelligence professionals, Harel told no one else in the defense and security establishment about Joklik's presence in Israel. Deputy defense minister Shimon Peres found out from his sources in the close-knit community, however, that Harel had "the Austrian scientist" stashed away. Peres insisted on meeting Joklik, so that the ministry's top men could question him.

Harel refused, establishing the tradition within the Israeli intelligence community that the agencies rarely share their secret sources with each other. The information is shared, but not the informants themselves. They are safer when fewer people know them.

Peres, however, complained to Ben-Gurion and threatened to resign. In his capacity as prime minister, "the Old Man" ordered Harel to make Joklik available to the defense ministry. Acting as defense minister, Ben-Gurion assigned the interrogation task to Binyamin Blumberg, chief of the ultrasecret Lakam agency. Because his staff included scientists, Blumberg would be in a position to judge Harel's contention that Egypt was close to an ABC-weapons capability that threatened the existence of Israel. This, of course, only made Harel resent Blumberg and Peres more than ever.

Blumberg's analysts, without anyone knowing they were attached to an agency named Lakam, rejected Joklik's information on the alleged dangers of the Egyptian missile project. They concluded that the Austrian's scientific credentials were doubtful.

Harel, however, was still certain that Nasser was planning the destruction of Israel. The Memuneh still believed in Joklik. Harel paired him with an Israeli named Yosef Ben-Gal and sent them on a secret mission to Switzerland. Their task was to frighten the daughter of Paul Görka, one of the German scientists working on Egypt's missile project. They told Heidi Görka there could be dire consequences if her father did not leave Cairo at once. She informed the Swiss police, who arrested the two Mossad agents outside a Basel hotel on March 15, 1963.

Just a few weeks earlier two Israeli agents had been arrested in West Germany, near the home of one of the rocket scientists. The Mossad had been lucky that its warm relations with the BND persuaded West German intelligence to arrange the quiet release of the Israelis.

Joklik and Ben-Gal were not so fortunate in Switzerland, and their trial was a public embarrassment to Israel. The Austrian and the Israeli were sent to prison, although only for short terms. If bad news comes in threes, this was the first.

Believing that the Germans and Egyptians were not being stopped, and that some explanation was required during the Swiss trial, Harel decided to go public. He hoped to persuade the world, or at least the Israeli people, that the heirs of the Nazi generation were now using Egypt as a base to pose a mortal danger to the state built by Holocaust survivors.

Mossad agents were sent on briefing missions to journalists in various European countries, and three leading Israeli newsmen — persuaded by Harel — undertook a special assignment, partly for their newspapers, and partly as an espionage mission to learn more about the German scientists.[34]

It was one of the few times, and probably the first, that the Mossad used Israeli journalists as agents. This was Harel's second major mistake. The articles that were published as a result of the semi-Mossad mission caused panic among the Israeli public about the ballistic danger from Egypt. Ben-Gurion was furious. He rebuked Harel for his unauthorized leaks to the press, blaming him for spoiling the developing ties between Israel and West Germany. These ties were of special interest to Ben-Gurion, Peres, and their circle, as a potential replacement for France as de Gaulle cooled toward Israel.

Harel did not care much about the diplomatic argument or how important West Germany was for Ben-Gurion's new foreign policy. The Memuneh was clearly persisting in his campaign, but "the Old

Man" was not going to allow anything to block better ties with Bonn. This was Harel's third major error.

Ben-Gurion demanded that Harel's private crusade come to an end. Harel refused, and he sought backing from other members of the prime minister's Mapai party. He attempted to recruit Foreign Minister Golda Meir and Finance Minister Levi Eshkol to his side. At the time, the political disputes over the Lavon Affair — coverups concerning sabotage in Egypt — were at their peak of ferocity.

For the first time since 1948, Harel joined Ben-Gurion's opponents and found himself in the enemy camp. Harel was still hoping to bypass his mentor's veto and to renew the holy war against the Nazi scientists. In Ben-Gurion's eyes, that was tantamount to treason.

Behind the scenes, there had been growing distrust between the prime minister and Harel over other issues. Ben-Gurion was not happy about Harel's zeal in pursuing Israel Beer, who had worked in the prime minister's bureau. His arrest in 1961 reflected poorly on Ben-Gurion himself. On the other side, Harel was not at all pleased with Ben-Gurion's putting Shimon Peres in charge of the secret nuclear project and Lakam.

The prime minister began to worry about the excessive authority enjoyed by Harel. Now, because of the German scientists, large cracks appeared in the relationship between the two old friends, and flood waters rushed into the breach to destroy their once-solid trust.

On March 25, 1963, nine days after Joklik and Ben-Gal were arrested in Switzerland, Harel submitted a letter of resignation. Harel hoped that Ben-Gurion would not accept the letter and would ask him to remain as Memuneh. He had come to believe the myth that he had created about himself. The little boy from Vitebsk had become a major player of the worldwide chess game. He met with powerful personalities such as Allen Dulles, confidant of President Eisenhower, and General Bachtiar, the head of Savak, who was also Iran's prime minister. Harel thought that he should enjoy the same powers and even become a cabinet minister. At the very least, he believed that he was irreplaceable as Memuneh. Ben-Gurion thought otherwise.

It was the end of an era. The great crusader had fallen on his own sword.

SIX

Amit Reshapes the Mossad

AN ARMY MESSENGER handed a slip of paper to Major General Meir Amit. "Contact the prime minister's office in Tel Aviv immediately," he read before folding the message neatly and slipping it into the breast pocket of his army uniform. It was March 26, 1963, and Amit was on a tour of military units near the Dead Sea.

He did as he was told, of course, hurrying to the nearest telephone and calling Ben-Gurion's office. "The Old Man wants to see you immediately, so we're sending an airplane," the prime minister's chief military aide told him.

About three hours later, Amit arrived at the prime minister's office in Tel Aviv. A branch of the main bureau in Jerusalem, it was a narrow, three-story stone building with a red tile roof and a tiny front porch. Amit knew the neighborhood well, as Ben-Gurion's office sat among similar houses along the tree-lined streets of the Kirya, the military zone that included the army's general staff and the headquarters of the fledgling intelligence community.

Ben-Gurion shook Amit's hand and then showed him a copy of a letter sent a few hours earlier to Isser Harel. It was the prime minister's acceptance of the Memuneh's resignation. Not even pausing to ask Amit if he wanted a new job, Ben-Gurion simply said, "You will be the next head of the Mossad." It was a command, and Amit accepted.[1]

General Amit was surprised by the sudden job offer, although he did believe that it was time for Harel to go after twelve years of wielding extraordinary power over the intelligence community. Yet another surprise was Ben-Gurion's decision that Amit would not have the same power as Harel. There would never again be a Memuneh in charge of both espionage abroad and counterespionage at home. The Shin Bet job would go to someone else.

Amit was, however, wearing two hats at first. A year earlier, he had been appointed head of Aman as the crowning achievement of a long career in uniform. He was born in Tiberias in 1926 as Meir Slutzki. Brought up as a socialist, Slutzki/Amit joined Kibbutz Alonim in the lower Galilee and enlisted in the underground Haganah. He was a company commander in the 1948 War of Independence, and after the victory he felt torn between his communal values and his commitment to defending Israel. Instead of returning to the kibbutz he chose to remain in the army, the new Israel Defense Forces.

Through the 1950s, Amit commanded infantry and tank units and he was one of the men who developed the principle of "Follow me," which became the Israeli army's trademark. The IDF officer does not remain in the rear but leads his troops into battle, setting an example of courage. Amit became a good friend of General Moshe Dayan and served as his aide-de-camp in the 1956 Suez campaign. Amit did take time off for a liberal arts education, including a degree in economics from New York's Columbia University.

When offered the opportunity to become Aman chief in 1962, perhaps Amit should have thought twice. The intelligence job had brought its incumbent nothing but bad luck. Three of Aman's four commanders had been forced out: Isser Beeri in 1949 for abusing civil rights, Binyamin Gibli in 1955 for directing stupid sabotage in Egypt, and Yehoshafat Harkabi in 1958 for mishandling a national mobilization exercise of army reservists.

Harkabi, however, was replaced by a living success story: General Chaim Herzog. He had earlier replaced Beeri at Aman, and in 1958 Herzog returned to the job to refurbish the image of military intelligence. He made Aman respectable again, but even Herzog could not move his agency out of the huge shadow cast by the Mossad during Harel's years as Memuneh.

With Herzog seeking to retire yet again from public service in 1962, Amit was offered the Aman job despite opposition from Harel. The Memuneh declared it was a mistake to choose a man with no intelligence experience, but he may also have felt potential competition from Amit's reputation as a general with his own band of loyal followers. Harel's influence over Ben-Gurion was already dwindling, however, and Amit got the job.

Shortly after taking over at Aman headquarters in the Kirya, Amit tried to lessen the hostility and competition between his agency and

Harel's Mossad. Saying that there was no room for rivalries when defending the Jewish state, Amit proposed that all the secret services work in close cooperation.

After a few weeks of attempted reconciliation, the tension and hostility between the two agency chiefs had only intensified. They did not simply have differences of opinion, but two entirely separate mentalities. Harel was a virtuoso of operations, while Amit specialized in military strategy. Harel happily ran around Europe for months on end searching for little Yossele Schumacher or some other quarry, while sleeping on cots and shivering on street surveillance. Military intelligence officers found the Mossad's methods laughable, because Israel's foreign spies were coming up with so little when it came to the military capabilities of the Arab countries.

Senior army commanders, naturally, expected vastly improved productivity when Amit became Mossad chief. He was one of their own, and it seemed inevitable that efficiency and coordination would be bolstered by his dual role at the Mossad and Aman. No one before had held those two posts.

The new job would not be easy. Amit also set a precedent as the first outsider to join the Mossad as head of the agency. Amit had the further handicap of replacing a man who had spent a dozen years shaping both the Mossad and Shin Bet in his own image. Most Mossad staffers could not and did not wish to forget Harel. They considered the Memuneh a legend in his own time, the patriarch of the clandestine community.

When Amit first walked into the Mossad's headquarters, not far from his military office at Aman, the reception was distinctly cold. Unlike his new subordinates in civilian clothes, Amit was wearing his general's uniform. He first had to confront Harel, who was waiting for him "as sour as a lemon," as Amit later recalled.[2] The outgoing intelligence chief said a few perfunctory words and then simply stood up and left. Harel's three secretaries burst into tears.

The next day, March 27, 1963, a decoded telex message arrived on the new Mossad chief's desk. It expressed distress at Harel's departure from the intelligence community and stressed that "every effort must be made to bring him back." The declaration was signed by the most senior secret operatives in Europe. They used codenames so as to observe security precautions in communications, and Amit had to ask his assistants to ascertain that the letter was from Shmuel Toledano, veteran of Moroccan and other adventures, Paris operations chief

Yitzhak Shamir, Mordecai Almog, and Yosef (Joe) Ra'anan.

Toledano and the others had considered a collective resignation, but in the end decided only to send the one harsh telex. Their protest was less severe than "the revolt of the spies" twenty-two years earlier when the foreign ministry's Political Department was reorganized. Still, Meir Amit was off to a difficult start in an atmosphere of bitterness.[3]

Amit had no sympathy or patience for letter writers and petition signers. He came from a different tradition, where the military chain of command was respected. If a commander falls in battle or departs for any other reason, he can be replaced and must be replaced.

The new Mossad chief shot back a strong response aimed at stopping the discontent from spreading. "I do not accept your behavior," Amit wrote. "I am not accustomed to collective protests."

The bad blood within the secret service prompted Amit to order that Harel's sabotage operations against the German scientists in Egypt be investigated. A special committee of cabinet ministers mounted an inquiry, and Harel was given access to the Mossad's files before testifying to the panel.[4] The clash of styles and personalities was never settled. Decades later it was difficult to get Amit and Shamir, by then prime minister, to say a kind word about each other. Amit and Joe Ra'anan did not hide their enmity when both were chairmen of Israeli economic conglomerates in the 1970s. The strongest mutual repulsion, however, was between Amit and Harel, which like old wine simply gained strength with each passing year.[5]

In 1963, however, Amit did fly to Paris on a mission of reconciliation with his European operatives. He also invited Yaakov Karoz, one of Harel's protégés, to serve as his deputy. Karoz was head of the Mossad's political action and liaison department and had been with the agency as an "alternative diplomat" since its earliest days. He accepted Amit's offer, a move that calmed the rage felt by Harel's loyalists.

Changes in Israel's government also helped reduce tensions. In June 1963, three months after Ben-Gurion forced Harel to quit, "the Old Man" himself resigned as prime minister. He was tired of fighting in the internal power struggles of the Mapai party over the Lavon Affair. The intelligence failure in Egypt had been eating away at Ben-Gurion, finally toppling him nine years after the sabotage ring was arrested.

Ben-Gurion stalked off to found a new, centrist political party called Rafi with his supporters Moshe Dayan and Shimon Peres. Still controlling a majority of Knesset seats, Mapai chose Levi Eshkol as the new prime minister.

Eshkol showed great interest in intelligence. He was literally awed by the work of the Mossad. From time to time, he would compliment Amit on the work of his agents. In return Amit made sure that Eshkol, who had been the minister of finance and understood government purse strings, enlarged the Mossad's budget. This enabled Amit to hire some of his own men and women and accelerate his reform of the secret agency.

Amit continued to serve in two posts, moving between the Mossad and Aman offices in Tel Aviv, until December 1963. He used the transition period to reorganize the Mossad structure — bringing Aman's élite operations arm, Unit 131, into the Mossad. Unit 131, its reputation sullied mainly by the Lavon Affair, needed a new identity and was integrated with the Mossad's two small operations units. Due to a chronic lack of manpower, they served both as operational teams that backed up Harel's worldwide missions and as collection departments that gathered information from Arab and foreign informers run by Israeli case officers. Yitzhak Shamir, head of the European unit, was expected to block the merger but resigned instead.[6]

In fact, within two years of sending their protest telex to Amit on his second day at the Mossad, all four senior field operatives who had signed the message left the agency. They knew that, having raised their flags of dissent, any hopes they had for promotion were dashed. After Toledano left the Mossad, he said that he had hoped to become agency chief. He had to settle for the post of Arab affairs adviser to Prime Minister Eshkol, an appropriate job for Toledano as a fluent Arabic-speaker but not for a man accustomed to covert work.

As for Shamir, he faced a difficult adjustment from the clandestine life he had led even before the State of Israel was born. From his command of the underground Stern Gang against the British and Arabs, to his roving Mossad job based in Europe, Shamir developed the ascetic strengths needed for a career in intelligence: he was suspicious, could happily make do with few creature comforts, and was willing to work extremely hard.

"Shamir was an introvert, very dedicated, thorough and hardworking," one of his Mossad colleagues recalls. "He taught himself French, hard as it was. You could always rely on him, but he did not come forward with brilliant ideas. He came to work in the morning and at the end of the day returned to his wife Shulamit and their two children."[7] Shamir's daughter, Gilada, was similarly attracted to intelligence work, while his son, Yair, became an air force colonel.

After leaving the Mossad, Shamir opened a factory but the business failed. There were few alternatives but to enter politics in 1972, at the relatively advanced age of fifty-five. Always used to melting invisibly into a crowd, this short and rarely smiling man with his small mustache had to learn to be a public figure. Even after mastering the political craft and attaining the post of prime minister, Shamir had fond memories of his days of drama and tension as a secret agent. "My days in the Mossad were among the happiest in my life," he said, "and even politics and the premiership cannot compare to them."[8]

To replace those who left, Amit installed his own top operatives. He brought many of them from Aman, including the head of the military's information-collecting department, Rehaviah Vardi.[9] Amit also arranged to raise the rank of the army's military attachés in Israel's overseas embassies, and to further boost their prestige he had some of them serve as Mossad station chiefs simultaneously.

The new chief aimed to transform the Mossad into a serious and modern intelligence organization focusing on what Amit considered to be its major task: the collection of military and political data on the Arab states. He regarded the Mossad as an information-gathering body that would henceforth eschew show-off operations, which he viewed as a waste of resources. Influenced by the economics and business courses he took in the United States, Amit wished to imitate the American corporate mentality and style of management.

Amit moved the Mossad's headquarters into modern premises, in a building in the center of Tel Aviv rather than in the defense ministry's Kirya compound. The agency chief granted himself a plush, American-style office with wood paneling and stylish new furniture.

Some Mossad veterans were enraged to see the budget spent on the kind of comforts that Isser Harel had always opposed. They preferred the former Memuneh's old, modest offices. From within the Mossad, the dissidents launched a new round of rumors, similar to those that had brought down Asher Ben-Natan and his Political Department men in 1951. They suggested that Amit was wasting money and even losing some to corrupt underlings. Stories circulated about the allegedly luxuriant lives led by senior Mossad officials who stayed in exclusive hotels and ate at the finest restaurants abroad.[10]

Amit resented the rumor mill and tried to shut it down, but otherwise he stuck to his guns, furniture, and carpeting. He was out to modernize the Mossad, and fresh new quarters were part of the plan.

Amit also changed the Mossad's methods of recruitment. Rather than relying on recommendations by friends, along the lines of a British "old-boy network," he preferred to use more systematic techniques than the mere luck of "feeling" that a longtime acquaintance who attended the correct school or army unit was the right sort of fellow to be a spy.

The new agency chief made an effort to spot potential candidates, not only in the army but in the universities, in the business world, and among new immigrants. Stress was placed on finding potential operatives who appeared European in manner and style of clothing, qualities that Israeli society generally scorned.

One of those who seemed to fill the bill was Charlie Mayorkas. He was born in Istanbul, to a father who grew up in Switzerland and a mother of Austrian origin. At age seventeen, he left Turkey to avoid military service there. He traveled to France to study medicine, but a year later his academic field was commerce. In 1965 this Turkish Jew moved to Israel, not for ideological reasons but because he discovered that the Jewish Agency was willing to finance his studies at Hebrew University.

On the campus in Jerusalem, Mayorkas caught the eye of the Mossad recruiters. They proposed that he join the agency, and he accepted with enthusiasm. After three years of basic training, his superiors discovered that Mayorkas was a homosexual. He was immediately dismissed from the Mossad.

"I wanted to serve the state, and then they hit me with this. What other Israeli would have such a perfect cover, with my family background, with my knowledge of eight languages, with access to all of Europe?" he complained. Many Mossad colleagues sympathized, but they were unwilling to take what was universally considered an unnecessary risk in the espionage world — always worried about sexual blackmail and compromising entanglements.[11]

The situation of women in the Mossad was hardly any better. "A woman cannot gather information in the Arab world," one of the senior men in the Mossad explains. "The different way in which women are treated in Arab society prevents us from employing women as operatives or case officers. The Arabs wouldn't accept them. They would see a woman like that and jump out the window."[12]

Most women in the Mossad are employed in administrative and service capacities. The Mossad has always been reluctant to send women on extended assignments overseas, even when these are the less dangerous jobs such as serving as liaison officers with the security agencies of other nations.

The inequality in who is sent abroad also affects promotions on the home front, because decision-making posts are generally reserved for those with experience in the field. For the Mossad's women, it is a vicious circle. Those who start out as secretaries may get to be managers — but office managers rather than captains of conspiracies and foreign plots.

To every rule there are exceptions, however. For example, Lily Kastel was a living legend, and years after her death in 1970 older men in the Mossad still speak of her extraordinary talent. She joined the agency in 1954, after previous experience in the prestate Shai.

Kastel spoke excellent Hebrew, English, French, German, and Russian, and she had a working knowledge of Arabic and Italian. She is remembered as attractive, intelligent, and trustworthy. Harel felt he was using both her brains and her looks on various assignments in Europe.[13] The precise nature of her work has never been revealed, however.

The changes in the agency under Amit did lead to some improvement in opportunities for women. The new boss's demand for proficiency and professionalism helped give women a fairer chance to be appointed to run "desks" covering specific regions or subjects. These were women who had slowly made their way up through the ranks, until they were finally made responsible for a single area of expertise.

The "desk manager" is the contact point between field operatives and the head office in Tel Aviv, supplying personnel abroad with whatever they need for their assignments. The desk person transmits orders and receives all material gathered in the field.[14] The East Africa desk, for instance, collects intelligence "product" sent from the large Mossad station in Nairobi and from agents in the countries neighboring Kenya.

Only when a specific mission requires women will a female be sent on an overseas assignment, and that is decided after all other avenues have been explored and dismissed. Despite the same reluctance that Israel's army feels about exposing its female soldiers to combat, intelligence chiefs recognize that using a woman can have distinct advantages. Alone, she usually provokes less suspicion. If she works with a male colleague, it is believed that an apparently married or courting couple attracts less attention than do single men in a surveillance operation.

The Mossad does send women into action for purposes of sexual entrapment, but again reluctantly. First, intelligence chiefs prefer to use single women for such assignments. Second, they are almost always used in this way only once. The Mossad hesitates before ordering its agents, male or female, to engage in sexual relations for the sake of the mission. This may be a hangover from Harel's puritanical spirit. The Memuneh is remembered for rebuking a married male operative who was seen hugging female secretaries in the Mossad headquarters.

The thinking on sex changed, however, and while there is no pressure on female agents to exploit their gender, it is expected of them to use sex as one of many weapons in the field.[15] If sexual blackmail or entrapment is an integral part of the mission, however, the Mossad often employs actual prostitutes. Some of Israel's streetwalking lawbreakers have proved to be surprisingly patriotic, although the secret agency does not tell them any details of the operation or even the identity of the men whom they are ordered to bed.

It is common practice, for instance, to debrief Arab informants run by either the Mossad or Aman by smuggling them across the border into Israel and bringing them to a quiet town. There, they are interviewed at length and then rewarded for their work by providing them with prostitutes. Their antics are occasionally photographed for potential blackmail leverage to ensure the Arab agents' loyalty in the future.

There is less hesitation in sending the men of Mossad abroad to the sexual hunting grounds. The appropriate, usually handsome operatives are chosen to befriend — and usually to become intimate with — an international array of embassy secretaries and airline stewardesses, for they can provide much valuable information about the diplomats, airports, and cities of the Arab world.

The system breaks down on occasion. One Israeli case officer had a tempestuous sexual relationship with the most important agent he was running, a young European woman. She would give him information, and they would sleep together. After a few years, a new case officer took over in Europe. The relevant desk manager was surprised to read the new man's first report, which noted that "the female source" expressed amazement and even complained that he was not willing to go to bed with her. The Mossad headquarters discovered that there had been two generations of case officers using the woman in more ways than one, and that she believed that having sex was an integral part of her employment by the Israelis. The Mossad decided not to bring disciplinary charges against the earlier case officers, judging that it would serve little purpose.

The use of sex and other Mossad working practices were refined during Meir Amit's tenure as agency chief. The Amit era also established many of the personnel principles and the organizational structure that would characterize the secret agency for many years to come.

Of the Mossad's eight sections, the Collection Department, the Operational Planning and Coordination Department, the Research Department, and the Department of Political Action and Liaison are the most important. The other departments — Training, Finance and Manpower, Technology, and Technical Operations — mainly provide assistance and support for the major departments.

The desks of the information-collecting and political departments are organized on both regional and functional bases, and they are highly specialized. The Mossad has a virtual monopoly on the collection of intelligence outside Israel, with the exception of certain military targets — usually not far from Israel's borders — on which Aman may spy.[16]

Mossad's modus operandi was shifting with time and personalities. Harel was a great believer in the power of human instinct. His own instinct was undoubtedly excellent, and he preferred unexplained, but well trained, inspiration to any dependence on cold, unfeeling technology. He did not hide his scorn for electronic gadgets, even though Israel was home to some of the world's greatest inventors.

Harel was always proud of the fact that his Mossad, unlike other intelligence agencies in the West, was an organization that relied on human resources and human intelligence. As such, it was almost universally acknowledged by experts as the world's finest example of *humint*.

The Mossad, under Amit, continued to be primarily *humint*-oriented, but other strengths were also stressed. Advanced computers were introduced to the agency in large numbers, based on the computerization of Aman under Herzog, Amit, and his successor Colonel Aharon Yariv. Yariv had been in charge of Aman's data-collection department when Amit was agency commander.[17]

Amit believed that raw facts and their organized analysis had to replace a reliance on human intuition, so as to improve the collection capability of the Mossad in the Arab "confrontation states" bordering Israel. In reviewing the work of the solitary secret agents, planted by Harel in the years after Aman's Unit 131 failed with great embarrassment in Egypt, Amit felt their record was only spotty.

A successful spy for the Mossad was Shaaltiel Ben-Yair, who lived in Egypt under deep cover from 1958 to 1962. Born to a Jewish family along Palestine's border with Lebanon, Ben-Yair had learned as a youngster to pose as an Arab. Only a teenager at the end of the 1930s, he joined Menachem Begin's extremist Irgun underground and was sent on missions posing as a young Arab cattle merchant.

Shaaltiel's father was alarmed by the dangers involved, however, and packed him off to a naval school in France, thinking it safer in Europe. But before long, the young Ben-Yair left school and ran off with an older woman. He did, however, learn French to an excellent standard. Back in Palestine, he attended a Scottish school and learned to speak English like a Scot.

In World War II he fought in a British commando unit in Egypt, and then in Yitzhak Shamir's Stern Gang against the British, before joining the Israeli army for the 1948 War of Independence. Unemployed except for bar-hopping in Tel Aviv, he heard in 1955 that Shamir and other friends from the prestate Jewish underground had joined the Mossad. Ben-Yair was happy to join, too, and without any trouble at all he assumed the cover identity of "François Renancoeur," a Belgian citizen who was an international "expert" on cattle. Ben-Yair/Renancoeur managed to secure an invitation from the Egyptian government to come to Cairo as an adviser on livestock.

One day near the end of the 1950s, the telephone rang in the Paris apartment of Israeli author Amos Kenan. *"Ici Charlie,"* said a voice he had not heard in years. That was one of Ben-Yair's codenames.

Kenan listened for a few seconds and then hurried off to meet his old friend from the Stern Gang on a tourist boat on the Seine River. To his surprise, the writer found that Ben-Yair no longer had a mustache and refused to speak anything but French.

"I am now an expert on cattle, and you must call me François from now on," the shadowy Israeli confided to Kenan. "Once a month I come to Paris for one evening, going to Brussels the next day and from there to Cairo. I have no one to talk to. My work is difficult. I was trained, and even if you shout to me in the middle of the night in Hebrew I would not wake up.

"Nobody in Egypt could imagine that I also understand Arabic. And in Belgium, they believe that I am Belgian. My French southern accent matches theirs. Just for safety's sake, I also tell people that I spent part of the war in southern France."

In Egypt, Ben-Yair/Renancoeur was one of Israel's most daring operatives. He was in charge of mapping Egyptian airfields and providing details of military installations. It was dangerous, but he was one of the Israeli agents who completed their missions and returned home — never caught and never causing a scandal. His most valuable attribute was that he was a natural lone wolf, a one-man spy network. But still, Ben-Yair had been unable to maintain total solitude and had breached security by talking to Kenan.

After returning to Israel in 1962, Ben-Yair found "overcover" life too boring — a common malady among former field agents who miss the excitement. He moved to Canada and changed his name. Having made his contribution to his homeland, he left it.

A spy story with a far unhappier ending is that of Jack Leon Thomas, an Armenian who grew up in Cairo and worked for Israeli intelligence without at first realizing it. He was an educated young man, handsome, with jet black hair and a perfect command of Arabic, English, French, and German. He moved to Beirut in 1956 and then on to West Germany, trying his hand at various commercial enterprises. In 1958 in Germany he met a young Lebanese man named Emil, and they became close friends. Enjoying the bars and restaurants of Cologne and Bonn, Emil was obviously wealthy and always picked up the tab. They talked about business and women, and when the chat drifted into politics Thomas did not hide his hatred for Egypt's President Nasser.

One evening, Emil offered Jack a huge amount of money and suggested that he return to Egypt to help overthrow the corrupt dictator. Thomas was told he would be working for one of the NATO countries. The method is called "false-flag recruiting," and the Mossad is especially good at it. Israel was never mentioned, and Thomas had always had a fondness for the West, so he swallowed the bait.

In a small apartment in Cologne, anonymous people taught him the basics of espionage: photographing documents and developing the film; hiding negatives in toothpaste tubes, shoe boxes, or books; writing with invisible ink; and passing coded messages by leaving them in "dead letter boxes" for unknown accomplices.

Full of enthusiasm, Thomas returned to Cairo in July 1958 and began recruiting informers into his network. From time to time, he would travel to West Germany for meetings with his operators, who continued to claim that they were "senior officials in NATO." In return for the military information he brought with him, his case officers gave him money and new orders.

On one of these trips, the young Armenian met a West German woman named Kathy Bendhof. After a whirlwind romance, they were married, and Bendhof joined Thomas in Cairo. He added his wife to his network, and she was his courier.

Thomas's case officer in Cologne eventually revealed the truth to him: "I have been running you for Israeli intelligence." The revelation did not come as a surprise to Thomas, nor did his lack of surprise entirely surprise his Israeli controllers. They knew they were dealing with an intelligent man, and indeed Thomas had suspected that he was working for Israel. Now that he knew for certain, it did not bother him a bit. He still hated Nasser, and he returned to his espionage work in Cairo with even greater enthusiasm.

Gradually, his network expanded. Thomas recruited two Armenians and a Jewish nightclub performer. Another informer was a childhood friend of Thomas's who had become an artillery officer. Kathy was sent to Amsterdam, where the Mossad taught her how to use a radio transmitter with great professionalism. The chosen code book was Pearl Buck's *The Good Earth.* The couple immediately received a pay raise, and the money was sent through a Belgian bank, allegedly as "help from relatives in Germany."

Their network amassed its own espionage equipment: five cameras, a suitcase with a false bottom, an electric shaver with a secret compartment for hiding documents, a hollow cigarette lighter for film negatives, and a sophisticated two-way radio hidden in the bathroom of their apartment in the Garden City section of Cairo. Every few days, Kathy Bendhof-Thomas would contact Tel Aviv and pass on information, at the same time picking up new orders.

In May 1960, the couple received an order designed to be a preview of a major project yet to come. They were to choose an Egyptian army officer whom they might later recruit into their network. The message warned them clearly to wait for further instructions, but they had already been infected by the most injurious of all occupational diseases faced by a spy: excessive self-confidence. They made overtures to a young officer of Coptic Christian extraction named Adiv Hanna Karolos.

Karolos appeared to have taken the bait, but he immediately informed his commanding officer of what had occurred. Egyptian counterespionage agents laid a trap for the Israeli network. At first, they fed false information to Thomas, who thought he was transmitting useful data to Tel Aviv.

Thomas, who evidently had begun to feel — with Isser Harel's favorite kind of instinct — that the ground was burning beneath his feet, prepared to disband the network and have everyone flee. He obtained false passports for himself and his wife. She managed to escape, together with the Jewish dancer, but Thomas and the other members of the network were arrested on January 6, 1961.

In a Cairo courtroom, Thomas claimed that he had been spying for Israel for a sense of adventure, for the money, and because he hated the Nasserite regime. "I am not a traitor," he said. "I never considered myself an Egyptian. We Armenians are oppressed in Egypt, because we are a minority." A military court convicted Thomas and two of his recruits of espionage and treason, and the three men were hanged on December 20, 1962.

During the trial, prosecutors revealed that the Thomas network had made serious attempts to offer pilots in the Egyptian air force a million dollars if they would agree to defect to Israel or Cyprus with a Soviet-made MIG jet.[18]

Israel's intelligence chiefs did not give up. Spurred on by the air force commander, the hyperenergetic General Ezer Weizman, they pressed on in their efforts to acquire a Soviet-made warplane. A number of possible methods were considered: intercepting an aircraft in midflight and forcing it to land in Israel; planting an agent as a pilot in one of the Arab air forces; or bribing an Arab pilot. But how could they bribe a pilot, already living as luxurious a life as any of the Arab armed forces could offer?

The prevailing opinion was that, while difficult, this avenue offered Israel its best chances of success. Aman and the Mossad had already amassed a tremendous amount of information on the air forces of Egypt, Jordan, Syria, and Iraq. The Israeli intelligence dossiers recorded every scrap of information on the enemy pilots, organized and stored by Aman and Amit's new computers. The information was so comprehensive that those in charge of the files felt as if they personally knew hundreds of Arab pilots.

That was why the Israelis were disappointed when an Egyptian pilot finally did defect to them in 1964. Captain Abbas Hilmi was indeed a pilot in Egypt's air force, and his plane was Soviet-made, but it was a Yak trainer of little interest to those who were dying to get their hands on a combat aircraft.

In spite of the disappointment felt in the Israeli intelligence community, Captain Hilmi was given a very warm reception. The information that he gave to Aman was an important addition to the data that had been painstakingly assembled about the Arab air forces. Hilmi was also used for other purposes. He publicly condemned Nasser's intervention in Yemen, where his army was trying to force another country into his sphere of radical Arab socialism, and Hilmi revealed that the Egyptians used poison gas against the Yemeni royalists.

The Egyptian turncoat was given financial assistance and a good job in Israel, but he was not able to acclimatize himself to life in the Jewish state. Rejecting the strong advice of his intelligence handlers in Tel Aviv, Hilmi decided to move to South America. The Mossad furnished him with new identity documents and gave him a large sum of cash to help him begin a new life in Argentina.

As soon as he arrived in Buenos Aires, violating the instructions the Israelis had given him, Hilmi made a number of literally fatal errors. First, he sent a postcard to his mother in Egypt, where the secret police intercepted the card and found out where he was hiding. Later, he befriended an Egyptian woman whom he met in an Argentine nightclub. She promised him her favors, and he agreed to go to her apartment. It was an Arab version of the "honey trap" which the Israelis and other espionage agencies use. Egyptian agents were waiting for

Hilmi in the woman's apartment. They subdued him, transported him in a crate to the Egyptian embassy, and from there smuggled him by cargo ship to Egypt. He was convicted of treason by a court-martial and shot.[19]

Even though the Hilmi episode was not the fault of Israeli intelligence, its reputation was harmed by his capture. The blow to morale led the Mossad and Aman to reconsider their plan to lure another Arab pilot to defect with a better airplane. There were a lot of discussions of the matter, but Weizman continued to insist that examining a MIG could be the key to winning a war. The efforts to snare a pilot continued.

A year later, at the beginning of 1966, another suitable target was found. This time it was an Iraqi pilot.[20]

Munir Redfa was a member of a wealthy Maronite Christian family in Iraq, where non-Moslems generally suffered discrimination. Trained by the Soviets, he was a pilot in a squadron of MIG-21's, the latest word in Soviet military aeronautics.

The Israelis, thanks to newspaper clippings, Iraqi communications they intercepted, and agents on the ground in Baghdad, were aware of Redfa's background. They learned that Redfa had been dismayed and upset about his air force's bombing and strafing raids on Kurdish villages in the north, as part of the suppression of that minority.

The Israeli agents chosen for this mission were selected with great care and sent to Baghdad, by way of Europe, to make contact with the pilot and his family. Of all the agents dispatched for the Redfa project — and there were many for what rapidly became a high-priority objective — the most successful was an Israeli woman who had been born in the United States and carried an American passport.

She posed as a rich tourist who attended some high-powered parties in Baghdad and managed to enchant the Iraqi pilot, even though he was married and had two children. Taking a position common with female Israeli spies over the years, the woman refused to have sex with Redfa in Iraq. He had to come to Europe with her, and then he could have his reward. The pilot agreed to accompany her to Paris, where romance would be in the air.

After two days in France, Redfa agreed to fly with the enchantress to Israel, where she said she had "some interesting friends." The Iraqi pilot harbored certain suspicions, but he did not seem to care very much and within twenty-four hours, holding a false passport provided by the Mossad in Paris, he was a passenger on an El Al flight to Tel Aviv.

In Israel, Redfa was treated as a VIP. He was taken on a tour of an Israeli air base. It was there that he met officers of the Mossad and Aman, who offered him one million dollars and asylum for his entire large family if he would defect to Israel with one of the new MIG-21's.

To demonstrate that their offer was authentic and authorized, the intelligence agents arranged a meeting for Redfa with General Mordecai Hod, commander of the Israeli air force, who had just taken over from Ezer Weizman. The Iraqi was amazed at how well the Israelis knew his air force. They knew the names of the Iraqi pilots and their Soviet instructors. The Israelis described in great detail the airfield and its runways, control tower, operations room, and living quarters.

In coordination with Redfa and with his consent, a date was set for his daring flight from Iraq nonstop to Israel. Hod helped plan a flight route and arrangements for communications on the day of the coup.

A few days later, the pilot and the Israeli agent, who he used to think was his American girlfriend, returned to Baghdad by way of Paris. As agreed in Israel, a down payment for Redfa was deposited in a Swiss bank account. Afterward, Redfa's family was smuggled out of the country into Iran, with the help of Kurdish rebels who regularly worked with Israeli agents. The Mossad station in Teheran then had the family flown to Europe and on to Tel Aviv.

Amit, meantime, flew to Washington to inform the CIA director, Richard Helms, that the United States would soon be able to feast its eyes on a MIG-21. The Americans had been trying for some time to examine this jet, with its secret technology, in order to improve their "top gun" fighter units and their simulations of U.S.-Soviet dogfights.

The planning was perfect. On August 15, 1966, Redfa flew the agreed route over Jordan, fleeing his homeland at high speed and landing his MIG-21 at an air base in the south of Israel. This was the first time that such a sophisticated Soviet warplane had reached the West. Decades later, the air forces of the United States and its NATO allies remained impressed by the feat accomplished by Israeli intelligence that day. Among Western military people, acquiring the MIG was one of the key events in building the Mossad's image into unassailable mythology. More than ever, Israel was seen as a master of *humint* methods.

The Redfa defection, known to some intelligence insiders by the James Bond monicker "Operation 007," gave Meir Amit great pleasure. Unlike the Hilmi affair, this acquisition of an Arab aircraft had a happy ending. Munir Redfa and his family were given new identities, the cash they had been promised, and everything they needed to lead happy lives in Israel. The American-born female operative left Iraq safely.[21]

The Americans, the NATO alliance, and other friendly foreign powers heaped great praise on Israel. The West enjoyed taking a close look at the MIG-21.

While plotting Operation 007, Meir Amit had to cope with disastrous setbacks in both Syria and Egypt. The Mossad's two most senior agents in the two most important Arab capitals were both lost in a single five-week period in 1965: Eli Cohen in Damascus, and Wolfgang Lotz in Cairo.

Until they were captured, Cohen and Lotz supplied Israeli intelligence with absolutely astounding information from the very heart of the Arab political and military power centers. They were extremely capable and courageous men, and both penetrated the highest ranks of the leadership in their respective espionage posts. Cohen became a personal confidant of the Syrian president, while Lotz befriended many senior officers in the Egyptian army.

Eliyahu (Eli) Cohen was born in Alexandria, Egypt, in 1924. He clandestinely helped other Egyptian Jews move to Israel and then took part in the ill-fated Israeli sabotage network that was smashed by the Egyptian authorities in 1954. It was pure luck that Cohen was not arrested with his friends.

He managed to get to Israel after the 1956 Suez campaign, and with great Zionist fervor he immediately contacted Israeli intelligence to volunteer. Military intelligence Unit 131 was still in charge of espionage in the neighboring Arab countries, although with better supervision after the 1954 fiasco. Cohen had always made a good impression.

Aman's standard psychological tests, however, indicated some disturbing signs. The agency concluded that Cohen had a high IQ, great bravery, a phenomenal memory, and the ability to keep a secret; but the tests also showed that "in spite of his modest appearance, he has an exaggerated sense of self-importance" and "a lot of internal tension." Cohen, the results indicated, "does not always evaluate danger correctly, and is liable to assume risks beyond those which are necessary."[22]

Israeli intelligence let Cohen get on with his life for a while, but when tension along the border with Syria increased sharply in May 1960, Aman urgently needed a spy in Damascus. Cohen was the man for the job.

Even with a sense of urgency, his training took over half a year in Israel followed by nearly a year more in Argentina — by now a favorite if out-of-the-way choice for building a spy's cover story. Cohen left Israel on February 3, 1961, and arrived in Buenos Aires as Kamel Amin Taabeth, a Syrian businessman invented by Aman. He was to blend in with the many Arab entrepreneurs in South America, and Cohen/Taabeth was dazzlingly successful at meeting rich and influential members of the Syrian community abroad.

By the time he moved on to Damascus on January 10, 1962, Cohen/Taabeth was armed with a pocketful of letters of introduction. He was the fascinating new man in town, recommended by all the Syrians of Argentina. Before long, in fact, one of his best friends from Buenos Aires, Major Amin al-Hafez, became the president of Syria. "Taabeth" was considered likely to get a cabinet post and perhaps eventually would be defense minister.

While running an import-export business, Cohen/Taabeth cultivated his political contacts. He was frequently invited to visit army bases and had a complete tour of the Syrian fortifications confronting Israel on the Golan Heights.

The information which he sent to Tel Aviv, mainly by tapping Morse dots and dashes on his telegraph key, covered all areas of life in Syria. Israeli intelligence was able to get a remarkably complete picture of an enemy country that had seemed impenetrable. Cohen's reports were always welcome at Aman headquarters. They contained vivid information on internal squabbles within the government leadership, as well as the kind of data on the Syrian military that was needed for the computerized files of military intelligence.

Smuggling documents out through Europe, Cohen was able to describe troop deployments along the border in detail, and he noted the specific locations of tank traps that might prevent Israeli forces from advancing if war were to break out. He furnished a list of all the Syrian pilots and accurate sketches of the weapons mounted on their warplanes.

If he and his Israeli controllers had only been more cautious, Cohen's chances of survival would have been much better. In November 1964 he was on leave in Israel, awaiting the birth of his third child. He missed his family and had taken to sending them indirect greetings through his espionage controllers, without revealing where he was. Cohen was getting to know his new handlers, because the Unit 131 operations team had been transferred from Aman to the Mossad after Meir Amit's move to the post of Mossad chief.

Cohen kept extending his leave and hinted to the Mossad that, after nearly four years abroad, he might want to come in from the cold. Cohen mentioned that he did not feel comfortable with Colonel Ahmed Suedani, head of the intelligence branch of the Syrian army.

Unfortunately, Cohen's case officers did not pay attention to the warning signs. There was renewed tension on the border and the real possibility of war on the horizon. It was vital to have reliable intelligence from Damascus, and the Mossad applied pressure on Cohen to return to his espionage post as soon as possible.

In the next two months, Cohen forgot the rules of prudence. It is possible that the unbelievable ease with which he had befriended the highest echelons in the land had made him complacent. He immediately resumed his coded broadcasts — which meant that a clever Syrian counterintelligence team could link their resumption with "Taabeth's" return from "abroad."

The broadcasts even became more frequent, and in the space of five weeks he sent thirty-one radio transmissions to Tel Aviv. Committing errors based on fatigue or some death wish, Cohen regularly sent his espionage messages at the same time, 8:30 A.M. This would make his transmitter easy to trace electronically.

Cohen sometimes sent two transmissions in a single day. Thus, for example, Tel Aviv asked him one morning, "What happened to the MIG-21 group that was on alert?" and that afternoon at four o'clock Cohen gave a detailed answer: "One of their pilots was killed when his plane hit a small plane on the ground, after a training accident in the air, and the third was grounded because of disparaging remarks he had made about his commander."

Cohen became almost irresponsible on the radio, as if deliberately courting his own demise. His case officers in Tel Aviv should have restrained him, but none of them did. The material he was sending was just too good to stop.[23]

Apparently guided by radio direction-finding equipment, most likely operated by Soviet advisers, Colonel Suedani's Syrian intelligence men broke into Cohen's apartment on January 18, 1965, and caught him red-handed, tapping his telegraph key in the middle of a transmission.

Suedani tried to deceive Israel by forcing Cohen to transmit fictitious information that had been encoded. After three days of this game, without response from Tel Aviv, the Syrians gave up and sent a final message — addressed to Prime Minister Levi Eshkol: "Kamel and his comrades are being hosted by us for a limited period of time. We will let you know in the future of his fate."

Several hundred Syrians whom Cohen/Taabeth had befriended were arrested. President Hafez was embarrassed to have known the man without knowing what he was. Cohen admitted he was an Israeli spy but, despite torture by the Syrians, told them nothing else that could help them.

Appeals made by Israel to the Pope and to European governments failed to win any clemency for Eli Cohen. A Syrian court sentenced him to death, and he was hanged from the public gallows of a Damascus square — to the cheers of a huge crowd — on May 18, 1965.

Considering that the Israelis had an intelligence asset so well placed as Cohen, it is all the more impressive that they had another at the same time: Wolfgang Lotz, in Egypt.

Lotz was born in Mannheim, Germany, in 1921. His mother was a Jewish actress, and his father was a Christian who managed a theater in Berlin. It turned out that for his own perilous espionage act, it was lucky that Wolfgang was not circumcised.

His parents divorced, Adolf Hitler rose to power, and young Lotz was brought by his mother to Palestine in search of a safe life as Jews. Wolfgang changed his name to Ze'ev Gur-Aryeh, Ze'ev being the Hebrew word for "wolf." While studying at the Ben Shemen agricultural school east of Tel Aviv, he developed such a love of horses that his friends nicknamed him Sus — Hebrew for "horse."

Lotz/Gur-Aryeh joined the Haganah underground in 1937 and fought for the British in World War II, infiltrating behind German lines in North Africa. He mastered Arabic and English, as well as German and Hebrew. In 1948–49 he was a lieutenant in the new Israel Defense Forces, fighting for his country's independence. Promoted to the rank of major, he commanded a company that captured Egyptian positions in the 1956 Suez campaign.

Only afterward did Aman approach him. Military intelligence officers were impressed by Gur-Aryeh, because they realized that he did not look Israeli. As he later recalled, "I was blond, stocky and . . . a hard drinker and the very epitome of an ex-German officer."[24]

The Aman recruiters asked if he could shed his Jewishness and even convince others that he was an ex-Nazi. In training that was "intensive and exhausting," Lotz was taught to forget he was now Gur-Aryeh and to return to West Germany to start building a cover story — steps similar to those taken by Max Bennett a decade earlier. Lotz was to play the part of a German businessman who had served in Hitler's army in North Africa and then had spent eleven years in Australia breeding racehorses.

His Aman handlers ordered Lotz into Egypt in December 1960, providing him with sufficient capital — a huge expense account, by Israeli standards — to establish a horse ranch. They felt it was unlikely that Egypt's *Mukhabarat el-Amma,* or "General Intelligence Agency," would dig deeply into the rich German's background. It was risky, as Lotz recalled, but he was "one of the few secret agents ever to have worked under his real name, with his own genuine papers."

A convivial and charismatic man, Lotz was the happy host of parties for senior army officers and all the "right people" in Egyptian society. He smoked hashish with them and encouraged them to talk about their defense-related work. Using a tiny radio hidden in the heel of a riding boot, he telegraphed detailed reports to Tel Aviv.

Lotz was also used in Isser Harel's ill-fated campaign against the German scientists in Egypt. He supplied their Cairo addresses to Mossad headquarters, and he sent them several anonymous letters warning them to quit the Egyptian rocket program — for their own safety. Lotz also stored explosives apparently intended to be used in letter bombs.

Every few months, the spy went to Europe to report to his Aman case officer. In Paris, for instance, he would go to a pay phone to call a number he had memorized. "After I'd given the code word, I was told to meet a friend at three o'clock in a certain café," Lotz recalled. "In fact, three o'clock at café X meant two o'clock at café Y."

On a night train from Paris in June 1961, Lotz met "a tall, extremely pretty, blue-eyed blonde with the curvaceous figure I always have a weakness for." Just two weeks later, Wolfgang married Waltraud. It is almost inconceivable that a trained and otherwise reliable agent would do such a thing, but Lotz said he did not consult his Israeli controllers and simply took his bride to Cairo.

Some reports, never confirmed, claim that the new Frau Lotz was simply part of his cover story, and that the chief of the BND, West Germany's intelligence agency, General Reinhard Gehlen — as part of his clandestine cooperation with Israel — assigned Waltraud, a BND agent, to work with Lotz in Egypt.[25] This possibility is reinforced by the little-known fact that Lotz, twice divorced earlier in his life, had a third wife in Israel to whom he was still married.

Lotz said that when he told his new wife he was a Jewish spy, she liked the idea and agreed to help him. They developed a code: "We always referred to Israel as Switzerland, and to Israeli intelligence as Uncle Otto." Together at their horse farm near an experimental rocket base, they would keep an eye on former Nazi officers and German scientists who were helping Egypt develop new weapons.

Once caught straying onto the base, Lotz had the authorities call all his friends in the Egyptian military and secret police. Duly impressed, the commander of the base gave the German horse farmer a tour of the missile facility. "We, too, will have a great Arab Reich one day," the Egyptian officer boasted. "The Israelis have an excellent intelligence service. They must not learn anything about [the rockets] until we strike the final blow. Now, let me show you around."

Lotz also detected some amateurism on the Israeli side. At parties in Cairo he saw Caroline Bolter, who claimed to be the half-Dutch and half-Hungarian wife of a German archaeologist. She would make a point of chatting with German scientists and would gently probe for information about the Egyptian missile project. Lotz noticed that when she drank too much, instead of speaking German she would lapse into Yiddish. Then somebody caught her taking pictures at a scientist's house. Lotz sent a message to Tel Aviv, saying that if Mrs. Bolter was an Israeli agent she had better be withdrawn immediately. She disappeared.

In Tel Aviv, meantime, the responsibility for running Lotz was transferred from Aman to the Mossad in 1963 — after Meir Amit moved from the military to the Mossad as agency chief. Case officers at Mossad headquarters did not immediately know how to handle their star agent's apparent polygamy, and they waited a long time before telling his wife in Israel that Lotz had married again.

The new case officers were also not pleased by their operative's habits: he drank too much, and he seemed too generous with gifts to his Egyptian contacts. The bills had to be paid in Tel Aviv, and based on the expense reports Lotz filed when he visited Europe, the Mossad accounting department dubbed him "the champagne spy."

The information he sent, however, was reliable and irreplaceable. Meir Amit's Mossad suffered a devastating blow when Lotz and his wife were arrested by Egyptian Mukhabarat agents who burst into their Cairo apartment on February 22, 1965.

It seems that Lotz's radio transmitter, hidden in his bathroom scale, was detected by direction-finding equipment, just as in Damascus. The Soviet military intelligence agency, GRU, was helping to plug security leaks affecting the two Soviet allies, Syria and Egypt.

There were clear differences between the Lotz and Cohen cases, however. Whereas Cohen admitted he was an Israeli spy and was hanged, Lotz stubbornly clung to the contention that he was a non-Jewish German who had helped Israel just to earn some money.

The Mossad was able to send a German lawyer to help Lotz and his wife at their espionage trial in Cairo. The lawyer said publicly that he had been sent by Lotz's Wehrmacht army buddies. "Since I had never served in the German army," Lotz recalled, "I had a fairly good idea who had sent him."

Even though sentenced to life imprisonment, Lotz and his wife were released after only three years in an Israeli-Egyptian swap of Six-Day War prisoners. Mossad chief Amit had been so frustrated at his inability to save Cohen that he insisted to Prime Minister Eshkol that Lotz be included in a POW exchange. Israeli political leaders were reluctant to admit publicly that Lotz was a spy for Israel, so Amit threatened to resign to win their approval of the swap.

Simply by virtue of being alive, Lotz was more fortunate than Cohen. But while Eli Cohen is a martyr and hero in Israel, Wolfgang Lotz became bored with life as a civilian in the Jewish state and moved to West Germany and then to California in pursuit of business opportunities that never quite panned out.

The Mossad had yet another senior agent in the Arab world at the time. Baruch Mizrahi was in Syria as the principal of a foreign-language school when Cohen was arrested by Syrian counterintelligence. Mizrahi's controllers in Tel Aviv immediately ordered him to return home.[26]

The Mossad's caution did not help Mizrahi seven years later, however. Mizrahi was posted in Yemen to spy on the Egyptian army, which was still involved in a civil war there, and to report on shipping traffic in and out of the Red Sea. The Yemeni authorities announced Mizrahi's capture in May 1972, and even though Egypt's troops had left Yemen sent the suspect to Cairo, where he was charged with espionage on behalf of Israel. Matters did not turn out too badly for him, because he was sent home in March 1974 in exchange for two Israeli Arabs who had been spying for Egyptian intelligence.[27]

The Mossad had long had an interest in Yemen, because of sea routes and Egypt's involvement there. Between 1963 and 1965, Israel joined with Great Britain — as did Saudi Arabia, a strange political bedfellow — in supplying finance and arms to the royalist forces in North Yemen who were battling the republican regime and Egyptian military units. The Israelis wanted the Yemeni civil war to continue, because it kept Egypt's army far away and busy.[28]

But the Israelis were wrong. The conflict in far-off Yemen did not prevent the war that Israeli intelligence had wished to avoid but for which it was also preparing.

SEVEN

The Road to War

EVEN AS HIS TROOPS battled in Yemen, President Nasser embarked on a political path that would take the entire Arab world over the precipice into a much larger war.

Carried away by his pan-Arab rhetorical fervor, Nasser knew that Egypt alone could not crush Israel. In January 1964 he convened a summit in Cairo, as host to all the kings and presidents of all the Arab nations. The summit declared the establishment of a new body, the Palestine Liberation Organization, which would fight to replace Israel with yet another Arab state.

Nasser also knew that new organizations would not be enough to achieve the goal, so the summit also decided to divert the tributaries of the Jordan River which were vital for the agricultural development of Israel. The diversion works provoked the Israelis into bombing the bulldozers in neighboring Syria, Jordan, and Lebanon.

Arab leaders realized that they would need armed might to defeat the Jewish state, so they set up a unified military command. That was the overt aspect of the gathering momentum toward war. There was also a covert side.

Egyptian and Syrian intelligence, never ranked among the world's best in espionage, did what they could to penetrate Israeli society. They hired a few of Israel's Arab citizens — a far from ideal choice, as they were naturally under suspicion and surveillance — and would occasionally send agents to the Jewish state posing as tourists.

The most daring technique used by the Arab secret services was a mirror image of the Mossad's modus operandi: an Arab agent would learn precisely how to pose as a Jew and would go to Israel as an immigrant, unnoticed in a wave of new and welcomed Jewish arrivals.

Kobruk Yaakovian, an Armenian working for Egypt, managed to effect this ruse. He assumed a false identity as "Yitzhak Koshuk" and moved to Israel in December 1961 — ostensibly from Brazil. The Israeli consulate in Rio de Janeiro granted him a visa, believing him to be a Jew making aliyah, "going up" to his biblical homeland.

In fact, Egyptian intelligence had recruited Yaakovian/Koshuk while he was in prison in Cairo for a minor criminal offense. The Egyptians even circumcised him to make him a physically convincing Jew. As Koshuk, he worked on a kibbutz for a while, settled in the port city of Ashkelon, and entered the Israeli army. Despite his desire to join the armored corps, he rose no higher than a transportation unit. Even so, he managed to send some information of value to Cairo before Shin Bet caught the spy in December 1963. Yaakovian/Koshuk benefited from Israel's lack of a death penalty for espionage. He spent only a few years in an Israeli prison and was then deported to Egypt.[1]

The Egyptians were more successful in the late 1960s, when they sent a man they claim was "one of the best" secret agents to Israel. He called himself Jacques Biton and opened a travel agency on Brenner Street in Tel Aviv. He, too, was posing as a Jew and was similarly circumcised. Unlike Yaakovian/Koshuk, Biton — his true identity remains unknown — was never caught. Instead, he was a spy who had the unusual luxury of choosing to retire. The Egyptians allowed him to move to West Germany, where he settled with his wife for the rest of their days.

Egypt's state television had a huge hit on the air in 1988 when it broadcast a movie based on Biton's life story. At first Israeli officials said it was "Arab fiction," but when more details emerged in Cairo they had to admit that an enemy agent had gotten away scot-free. The Israelis still insisted that he had caused little or no harm.

The first assumption that Biton had to have been harmless, that the Arabs could not run a successful operation within Israel, was a natural result of the traditional belief in total Arab fallibility. The Israelis became convinced that their enemies could not do anything right, especially after the Six-Day War of 1967.

The lightning victory over Egypt, Jordan, and Syria was largely Meir Amit's triumph, made possible by the Mossad director's own obsessions. Different from those of his predecessor, Isser Harel, Amit's focused on obtaining as much information as possible about the neighboring Arab states and their armies so as to be thoroughly prepared for war at any moment.

Intelligence could be acquired from many sources, and Amit believed that friendly foreigners could help. That is why he made sure, after taking over as Mossad chief in 1963, that the agency forged ties with its counterparts throughout the Western world.

The Mossad's political action and liaison department became a second, secret foreign ministry, occasionally outmaneuvering the genuine one. In his memoirs, Miles Copeland, the self-proclaimed "CIA's original political operative," defined "political action" in the intelligence sense. He said it involved lobbying by "lining up industrial and commercial concerns in target countries, inducing them to organize discreet means of pressuring their government," sending advisers, and employing local personages as agents of influence.[2] While defined by a CIA man, the job was carried out worldwide by Israelis.

There were many countries — for instance, thirty developing nations in Africa — where Israel happily opened embassies after establishing diplomatic relations and various aid programs. As almost any country would do, Israel had Mossad agents working in the embassies under diplomatic cover.

Where official relations were not established or were later cut owing to overt political disputes, the Mossad's alternative diplomats performed functions that are not customarily handled by secret services. Specifically in Africa, Amit persuaded the CIA to provide millions of dollars to underwrite Israel's clandestine activities. They were judged to be in the general interest of the West. On the CIA's books, the project was codenamed "K K Mountain."[3]

The "peripheral concept" of the first Mossad director, Reuven Shiloah, gained great momentum in the Amit years. Israel's secret links with Ethiopia, Turkey, and Iran were strengthened. Both Israel and Iran aided the Kurdish revolt against the government of Iraq. Israeli agents in South Yemen helped the royalists fight off the Egyptians. In southern Sudan, Israeli aircraft dropped supplies for Christian rebels. Even deeper in Africa, the Mossad was working as far afield as Uganda by October 1970 to help Idi Amin depose President Milton Obote.

In coordination with Shin Bet, the Mossad also established ties with a large number of foreign security services by joining "Kilowatt," a secret group formed to combat international terrorism. Its members were representatives of the espionage agencies of Italy, Belgium, West Germany, Britain, Luxembourg, Holland, Switzerland,

Denmark, France, Canada, Ireland, and Norway, in addition, of course, to Israel. The Mossad also has ties with other states in Europe, such as Portugal, Spain, and Austria.

In most of these states, there are Mossad stations. The station generally operates under diplomatic cover within the Israeli embassy, but the head of the station does not inform the ambassador of his activities. Instead, he sends his reports directly to Tel Aviv. Every station has representatives of the two important departments of the Mossad: collection and liaison. The agents abroad are strongly insistent on compartmentalization, so that the members of one department do not know, and should not know, about the work of the others. Their tasks include official liaison exchanges with the host country's secret services, but they also operate their own networks, without informing the host service.

Amit's emphasis on quasi-diplomatic activities concentrated primarily on two continents: Africa and Asia.

The nascent, newly independent black African states of the 1960s opened their eyes to see Israel the beautiful: an example to copy. While the United States and the Soviet Union were regarded as expansionist superpowers, and Britain, France, and the other European countries were still disliked as colonialists, Israel was a young nation that had mastered the process of rapid development in the modern age. Africa's leaders could see the pioneering spirit at work in Israel, with initiative and proven ability that they hoped might rub off on them.

Over a dozen African states welcomed Israeli technicians and instructors in agriculture, industry, commerce, and defense. Hundreds of experts started development projects, and Israel's traveling politicians were not far behind. Foreign Minister Golda Meir toured the continent, and Prime Minister Levi Eshkol was also an honored guest in a number of African countries.

The number of Israeli advisers grew exponentially, and naturally quite a few of them were Mossad agents. The governmental hosts in Africa were usually more than understanding of this fact of life, and Israel quickly developed excellent intelligence cooperation with Kenya, Zaire, Liberia, and Ghana. In each country, espionage agencies or security services were trained or assisted by the Israelis.[4]

The Mossad's leading force in Africa was David (Dave) Kimche. Kimche, whose Eastern European family had moved from Switzerland to England, was a Zionist and moved to Palestine in 1946. But he kept his British habits. He is quiet and cultured, and wears thick, black-rimmed eyeglasses. His is an intelligent, often friendly face, topped with dark hair. He does not sound Israeli, as he speaks English perfectly and with an accent that would lead anyone to believe he is an English gentleman.

Kimche was recruited by the Mossad in 1953, after a few years in academe, and quickly gained a reputation in the intelligence community for keen perception, excellent analytical ability, and a tendency to keep his feelings to himself. He is the true-life Israeli equivalent of John le Carré's fictional British spy George Smiley. His interests lay in forging relations with non-Arab or non-Moslem minorities in the Middle East, but his specialty was Africa.

He worked all over the continent under various guises, including that of "David Sharon," Israeli diplomat. Kimche/Sharon was a reliable and friendly source for foreign journalists, and he was always able to supply them with the latest gossip on African regimes in the oddest places.[5]

One of those was the small island of Zanzibar, off the East African coast. Until 1964 it was ruled by a sultan, and the members of his court were descendants of Arabian slave traders. The rest of the population is black. A bloody revolution broke out that year on Zanzibar. The black majority seized the government from the Arab minority. The sultan and his family were killed or fled from the island.

In Israel, no tears were shed over the departure of the sultan. Another Arab stronghold in Africa had fallen, and another state had been opened to Israeli influence. Dave Kimche "happened" to be in Zanzibar on the day of the revolution. His presence enhanced the reputation of the Mossad, among Western diplomats and intelligence analysts, as being able to do anything.

Amit made sure that the Mossad also extended Israel's secret diplomacy to the Far East, opening an intelligence station in Singapore — a former British colony that was then part of the newly formed Malaysia, before turning itself into an independent and wealthy city-state. Always fearful of neighboring Malaysia and their own Malayan minority, the ethnic Chinese leaders of Singapore welcomed Israel's advice in the military and defense fields.

The Mossad set up a permanent Israeli military delegation in Singapore led by Colonel Binyamin (Fuad) Ben-Eliezer, a highly experienced commando-unit officer who was later promoted to brigadier general. Ben-Eliezer and his team provided consultations, training, and then weapons to Singapore's army and secret police.

Tiny Singapore, with its population of barely two and a half million, became the launching pad for the Mossad's alternative diplomats throughout Asia. Their first huge success in Asia was Indonesia — a nation of 180 million people, of whom ninety percent are Moslems.

President Sukarno, who fought for his country's independence from the Netherlands after World War II, was a leader of the anti-Western "non-aligned" movement and was firmly opposed to Israel. He was toppled in 1968, however, after suspending democracy and allegedly cooperating with the powerful Indonesian Communists in an attempt to take over the multi-island nation.

After supervising the slaughter of three hundred thousand Communists, the top army commander General Suharto became president. He would do almost anything to solidify his rule, and just the previous year Israel had managed to defeat the larger Arab armies in only six days. Suitably impressed, Suharto contacted the Israelis. The Mossad sent a team from its Singapore station southward to Jakarta, where possibilities of cooperation were fully and fruitfully discussed.

Before long, Israeli advisers — usually pretending to be Europeans or Americans — were training the Indonesian army and Suharto's intelligence service. The domestic security agency in Jakarta was convinced that it could vastly improve its capabilities with Israeli advice.

Because of their country's firm anticolonialist policies, the Indonesians did not trust the CIA or other Western secret services. The Mossad was therefore a perfect choice, and the Israeli agency was allowed to open a fairly large station in Jakarta under "commercial cover" — the intelligence analyst's term for posing as a business.

President Suharto and his aides told the Israelis that, as an Islamic nation, Indonesia could never consider formal diplomatic relations. But clandestine links became very close. Indonesian military and intelligence officers were sent to Israel for training, and they focused especially on anti-insurgency tactics to search for Communist guerrillas — techniques mastered by the Israelis to protect their own borders and to counter Palestinian terrorism.

By the 1970s, the Mossad brokered significant arms sales from Israel to Indonesia. These included a dozen American-made Skyhawk bombers, which Israel's air force no longer required. In addition to the revenues from such sales, Israel benefited from yet another intelligence toehold in the Islamic world. Indonesia proved to be a valuable base from which to observe Arab diplomats and Palestinian activists.

India, even more populous, was another useful contact point for Meir Amit's Mossad, even though the Indian government was also unwilling to tell its 800 million Hindu and Moslem people about the secret relationship with the Jewish state. Clandestine cooperation is always based on common interests, leading to an exchange of information. For India and Israel, the common potential enemy was Pakistan — a Moslem nation committed to helping the Arab countries of the Middle East.

The Mossad was deeply concerned to learn that Libya's Colonel Muammar Qaddafi had offered to finance the construction of a nuclear reactor in Pakistan, on condition that it be used to develop an "Islamic bomb" to be given to Qaddafi. Israeli operatives even explored the possibility of acting together with Indian forces to destroy the Pakistani reactor.[6]

The Mossad's ability to foster foreign contacts on Israel's behalf has been most striking in the unique relations Israel has with an Arab state, Morocco. As a Moslem nation and leading member of the Arab League, Morocco has always offered vociferous support to the Palestinian cause. Secretly, however, it established mutually beneficial ties with the Jewish state. King Hassan II has a personal, pro-Western inclination and felt threatened in the 1960s by the radical and anti-royalist regime in neighboring Algeria and by the extremist Nasser in Egypt.

Mossad experts helped Hassan establish a secret service, and in return Israel received the king's assurance that he would protect the Jews in his country and would permit those who wished to emigrate to Israel to do so. The relations between the two nations were secret, but they were good — even ideal. Amit, however, soon found that there was a price to pay for all this bounty: the head of Mehdi Ben-Barka.

The leading Moroccan dissident, Ben-Barka was sentenced to death in absentia. The Moroccan security service, led by General Muhammad Oufkir, decided to carry out the sentence wherever Ben-Barka might be. Oufkir asked for the assistance of his Israeli friend, General Amit.

The Mossad chief agreed to help, because he was concerned that refusing the request would adversely affect Morocco's Jews. Amit met Oufkir in France in the early autumn of 1965 to clarify final details of the agreement. The Mossad would help set the trap for Ben-Barka.

On October 29, 1965, Israeli agents lured the Moroccan dissident into leaving Geneva for a bogus meeting with a film producer in Paris. There, just outside a fashionable brasserie on the Left Bank, three French security officers who were cooperating with the Moroccans "arrested" Ben-Barka. When the Israelis saw that too many French and Moroccan agents were involved, they stepped out of the picture. The Mossad station chief in Morocco, however, had the distasteful task of sticking with Oufkir because Amit insisted that the Moroccan security boss not be snubbed. The Israeli agent, traveling on a false British passport, did not know the full purpose of the mission and was surprised when Oufkir and his men shot Ben-Barka dead and buried him in the garden of a villa outside Paris.

Amit and Oufkir believed that the secret had been buried together with the corpse. Who would pay attention to a disappearance — or even an isolated murder that was entirely within the norms of Middle Eastern politics? The two intelligence chiefs did not, however, take into account the reactions of two other people, of very different outlooks and temperaments — Isser Harel in Israel, and General de Gaulle in France.

The French president immediately ordered an investigation as to how Ben-Barka could have vanished in the very heart of Paris. The investigation uncovered not only the Israeli-Moroccan connection, but also the involvement of the French equivalent of the Mossad, *Service de Documentation Extérieure et de Contre-Espionage.*

De Gaulle, who suspected that his secret agency might be plotting against him, was absolutely furious. He immediately ordered that the secret service's house be put in order. He also directed his anger at Israel. How could France's allies, with whom de Gaulle had cooperated, work behind his back?[7]

As a reaction to the Ben-Barka killing, the French president ordered that the Mossad's European command be removed from Paris, and he also ordered a cessation of all intelligence cooperation between the two nations. His decision simply sharpened the knives that had been drawn in Israel, where a scandal was brewing over the Mossad's involvement in murder.

There was already a major internal struggle in Israeli politics, as the election set for November 1965 approached. Labor was sure to win, as usual, but the Labor movement was bitterly divided between Ben-Gurion's Rafi party and the Mapai party of Levi Eshkol and Golda Meir.

Having learned lessons from the Lavon Affair and wider scandals stemming from botched espionage operations in Egypt, Mapai leaders decided that, come what may, they would not permit the Ben-Barka affair to grow — or even to become public knowledge. The killing had led to a noisy scandal in France; Israeli involvement was kept totally secret.

When a sex-oriented Israeli magazine called *Bul* hinted that there could be "Israelis in the Ben-Barka case," Shin Bet impounded all thirty thousand copies of the issue just before their scheduled distribution. Only five copies reached the newsstands. The editors of the magazine, Shmuel Mor and Maxim Gilan, were placed in administrative detention.[8] Article 23 of the Israeli security laws was invoked, even though this section had never been used before for anything other than espionage against the Jewish state. This was the first — and, as of this writing, the only — occasion on which this law was invoked against Jewish journalists in Israel.

As in the Lavon Affair, the key question was: Who gave the orders? Amit claimed that he had been given the go-ahead by Levi Eshkol. The prime minister claimed that he had never done any such thing. A demand to set up a commission of inquiry began to gain momentum when Isser Harel joined in calling for one. His voice was authoritative, not only because of his past, but also because the ex-Memuneh had just been appointed to a new job as adviser to the prime minister on intelligence.

Harel's surprising return to active duty came in September 1965, a month before Ben-Barka was killed. Eshkol may have been motivated by a desire for one-upmanship against his constant rival, David Ben-Gurion. It was as if he were sending a message: I, Levi Eshkol, having taken the place of "the Old Man," am restoring to the Israeli secret services the person who had once been Ben-Gurion's protégé but was thrown onto the scrap heap.

Eshkol ignored Amit's protests over the appointment, and the dirty war between Amit and Harel was renewed from the first instant of the new arrangement. The intelligence community found itself pulled in opposite directions. Amit refused to cooperate with Harel. Harel found ways to bypass Amit. Using personal contacts and his knowledge of the secret agencies' archives, Harel managed to borrow secret files from the Mossad's safes. Harel brought the heads of Mossad departments directly to Prime Minister Eshkol for meetings, and the subjects often included their assessments of Amit's ability — concentrating on his deficiencies.[9]

Proposals for secret operations, which were brought to Eshkol by Amit, were vetoed by Harel. That was the fate of a bold plan put forward by Amit in 1966 to travel to Cairo for a secret meeting with President Nasser's deputy, Field Marshal Hakim Amar. The idea had been suggested by a foreign Jewish businessman who was acquainted with senior Egyptian officials. Amit was extremely interested.

Harel chimed in that the proposed Cairo talks could be a trap, adding that it would be insane and irresponsible for the Mossad chief to fly into the enemy's hands. If arrested and interrogated in Egypt, Harel suggested, Amit might be compelled to reveal vital Israeli secrets.

Torn by the battle of the giants, Eshkol sided with Harel. The suggested negotiations with Egypt never took place. Amit believes, with regret and bitterness, that if he had flown clandestinely to Cairo the war that broke out in June 1967 might have been averted. There was no time for the intelligence community to ponder such questions, however. Tension along Israel's borders with Egypt and Syria was increasing sharply, and the secret agencies had to devote all their resources to the new threat.

There was also no time to settle the argument over who was in charge of Israeli intelligence, Harel or Amit. A compromise suggestion, to put cabinet minister and 1948 war hero Yigal Allon in charge of the intelligence community, also did not get the attention it deserved with war on the horizon.

Amit's biggest embarrassment, the Ben-Barka killing in Paris, was also swept under the carpet in Israel. This was more than Harel could tolerate, after his repeated calls for a full investigation. He had laid his prestige on the line and felt no choice but to resign in June 1966. To the immense relief of Amit, Harel's attempt at a comeback abruptly ended after only nine months in the prime minister's office. The former Memuneh's new crusade had gotten nowhere, except for the cancellation of the peace mission to Cairo, and this time Harel left secret service for good.[10]

Amit clung to his Mossad job by the skin of his teeth, lucky that miscellaneous matters were shoved aside when full attention was devoted to the foremost purpose of intelligence: preparing for war.

Aman's commander, Colonel Yariv, Amit's former deputy in military intelligence, did a phenomenal job at collating every available tidbit of information about the Arab armed forces as they prepared to attack Israel in 1967. Using computer systems developed by Aman Colonel Yuval Ne'eman among others, the intelligence community was able to provide Israel's military planners with lists of targets and potential trouble spots should war break out.

When Egypt's Nasser blockaded the Straits of Tiran in May, preventing access by sea to Israel from the south, Prime Minister Eshkol explored diplomatic options for three weeks before declaring the blockade an act of war. Nasser, meantime, had ordered United Nations peacekeepers to leave Egypt's Sinai Peninsula.

Israel's response came by air on the morning of June 5, 1967. The Israeli air force, armed with both bombs and the intelligence community's list of targets, guaranteed the six-day victory in less than six hours. The Egyptian air force was destroyed on the ground. Syrian and Jordanian forces suffered similarly devastating blows.

The first hours of the brief war were confusing. While Arab radio stations gloated over their imaginary victories, John Hadden, the CIA station chief in Israel, was able to report to his headquarters in Langley, Virginia, that "the war is over." He was on excellent terms with the Mossad — for fun, his official Israeli liaisons addressed him by the Hebrew-sounding equivalent of his name, Yochanan Ha-Dan — and he had access to the latest, honest battlefield reports.

Amit had been at the new CIA headquarters only a few days earlier, on a special assignment for Eshkol. His mission: to tell the Americans that war was inevitable, that Nasser started it by trying to strangle Israel, and that Israel would have to launch the first armed attack in order to survive.

CIA director Richard Helms listened to Amit, and so did President Lyndon B. Johnson. The United States understood Israel's reasoning and did not object to the preemptive attack. Amit's achievement in secret diplomacy was built upon the international intelligence links which the Mossad had worked so hard to foster for years. The air force and army then did the rest, and even overdid it.

In one of the most mysterious and controversial incidents of the war, Israel's air force and navy raced to attack an American ship. The USS *Liberty* was a naval spy vessel with sophisticated radios, antennas, and dishes, working for the National Security Agency (NSA) in the Mediterranean. On Wednesday, June 8, the *Liberty* was off the coast of the Sinai Peninsula, monitoring the advance of the Israeli conquerors. Although it flew the Stars and Stripes, Israeli warplanes and ships bombed, strafed, and torpedoed the surveillance vessel. Thirty-four American sailors were killed, and many more wounded.

Nearly a quarter of a century later, neither the United States nor the Israeli government provided a coherent explanation and left the way open for rumors, speculation, and natural anger felt by many U.S. Navy veterans. How, they wondered, did the Israelis dare to attack their chief ally's ship? Why did they do it?

The survivors and the bereaved families believed that it had to be intentional: that the Israelis knew what they were doing, to blind and deafen the NSA's electronic eyes and ears just when Israel was shifting its armed might from the Egyptian front to the Syrian.[11]

CIA station chief Hadden and the U.S. naval attaché in Tel Aviv, Captain Ernest Castle, were assigned to find out. The Israelis said their forces had simply made a mistake. After a thorough investigation, Hadden and Castle believed them. In the heat of battle, the Israeli navy and air force had ingloriously competed to be first to eliminate a ship which in the official battle plan simply did not belong there. And when they saw the U.S. flag, the Israelis thought it was probably the Egyptians pretending to be Americans and did not bother to check. The United States was further annoyed for many years by the Israelis' seeming arrogance in refusing to pay compensation to the families of the victims.

By June 11, euphoric Israel was the master of Jordan's West Bank, Egypt's Sinai and Gaza Strip, and Syria's Golan Heights. The capture of these huge territories erased forever the notion of a tiny Jewish state barely managing to survive among the large and powerful Arab nations.

The triumph marked a watershed in Israel's history, and the intelligence community was not immune to the sweeping changes that followed.

EIGHT

Shin Bet Has Its Day

THE BED WAS STILL WARM, the sheets and blankets lay strewn all over the floor, the water had boiled in the kettle, and the tea in the cups was still hot, but the man known as Abu Ammar was not to be found. A few seconds before Israeli troops and security men broke into the three-story villa in Ramallah, on the West Bank, the leader of the Palestine Liberation Organization — better recognized in the outside world as Yasser Arafat — had fled.

From his second-floor hiding place, he heard the voices of the Israelis as they surrounded the villa and began their search. Arafat leaped from a window and hid in a car parked nearby. When the men who were after his scalp had left, he hurried eastward and crossed the Jordan River for the last time.[1] It was mid-December 1967, six months after Israel captured the area from Jordan. Since then, Arafat has never set foot on the West Bank.

Shin Bet director Yosef Harmelin was disappointed. It was the seventh time that his men did not ensnare the PLO leader. The guerrilla organization had become an important focus for Israeli intelligence since the PLO's establishment in 1964. On January 1 of that year, Harmelin had taken over from Amos Manor at Shin Bet. Manor had been disappointed not to replace Isser Harel as Memuneh in 1963 and felt he could not compete with Mossad chief Amit for the attention of Prime Minister Eshkol.

Despite the failure to capture Arafat, Shin Bet had plenty to be proud of in 1967. Most importantly the security agency had quickly managed to quash the PLO's attempt to launch a "popular uprising" — almost before it could begin.

Most of the territories seized by Israel in June presented few difficulties in holding. Almost all of the Syrians in the Golan Heights, except for a few thousand Druze, had fled the area. The Sinai was home to almost no Egyptians, except for a few wandering Bedouin tribes.

The real problems, for Israel as an occupying power, were found in the West Bank and the Gaza Strip. In other words, that is where the people were.

The West Bank, an area of less than three thousand square miles, was home to around six hundred thousand Palestinians, while another four hundred thousand resided in the overcrowded poverty of the Gaza Strip, which comprised barely one hundred square miles.

The Palestinians were confused and frightened as Israel set up the structure of its military occupation. The intelligence community formed a task force, made up of the Mossad's David Kimche and Shin Bet and Aman men, to explore the politics of the local inhabitants. The group proposed granting the Palestinians autonomy leading to a separate state, but Eshkol and his government ignored the advice. Some of the Arab dignitaries were polite, asking only that the Israelis permit a rapid return to normal commerce and day-to-day civilian life, but it was clear that most West Bankers would prefer to return to King Hussein's Jordanian administration. Even the Gazans, who had done poorly when governed by Egypt, would opt for an Arab ruler rather than Israel.

Hoping to capitalize on popular discontent, the PLO and splinter groups of guerrillas planned to emulate the Vietcong, who were successfully confronting the powerful American armed forces in Vietnam, and the FLN, which had driven the French from Algeria. Arafat and his comrades called upon the Palestinian population to rise against the Israeli-Zionist occupation.

Their plan, after the crushing defeat of 1967, was to make the territories ungovernable for the Israelis. The PLO would control daily life in the five hundred towns and villages of the West Bank and Gaza, and left-wing theorists among the guerrillas believed a Palestinian revolutionary government would inevitably follow.

Immediately after the Six-Day War, a PLO pamphlet which was defiantly distributed in the West Bank used classic, Communist-inspired language: "We must set up secret resistance in every street, village, and neighborhood. Each person is obliged to fight the enemy. Roll large rocks down from the heights of mountains, in order to block the enemy's traffic arteries. Try to cause the enemy's cars to burst into flames. We must impose a boycott on the economic and cultural institutions of the occupation forces." The circular ended with instructions on how to prepare a Molotov cocktail.[2]

What the guerrilla groups had in mind was a "popular liberation struggle" of which Mao Zedong or Fidel Castro could be proud. The PLO borrowed not only foreign concepts but also operational tactics from China, Cuba, Vietnam, and Algeria. The Palestinians had active assistance from Colonel Ahmed Suedani, the head of Syrian military intelligence who was credited with catching the Mossad's Eli Cohen in Damascus. Suedani was known as an enthusiastic supporter of "popular struggle" anywhere in the Middle East except Syria.

Militant PLO factions infiltrated dozens of their members, armed with guns and explosives, into the occupied territories and set up command posts under the noses of the new Israeli administrators. Arafat was personally involved in recruiting fighting men for various operations, and his approval was required for almost every tiny detail. Guerrilla cells were sent out on hit-and-run operations against army vehicles and patrols. The Palestinians staged ambushes on the narrow streets of West Bank towns.

In Israel itself, the Palestinians detonated bombs in markets, movie theaters, bus stations, and restaurants. Whether the targets were civilians or military men meant nothing to the attackers. Arafat and his strategists believed they were engaged in a pure form of honorable armed struggle, whereas in the eyes of Israel and most of the outside world there was one simple word for the PLO's tactics: terrorism.

Shin Bet had no time to argue about terminology. Prime Minister Eshkol and Defense Minister Dayan — while putting the army in charge of the daily affairs of military and civil administration in the occupied territories — assigned Harmelin's secret service to fight subversion and to preserve law and order. There were many, however, in both the government and the army who doubted Shin Bet's ability to accomplish these aims.

At the time, the agency was a small and self-contained body working in virtually total anonymity. The general public had not heard of Shin Bet by name, details of its operations had been censored out of the press, and it was illegal to identify any of its personnel. The entire force numbered around five hundred people, and the atmosphere within was that of a close family in which everyone knew everyone else. Family secrets were never divulged to outsiders.

It was also, however, a lackluster agency that had always been overshadowed by the Mossad and by Aman. Only rarely were a few crumbs of excitement tossed to Shin Bet by the operations department which it shared with the Mossad. These were some unusual overseas assignments, such as the capture of Adolf Eichmann or the search for little Yossele Schumacher.

Shin Bet's main task was the usually unglamorous business of watching vigilantly for foreign spies and domestic subversives. Naturally, the Arab minority in Israel had always constituted the main pool of suspects.

Just two years before the Six-Day War, the government abolished the military administration that had been in effect in Israeli Arab towns and villages since the 1948 War of Independence. While the Arab citizens of the Jewish state always enjoyed the right to vote for Knesset members, they had not been governed by the same civilian systems as Jewish-dominated areas. There had been military governors for the Arab-populated sectors, mainly the Galilee region in northern Israel, and the residents had been closely watched by Shin Bet.

The recommendation in 1965 to do away with military rule in specific regions of Israel came from former Mossad operative Shmuel Toledano, in his role as Eshkol's adviser on Arab affairs. Harmelin of Shin Bet supported the proposal, not because the agency suddenly took a liking to Arabs and their civil rights, but because the interests of the state and its security could be served better.

Shin Bet's job was to prevent the Arabs from acting as a fifth column that could help their brothers across the border. Abolishing military administration, Shin Bet claimed, would offer the Arabs an incentive to become integrated into Israeli society, to study in its universities, to set up businesses, to launch careers, to increase income, and no longer to feel the discrimination, frustration, disappointment, and hopelessness that fostered subversion. Shin Bet believed that lifting official restrictions on Israel's Arabs would calm that sector of society, and would isolate the minority of extremists who claimed that life in Israel was bad.[3]

Toledano's proposal was approved. With the ensuing readjustment of Shin Bet's tasks, Harmelin's era had truly begun. Until he was promoted to replace the colorless and businesslike Manor, Harmelin had been in charge of the Shin Bet counterespionage department. He planned to make spycatching the main focus of the entire agency's activities.

The new chief liked the mental cut and thrust of trapping foreign agents. Shin Bet's success at it demanded a great deal of sophistication, and interrogations were an especially interesting intellectual challenge. Confronting suspects involved an unceasing effort to identify weak spots in their personalities and human frailties in general. The Shin Bet interrogator and the person being questioned — an alleged traitor or spy — would sit together drinking coffee, without violence, and would engage in a battle of wits.[4]

No one had a better poker face than Yosef Harmelin. He was an impressively tall man, but the ability to maintain an expressionless countenance was his most memorable quality. Hiding one's feelings is an excellent attribute for an intelligence man. He was probably born with the talent when he entered the world in Vienna in 1923.

After the *Anschluss* in 1938, when Austria was annexed by Nazi Germany, Harmelin's parents escaped the approaching Holocaust by moving to Mexico. The teenaged Yosef, more Zionist than his parents, moved to Palestine instead. He studied at the Ben Shemen agricultural school, which produced future political leaders such as Shimon Peres and future spies such as Wolfgang Lotz. Like Harel and Amit, Harmelin joined a kibbutz before enlisting in the British army in World War II. After the war he joined the Haganah, where he met Harel, and a few years after Israel's independence Harmelin was recruited by Shin Bet. He gradually worked his way up to the top.[5]

His relationship with Levi Eshkol, who appointed him Shin Bet chief, was very formal. Eshkol had wanted something entirely different. As prime minister, directly responsible for the Mossad and Shin Bet, he tried to develop a close, almost paternal relationship with Harmelin — to contrast with the troubles Eshkol was having getting along with Mossad chief Meir Amit.

Eshkol found Harmelin to be honest to a fault, sincere, and a perfectionist. On the other hand, Harmelin was also too dull for Eshkol, who was a canny politician, an expert manipulator of party intrigues, and a man who enjoyed a good joke. The prime minister's sense of humor cut no ice with Harmelin, despite repeated attempts by Eshkol to enliven their conversations with wit and wisdom in his beloved Yiddish language.

On one occasion, after Shin Bet detected indications of an assassination threat, the guard around the prime minister was doubled. Almost every week, there were suggestions and threats that Eshkol might be killed. In general, these threats were ignored, because the

Israelis have always believed that genuine assassins do not write warning letters. After President John F. Kennedy was murdered in November 1963, however, Shin Bet was unwilling to take any unnecessary chances.

Harmelin, whose responsibilities included protecting the prime minister and other government officials, told Eshkol soon after Kennedy's assassination that as the result of a security review, the prime minister would now have two around-the-clock bodyguards rather than one.

"But you can trust their utter discretion," the Shin Bet chief promised, remembering that Eshkol was a widower and might demand privacy when seeking female companionship. "Even if you have any very intimate meetings," Harmelin explained, "they won't breathe a word."

Eshkol, with his typical chuckle, responded: "On the contrary. Let them tell."[6] Harmelin did not laugh at such jokes. He treated his work with complete seriousness. That was also how he behaved when he was given a new assignment: the occupied territories.

The decision to put Shin Bet in charge of law and order in the captured lands, thus extending its internal security role beyond Israel's formal borders, was made on June 19, 1967, at a meeting of Varash — the committee of all the intelligence chiefs. The Six-Day War had ended in triumph only a week earlier, and the flush of victory was still strong. By Varash tradition, Mossad director Amit chaired the meeting, and around the table sat Aman chief Aharon Yariv, Harmelin for Shin Bet, the national police chief, and the director-general of the foreign ministry.[7]

The Israeli government was finding it difficult to decide on a status and future plans for the territories captured that month. Were they "liberated" portions of the biblical Land of Israel, or "occupied" pieces of hostile, foreign territory?

Lacking a political decision about the land, the Varash committee was forced to adopt an administrative policy of "carrot and stick" designed to preserve the status quo while maintaining order as the highest priority. In an attempt to drive a wedge between the majority of the Palestinians and the dangerous, subversive minority, the intelligence chiefs decided that the inhabitants would be permitted to conduct their lives normally. That was the carrot.

The stick was the policy to punish, strongly and surely, anyone participating in subversion or outright violence. Palestinians who aided guerrilla groups were punished by imprisonment and the destruction of their houses — usually by dynamite, in loud explosions meant to serve as examples to others. Losing one's home was severe punishment, but the most serious and decisive penalty available to Shin Bet was expulsion. From the early weeks of running what Israel called "the administered territories," Arab residents believed to have ties with PLO terrorists were escorted across the bridges into Jordan and banned from returning.

Transforming the carrot-and-stick theory into practice was no simple task. Shin Bet agents were not prepared for it. The new territories in Israel's hands were terra incognita to them — an unknown world where the agency had no men in the field and did not know the population. Shin Bet had to start from scratch.

As a first step Harmelin's operatives, with the help of Yariv's military intelligence staff, used psychological warfare to spread rumors of how tough the Israeli hard line would be. These were not so much accurate as they were chilling.[8]

After it was clear that Israel's determination to remain in the territories was known to their inhabitants, Shin Bet turned to the second and major stage: preventing the attempted Palestinian uprising and combating terrorism. Harmelin assigned the task to Avraham Ahituv, the head of the small Arab affairs department of Shin Bet. Filling some of the gaps left by the abolition of military administration in Galilee in 1965, Ahituv's department had ensured that the Israeli Arabs did not engage in subversive acts, incitement, or violence.

Ahituv was a lawyer by training and worked with the meticulousness required in legal work. His work was of dubious legality, however, although there was nothing but praise from his Shin Bet colleagues as he established a widespread network of informers among Israeli Arabs. It appeared that nothing escaped his men's eyes. A secret report compiled by the CIA called Ahituv "extremely bright, hard-working, ambitious, and thorough," but also "headstrong, abrasive, and arrogant."[9]

Ahituv had previously been in charge of Shin Bet operations in the Gaza Strip after Israel briefly seized it from Egypt in 1956. The Palestinians there had been kept in control, and Ahituv had built his reputation. In 1967, he was asked to use his talents to achieve —

throughout the occupied territories — similar results to those he had achieved in Gaza and in Israel's Arab sector.

Ahituv's most able assistant was Yehudah Arbel, a short man with prematurely gray hair and hypnotic eyes. His eyes were the bluest of blue, but they were ice cold. He was a romantic and an aesthete who loved music, art, beautiful women, and good wine. Although Arbel was striking in his individuality, his biography was similar to that of others in the Israeli intelligence community. He was born in Transylvania, then part of Hungary but now in Romania, moved to Palestine, served in the British army, and fought for Israel's independence in 1948. Until he joined Shin Bet in 1955, he worked as a police officer. When the 1967 war broke out, Arbel was the Jerusalem district head of Shin Bet. It was a small, uneventful district, with relatively little work to do. Generally, since Israel's western sector of Jerusalem had very few Arabs until then, this work consisted of counterespionage and surveillance of foreign diplomats.

Arbel was so bored that for a time he considered resigning. Following the Six-Day War, however, his new role as an antiterrorist combatant was quickly recognized as one of the most vital in Israeli intelligence. It was like a sudden shot of adrenaline. It was as if he had been reborn. Arbel drove incessantly from one village to another in the West Bank, recruiting informers and coordinating the penetration of resistance cells.[10]

In no time flat, Shin Bet licked the immediate problem facing Israel in the territories. The Palestinians would not manage to mount a popular uprising in the newly occupied lands. Shin Bet had excellent inside information, and that was the essential weapon in waging a successful war against underground opposition.

Ahituv and Arbel managed to crisscross the entire West Bank and Gaza Strip with networks of informers and secret agents. Most of them were Arabs, recruited either by money or intimidation, but there were also a few Israelis who were excellent Arabic-speakers. The agents often gave Shin Bet advance information of attacks planned by guerrillas.[11] It was the continuous flow of information that had nearly enabled Shin Bet to lay its hands on Arafat that December 1967 night in the Ramallah villa.

Shin Bet operatives, acting on tip-offs, were able to swoop down on subversive meetings and laid ambushes to capture Palestinian squads on their way to staging attacks. The system that permitted these successes became known as "preventive intelligence," which is the greatest desire of every internal security service having to deal with violence and terrorism. The ultimate aim is not to have to search for the perpetrators after the crime, but to prevent the terrorists from carrying it out in the first place.

By December 1967, Shin Bet had chalked up an amazing record of triumph: most of the PLO cells collapsed, and their headquarters within the West Bank were forced to retreat to Jordan. Two hundred Palestinian guerrillas were killed in battles with army and Shin Bet units, and more than one thousand were arrested.

The failure of the attempted Palestinian uprising in 1967 was not, however, due solely to the efficiency of the Israeli secret services. The Palestinians were also to blame, because of their lack of professionalism. They did not obey the rule of compartmentalization that is so basic in spycraft and underground movements. Instead, they organized in relatively large groups, knew one another, and relied on local Arabs not to turn them in to the authorities. Arafat himself and his senior commanders, in total violation of the rules of a good conspiracy, knew most of the members of the cells. Their communications system was primitive, and their codes were simple. No escape routes were planned. Their "safe houses" were not really safe. Nor were the members of guerrilla squads prepared to withstand interrogation, when captured. As soon as they were picked up by Shin Bet, they would tell everything they knew.

Their codes were broken, and their weapons and explosives were confiscated. Like dominoes, the cells fell one after another. Above all, failing to honor Mao Zedong's Chinese dictum that a guerrilla fighter must have the support of the population and feel "like a fish in the water," the Palestinian fighters could not "swim" unnoticed among their neighbors who swept them to the Shin Bet shore. Motivated by Israeli carrots and sticks, the local populace preferred peace, quiet, and prosperity — rather than collaboration with the underground.[12]

Full credit was given, however, to Shin Bet. The importance of Harmelin's agency within the intelligence community was growing, and Ahituv's case officers became known as the "kings of the territory." Almost as in a feudal regime, each Israeli operative was given his own region, generally a village or a group of villages. He had to be Israel's eyes and ears, knowing everything that happened in his fiefdom. The operative was trained to know most of the villagers by name, while they knew him only by an alias — usually an invented Arabic name such as Abu Musa, "Father of Moses."

If a Palestinian wanted a building permit, the military government in the occupied territories would first check with the local Shin Bet case officer. An Arab merchant who wished to export his citrus crop from Gaza or his olive oil from the West Bank was able to obtain the necessary licenses only with the assent of Shin Bet. Almost every daily activity, almost every minute of the Palestinian's life, was supervised by Shin Bet in a kind of business transaction. The Arabs supplied information, and in return they were given security and fringe benefits.[13]

Shin Bet's success came at a price, however. Israeli society, to its cost, was judged in the outside world by what could be seen of its security policies. Subversion was crushed, but Israel's goodwill around the world was being squandered. Instead of being an admired favorite of international public opinion, the Jewish state became the Ugly Israel. All the good the country had done was swept aside by negative headlines. The underdog of 1967 was now seen as a brutal occupier of another people's land.

Just as most intelligence agencies reflect their societies' ethics, values, and morals, the change in Israel's image inflicted damage on Shin Bet. Until the Six-Day War, the agency's personnel were like a small family sharing a common background: they had served in the British army or the Haganah and were primarily from the European, Ashkenazic sector of the Jewish population.

After the 1967 war Shin Bet was forced by circumstances to transform itself into an oppressive force, playing a central role in governing the territories and their people. Shin Bet became the security service of an occupying power, self-confident and even arrogant. Having to cover a lot more ground, perfectionism and meticulous work had to give way to hasty improvisation.

In order to set up Shin Bet's large intelligence networks, there was an urgent need to expand its manpower. A new and modern complex of buildings was built in a northern suburb of Tel Aviv to house Shin Bet headquarters and to replace the old one in Jaffa. The recruiting criteria were made easier with less emphasis on high standards. Everything was done in a hurry, and the social profile of Shin Bet's personnel changed. The Arabic-speakers who were now so essential were to be found among the Oriental, Sephardic sector of the Jewish populace. There were exceptions, of course, but these were generally less educated men who built their careers more on brawn than brains.

Until then, most of those selected were soldiers from élite combat units of the army. Unlike most countries, where the special forces or commandos are considered the most aggressive and bloodthirsty troops, overeager for battle, the Israeli élite fighting men have been trained to be soul-searching and aware of morality. Shin Bet, in its haste to expand, added to its ranks from mere support units, where soldiers were less inculcated with the finer aspects of morals and ethics.

Even senior Shin Bet commanders, who normally had a good eye for spotting problem applicants, made mistakes. Yossi Ginossar, who two decades later would feature in two of the worst scandals in the history of the Israeli intelligence community, was one of those "errors." Ginossar came from the adjutancy — a staff officer who assisted at the rear, rather than battling at the front.

The changed nature of the work also dictated new methods. At a time when two thousand Arabs were being detained for questioning, when booby-trapped cars were exploding, and when hotels and airliners were terrorist targets, it was essential to extract information as quickly as possible. The time factor became the most important element of preventive intelligence. Fast action seemed to require brutality without pausing for a second thought.

At first, Shin Bet found it difficult to adjust to this new reality. When Yosef Harmelin once saw one of his young interrogators slap the face of a Palestinian suspect, the agency chief fired his employee on the spot. Harmelin did not agree that physical violence was necessary.[14]

The new circumstances, however, dominated. Shin Bet operatives learned the hard way what the occupation meant. Theirs was dirty work in the service of a perhaps noble cause. Harmelin and his deputy Ahituv did manage to suppress terrorism, but they had to do it by introducing what their men called "the System."

The security methods were indeed systematic in creating a double standard of justice. One, democratic by nature, applied to Israeli citizens; and a totally different one, operating in the gray area between the permissible and the forbidden, was used against Palestinian troublemakers and suspects in the occupied territories.

The System and its double standard created a new frontier, "Shin Bet country." In Shin Bet country the agency had its own detention centers as well as separate, Shin Bet–run wings of Israeli civilian prisons. Whenever Palestinian prisoners were arrested, they were brought directly to the special wings or detention centers. The police and national prisons authority never took a look at what was occurring in the cells behind those walls.

Arabs accused of terrorism faced brutal interrogation. Physical blows were rare, but there were other forms of coercion that left no marks. Once the gates of Shin Bet closed behind them Palestinian prisoners typically had their heads covered by a black sack, and then they were left, exposed to the hot Israeli sun or winter cold, waiting for the interrogators. The questioning then went on for hours. The suspects were usually deprived of sleep and sometimes soaked with cold water.

Some Shin Bet personnel did not like what they had to do, but they regarded it as necessary in the struggle for national existence. They believed that they were defending Israel, which faced cruel terrorism. "What do terrorists that kill women and children expect? That we should knock on their door and invite them for a cup of coffee?" said a Shin Bet veteran who headed the agency's interrogation department for many years. He never used his real name and only called himself Pashosh, which means "warbler" and reflected his goal of having all suspects "sing" the whole truth.[15]

A highly unusual project in which Shin Bet cooperated with Aman and the Mossad was aimed at countering the "demographic problem," the expectation that with their much higher birthrate the Arabs would outnumber the Jews in Israel and the occupied territories by the end of the twentieth century. The intelligence community was assigned to encourage Palestinians to emigrate. A special Israeli unit set up phony corporations in Europe that bought land for Arabs from Gaza and the West Bank who agreed to move abroad. The properties were in Brazil and Paraguay, and even in Libya for those who preferred to live in an Arab country.

Doing business in Libya gave the Mossad a good opportunity to watch political developments there, so it came as no surprise to agency chief Zvi Zamir when the pro-Western King Idris of Libya was overthrown in September 1969 by a band of young military officers who modeled themselves after Colonel Nasser and his Egyptian coup of 1952. The new Libyan leader was Colonel Muammar el-Qaddafi. Zamir could not know, when he heard the news from Tripoli, that Qaddafi would become one of Israel's most vicious enemies.

The Mossad chief did realize that the Libyan king's departure was bad news. The West had lost a strategic bastion in North Africa. "We told them, we warned them," Zamir said to a colleague in Tel Aviv, hinting that Israeli intelligence had issued advance warnings to Idris and his friends in the American, British, and Italian governments.

The loss of Libya as a place to resettle Palestinians did not spell the end of the secret program to send them abroad. Its demise came after a murder in Asunción, the Paraguayan capital, in 1970. Around midday on May 4, a young Arab stormed into the Israeli consulate there and angrily demanded to see the ambassador. When one of the Israeli secretaries tried to calm the man, he pulled out a pistol and shot her dead. The gunman and two accomplices who were waiting outside apparently fled the country and were never caught.

Israel's official spokesmen quickly declared that the killing was yet another in a wave of Palestinian terrorist attacks. It was in fact something quite different: an act of vengeance by three Palestinians who had been resettled in Paraguay as part of the secret intelligence community program. The three men were unhappy at what they believed was a raw deal from the Israelis.

The killer was identified by police investigators in Asunción as Talal ibn-Dimassi, who was born in the Gaza Strip. He and his two friends had lived in the Jabaliya refugee camp in Gaza when the area was captured by Israel in 1967 and were quickly fed up with life there. They accepted an invitation to visit the Israeli military governor's office in Gaza, not far from Dimassi's appliance store on el-Mukhtar Street in Gaza City, and thus began their journey into voluntary exile.

Israeli intelligence officers had worked intensively to find Arabs like Dimassi who were so disappointed with their lot that they might be candidates for departure. Hundreds of refugee families accepted the offer, clutching new passports, start-up funds, and one-way tickets from an Israeli travel agency as they headed for the new homes they were promised in South America or North Africa.

Dimassi and his friends arrived in Paraguay in April 1970, expecting Israel to honor a pledge to help them find jobs. The promises unfulfilled and their pleas to the Israeli embassy and consulate unanswered, the three Palestinians decided to lodge a violent protest. They intended to kill the Israeli ambassador, but Dimassi panicked and shot the secretary instead.

Unwilling to risk any publicity, the Israeli cabinet ordered the intelligence community to shut down the refugee resettlement program quickly. Cabinet ministers had known all along that sending a million or more Arabs overseas would be prohibitively expensive, but they had been willing to give the idea a chance until the Paraguay murder soured the operation and endangered its secrecy. In all, around twenty thousand West Bank and Gaza residents emigrated in the first three years after the 1967 Six-Day War. About a thousand received aid from the secret resettlement program.[16]

A huge majority of Palestinians, however, remained in their homes and learned to live with the Israeli occupation. A few stayed and fought, but they found that battling Shin Bet and the Israel Defense Forces was fruitless.

After failing to ignite an uprising in the territories, Palestinian militants shifted their battle to other locales. Israeli intelligence received fragmentary reports in 1968 from friendly secret services in Europe, indicating stepped-up efforts by Palestinian groups to attract volunteers from radical left-wing circles in Europe. Most of the recruiting was done by Georges Habash, who led a Marxist-Leninist wing of the PLO known as the Popular Front for the Liberation of Palestine (PFLP).

Impatient emissaries, on behalf of Arafat, Habash, and others, hopscotched across Italy, Holland, France, and West Germany, using ideological comradeship and financial incentives to persuade young Europeans to come to the Middle East and fight "the Zionist occupation" and "its imperialist allies." Dozens of highly motivated volunteers answered the PLO call, were brought to Jordan and Lebanon, were trained in guerrilla camps, and went in some cases into battle as terrorists against Israel.[17]

Even as Israeli intelligence tried to figure out what the Palestinians had in mind outside the Middle East, Habash's radicals sprang a surprise by targeting Israel's national airline. In the first, memorable report of its kind, Shin Bet's Harmelin informed Prime Minister Eshkol: "An El Al Boeing 707 plane, on a flight from Rome to Tel Aviv, has been hijacked and has landed in Algeria." The hijackers were three Arabs. It was July 23, 1968, and the PFLP was launching a major terror campaign that day.

Shin Bet and the rest of the intelligence community were powerless, in the short term, to do anything except monitor developments. The passengers and crew of the Israeli airliner were held prisoner in Algiers for three weeks, and only when Israel agreed to free a dozen wounded guerrillas from jail did the first Palestinian hijacking end with the release of the hostages.

It was also the last successful hijacking of an Israeli airliner. Israeli decision makers quickly drew conclusions from the humiliation of succumbing to blackmail. They vowed never again to surrender to the demands of terrorists, but the Israelis also knew that defiant statements of intent are insufficient in such matters. Rather than words alone, they would need a new art: counterterrorism.

The Palestinian gunmen and bomb makers seemed to have seized the initiative. On December 26, 1968, two PFLP men threw hand grenades and opened fire at an El Al airplane at Athens airport, killing one Israeli passenger and wounding two stewardesses. An almost identical attack took place at Zurich airport the following February 18, when four PFLP gunmen killed an El Al pilot and wounded five passengers. Other airlines flying to Israel became targets of hijackings and bombings, as the entire earth seemed to be transformed into a global terrorist village. No target, especially if connected to Israel or Jews, was off limits.

When the PLO and its extremist men of violence moved abroad, Shin Bet followed. Despite interagency rivalries and its near monopoly over foreign operations, the Mossad reluctantly accepted that Shin Bet had the legal and professional obligation to expand its activities abroad in the hot pursuit of terrorism. Therefore, Shin Bet officers and agents were either attached — on loan — to embassy-based Mossad stations, or were assigned to Europe independently by Shin Bet. In what became an undercover, no-holds-barred war fought with innovation and improvisation, Israeli operatives played a deadly game of cat and mouse with the Palestinians.

Shin Bet's responsibilities focused on developing antiterrorist defenses. Harmelin recalls: "We were on the verge of total desperation. The struggle against terrorism, especially aviation terror, seemed to us like mission impossible."[18] His agency had to build, from nothing, an effective and sophisticated system to protect Israeli interests abroad: embassies, banks, tourism offices, and the national airline. It was not only the fleet of airplanes but the ground facilities that had become terrorist targets. Check-in counters and offices in all airports abroad had their defenses "hardened" and were given armed guards.

Israel introduced a radically new type of security setup by posting armed sky marshals on every flight, sitting in ordinary seats in the guise of ordinary travelers in plainclothes. These were young men who had served in élite army units and had learned to be quick on the draw. Officially they were airline employees, but Shin Bet trained them and set the strategy. With an investment of hundreds of millions of dollars, El Al became the most secure airline in the world.

The world only learned about it when one of the sky marshals shot back during the Zurich attack in February 1969. Armed El Al man Mordecai Rachamim drew a revolver during the PFLP's onslaught and shot dead one of the Palestinians on the tarmac of Kloten airport. Rachamim and three wounded terrorists were arrested by the Swiss authorities. The young Israeli spent a few months in jail, before returning to Israel as a national hero. Because his identity had been "burned," with his photograph appearing in international newspapers and on television, Shin Bet assigned him to be personal bodyguard to Golda Meir — a job that does not require undercover anonymity.*

The Mossad had recently gotten a new director, appointed in 1968 with the usual cloak of official anonymity. Zvi Zamir had never been a headline maker, anyway. The most surprising aspect of the change in command was that Meir Amit did not retain the job beyond what was informally considered a first, five-year term. Amit asked Levi Eshkol for a second term, but the prime minister refused. In part, he was still bitter over the Ben-Barka affair and Amit's excessive autonomy.

All, including Eshkol, had to admit that Amit was talented. He may, in fact, have been forced out because he was too efficient. Eshkol, Golda Meir, and other veteran leaders of the Labor party began to fear Amit's increasing power. Just as Ben-Gurion eventually became suspicious of the power accrued by Isser Harel, the new party leaders did not want to have an intelligence chief who was too strong.

Another cause of Eshkol's suspicion was a minor conspiracy by Amit with his longtime friend, Defense Minister Moshe Dayan. In

*Meir had become prime minister in March 1969, after Eshkol's death.

March 1968, Dayan wanted to make a secret trip to Iran to see the shah. He turned to Amit, because the Mossad was responsible for ties with Iran, to arrange the visit. When Eshkol found out, he was livid. He demanded an explanation from Amit.

"What's happening here?" Eshkol asked the head of the Mossad. "How dare you do a thing like that? The Mossad and you are subordinate to me, and not to the defense ministry or Moshe Dayan."[19]

Amit did not have a good answer, and the seemingly minor clash over bureaucratic prestige sealed his fate. When Amit asked a short while later for another five years as Mossad chief, Eshkol explained to him politely that he had decided to replace him with Major General Zvi (Zvicka) Zamir. Amit and many others were surprised that Zamir got the job. The fact that he had no previous background in intelligence made him a surprise choice, even to himself.

So why was he selected for one of the most important and sensitive jobs in Israel? Because leaders of the Labor movement considered Zamir "one of us." Similar to many Labor figures, he was born in Poland in 1925 and arrived in Palestine at the age of seven months with his family, whose name was then Zarzevsky. He joined the Palmach at eighteen, fought in the 1948 war, and made his career in the Israeli army. He attained the rank of major general, was placed in charge of the Southern Command, and, to cap off his career, was appointed Israel's military attaché in London in 1966.

There was another reason for Eshkol's decision: in a sense, Zamir's strength could be found in his weakness. After two decades of strong, overconfident master spies, the prime minister wanted to appoint a completely different character. Zvi Zamir fit the bill. His London post meant that he missed the Six-Day War and the limelight of glory cast upon other Israeli generals. Zamir lacked glamour and was one of those colorless, boring, expressionless faces of the Israeli military.[20]

Zamir did manage to cooperate well with Shin Bet's Harmelin in the fight against Palestinian terrorism, and the joint effort brought the ostensibly domestic security agency into foreign battlefields more than ever before.

When the PLO began to attack Israeli embassies and diplomats in Europe and Asia, Shin Bet was ready to respond. The embassies and consular offices were transformed into fortresses: double-thickness steel doors protected entrances, television cameras scrutinized all visitors, building perimeters were surrounded by electronic sensors, and Shin Bet guards were assigned to keep watch over buildings and their staff. The expanded "protective security" department of Shin Bet did everything possible to defend Israeli facilities abroad, but the intelligence chiefs realized that to deter terrorism they needed stronger measures.

Moving beyond passive defense, Israeli intelligence moved full speed ahead into active defenses. More accurately, it was offensive action. The first foray into retaliating against terrorism came in 1968, after the attack at Athens airport on December 26. The Israeli public cried out for some relief to the frustration of feeling victimized. The Israelis feared that their defenders had no adequate response to the export of Palestinian terrorism from the Middle East to Europe.

It was with that dark mood dominating the country that Prime Minister Eshkol called a special meeting in his office with military and intelligence chiefs. Eshkol set the tone himself: "We can't just ignore this," he exclaimed. They decided to send the army on a retaliatory mission to Beirut, from where the Athens attackers had come.

Israeli special forces were landed by helicopter at the international airport just south of the Lebanese capital on December 28 at 9:15 P.M. Undeterred by a gun battle with Lebanese troops, the Israelis blew up thirteen empty civilian aircraft belonging to Lebanon's Middle East Airlines and other Arab companies. The world was shocked by the audacity of the move and condemned Israel for engaging in what was referred to as state terrorism. It emerged that as in the old days of the Lavon Affair and the Ben-Barka murder, the prime minister was not told everything. Defense Minister Moshe Dayan had deceived Eshkol, by promising him that only four airplanes would be blown up in the action.[21]

Behind the condemnation, the world had to admire Israel's military prowess. The Beirut raid was a clear sign that Israel could strike with astonishing accuracy at the heart of the Arab world. The credit for the operation, which was commanded by Brigadier General Raphael (Raful) Eitan of the paratroops, went to the Israeli special forces. Each of these élite units is known as a *sayeret.* The word derives from the Hebrew for "reconnaissance," but the soldiers in a sayeret are expert in much more than just looking around. They have to undergo tough training including guerrilla warfare, nighttime combat, parachute drops, and the use of a variety of firearms.

Almost every sector of the Israel Defense Forces (IDF) has its own sayeret. Thus the paratroops, the infantry, the navy, and the tank brigades each have a sayeret. Above all of these is another sayeret — the élite of élites — known as the *Sayeret Matkal.*[22] *Matkal* is the Hebrew acronym for the "general staff" of the army, and this particular sayeret is officially under the direct command of the chief of staff, Israel's highest military officer.

In reality, however, the Sayeret Matkal carries out its dangerous and complex missions at the behest of both the chief of staff and the commander of Aman. The top commando unit was set up in 1960 to enable military intelligence to put some of its plans into action, especially behind enemy lines — meaning, in peacetime, across the borders inside Arab countries.

The existence of the Sayeret Matkal is officially a secret, and Israel's military censor still bans all reports of the unit's activities. In the 1960s only a few senior officers knew the truth about the special team referred to by its army designation, Unit 269.

It was founded by a senior Aman officer, General Avraham Arnan, who handpicked the bravest and smartest soldiers from throughout the IDF. Arnan trained them to perfection in the art of solitary combat — the loneliness of the long-distance fighter. Taking various routes in pitch darkness, the sayeret commandos had to learn to survive on their own for long periods of time, trekking for many miles before staging a picture-perfect military assault.

Their missions are usually carried out in small teams of three or four men, silently crossing the border to set up an observation post, to plug into the Arab country's telephone system, or to assassinate or abduct a specific target: a person or an inanimate object.

During the 1969–70 War of Attrition, in which artillery exchanges killed hundreds of Israeli troops and thousands of Egyptians, Israel's commandos scored an astounding coup with an assault on a Soviet-made radar station on Egypt's side of the Gulf of Suez. Blowing up the high-tech, newly supplied radar complex would have been difficult enough, but it would have been easy compared with what the Israelis did instead: on the night of December 26, 1969, they used two helicopters to lift the entire radar station, weighing seven tons with its rotating antennas and control panels, high into the air and across to the Israeli-held side.[23]

From the Sinai, the Soviet-Egyptian radar station was rushed to a top-security Israeli base, where Aman analysts had a field day with their finest "catch" since the defection in 1966 of the Iraqi pilot with his MIG-21. They shared their catch with the CIA and U.S. Air Force intelligence officers, and this was a useful beginning of the military cooperation between the two nations that would reach its peak after the 1973 war.

The Sayeret Matkal was the first commando force in the world to use helicopters routinely in cross-border missions. But despite advances in technology, including night-vision goggles and lightweight two-way radios, the commando's most important assets were his map and his legs. Ironically, the Israeli army never came up with brilliant ways to use its sayeret units during wartime. They fought well in the Six-Day War, and later in the 1973 war, but their outstanding moments came in between the Middle East's major fighting.

Despite the ban on any publicity at home, foreign journalists heard about some of the commando exploits and wrote about "one of the select units of the Israeli army" or "the élite unit." Hidden, still, was the fact that the Sayeret Matkal is connected to the entire Israeli intelligence community — not only to Aman, its military wing. The unit, under orders from the chief of staff, acts as an operational subcontractor for the Mossad and Shin Bet, too. It is an example of the remarkable cooperation, which rarely breaks down, between the army and the intelligence agencies.

Sayeret veterans, generally after three hard-working years of active service, are often prime candidates for jobs in Shin Bet or the Mossad. They are just the sort of recruits desired by whoever — probably the Mossad — placed this anonymous advertisement in the "jobs available" column of an Israeli newspaper: "Young ex-members of combatant units for interesting work abroad. Priority will be given to those who possess a foreign passport and who know a foreign language."[24]

Sayeret units, which recruit volunteers from among newly enlisted soldiers, hold a powerful attraction for Israeli boys, who are nearly all drafted at the age of eighteen. Israel does not have a military tradition, as do other Western countries, in which generations of the same family serve proudly in certain units or study in military academies such as America's West Point or Britain's Sandhurst. Israel does have, however, a tradition of personal and family contacts and *protektzia* — a term in both Russian and Hebrew for what Americans call "pull." Often, such contacts are put into action for positive ends. The sons of celebrities or politicians, when highly qualified, are commonly brought into a sayeret.

One example is Colonel Uzi Dayan, who took part in the raid on the Beirut airport. He is the nephew of General Moshe Dayan and was able, in spite of being seriously injured before joining the army, to be accepted into a very select sayeret.[25]

The ongoing war against terrorism took a turn for the uglier in 1972, after four Palestinians hijacked a Belgian airliner on May 8. Sabena flight 571 was bound from Brussels to Tel Aviv, and the hijackers had it land as scheduled at Lod airport. They held nearly a hundred passengers and crew at gunpoint in the Boeing 707, demanding that Israel free 317 imprisoned guerrillas. Aman's chief, General Aharon Yariv, negotiated with the two men and two women who had commandeered the airliner, demonstrating his talents as a talker while the Israel Defense Forces prepared their true response.

On cabinet orders, a sayeret specially trained in storming airliners and rescuing hostages went into action on May 9 at 4:22 P.M. The army commandos, dressed in white overalls as airport maintenance men, broke into the Boeing jet through every conceivable entrance and, with pinpoint marksmanship, killed the two male terrorists, wounded the two females, and freed ninety-seven hostages. In the exchange of fire, one Israeli passenger also died.

Theory quickly followed from practice, and as Israel developed a new theory of war on terrorism, the rest of the world hurried to learn from the Israeli experience. West Germany, Britain, and other states sent security agents and military commandos to Israel, where IDF experts were assigned to teach friendly foreigners. Many nations then established commando units of their own, based on the Israeli model. Britain's hostage-rescue specialists were units of the SAS, the Special Air Services, while the West Germans formed a force called GSG-9.

On May 30 three gunmen of the Japanese Red Army slaughtered twenty-seven passengers, most of them Christian pilgrims from Puerto Rico, who had just arrived at Lod airport. After initial confusion, security guards fought back, leaving two terrorists dead and Kozo Okamoto captured. He confessed, during his trial, that he and his colleagues — to display solidarity — had acted on behalf of the PFLP. The massacre was revenge for the failure of the Sabena hijack, three weeks earlier, on the Lod tarmac just a few hundred yards away from the carnage the Japanese terrorists caused in the terminal.

Five weeks later, it was Israel's turn to retaliate. A letter bomb that arrived in Beirut killed Ghassan Kanafani, a poet, writer, and PFLP spokesman accused by the Israelis of planning the Lod massacre. Two days later another letter exploded in the hands of PFLP official Bassam Abu Sherif, who lost an eye and several fingers. These attacks were in the tradition of the parcel bombs that killed the Egyptian officers in the 1950s, and the letter bombs sent to German scientists in Egypt in the early 1960s.

The vicious circle of violence and retaliation reached its peak at the Olympic Games in Munich on September 5, 1972. Under the cover of the shadowy "Black September" group, named for the month in 1970 when Jordan's King Hussein crushed the Palestinians, seven Arab terrorists seized eleven Israeli athletes in the Olympic village. The original aim of Black September, which was a secret branch of the PLO although pretending to be a separate entity, was to take revenge against Hussein. Jordanian targets were attacked, but Black September quickly turned its guns against Israelis, too.

As in other hostage incidents, the Olympic terrorists demanded that Israel free 250 of their comrades from prison. The Israeli government, true to its firm policy, declined to cave in and refused to free any guerrillas.

As the world's media broadcast live coverage of the siege into homes around the globe, simultaneously publicizing Palestinian demands while generating sympathy for Jewish victims suffering on German soil, Prime Minister Golda Meir handed responsibility for the Munich events to her trusted Mossad chief, Zvi Zamir. He immediately flew to Munich and held urgent discussions with West German security officials.

Under Prime Minister Meir's direct orders, and armed with the experience of rescuing the hijacked Sabena passengers only four months earlier, Zamir pleaded with the West Germans to permit a specially trained Israeli sayeret to deal with the siege. Chancellor Willy Brandt probably would have agreed, but the German federal constitution left the decision in the hands of local state officials, who refused.

Zamir, therefore, was left to watch helplessly from the control tower of Munich's military airport as inexperienced and ill-equipped German sharpshooters opened fire but failed to kill all the terrorists in the first volley. Three were still alive, and they fired their guns and tossed their hand grenades to kill the handcuffed hostages, slaughtered as they sat in helicopters on the tarmac.

Waves of shock reverberated around the world, with the massacre seen as both a human tragedy and a warning that terrorism was growing out of control. In Israel an inquiry committee decided that the head of Shin Bet's protective security department, who had been responsible for guarding the Olympic athletes, should be dismissed. Agency chief Harmelin stood firmly against pinning the blame on the department head, however, and for the only time in his career Harmelin threatened to resign. Prime Minister Meir insisted that the dismissal was a cheap bureaucratic price to pay, and Harmelin reluctantly fired his subordinate.[26]

While the investigation continued, five days after the Munich massacre, Zadok Ofir received an urgent phone call at his desk in the Israeli embassy in Brussels. He rushed to the Café Prince, where an Arab carrying a Moroccan passport, who was a member of Black September, shot him at point-blank range. Later it became clear that Ofir was a Shin Bet officer, working undercover as first secretary at the embassy. Ofir was wounded in the abdomen, but he survived. It also emerged that the Israeli knew his assailant. The Arab was a double agent, and Ofir was his case officer. The embassy in Brussels was the center of Israeli espionage activity in Europe, a role it had since de Gaulle expelled the Mossad from Paris after the Ben-Barka killing.[27]

The Brussels shooting should have lit huge warning lights in the Mossad and Shin Bet headquarters. For the first time, an Israeli intelligence officer on active duty abroad had been shot. The massacre at Munich, however, was overshadowing all other incidents and considerations. Even Zamir, returning from Munich, did not recognize the importance of the assault on Ofir.

Returning from Germany, Zamir hurried from Lod airport to Jerusalem, where he told the prime minister of the disaster he had witnessed. There were tears in Golda Meir's eyes. Meir, a hardened politician but nevertheless a sensitive woman who was a typical "Jewish mother," was torn between cool logic and a desire to avenge the lives of her murdered "boys." Before long, both converged in a cold, calculated decision to kill those who had killed.

Meir created the new post of "prime minister's adviser on counter-terrorism" and chose General Aharon Yariv for the job. He had just retired after eight years as Aman director, his place in history assured by the six-day victory of 1967.

Arab terrorism became an obsession for Meir, Yariv, and Zamir, and at their urging the Israeli cabinet formed a top secret committee, chaired by Golda Meir and Moshe Dayan, to decide on a response to Munich. The panel was known only as "Committee X," so that not even the other cabinet members and civil servants would know of its purpose. Committee X made the historic, but top secret decision to assassinate any Black September terrorists involved, directly or indirectly, in planning, assisting, or executing the attack at the Olympics.[28]

The mission was not to capture anyone. It was out-and-out revenge — to terrorize the terrorists. Meir assigned the task to the Mossad. Zamir summoned Mike Harari, one of the senior agents in the operations department, and put him in charge of the assassination squads. Harari handpicked a team of operatives, both men and women, and established his European command post in Paris. He adopted several false identities, including a passport that identified him as French businessman Edouard Stanislas Laskier. Harari and Mossad operative Avraham Gehmer, whose cover job was as first secretary of the Israeli embassy in Paris, were in charge of the planning.[29]

First, the Israelis compiled a list of Arabs who had been involved in the Munich operation. The team then began to trail the men on its "wanted" list, most of whom had remained in Europe in various overt professions and covert terrorist activities. When Harari and his team felt ready to attack, they contacted Zamir in Tel Aviv, and he turned to Committee X for permission to give the go-ahead. Prime Minister Meir and her secret panel had to approve each individual killing.

The first to die, in October 1972, was Adel Wael Zwaiter, a Palestinian intellectual in Rome who worked for Black September. Within ten months, Harari's men and women took the lives of twelve Palestinians who were linked to terrorism against civilians. They were killed by guns with silencers, sometimes fired from cars or motorbikes in Paris and Rome, or by remote-controlled bombs detonated by high-tech, high-pitched tones transmitted by telephone or radio in Nicosia and Paris.

Black September, which saw that its top men were being killed, attempted to mount a response. On November 13, 1972, a Syrian journalist in Paris named Khader Kano was shot dead. He had been an informer for the Israelis. On January 26, 1973, Israeli businessman Hanan Yishai was shot dead as he stood in a doorway on the Gran Via, the main street of Madrid. After his death it was revealed that his real name was Baruch Cohen, and that he had come to Madrid from Brussels on a mission for Israeli intelligence.

Cohen was the black sheep of a well-known family in Haifa, most of whose members identified with right-wing political parties. One of his brothers, Meir Cohen, was deputy chairman of the Israeli parliament as a member of Menachem Begin's Likud party. Only Baruch followed a different course. He lived on a kibbutz, identified with socialism, and joined Shin Bet. Until the 1967 war, he worked in Avraham Ahituv's department of Arab affairs, mainly as a field agent in the upper Galilee region.

After the war, because of his knowledge of Arabic, he was put to work in the West Bank. Although only a sergeant in the military reserves, Cohen was immediately promoted to captain in order to serve as military governor of the occupied territory's largest town, Nablus, where naturally he was to focus on suppressing terrorism. Almost as soon as he arrived, in July 1967, he nearly captured Yasser Arafat, who on that occasion had to dress in women's clothing, including the traditional dark veil, to escape Cohen and his men.

In 1972 he was involved in exposing a Jewish-Arab spy ring that worked under Syrian intelligence orders, and he was later sent to Europe to operate a network of young Palestinian informers there. One of his operatives was a double agent whose ultimate loyalty was apparently to Black September, because he shot his Israeli case officer, Cohen. Zadok Ofir had survived a similar attack four months earlier, but Cohen became the first Israeli intelligence operative in Europe killed by a Palestinian.

Some members of Cohen's family claimed later that his death could have been prevented. In violation of all security precautions, Cohen's photograph had been published — ironically, in an official army album celebrating the 1967 victory — and the snapshot showed Cohen in military uniform with his best friend Zadok Ofir, also in uniform. Arab intelligence services collect such clippings, and it is considered vital that Israeli operatives never show their faces. Enemy agents can put two and two together. Even if Cohen concealed his identity as an Israeli when operating his Palestinian network, that photograph may have given him away.

The fact is that a few months before his death, Arab newspapers carried stories that Black September had sentenced an Israeli agent to death. Reading those reports should have alerted Shin Bet that Baruch Cohen's identity might have been discovered, and his life should not have been endangered by sending him to Madrid. It is equally disturbing that while other Israeli agents were "covering" Cohen by observing him, they did not spring into action when he was shot for fear that they themselves would be exposed.

Family members, who felt that Cohen was a victim of his superiors' failures, took no pleasure from indications that the Mossad was avenging the death of Baruch Cohen. His widow, Nurit, revealed: "Occasionally, service officers would come to visit me and ask 'Have you read in the newspaper that this-and-that guy has been killed or this-and-that guy has been blown up?' What can I say, that it consoled me?"[30] Word spread that three members of Black September who had been involved in Cohen's murder were liquidated.

Cohen's death should have served as another warning to Israel. The intelligence community should have linked the assassination of Cohen to the attempt on the life of Ofir and the murder of the Syrian double agent Kano. The Mossad should have concluded that its Palestinian enemy was displaying a high degree of professionalism in penetrating the operational heart of Israeli intelligence overseas.

Instead, the intelligence community behaved as though still trapped by obsession. It had adopted vengeance as its creed. Members of Black September were killed one after another in Europe.

Seven months after the Olympic massacre, the Israeli assassins brought their vengeful teamwork into the Arab world. Their targets were two Black September commanders, Muhammad Najjar and Kamal Adwan, and the PLO spokesman Kamal Nasser. On the night of April 10, 1973, all three were shot dead in their own separate apartments in downtown Beirut. The gunmen were crack Israeli troops led to the targets by Mossad men. The army operation featured the nocturnal landing of members of the top sayeret commando unit on the Lebanese beach, and it was a masterpiece of precise military planning.

Even more impressive were the preparations by Israeli intelligence. The commandos had the addresses of all three leaders; the attackers were able to land at locations convenient to all three homes; and there were rented Mercedes cars waiting on the beach for the plainclothes soldiers. It showed an impressive degree of cooperation between Aman and the Mossad agents, and this in an Arab capital where there was no Israeli embassy to provide diplomatic cover to a spy and where no Israeli could even visit owing to the official state of war.

The operation was the second assault on Beirut in four and a half years. It was codenamed Aviv Ne'urim, "Spring of Youth." The men who again demonstrated Israel's military prowess included young officers such as Ehud Barak and Amnon Lipkin-Shahak, who would both later rise to the top of Aman.

The warm glow of a job well done lasted barely three months and was extinguished in a place called Lillehammer. At the beginning of July 1973, most of the members of Mike Harari's hit team, authorized by Prime Minister Meir and Committee X, gathered in that small town in northern Norway. They had come from various locations in Europe to settle a score with "the Red Prince," the codename given by the Mossad to Ali Hassan Salameh.

Salameh was Black September's operations officer in Western Europe, and he planned both the attack on the Israeli athletes in Munich and the assassination of Baruch Cohen. His importance extended beyond the shadowy Black September. Salameh, the son of a high-ranking Palestinian militia commander who had been killed in the war against Israel in 1948, was in reality the commander of Force 17, the PLO unit specifically responsible for the protection of Yasser Arafat — so named simply because 17 was its telephone extension at PLO headquarters in Beirut. Mainly because of Salameh's involvement with the Olympic massacre, the Mossad wanted to put a violent end to his career.

Salameh was a self-confident playboy and a womanizer, but also a very difficult man to catch. After months of searching for him, Mike Harari's gunslingers headed to Norway with great enthusiasm because agents on a prior reconnaissance tour were certain they had finally found Salameh. The Harari team located its quarry in Lillehammer, tailed him for several hours to be sure he was the Red Prince, and then shot him dead on the evening of July 21. The gunmen themselves quickly fled the country, as the rest of the Israelis headed for safe houses in Oslo.

Only the next day did the Israeli agents discover that they had made a terrible mistake. They had killed the wrong man, a Moroccan waiter named Ahmad Bouchiki who was married to a Norwegian — a pregnant woman who witnessed the shooting.

The Israelis might have gotten away with murder, keeping their error an absolute secret, had it not been for the stupid behavior of the Israeli support agents, the men and women who did the surveillance and some of the planning for the gunmen. They made every conceivable mistake, as if seeking to be caught by the Norwegian police.

The police were not even making any great efforts to capture the killers. The fact is that the Mossad agents — although carefully trained to disappear at a moment's notice — inexplicably left a clear trail at every step. They drove around in Lillehammer in cars they themselves had rented, rather than using go-betweens who would never know the true nature of the murder mission. In trailing Bouchiki, they had been as graceful as a herd of elephants in a china shop. They did not observe the rules of compartmentalization but instead knew one another.

The unfortunate waiter's neighbors had reported a license-plate number to the police, and two of the Israeli operatives were arrested as they returned their rented car to Oslo's airport. Traveling as Dan Ert and Marianne Gladnikoff, they both admitted they were working for Israel and provided the address of an apartment used by the Mossad. The police found two more members of the hit team there.

Norwegian investigators were amazed at the amateurism displayed by the espionage agency considered to be the world's best. The Israelis fell into the hands of the police, one after another, like overripe fruit off a tree. Harari himself managed to flee, but Avraham Gehmer and five other Mossad operatives were arrested.

The interrogations in Norway exposed the modus operandi of the other post-Olympic assassinations. One of the Mossad men was carrying a key to an apartment in Paris, where the French secret service found keys to even more safe houses used by Israeli operatives. Evidence was found that connected the Israelis with the unsolved murders of Palestinians in several countries. Western intelligence agencies looked into how the Israelis had deployed hit teams in Europe and found that the Mossad had employed part-time help to mount surveillance and work out logistics.

One example, and by far the most talkative when questioned in Oslo, was Ert — not a member of Mossad's staff but a businessman of Danish extraction who lived in Herzliyya, north of Tel Aviv, under his apparently genuine name, Dan Aerbel. He was called upon by the Mossad, from time to time, for various missions. As soon as the Norwegians placed him in a solitary, darkened room, he told them everything. The interrogators were unable to conceal their amazement when Ert/Aerbel revealed that he suffered from claustrophobia, a definite handicap for a secret agent. In return for being moved to a larger cell, he was willing to confess all — not only about the Lillehammer operation, but also about his involvement in the mysterious transfer of a shipload of uranium to Israel in 1968.

Ert/Aerbel said he had been the front man for the Mossad's purchase of an old freighter called the *Scheersberg A,* which had 560 metal drums of uranium oxide when it left Antwerp, Belgium, but showed up at its next port without the nuclear raw material (see Chapter 9).

Another of the Israelis arrested in Norway was Sylvia Raphael, but she was far more professional than Ert/Aerbel. Under her cover name, Patricia Roxborough, she traveled the world as a newspaper photographer with a forged Canadian passport. Raphael had been born in South Africa and was recruited by the Mossad after working as a volunteer in an Israeli kibbutz. Only in her case, incidentally, was there a happy ending to the Lillehammer affair. Raphael/Roxborough fell in love with her Norwegian lawyer and married him. First, though, she and four of the other Mossad operatives had to spend time in jail. Despite the punishments handed down by the court, prison terms ranging from two to five and a half years, the sympathetic Norwegians released the Israelis after no more than twenty-two months.

The Mossad was lucky that Norway did not press very hard in its investigation of the complicated case, clearly preferring not to add public humiliation to Israel's embarrassment. Despite the incriminating information that emerged at the trials in Norway, the French and Italian security services also displayed a great deal of solidarity with the Mossad. They ignored the PLO's demands to renew the investigation into the violent deaths of Palestinians in those countries.

The intelligence agencies of Western Europe felt compassion for the Mossad. They realized that they, too, could just as easily be caught "with their pants down," and it was professional courtesy not to make things worse. There was also a strong element of sympathy for Israel in its fight against Arab terrorism. Western secret services respected the Jewish state's willingness to show the world an alternative to appeasement and submission, in the war against terror.

This was small consolation for Israel. The Mossad could not be satisfied until it finally did catch up with Salameh five and a half years later. A small team of Israeli operatives, again including a woman, flew into Lebanon on British and Canadian passports. On January 22, 1979, they parked a car filled with explosives along a roadside in Beirut and detonated the powerful bomb by remote control as the Red Prince drove by. He and his car were vaporized.

The CIA was not very pleased with that operation because Salameh, it became known after his death, had been helpful to the Americans. He had been the secret liaison between the PLO and American intelligence.[31]

Memories of the publicly exposed failure in Norway continue to haunt Israel. Many in the Israeli intelligence community refer to Lillehammer, in an unhappy pun, as *Leyl-ha-Mar,* "the Night of Bitterness." Every time it is mentioned, Israeli secret agents cringe. They all agree that killing the wrong man — and then getting caught — was their greatest operational failure.

The obsession with revenge had made Israel misplace its keen judgment. Senior officials in the intelligence community bitterly complained that it was not their duty to become a branch of Murder Incorporated. They claimed that a significant portion of the human and technological resources of the Mossad and Shin Bet were tied up in the manhunt, rather than being involved in the more important and more traditional work of collecting information on the military potential of the Arab states.

The internal dissenters claimed that Israel was exaggerating the importance of Palestinian terror, for in the final analysis it was not this which would imperil the country's existence. At worst, it was like a pesky fly annoying Israel without posing a huge threat. Others stressed that there was no use in wiping out the heads of Palestinian guerrilla groups, because there was no guarantee that their replacements would be more moderate or less able.

The angry dissidents further charged that the Lillehammer debacle was hushed up. No one bore the consequences. Even Mike Harari simply resumed his operations job in Tel Aviv.

These, however, were like voices crying out in a vast desert. Mossad chief Zvi Zamir had been at the airfield in Munich. He had seen the Israeli Olympians slaughtered while handcuffed inside helicopters. He was angry and absolutely in harmony with Golda Meir's desire for revenge.

Black September was being dismantled by the campaign of assassinations, and now Israeli intelligence wished to deal with its old PFLP nemesis, Georges Habash. On August 10, 1973, fighter planes intercepted a Lebanese civilian airliner and forced it to land at a military base in Israel. The passengers were led out single file and individually questioned, but there was no terrorist chief among them, so everyone was set free — with considerable embarrassment to the Mossad.

A tip that Habash would be on the airliner had apparently come from one of Israel's best-placed agents within the Palestinian guerrilla hierarchy: a woman named Aminah al-Mufti. Born in 1935 to a Circassian Moslem family in Jordan, she was recruited by the Mossad in Vienna in 1972 — reportedly after she fell in love with an Israeli pilot visiting Austria. The pilot is likely to have been on a mission to find a potential Arab agent, and Mufti would have been an attractive choice. Circassians living in Israel were already serving the Jewish state's intelligence community by penetrating Arab society.

Her assignment, which she accepted in part because she hated the PLO and blamed its extremism for perpetuating the Middle East conflict, was to move to Beirut in early 1973 and meet as many Palestinians as possible. Mufti had already had some medical education, so the Israelis helped her set up a clinic. Her facility became busy when the Lebanese civil war broke out in 1975, treating Palestinians wounded in the defense of their neighborhoods and refugee camps. The Mossad, ironically, was secretly financing medical care for the PLO in Lebanon.

Mufti befriended top PLO officers, and when alone at night she wrote lengthy accounts of everything she saw and heard. She never met any Mossad contact in Lebanon, however, because she left her reports and photographs in various "dead letter boxes" in Beirut — locations such as hotel corridors or restaurant rest rooms where a small envelope could be left to be picked up later by an unseen courier. She transmitted urgent information to Israel by using a favorite Mossad piece of technology, an amazingly tiny radio set.

The flow of information stopped in 1975, when Mufti was caught by the Palestinians. She was tortured by PLO radicals and was questioned by Soviet KGB and East German intelligence agents during five years of imprisonment in a cave near the Lebanese port of Sidon. Negotiating through the International Committee of the Red Cross, Israel arranged a prisoner swap and freed two PLO terrorists — who had been sentenced to life in prison — in exchange for Mufti. After the Red Cross handed her to a Mossad team in Cyprus, she was given a new identity and a job as a doctor in northern Israel.[32]

Through the five and a half years that Zamir was in the Mossad as agency chief, the emphasis was on the struggle against terrorism. Together with Shin Bet and Aman, Mossad had great harmony on this score. But they were playing the wrong tune. Obsessed with the desire shared by Golda Meir and her cabinet, they saw the Palestinians as a bunch of killers and believed the problem could only be solved through counterterror.

With the benefit of hindsight, it can now be seen that Israel should have been on the lookout for a larger threat: the Arab military buildup, not Salameh or Habash. But Israel's leaders were complacent on the dangers of war because they did not believe the Arabs had the ability to launch one. And Israel's scientists had secretly made great strides in developing the ultimate deterrent: a nuclear arsenal.

NINE

The Secret Weapon

THE CIA STATION CHIEF in Tel Aviv through the mid-1960s, John Hadden, had a full plate: maintaining a mutually beneficial liaison relationship with Israeli intelligence while monitoring the many events that the authorities did their best to hide. Naturally, Hadden was especially active in trying to keep up with Israel's most secretive project. He knew that the Israelis were not telling the truth — not even to him, their official local "friend" — on the atomic issue. Like any professional in the field, he never expected openness anyway. Intelligence agencies, like nations, have no friends; only cold, hard interests.

The words "truth" and "atomic" never went together in Israel. Prime Minister Ben-Gurion had told President Kennedy at the White House in 1961 that the Jewish state was working on nuclear power but not on a bomb. Washington was not buying that story.

In April 1963, Shimon Peres was summoned to the Oval Office by Kennedy, who pressed him for information: "You know that we follow with great interest any development of nuclear potential in the region. That would create a most dangerous situation. For that reason, we have been in close touch with your effort in the nuclear field. What can you tell me about that?"

Peres replied with what would be the repeated refrain of Israel's political tunesmiths for decades. "We will not introduce nuclear weapons into the region," he told the President. "We will not be the first to do so."[1]

The CIA station chief certainly heard a new melody when Prime Minister Levi Eshkol, as a former finance minister, barely concealed his opposition to spending money on developing nuclear arms. In his visits to Washington, Eshkol reached a tacit agreement with the Johnson administration that Israel would receive stepped-up conventional military aid in exchange for slowing down the nuclear project. The Israelis for the first time received advanced Phantom and Skyhawk jets, and the Americans totally supplanted the French as the Jewish state's arms suppliers.

Hadden still detected deception by the Israelis. His most alarming reports to CIA headquarters in Langley, Virginia, concerned Moshe Dayan's attitude toward Israel's so-called bomb in the basement. Dayan, in the U.S. intelligence assessment, had a nonchalant attitude toward the secret project, referring to it as "just another weapon." Red lights began to flash when the Israeli strategist was heard to remark that it could even be the weapon to end all wars in the Middle East.

When Hadden traveled to the Negev, as he and other CIA agents did in their effort to keep an eye on Dimona, he was shadowed by Israel's Shin Bet. On one occasion, the American — officially an embassy diplomat — was on a road near the nuclear facility when a military helicopter landed near his car. Security personnel asked to see identification, and after flashing his American diplomatic passport he drove off still convinced that there was a lot more going on in Dimona than was ever admitted by Israel.

The CIA detected signs of an Israeli nuclear strategy that called for developing weapons of all types and all sizes for maximum flexibility of eventual use. These could range from atomic bombs to be dropped from airplanes to hydrogen bombs meant to be packed into missile warheads. The scientists were believed to be considering almost anything, and the CIA concluded that Israel wanted to have many delivery systems and especially ones that could be protected.

The Dimona reactor seemed well guarded, and antiaircraft missile batteries hidden in the desert hills around it even shot down an Israeli air force jet that mistakenly strayed nearby on its way back from a bombing mission in Jordan during the June 1967 war.

But whether it was in Dimona or stationed with Israel's air force, the secret nuclear arsenal was not considered as safe as it ought to be. Even tiny Israel formulated its nuclear strategy along the same concepts adopted by the superpowers: deterring war as a primary interest, but also devising an ability to deliver a successful second strike in case the enemy should attack first. The CIA detected a strong Israeli desire to put at least part of the arsenal offshore.

Based on intelligence gathered in Israel and elsewhere, CIA analysts concluded that the Israelis were developing a submarine-based nuclear strike capability. In strategic terms it was only natural, although highly ambitious for a small state, that the most secure launch platforms be used: submarines, which would be extremely difficult for the Arab enemy to locate, would be relatively safe storage facilities for the secret arsenal. And whereas Dimona or air force bases might be bombed, shelled, struck by missiles, or even overrun by the Arabs, the submarines would still be out there at sea, ready to retaliate.

The CIA believed that Israel eventually managed to develop that capability to station compact but powerful nuclear arms aboard its navy's three British-made submarines. These were generally on patrol in the Mediterranean, and technically might be considered a way of avoiding a breach of the official policy that Israel would not be first to introduce nuclear weapons into the Middle East.

In any event, such promises are for politicians and not for intelligence agencies or nuclear scientists. They simply persist in their work, silently and diligently.

When Israel's support from de Gaulle's France dried up in the 1960s, the chief of the ultrasecret Science Liaison Bureau had a problem but did not let it faze him. From his anonymous desk at Lakam, Binyamin Blumberg sought alternative sources when diplomatic troubles were brewing with France, until then the chief supplier of Israel's nuclear materials and know-how. His first success was with Norway. The Oslo government agreed to a secret sale of twenty-one tons of heavy water to Israel. As soon as this supply was guaranteed, Lakam began to look for uranium. An important source was found in the person of Zalman Shapiro.

Shapiro was born in 1921 in Canton, Ohio — an American with a keenly felt Jewish background. His father was an Orthodox rabbi of Lithuanian origin, many of his relatives perished in the Holocaust, and even in America Zalman suffered the indignity of anti-Semitic insults. He earned a Ph.D. in chemistry in 1948. The State of Israel proclaimed its independence that same year, providing great inspiration to Shapiro. He joined the Zionist Federation and the Friends of the Technion, Israel's top technological university.

He worked for the Westinghouse Corporation, helping to construct the U.S. Navy's first nuclear submarine, the *Nautilus*. In the mid-1950s he started up his own company, Numec, the Nuclear Materials and Equipment Corporation, in Apollo, Pennsylvania.

Shapiro's company supplied uranium for nuclear reactors in the United States, but the company seemed to have an inordinate number of foreign visitors. They came mainly from France and Israel. These tours of Numec did not escape the notice of the U.S. Atomic Energy Commission, which in 1962 rebuked the company for its lax security precautions and its slipshod record keeping. It was only in 1965, however, that a routine AEC inspection made a significant discovery: Numec's warehouse records showed that more than 110 pounds of enriched uranium were inexplicably missing. Enriched uranium is used in manufacturing nuclear weapons.

The AEC investigators were unable to obtain clear proof that the material had been sent anywhere or that Numec had committed any crime. But in official probes that lasted fifteen years, the AEC reported that a total of 587 pounds of uranium had disappeared — in theory, enough to make perhaps eighteen atom bombs.

The FBI also investigated, concentrating on Shapiro's ties with Israel, but could not arrive at any clear conclusion. Other federal authorities considered Shapiro's case but ruled that his limited ties with Israel did not require him to register as a foreign agent. Still, the suspicions had grown to near certainty by 1968 that the missing uranium had been sold or somehow shipped to Israel.[2]

The American intelligence community, believing that Israel had obtained a large quantity of enriched uranium, went into action. The CIA and the FBI began a more thorough investigation, placing Shapiro under surveillance and tapping his telephones. He was brought in for questioning, and some of the more interesting tales he told had to do with meetings he had with Avraham Hermoni, scientific counselor at the Israeli embassy in Washington — in other words, although the agency name was not known, the Lakam station chief.[3]

Israel was concerned about the new American attitude on nuclear questions. In previous years, largely owing to the influence of the Mossad's best friend, James Angleton in the CIA, the U.S. authorities had been content to let the Israelis do as they wished. In effect, Angleton had been protecting Israel's nuclear secrets.[4] By 1968 Angleton's influence had diminished, and the new CIA director, Richard Helms, was far more suspicious about Israeli actions and motives.

To explore the situation in Washington, four Israelis — including Hermoni, Rafi Eitan of Mossad, and Avraham Bendor (later Shalom) of Shin Bet — dropped in on Shapiro's Numec plant on September

10, 1968. In an application for U.S. government clearance, Eitan and Bendor listed themselves as "chemists" with the Israeli defense ministry.[5] They were on special assignment for Lakam, after Blumberg's success in repairing relations with the other Israeli secret agencies.

When they returned home from their damage assessment mission, Eitan and Bendor/Shalom reported that Israel would still enjoy the benefit of any doubt and would get away with its uranium procurement. So there was no reason to stop such extralegal activities.

In November 1968, in a joint operation with the Mossad, Blumberg's agents spirited away two hundred tons of uranium oxide — in 560 drums labeled PLUMBAT — from the deck of a cargo ship. Based on the confessions of Dan Ert/Aerbel in Norway in 1973, investigators established that a German chemical corporation named Asmara, through subsidiaries, had bought the uranium from a Belgian company, Société Générale de Minaro. The uranium was loaded at Antwerp harbor onto a ship named the *Scheersberg A*, which flew a Liberian flag of convenience. Its captain declared that its destination was Genoa.

It never arrived in Italy, and instead the *Scheersberg A* simply "disappeared" from the registry. After entering the Mediterranean, it had sailed east rather than north, where it should have been headed, based on its declared destination. Somewhere between Cyprus and Turkey, it had rendezvoused with an Israeli cargo ship. At the beginning of December, a few days after its brief disappearance, the *Scheersberg A* anchored in the port of Iskenderun in Turkey. There was no longer any uranium on board.

The ship was in fact owned by the Mossad, and from amid this confusing collection of countries and companies Israel had managed to obtain fuel for the Dimona reactor. The atomic energy agencies of the European Economic Community were so astounded and puzzled by the incident that they decided not to publicize it.[6]

Another coup enabled Israel to produce in its nuclear reactor uranium extracted from its huge phosphate reserves. Israel's acquisition of all of these materials, plus the fact that the country bought uranium directly from South Africa,[7] make it clear that Israel was constructing something extremely secret at Dimona: an arsenal of weapons. South Africa would become Israel's partner in clandestine projects including nuclear and missile research.

There was by then no doubt that Israel had become the sixth nation in the nuclear club, joining the United States, the Soviet Union, France, Britain, and China. Israel made no announcement of the fact, but it was certainly clear to the United States.

From the late 1960s onward, America's intelligence community kept tabs on nearly every scientist who visited the United States from Israel. Professor Yuval Ne'eman, who happened to have developed a host of useful gadgets and technical systems for Aman, found himself face to face with suspicion after arriving in Pasadena, California, for a semester of physics research.

"Professor, I am from the department," an unfamiliar voice on the telephone announced. "Can we meet?"

Ne'eman assumed that the person on the other end of the line was a member of one of the University of California's academic departments. To his consternation, the man who arrived for the appointment introduced himself instead as an investigator for the U.S. Justice Department. "Are you Colonel Ne'eman?" the American asked.

"Yes," Ne'eman replied, somewhat surprised to be addressed by his military rank and realizing that the investigator was in fact an FBI man. The Israeli explained that until the early 1960s he had indeed been a colonel in his country's military intelligence service, but had left and now worked at Tel Aviv University.

"But we know that you are still involved in spying," said the American. "I'd advise you to stop immediately."

Ne'eman vehemently denied the allegation and the conversation ended on the spot. It had obviously been an attempt to intimidate him, probably in reaction to Ne'eman's visit to the federal laboratories in Livermore, near San Francisco. Considering what the United States was starting to figure out about Israel's Dimona facilities, a tour of Livermore Labs seemed important because of the nuclear research conducted there.

A few weeks later Ne'eman moved to the University of Texas at Austin, where another Justice Department official paid a visit — this time demanding that Ne'eman register as a "foreign agent" of the Israeli government.

Doing so would have harmed Ne'eman's reputation as a physicist and his ability to meet with colleagues. If he were an official agent for a foreign government, his movements could be restricted by the U.S. authorities. Ne'eman tried to mobilize all his American contacts to avoid having to register. He turned to old friends for help, including the father of America's hydrogen bomb, Professor Edward Teller, and the influential Senator John Tower of Texas.

In the end, it was the U.S.-Israeli intelligence connection that helped Ne'eman. The Mossad's liaison officer in Washington lodged a direct and secret appeal with the CIA, which was able to cancel the requirement that the Israeli scientist register as an agent.

Other Israelis, some with an intelligence background and others merely dabbling in the secret art, have collected information for their country while visiting the United States. When the targeted information touched on scientific affairs, Lakam was usually in charge.

The astonishing aspect of Lakam's history is that, despite all of its espionage activities, foreign intelligence agencies were not aware of its existence. A secret report by the CIA, written in 1976 and purporting to survey the entire intelligence community of Israel, referred to the community's high interest in science and technology but never mentioned a Lakam or a Science Liaison Bureau.[8]

Blumberg suggested that his agency coordinate covert support, not only for the nuclear project, but also for the entire Israeli defense industry. His offer was accepted, and Lakam's budget was immediately boosted by contributions from clients including Israel Aircraft Industries, the weapons development firm Rafael, and Israel Military Industries. They all were either owned or controlled by the government, but company officials did not necessarily know how they came across their blueprints or production manuals from abroad. They certainly did not know the name "Lakam."[9]

One specific objective for Israel, while developing its nuclear potential, was acquiring the technology and hardware to manufacture ground-to-ground missiles. This was not mere coincidence, for there would be little sense in developing nuclear weapons if there were no reliable means to deliver them to their targets. As Ezer Weizman once said, in a secret meeting when he was defense minister, "All missiles can carry an atomic head. All missiles can carry a conventional head. They carry all sorts of peculiar heads."[10] Israel's homemade arsenal could be used for either nuclear or conventional purposes.

Blumberg's men managed to obtain missile-related know-how from various sources, and they kept up to date with the latest technology to know what was worth buying. A large step forward came when France agreed to sell ground-to-ground missiles to Israel. Israel's specialty was adapting — not quite copying — the inventions of others so as to synthesize its own breakthroughs. In Weizman's words, referring to the French: "We improved their equipment." Thus the MD 660 missile provided by France begat a family of Israeli missiles: first the Luz, then the Jericho. In addition, Weizman spoke secretly of "the Flower Project" to develop a long-range sea-to-sea missile.[11]

The Six-Day War marked a turning point for Lakam, as for almost every other institution in Israeli life. Thanks to the secret agency's success in acquiring needed nuclear materials, Lakam's assignments were extended to other fields of science and technology. A new challenge was the fact that President de Gaulle imposed an arms embargo after the 1967 war, and he refused even to deliver munitions, boats, and aircraft previously paid for by Israel.

The small Israeli navy was frustrated by the fact that five missile boats, purchased by the Jewish state before the embargo announcement, were tied up in the harbor of Cherbourg with strict instructions to stay put. France and Israel reached a diplomatic standoff when they discussed the missile boats, and the deadlock was resolved only when the Israeli intelligence community took direct action.

In a plan concocted by both the Mossad and the military, working in close concert, a few dozen Israeli navy men flew to France in late 1969 as ordinary "tourists" with uniforms cached in their suitcases. Secret agents, who had previously explored all the weak points in Cherbourg's shipyard security, then led the sailors to the missile boats in the harbor area. The operation was perfectly timed: the Israelis repossessed their property on Christmas Eve, when French guards were few and barely vigilant.

The navy men, with Mossad operatives aboard, simply sailed off into the Mediterranean aboard the five ships which they believed to be rightfully theirs. The business side of the operation, including false contracts and other documents, was handled through Mossad-controlled companies in Panama. The Latin American country, with the strategic canal cutting through it, had become an important center for Israeli intelligence in shipping and financial transactions.

Snatching missile boats from their nests, within sight of the French shore, could not be kept secret. The vessels were obviously missing from Cherbourg, and within hours French authorities responded to a multitude of questions by blaming Israel.

Israel saw no reason to hide the fact that it had recovered the war ships it had paid for. When the Israeli sailors completed their three-thousand-mile voyage to Haifa, they were honored by a jubilant crowd that gathered on the docks. The Mossad had scored another success, and the chutzpah and the operational skill were flaunted by the secret and occasionally bashful intelligence community.

With a prevailing sentiment in favor of taking whatever Israel felt it needed but could not obtain by negotiation, Lakam's business flourished. Theft, bribery, and other schemes bordering on the illegal were used to procure valuable treasures that no one was willing to sell.

An outstanding coup came in Switzerland, where the Israelis penetrated a company manufacturing engines for the French Mirage warplane. A joint operation of Lakam, the Israeli army, and the air force performed the classic intelligence procedure of identifying and then exploiting the personal weaknesses of a Swiss engineer, Alfred Frauenknecht: his resentment of his company, his need for money to afford having a mistress, and his sympathy with Israel after the Six-Day War.

Colonel Dov Sion, Israel's military attaché in Paris, who happened to be Moshe Dayan's son-in-law, took the first step. He met Frauenknecht a few times, took him out to dinner, and sized him up. Before long, Lakam's agents persuaded the Swiss engineer to supply a complete set of blueprints for the Mirage. He accepted payments but insisted that he was not acting only for money, but also for ideological reasons. Frauenknecht was not Jewish, incidentally, so employing him was not a violation of the lesson learned by Israeli intelligence after fiascos in Iraq and Egypt: not to employ foreign Jews to spy on their own home countries.

At first, Frauenknecht met Israeli operatives in hotels or restaurants, where he would hand over photocopies of the blueprints. To speed up the operation, Frauenknecht got his nephew to help him photograph documents, place them into boxes, and deliver them to Israeli agents who brought them to Germany. Eventually these activities were noticed by the Swiss authorities, who arrested the engineer and quickly elicited a confession.

Frauenknecht said he had been promised a million dollars for the Mirage plans and had so far received $200,000 from the Israelis. On April 23, 1971, a Swiss court found him guilty of espionage, but the judges seemed to respect his motives — as he still stressed his affection toward Israel rather than greed — and the convicted spy spent only a year in prison.

Within half a year Israel was flying a new warplane, the Nesher, which had the benefit of some of the Mirage technology. On April 29, 1975, Israel proudly unveiled its latest jet fighter: the Kfir. It bore an uncanny resemblance to the French Mirage, and the man responsible for that — Frauenknecht — made his first visit to the Jewish state to see the inaugural flight, looking up in the air and knowing he had something to do with that silver streak across the Middle Eastern sky.

Israeli intelligence chiefs were ambivalent, however, in their attitude toward him. No one likes to be reminded of the negative side of an operation, the man who was caught and served time. The Israeli government did not even pay his airfare from Switzerland and refused to extend a formal welcome to him. Overall, he felt he had been forgotten and abandoned by his operators.[12]

While Frauenknecht was bitter, Binyamin Blumberg's reputation within the intelligence community grew to mythic proportions. Few knew exactly what he did, but senior operatives and defense staffers knew he was good at it. Only the highest officials linked Blumberg with the top secret nuclear project.[13] But almost every knowledgeable analyst knew that the Dimona reactor had a military function, and there was a widespread belief that Israel had achieved its goal of joining the select group of nuclear nations.

On the other hand, if the Israelis thought such a secret, but special, status would keep them safe, they were dead wrong.

TEN

The Surprises of War and Peace

SYRIAN TROOPS WERE KNOCKING on the thick steel doors, but lest that sound polite there is no etiquette in the explosion of hand grenades. The doors were built to withstand such an attack, and for a few hours the Israeli soldiers inside the Mount Hermon bunkers were beyond the reach of their rapidly advancing enemies.

The soldiers worked for Aman. They were not fighters. They were military intelligence professionals, posted on the snow-capped mountain in the occupied Golan Heights to spy on Syria.

The Aman men were working even on Yom Kippur, the holiest day of the Jewish calendar, when Israel normally stands still. It was Saturday, October 6, 1973, at two o'clock in the afternoon.

The Hermon post commander, young Lieutenant Amos Levinberg, had just been on the radiotelephone to his superior officer to report incoming artillery fire. Levinberg recalls: "I told him I wasn't worried, that everything was under control, and once the shelling stopped we would repair the damaged aerials outside." But within hours, Levinberg and the survivors of his unit would be in the hands of the Syrians.

The invaders were Syria's best troops, commandos who landed from helicopters. It took them until around midnight to break in, kill eighteen of the Israelis, wound others, and capture thirty-one in all — with a valuable pile of Western- and Israeli-made electronic equipment, which Syrian and Soviet experts would later examine in minuscule detail.

The loss of Mount Hermon, without regard to the setbacks suffered on the wider fronts that day, was a major blow to Israel's defenses. It had been the ultimate high ground: a mountain equipped with massive antennas, dish aerials, telescopes, ultramodern binoculars, and night-vision devices. Hermon had been the Jewish state's top secret eyes and ears in the north.

The post was one of many Aman listening units that monitored all radio traffic in the region, and from the mountain on a clear day you could watch the full deployment of Syrian forces all the way back to Damascus, twenty-five miles away.[1] It was the latest word in *sigint,* signals intelligence, and *comint,* communications intelligence: professional terms for high-technology means of detection and interception of every audio source ranging from radio transmissions to telephone conversations.

The sophisticated listening post was supposed to see and hear everything the enemy was doing. The system had failed. Even worse, capturing Hermon yielded an intelligence bonanza for the Syrians. The Israelis had kept an entire set of military codes there, allowing an enemy to monitor all air force communications. Aman had to admit this was a gross error. POW Amos Levinberg's tale — of complacency, the failure to detect the danger, and the shock of being taken captive — illustrates the humiliation shared by the entire country that day.

The armies of Egypt and Syria, in a carefully planned attack, totally surprised the Israeli defensive positions in the territories which the two Arab states had lost six years earlier. Israel's intelligence community failed for the first time in its primary mission: giving advance warning of war. It was Aman's responsibility above all, but the blame — and the nation's feeling of having been let down — extended to all of Israel's security agencies.

The intelligence chiefs in the Varash committee should have known the war was coming. They had every reason, even five months before Yom Kippur, to know of the aggressive preparations made by "the other side."

They simply did not believe what some of their junior agents and analysts were seeing. Everyone, it seems, had their brains manacled by what strategic experts in Israel called *ha-Konseptzia,* "the Concept." This informal but forceful doctrine developed rapidly in the euphoria that followed the stunning six-day victory of 1967. It held that the Arabs would never launch an all-out war, since it was so clear that they could not win. In the unlikely event of war, the Israelis were utterly convinced that they could smash the enemy lines and march on the Egyptian and Syrian capitals, Cairo and Damascus.

The intelligence agencies were, as always, amassing detailed information on troop movements in Egypt and Syria, but the Concept dictated that any military activity was just an exercise or a hoax aimed at prodding Israel into ordering an expensive and disruptive mobilization of army reserves. The Concept was convenient and reassuring, and it spread up and down the military, intelligence, and political chains of command.

Aman is part of the army's general staff, reporting to the chief of staff and the defense minister. Although it has been overshadowed by the headline-making exploits of the Mossad and Shin Bet, Aman is the largest and most important intelligence agency in the defense of the Jewish state. In that way — and not only in its responsibilities for electronic and radio monitoring — Aman resembled the U.S. National Security Agency. Called "the Puzzle Palace" by James Bamford, author of the book of that title, the huge NSA lives in the CIA's shadow while laying the groundwork for American intelligence successes.[2]

Aman is well organized, as might be expected from a military unit. It comprises six departments, dominated by the two called Collection and Production.

The Collection Department is responsible for the *humint* running of agents and informers just over the borders, for *sigint* radio interceptions, and often for plugging into the telephone systems of Arab countries to eavesdrop and record "landline" conversations. Part of the six-day success in 1967 was the quick interception of Arab planning sessions, including a telephone call between Egypt's President Nasser and Jordan's King Hussein, and efficient distribution of the details from Aman to the appropriate Israeli generals.

Aman works closely with the air force in electronic warfare, known to intelligence analysts as *elint.* Radar and even more sophisticated signals are sent to disturb and deceive enemy forces.

The Production Department is the largest, employing nearly three thousand of the seven thousand men and women in Aman. Their task is to receive and analyze the information that has been collected.

They are organized into "desks," and as in the Mossad these are divided along geographical and functional lines: the Western area for Egypt, Sudan, and Libya; the Eastern area for Iraq, Syria, and Lebanon; a separate desk for Jordan and the Arabian Peninsula; a Palestinian desk to track guerrilla groups; analysts of inter-Arab relations; and a desk for Middle East economics. The Production Department "produces" analyses, including advice for political decision makers.

Aman is also responsible for sending military attachés to Israel's overseas embassies, for administering the military censorship of the press, and for "field security" to prevent the leakage of secrets from army units. There is a small Research and Development Department that devises hardware and software to help in the collection of intelligence, and the navy and the air force have their own tiny, specialized intelligence units.[3]

This structure provides the prime minister and the cabinet with an annual National Intelligence Estimate — signed by the Aman chief — designed to review and predict the wide range of military, economic, and political factors that add up to war or peace. In the years between the 1967 and 1973 wars, these estimates were riddled with the bias of the Concept.

The perceived truth was put to the test in November 1969, when Aman received information from Egypt that seemed to conflict with the Concept. Less than two and a half years after their humiliating defeat, the Egyptians were reportedly rebuilding their forces more successfully than Israel had believed. Intelligence analysts, unable to accept such information, did nothing with it.

Despite the early tip-offs, Israel was entirely surprised in February 1970 when the details of a massive Soviet military involvement in Egypt came to light. Russian advisers were attached, for the first time, to Egyptian combat units — a fact that greatly altered Israel's calculations in defending the western edge of the occupied Sinai Peninsula.

Aman had apparently failed to give advance warning of the most serious superpower involvement in the region in over thirteen years, and it seemed obvious to Israeli politicians that an independent commission of inquiry should look into the failure. Instead, Aman set up its own internal review panel, led by Brigadier General Yoel Ben-Porat, the commander of Aman's eavesdropping units. The results of the mild questioning were never taken seriously.

The commander of military intelligence, General Aharon Yariv, sensed that something was wrong with his staff of analysts at Aman. Officers working with Yariv were surprised to find their chief short-tempered whenever the subject of analysis arose. Usually quiet and unemotional, the general would suddenly shout at his subordinates. Waving a file containing raw intelligence reports from the front, Yariv might yell at an Aman analyst, "For God's sake, the reports differ from your estimates!"

Yariv's angry and frustrated cries came too late to do any good.

After eight years as Aman chief, the general left the army in November 1972 to become Prime Minister Meir's adviser on terrorism. Yariv left an agency that had become complacent and arrogant.

No one clung to the Concept of Israeli invincibility more than the new head of Aman, Major General Eli Zeira. He was, from a bureaucratic point of view, on top of the world. Military intelligence, after all, had made the triumph of the Six-Day War possible. The unanimous praise of the political and defense establishments had gone to Yariv, and Zeira shared in the warm glow because he was Yariv's deputy until he inherited the top job.

Such was the high-flying reputation of Aman that when Zeira said in 1973 that Egypt was far too distracted and disorganized to attack Israel, that was accepted as ultimate authority in Jerusalem. Zeira said it in May of that year, when the Egyptian army went on alert and prepared its units along the Suez Canal for a possible offensive. When nothing further occurred and the Egyptians wound down their alert, Zeira and the Concept were seen to be vindicated. Some Israeli reserve troops had been mobilized, but this was considered to have been a waste of money.

Similar army preparations by both Egypt and Syria were noted in late September 1973, but the omnipotent Concept said these had to be harmless. Even in the United States the CIA, according to then president Richard M. Nixon, reported that "war in the Middle East was unlikely" on October 5, "dismissing as annual maneuvers the massive and unusual troop movement" by the Arabs.[4]

Unfortunately, the CIA was getting much of its data on Middle East events from Israeli intelligence — through the long-standing direct link from the Agency headquarters in Virginia to the Mossad building in Tel Aviv. In other words, the Americans had been taught the Concept and it blinded them, too.

Even as the Israelis gathered data covertly, Egypt's President Anwar Sadat gave overt hints of his intentions in a string of bellicose speeches. On the third anniversary of his predecessor Nasser's death, September 28, Sadat told his nation: "We shall spare no efforts or sacrifices to fulfill our objective. I shall not discuss any details, but the liberation of the land is the first and main task facing us."[5]

Zeira and his Aman analysts had decided long before to ignore the flood of Arabic hyperbole heard from politicians such as Sadat —

even when other information seemed to confirm Egypt's plans for war. Aman chiefs considered but rejected a startling report by an intelligence officer attached to the army's Southern Command, monitoring the occupied Sinai all the way to the Bar-Lev Line defending the Israeli-held side of the Suez Canal. Lieutenant Binyamin Siman-Tov reported on October 1, in detail, that Egypt was preparing to launch an attack across the Suez within days. Zeira was unmoved.

The Mossad, on the other hand, was more alert. More than two days before the Egyptian and Syrian attack, a Mossad agent in Cairo reported that war was on the immediate horizon. Mossad chief Zvi Zamir took the warning seriously, but he did not fight for his point of view.

Precisely how the Israeli intelligence bureaucracy handled — or mishandled — the signals of war remains a mystery, with retired officials still vehemently defending their honor. According to the system as it then stood, the Mossad's Zamir was the prime minister's chief intelligence officer with responsibility for reporting such information both to Golda Meir and, in writing, to Aman.

Aman and other intelligence veterans charge that Zamir, although he was convinced that war was "imminent," merely told Zeira by telephone and assigned an assistant to report to the prime minister's office. The Mossad assistant believed that all he had to do was verbally transmit the information to Meir's office, yet he was unable to reach the appropriate official by phone.

The information did not reach its intended recipient, and Zamir was not around to check. He left the country, presumably to meet and make a personal evaluation of the Mossad source — who was brought briefly out of Egypt. Prime Minister Meir could not find Zamir on Friday, October 5. And only on Saturday morning did the Israeli intelligence community reach its conclusion that a war would start that day. By then it was too late.

True, Israel still could have used its air force for a preemptive strike along the 1967 pattern, but Meir and Defense Minister Dayan decided not to do it. They knew that the United States would disapprove, and for the sake of American support they sadly concluded that Israel would have to absorb the first blow.[6] It was the ultimate, costly example of what had become a repeated pattern in Israeli foreign and defense policies: the increasing dependence on the U.S. government. In 1967, it was vital that Mossad chief Meir Amit return from Washing-

Above left: Reuven Shiloah, first director of the Mossad, never received the recognition he deserved as Israel's "Mr. Intelligence." *Ma-Aviv Library*

Above right: Isser Harel, the unique "one in charge" of the intelligence community. He was director of Shin Bet 1948–1952 and of the Mossad 1952–1963. *Hadashot Library*

Left: Shaul Avigur, the founder and first head of the Liaison Bureau (1953–1970), was in charge of smuggling Jews to Israel. *Hadashot Library*

DIRECTORS OF THE MOSSAD AND COMMANDERS OF SHIN BET

Left: When Ben Gurion ordered Meir Amit to lead the Mossad, he brought in American-style management. Amit was director of the Mossad 1963–1968 and of Aman 1962–1963. *Alex Libak*

Center: Nahum Admoni, commander of the Mossad 1982–1989, let the agency's power slip away. *Alex Libak*

Right: Amos Manor, head of Shin Bet 1953–1963, obtained Khrushchev's secret speech in 1956. *Uzi Keren*

Yosef Harmelin (Shin Bet commander 1964–1974, 1986–1988) insisted on high standards in a world of vicious terrorists. *Uzi Keren*

Avraham Ahituv *(right)*, Shin Bet director 1974–1981. He had trouble with Prime Minister Menachem Begin *(left)* because of Jewish terrorists. *Uzi Keren*

Above: Avraham Shalom on his yacht. As director of Shin Bet 1981–1986, he ordered the killings of two captured Palestinian terrorists and was forced to resign. *Alex Libak*

Left: A Palestinian bus hijacker (*center*), being led to his death by two Shin Bet agents in April 1984. This photograph sparked a scandal in 1985–86. *Alex Libak*

Binyamin Gibli (1950–1955), whose downfall was brought about by a sabotage operation in Egypt. *Uzi Keren*

Yehoshafat Harkabi (1955–1959) ordered Israeli intelligence's first assassinations. *Kim Nave*

President Chaim Herzog *(center)*, veteran commander of Aman (1949–1950, 1959–1962), with Ehud Barak *(right)*, Aman commander 1983–1985. *Israeli Defense Forces*

Aharon Yariv, commander of Aman 1962–1972, was responsible for the Six-Day War triumph. *Uzi Keren*

Eli Zeira, commander of Aman 1972–1974, whose career was destroyed by an intelligence failure in the Yom Kippur War. *Uzi Keren*

Shlomo Gazit, commander of Aman 1974–1979, was taken by surprise by Anwar Sadat's peace initiative. *Uzi Keren*

Amnon Shahak, commander of Aman since 1986, participated in raids against Palestinian terrorists. *Alex Libak*

Amiram Nir, former television reporter and the prime minister's adviser on counterterrorism 1985–1988, involved in the trade of American hostages for arms, briefed Vice President George Bush. He died in a mysterious airplane crash in Mexico. *Uzi Keren*

Jonathan J. Pollard, the American who spied for Israel until his arrest in November 1985. The revelation of his activities deeply troubled many Jews in the United States and embarrassed Israeli intelligence. *CBS News*

Mike Harari *(wearing dark glasses)*, who led the Mossad hit team in 1973, during a military ceremony in Tel Aviv in 1985 honoring his friend, Panama's Colonel Manuel Noriega *(second from right)*. *Hadashot Library*

A French warehouse containing nuclear cores bound for Iraq, its windows blown out by a bomb explosion in April 1979 as a warning before Israeli war planes destroyed the Iraqi reactor in Baghdad. *Agence France Presse*

Sudan's president, Gaafar Numeiri *(left)*, Israel's defense minister, Ariel Sharon *(center)*, and Saudi tycoon Adnan Khashoggi meeting in Kenya on May 13, 1982. Acting behind the Mossad's back, they secretly plotted a coup in Iran. Numeiri also agreed to let Ethiopian Jews move to Israel through Sudan.

Mordecai Vanunu, the Israeli who slipped through the Shin Bet net, sold his country's nuclear secrets. He was kidnapped by the Mossad in September 1986. *Agence France Presse*

A villa in Tunis, where a Mossad team and Sayeret commandos assassinated PLO military commander Abu Jihad in April 1988. *Agence France Presse*

Hafez Dalkamoni *(right)* of the PFLP-GC and two of his Arab contacts in West Germany. Intelligence agents took this photo approximately three months before members of Dalkamoni's cell allegedly blew up Pan Am flight 103 over Lockerbie, Scotland. Dalkamoni had been watched by the Mossad since his release from an Israeli prison in 1979.

ton to report his impression that President Johnson would give a "green light" for a preemptive strike. In 1973, Meir and Dayan took the opposite decision based on the same factor: the Americans, whose support was considered an unsacrificeable holy of holies.

The Yom Kippur surprise was similar to what American historians have written about the Japanese attack on Pearl Harbor in 1941. The information was there, but intelligence chiefs either chose to ignore it or wrongly analyzed it.

Israeli foot soldiers in the Sinai and on the Golan Heights had to compensate with their lives for the complacency of their leaders and the mistakes of the intelligence community. In fierce battles, the Syrians recaptured part of the Golan Heights, the Egyptians crossed the Suez Canal and gained a foothold in Sinai, and Dayan — the hero of the 1967 war — panicked. He was so gloomy that on the third day of the war, he muttered darkly about the possible destruction of "the Third Temple" of Israel.[7] Jewish history, of course, tells of a first holy temple in Jerusalem that was destroyed by the Babylonians in 586 B.C., and a second decimated by the Romans in A.D. 70. The third temple was the State of Israel itself, and Dayan rated its chances of survival as very low.

There was talk among Israeli generals of using "unconventional" weapons.[8] Serious consideration was given for the first time, that week, to the possible need to use Israel's nuclear bombs as a last act of almost suicidal defense. The secret arsenal, which the invisible agency Lakam had worked so hard to acquire, was then untested and still "dirty." But on Dayan's orders, Jericho missiles and special bomb racks on Phantom aircraft were prepared for the possible launch of atomic weapons.[9]

The defense minister's despair weighed heavily on Golda Meir's spirit. She seemed to be considering suicide, as her confidante Lou Kaddar recalls: "I never saw her so gray, her face as in mourning. She told me, 'Dayan wants us to discuss terms of surrender.' I thought that a woman such as she would never want to live in such circumstances. So I prepared it for both of us. I went to see a doctor, a friend of mine who would agree to give me the necessary pills so that we both — she and I — would go together."[10]

Meir pulled herself together and with her army chief of staff, Lieutenant General David (Dado) Elazar, who was strong as a rock, she directed the counterattacks that eventually brought victory. The short-term damage represented an extremely heavy price for Israel: 2,700 soldiers killed — equivalent, by proportion of population, to 170,000 dead Americans. In a nation of just over three million people, the loss was traumatic.

The long-term damage was that the entire State of Israel lost confidence in its once legendary intelligence community. It was not just a feeling. It was in writing. Prime Minister Meir commissioned an official inquiry into the Yom Kippur War and the *Mechdal,* or "Omission" — the instantly coined euphemism for the intelligence blunder that made the war a total surprise. The investigators were known as the Agranat Commission and they were led by the Chief Justice of Israel's supreme court, Shimon Agranat.

As usual, the politicians escaped the full brunt of the investigation — for which they themselves set the terms of reference — and the blame was placed on the military and on the intelligence community. The commission cleared Meir and Dayan of "direct responsibility" for the Mechdal. Agranat's panel instead made Chief of Staff Elazar and his Southern Command general, Shmuel Gorodish-Gonen, the scapegoats, and the official report scathingly destroyed the careers of Aman chief Zeira and three of his assistants. They were replaced by new officers, and Major General Shlomo Gazit became commander of Aman.

The Agranat Commission recommended a structural reorganization for the entire intelligence community, including formation of a new unit. As a result, the foreign ministry's Research and Political Planning Center — which had existed only on paper since 1951 — was brought to life. Its mission is not to collect intelligence but to provide a further, independent assessment of the data already collected. The center has its own office, in a separately fenced-in compound within the ministry of foreign affairs in Jerusalem. This is not because it has secret agents; it is to protect the raw intelligence material that is provided by the Mossad and Aman.[11]

Other changes included enlargement of the tiny research department of the Mossad, so as not to depend solely on Aman's analytical powers. As suggested by the Agranat Commission, the Mossad "researchers" began to have a hand in assembling the National Intelligence Estimate prepared each year for the prime minister.

On the political level, Meir and Dayan took the heat of sharp criticism for a few months after the near defeat of October 1973. The heat became unbearable, and in April 1974 they resigned.

Yitzhak Rabin became Israel's new leader. As the army chief of staff in the 1967 war and then ambassador to Washington, Rabin was no stranger to intelligence reports.

As prime minister, he asked to see much of the raw data collected by the secret agencies rather than the digested summaries favored by many civilian politicians. This was not only because of Rabin's military background. The CIA, in a secret profile, considered him "introspective" and "having a tendency to worry."[12] He had the distinct personal habit of not relying on others, and Rabin was certainly not going to trust the judgment of intelligence agencies after the total failure of their analysis in 1973. He was simply acting within the new national mood.

Aman's morale was at its nadir. The Mossad, on the other hand, escaped almost unscathed from the Yom Kippur debacle and the investigations that followed. This was because Zvi Zamir had known the October war was coming and was forgiven for his failure to shout a warning. Rabin in effect rewarded the Mossad with a new assignment: coordinating his clandestine meetings and other official contacts with Jordan's King Hussein, surely the most sensitive and secret aspect of Israel's foreign policy.

The monarch whose land bordered Israel to the east had, after all, stayed out of the Yom Kippur War despite his public demand for the return of his former West Bank. Behind the scenes, Hussein had been having face-to-face meetings with the leaders of Israel since 1963, at first aimed at hammering out a peace treaty but later finding satisfaction in a solid but undeclared de facto peace.

The Mossad, in its contacts with the CIA to arrange the details, referred to the clandestine meetings by a codename — Operation Lift.[13] Perhaps unknown to the Israelis, Hussein happened to be on the CIA payroll as an "asset" in the Middle East.[14] The Mossad's role traced the old footprints of Reuven Shiloah, the Mossad founder who had conducted secret talks with Hussein's grandfather King Abdullah until 1951.

Rabin and Hussein intensified the relationship, and the Jordanian monarch even went so far as to visit the Israeli prime minister in Tel Aviv — a secret never disclosed, even in the memoirs of the few officials who knew of the hidden diplomacy. The king felt very much in command after his Arab Legion defeated Yasser Arafat's PLO in the 1970 civil war. The Israelis had indirectly helped Hussein, by moving their troops — as coordinated by the United States — so as to deter Syria from intervening on the PLO's behalf.

One of the results was a top secret but highly useful intelligence exchange between the Mossad and the Jordanian secret police, known as the Mukhabarat, Arabic for "intelligence." Their common enemies were the Palestinian terrorist organizations, and the Israelis happily informed Hussein of PLO plots against him and his cabinet ministers. There were quite a few.

Jordan's Mukhabarat, meantime, provided the Mossad with a window on the politics and the dangerous radicals of the Arab world. They did not give each other everything, and the Israelis were especially careful not to put their own agents and informers in any danger, but senior officials of the two agencies met frequently — on both sides of the Jordan River and on neutral ground in Europe.

Hussein met Rabin in May 1975 along their desert border in the dusty Arava plain. When the king was flown by helicopter to a Mossad-operated guest house just north of Tel Aviv in March 1977, the Mossad recorded the talks with hidden cameras and microphones. The official tapes and files have been locked away in Israel's government archives with absolutely no plan ever to release them.

The Mossad also had the privilege of arranging a secret visit by Rabin to another Arab state, Morocco. Rabin was hoping to break the Middle East deadlock, after finding that Jordan would not sign an overt peace treaty and deciding that the Egyptian front required something more permanent than a mere disengagement of forces.

The prime minister flew to Rabat in 1976, by way of Paris, wearing a wig as a disguise. Rabin asked King Hassan II to try to persuade Egypt's Sadat to come to the negotiating table. There was no immediate result from the initiative toward Cairo, but the clandestine cooperation between Israel and Morocco was reaffirmed. Both the Mossad and the CIA had the freedom to roam Morocco, making contact with other potentially useful Arabs, running listening posts to keep an electronic ear on North Africa, and advising the king and his top officials on internal security.[15]

In full public view Israel's diplomats were busy, working with Henry Kissinger and other American go-betweens to hammer out separation-of-forces accords with Egypt and Syria. U.S.-Israeli concerted action was not confined to diplomacy. Behind the scenes, far wider fields were being explored. Because Kissinger and the Nixon administration were satisfied with Israel's restraint on the eve of the 1973 war, they rewarded their client with the latest models of tanks, aircraft, and missiles.

The golden era of military cooperation had begun. Encouraged by Nixon officials and later by President Gerald R. Ford's administration, U.S. corporations followed their government's lead by investing in Israeli industries and setting up joint ventures to produce both military and civilian hardware and know-how.

Contacts between the armed forces of the two nations increased, with military personnel taking part in exchange programs to the benefit of both sides. Israel provided the United States with excellent insights into the state of Soviet technology based on weapons captured by the Israelis in their wars against the Arabs. The Americans examined the armaments, developed the appropriate countermeasures, and then sent the new arms to Israel to be tested. These included missiles meant to pierce tank armor, jamming devices to outwit radar and guidance systems, and upgraded computer avionics in warplanes. U.S. military products could thus be "battle proved" by authentic combat units in genuine firefights.

Even as the United States became its undoubted chief ally and guardian angel, Israel was drifting in a transition period after 1973 without any clear direction in shaping its relations with its Arab neighbors. The failure to sign any peace treaties, contrasted with the achievement of more modest troop-restriction agreements, reflected the twilight between peace and war during Rabin's period as prime minister. Similarly, when he selected a new Mossad chief it was not seen as a matter of life and death. The changing of the guard made no real difference. One army general left the post, and a new one came in.

After serving five years as Mossad chief, just as his predecessor Meir Amit had done, Zvi Zamir retired from the agency — as colorless and unnoticed as he was when he joined it. His term ended in 1974 and was dominated by two failures: the Lillehammer disaster and the Yom Kippur War, even though the latter did not besmirch him personally.

Rabin chose an old acquaintance, Major General Yitzhak (Haka)

Hofi, to serve as head of the Mossad. The appointment reflected the lingering memories of the 1973 intelligence failure, because Hofi could only be proud of his own actions at the time. In charge of the army's Northern Command, Hofi was probably the only general who urged his superiors to take notice of Syria's threatening troop movements in the weeks before Yom Kippur. He asked that his tanks and artillery units be reinforced, but his pleas were ignored. During the war Hofi and his soldiers fought well, recaptured Mount Hermon and the Golan Heights, and even advanced deeper into Syria.

Born in 1927, Hofi became the first Sabra Mossad chief. (Sabra, Hebrew for "cactus fruit," is the term used for Israeli-born citizens because they, too, are said to be prickly on the outside but sweet within.) Like many of his generation, Hofi joined the Palmach special forces, fought in the 1948 war, and — as did Amit and Zamir — decided to stay in the army. As a paratroop commander he was involved in several daring Israeli operations in the Sinai and Gaza Strip before the 1956 war, and ten years later he was a planning officer in the preparations for the Six-Day War. In July 1974, the heavyset, round-faced Hofi left the army and simply disappeared. Israeli authorities refused to comment on his whereabouts, but the former paratrooper had landed in Mossad headquarters in Tel Aviv.[16]

He was no intelligence genius, but Hofi had always been highly respected by his men, and he was hard-working and serious. His relationship with the prime minister was greatly helped by the fact that he had spent his teenage years in the same wing of the Labor movement as Yitzhak Rabin.

While the Mossad continued to pursue the traditional Israeli policy of surrounding the hostile Arab states with "peripheral" friends, it became clear under Hofi that Israel had an even greater need to come to terms with the Arab nations themselves. In addition to Jordan, Morocco, and initial contacts with Egypt, it was Lebanon's turn.

The main motive was still the old peripheral notion of ties with the Maronite Christian minority in Lebanon, but making connections in Beirut gave the Mossad another channel of communications with the Moslem world as well.

At the same time, the Mossad's secret diplomacy dovetailed with the war against terrorism — reaching the pinnacle of success as far south as the heart of Africa. The clandestine links made by David Kimche and other "alternative diplomats" in the continent were called upon when Israel was faced with the hijack of a French jet to Entebbe, Uganda, on June 27, 1976. It seemed an impossibly helpless situation for the Israelis. Air France flight 139 had left Tel Aviv, originally bound for Paris when it was commandeered by two members of the Popular Front for the Liberation of Palestine and two West German "urban guerrillas" — heirs to the notorious Baader-Meinhof gang.

The French airbus had over 250 passengers and crew, and at least 83 of the hostages were Israelis. The heavily armed hijackers chillingly chose to hold only Israelis and Jews as their captives, while freeing all the other passengers. The segregation, as related to intelligence debriefers in France by those who were released, angered normally cool-headed Mossad and Aman analysts. It reminded them of the Nazi "selections" of gas-chamber victims from among the Jews arriving at concentration camps in cattle cars.

Mossad operatives were also irked that one of the black African leaders whom they had cultivated was now biting the Israeli hand that used to feed him. Many African rulers abandoned their friendship with Israel after the 1973 war, including Ugandan president Idi Amin, who had taken power three years earlier in a coup with the help of Israeli military advisers. But now the murderous madman — a former British army sergeant and boxer who threw his political enemies to the alligators — realigned his mercurial policies in favor of the Arab world.

Rejecting the outright capitulation of freeing forty convicted terrorists, as demanded by the hijackers, Israel saw only a military option — difficult as it was. On the night of July 3, 1976, the air force flew several sayeret commando units well over two thousand miles to end the hijack. They deceived the Entebbe airport control tower by landing Hercules transport planes full of troops, weapons, and a field hospital without making a sound.

Some of the troops even deplaned in a duplicate of Amin's black Mercedes limousine, as the assault force burst into the old passenger terminal and killed seven terrorists within minutes. Three others — in the PFLP band reinforced in Entebbe with President Amin's complicity — are believed to have been secretly taken prisoner by the Israelis.[17] Over one hundred hostages were rescued, although two were killed in the spray of sayeret gunfire. Lieutenant Colonel Yonatan Netanyahu, commander of one of the elite units, was the only

Israeli soldier lost, cut down by a Ugandan sniper in the control tower. Forty-five Ugandan soldiers were killed.

Israel's famous and startling success — a bold, long-distance version of the Sabena hijack assault in Tel Aviv four years earlier — is part of the Jewish state's nonfictional folklore. Even in the United States on that July 4, the Entebbe rescue nearly overshadowed the celebrations of America's Bicentennial.

Not celebrated publicly, in fact untold amid the rejoicing in Israel, was the excellent preparatory legwork by anonymous Mossad agents. The Israeli cabinet had instructed its intelligence community to devise possible responses, from the moment that the French airbus was hijacked.

The Mossad immediately knew that the man to contact was Bruce Mackenzie. A British businessman and farmer who had settled in Kenya, Mackenzie was a good friend of President Jomo Kenyatta and was the only white man in Kenyatta's cabinet. Mackenzie helped organize his adopted country's defense and security, while keeping Britain's MI6 informed of events in Africa. He also knew the Israelis very well.

The Mossad, through its station in Nairobi, has long maintained excellent ties with the Kenyan security service.[18] The special interest for Israel is that Nairobi is not far from the Horn of Africa and is one of the most important capitals on the continent, with diplomats and spies of all nationalities and allegiances at offices of the United Nations and the Organization of African Unity. Together with Zaire in Central Africa and Nigeria to the west, Kenya became one of the three strategic centers of Israeli intelligence activity in Africa.

Such cosmopolitan crossroads inevitably attract terrorists, too. On January 18, 1976, less than half a year before the hijack drama at Entebbe, Kenyan police arrested three Palestinians on the edge of the Nairobi airport with two Soviet-made shoulder-fired SAM-7 rocket launchers. The Arabs had been planning to shoot down an El Al airliner, with 110 people aboard, which was due to land an hour later. Based on their interrogation, Kenya's secret police arrested a West German couple, Thomas Reuter and Brigitte Schulz, both twenty-three years old, as they arrived in Nairobi three days later. All five suspects — the three Palestinians and the two Germans, who were another example of cooperation between Arab terrorists and European radical youth — then vanished.

Schulz's family tried to discover her whereabouts, but the Kenyan government denied holding any foreign prisoners. Eventually, Israel confirmed that it had all five under arrest. Mackenzie had arranged an extrajudicial extradition, whereby the Kenyan authorities handed the terrorists over to the Mossad. In Israel they were secretly tried, convicted, and jailed.[19]

At the end of June, with Israelis among the hijacked passengers in Entebbe, the Mossad turned to Mackenzie with a need for even greater assistance. He secured President Kenyatta's approval for the use of Kenya by Israeli intelligence. Within a few hours, ten Mossad and Aman agents flew to Nairobi and set up a planning center, laying the ground for dozens more intelligence and military operatives. The Israelis, some posing as businessmen and others rowing tiny boats, crossed the border into the Entebbe area — just across Lake Victoria from Kenya — on reconnaissance missions needed to watch the airport and map out entry and exit routes.

Kenya also allowed the Israeli aircraft that served as a field hospital to stop in Nairobi after the successful rescue. The clandestine connections forged by the Mossad paid off with the success of the lightning raid on Entebbe, as Israel gave the world a demonstration of its talents in combating terrorism.

The Jewish state also showed, as it did toward the CIA's James Angleton, that it could honor its clandestine friends. Two years after the Entebbe assault, Mackenzie was killed because of his cooperation with Israel: Libyan agents working for Uganda's dictator planted a bomb that destroyed Mackenzie's private jet. It was Amin's revenge.

Israel's tribute was green and lives on. The Association of Israeli Intelligence Veterans, headed by former Mossad chief Meir Amit, raised money to plant a forest of ten thousand trees in the hills of lower Galilee in memory of their British-Kenyan ally.[20]

The Entebbe success was, quite naturally, a morale booster for the intelligence community three years after its Yom Kippur humiliation, but a single spectacular was not enough to keep Yitzhak Rabin in power. In May 1977, the Israeli electorate unexpectedly rejected Rabin and his Labor party. All the failures and scandals, ranging from the Lavon Affair to the Omission of 1973, mixed with the further spice of financial corruption, finally caught up with Labor after governing Israel for an unbroken twenty-nine years. The right-wing

Likud bloc won the election, and Menachem Begin was the new prime minister.

As much as other Israelis, senior members of the intelligence community were shocked by Begin's victory. The secret agencies had become accustomed to working with the famous faces of Labor, and most intelligence officials came from the Labor movement's ranks. Although their objectives were meant to be nonpartisan, the top echelons of the community had established familiar, almost intimate relations over the years with their political masters.

Now there was uncertainty and even fear that Likud's lust for power, which they naturally expected of a party that had been in the political wilderness for three decades, would lead to a purge of the Labor-appointed civil service. The intelligence chiefs had no reason to believe that they would be excepted. Their fears were not without foundation, because there were indeed Likud leaders who urged Begin to launch just such a purge.

Both Mossad chief "Haka" Hofi and Shin Bet chief Avraham Ahituv conveyed almost identical messages to the new prime minister: if he wanted them to, they would resign. Although both were civil servants who could retain their jobs, they recognized the right of the new leader to appoint his own people to these sensitive positions.

Begin, however, told them to stay. He did not wish to cause any unnecessary disturbances or discontent in government agencies. In fact, Begin very quickly fostered close relations with Hofi and Ahituv. The two men, especially the Mossad chief, were often in the prime minister's private office.

Begin was fascinated by the Mossad's secret operations, which apparently reminded him of his past as head of the Irgun underground in the 1940s. With almost boyish enthusiasm, he frequently asked Hofi to tell him "everything" — not to spare any details. Hofi showed great patience, even though he was astounded time and again by Begin's ignorance of intelligence and military matters. As the ultimate outsider since 1948, the Likud leader had not acquired the background information gained by Labor party insiders. As Hofi later put it, Begin's lack of knowledge forced him and the Aman chief to go into great detail in their explanations so that the prime minister would get the full picture.[21]

Begin loved the glamour of the intelligence agencies, and he enjoyed being their new boss. He had other reasons for his high interest.

Begin was out to change history, and he was going to use Israeli intelligence to do it. Begin had his own vision for his first years in office. His political enemies in the Labor party had portrayed him as a demon, as a satanic figure "who would devour Arabs," and as a warmonger who would bring about a terrible conflict with Israel's neighbors.

Begin was aware of his image problem and tried with all his might to prove everyone wrong: he would be a great peacemaker. One step was to make Moshe Dayan, until then a Labor stalwart, his foreign minister. Another step was to send Hofi to Morocco.

The Mossad chief, accompanied by his assistant, David Kimche, arrived at King Hassan's secluded Ifran palace within weeks of Begin's taking office. The new prime minister was hoping to achieve what Rabin had failed to do in his trip to Morocco the previous year: to make peace with Israel's largest enemy, Egypt. Hofi had secured Hassan's agreement to play host to a unique encounter. The head of the Mossad, hated and feared throughout the Arab world, was about to meet senior Egyptians to pave the way for future negotiations.

The same day, two top officials from Egypt arrived in Morocco. They were General Kamal Hassan Ali, head of the Egyptian equivalent of the Mossad, and Hassan Tohami, the religious deputy prime minister occasionally ridiculed for his spiritual visions but quietly respected because he had been a confidant of Nasser in the 1950s and his liaison to the CIA. Years later General Ali would recall how President Sadat instructed him by telephone to fly abroad with Tohami without any explanation. All through the flight, Tohami was absolutely silent. All Ali knew was that their destination was Morocco.

The Egyptians entered Ifran palace and shook hands with the two foreigners, but Ali was not told who they were and was then astonished to be dismissed from the room by Tohami. Ali, nominally in charge of Egyptian foreign intelligence, did not know what his own government was doing under his own nose — while the king of Morocco did know.

When the meeting ended, Ali waved an angry finger at Tohami and said that he would not have come if he had known he would be excluded. Tohami replied that the two strangers were French, and the talks were about arms deals.

General Ali was even more offended: "I am a military man. There is no reason I should not take part in such talks."

When they returned to Egypt, Ali complained to Sadat about Tohami's mysteries. "The president laughed as I've never seen him before," Ali recalled, "and then he told me the real purpose of the trip."[22]

Hofi's purpose was to convince the Egyptians that Begin was sincere about making peace and was strong enough to pull it off. Hofi and Tohami agreed there should be more secret meetings. On September 16, 1977, Tohami flew again to Morocco to meet this time with Moshe Dayan — the new Israeli foreign minister, but also the old feared general who was a living symbol for the Arabs of Israel's military superiority.[23]

Dayan, with the Mossad's Kimche at his side, gave Tohami the impression that in return for a peace treaty Israel would be willing to withdraw from the entire Sinai — ceding valuable oil fields, air bases, and settlements. This was jarringly unexpected, because Begin had built his reputation as an unyielding ultranationalist.

That meeting in Morocco paved the way for the historic visit of President Sadat to Jerusalem just two months later.

Even though Israel's intelligence chiefs were in on the peace process with Egypt from the beginning, they were skeptical about its chances of success. Hofi returned from Rabat, still suspicious about the real intentions of the unpredictable Egyptian president.

As for Aman, its annual National Intelligence Estimate predicted that Sadat would again resort to war — not to peace. Aman analysts explained later that they had been unable to foresee the personal decision of an individual man. Intelligence, in such circumstances, had very little to go on. Sadat made "a decision that was not considered beforehand or decided by any forum of the senior government echelon in Cairo," said Aman chief General Gazit, trying to excuse his agency's being surprised — this time not by war, but by peace.[24]

Even as the Egyptian president prepared for his short but momentous journey to Ben-Gurion airport, Aman advised the army chief of staff, Lieutenant General Mordecai Gur, that Sadat's incoming flight from Cairo could be a decoy for a military assault. Israel's army was placed on alert as the Jewish Sabbath ended that Saturday evening, November 19, 1977.[25]

General Gur even embarrassed Begin by publicly doubting Sadat and stressing that Israel was ready for war. Sadat was not at all embarrassed, and just after coming down the steps of his airplane at Ben-Gurion airport he shook hands with Gur and told him with a smile, "I come for peace, not war."

Aman, still suffering the shellshock of its 1973 failure to predict war, was ultracautious to the last moment. Paralyzed by the stench of failure and the fear of failing again, military intelligence officers had become almost paranoid. They saw war behind every door. Fortunately, this did not become a new "Concept."

On the contrary, the concept was now not to have a "Concept." Instead of overconfident faith in success, the new psychology led to a worst-case analysis of almost everything. Raw data, however, was being handled much better than in 1973. There was a new emphasis on long-distance military monitoring, using technological advances such as unmanned flying drones that could transmit live television pictures from above the enemy lines.

In any event, the failure in 1977 to predict peace was not so bad as the intelligence Omission that cost the Israelis thousands of lives. At least it was peace and not war.

Three years later, after the Camp David peace treaty was signed, a strange scene was played on the fringes of another Sadat visit to Israel. In 1980 the Egyptian leadership was in Haifa, and Deputy Prime Minister Tohami was waiting to enter an official banquet. Six feet away stood Mossad chief Hofi and his wife. Tohami and Hofi pretended not to know each other — not a handshake or even a nod of the head.

An Israeli television reporter, who knew that the two men had secretly launched the peace process in Morocco, nudged Tohami: "Enough of the play-acting. It's already in the history books."[26]

ELEVEN

For the Good of the Jews

"YEHIEL, PLEASE INVITE Harry Hurwitz in," the prime minister asked his dedicated political secretary, Yehiel Kadishai. It was July 1977. Menachem Begin was leader of Israel and determined to become champion of the Jewish people everywhere.

Kadishai, an enthusiastic conversationalist easily recognized by his white hair and dark-rimmed thick glasses, had been Begin's private secretary ever since their underground days in the Irgun. Together, they had known the long frustration of serving in the parliamentary opposition against an unbroken string of Labor-led governments. Having finally won a general election, Begin and his men were more than eager for real action.

Kadishai picked up the internal telephone, dialed extension 211, and asked Hurwitz to come to the prime minister's office immediately.

In the short time that the South African–born Hurwitz, dark-haired, bespectacled, and heavyset, had been working for Begin as his adviser on Jewish affairs, he had learned to understand his boss. Begin would only rarely invite him to his office, and this was usually when he needed Hurwitz's skill in wording letters and sensitive documents in English.

Although born and educated in Poland, Begin had little trouble with the English language and sharpened it daily by listening to the BBC World Service — a private tribute to London from the man who was a wanted terrorist during the British Mandate in Palestine. Begin admired Britain and wanted Israel to emulate its democracy. Still, when he wanted something especially eloquent, Begin would turn to Hurwitz.

The adviser hurried past several Shin Bet bodyguards in the round-the-clock protection detail. "Harry," the prime minister greeted him as he entered Begin's office on the second floor, "I would like you to write a letter which is not only important, but is dear to my heart." The letter was addressed to the new Marxist president of Ethiopia, Colonel Mengistu Haile Mariam, and in exceptionally polite language Begin asked Mengistu to permit the Jews of Ethiopia to move to Israel. Begin framed his request as a humanitarian plea to the leader of the "Provisional Military Administrative Council" in Addis Ababa. The army had overthrown Israel's old peripheral ally, Emperor Haile Selassie, in 1974.[1]

Begin felt there was an opening for him to pursue his special interest in liberating the Jews of the world, because Jerusalem had just received a request from Colonel Mengistu to renew Israeli arms sales to Ethiopia. The Marxist leader indicated, through clandestine channels, that he hoped Israel could persuade the United States to aid him in his wars against neighboring Somalia and against the rebels of the Eritrean Liberation Front.

On his first visit to Washington as prime minister, in July 1977, the first question Begin raised with President Jimmy Carter had to do with Ethiopia. It was not focused, however, on arms or African wars. Begin spoke for several minutes, to arouse the sentimental Carter's sympathy for the yearning of Ethiopia's Jews to realize their ancient dream of moving to the land of their forefathers.[2]

In Africa and elsewhere, the Begin government brought about a sweeping change in Israel's perception of the Jewish Diaspora — the majority of the world's Jews dispersed around the globe, residing outside the biblical homeland of their people.

The new prime minister summoned Mossad chief Yitzhak Hofi and Nehemiah Levanon, who was new head of the Liaison Bureau that coordinated all of Israel's efforts to help Soviet Jews win the right to emigrate. Begin told them that he regarded immigration to Israel as no less important than peace with Egypt, combating terrorism, or issuing military assessments — the vital tasks that were normally the highest priorities of the intelligence community.

Levanon had replaced Shaul Avigur at the Liaison Bureau in March 1970, thus filling the oversized shoes of one of the founding grandfathers of Israeli intelligence. Avigur had been cofounder of Shai, the prestate intelligence force, in 1934 and had finally retired, in his seventies and in poor health, after seventeen years of directing the bureau in its clandestine fight for Soviet Jewry.

The new head of the bureau had worked for Avigur both there and previously in the Institute for Aliyah B. Posted to Moscow as a diplomat in the 1950s, Levanon was expelled by the Soviets for clandestine contacts with Jews. These included delivering a letter from an Israeli cabinet minister to his sister in Russia. The unfortunate woman was sentenced to three years in prison. Two other Israeli diplomats were declared persona non grata in separate but similar incidents.[3]

Levanon returned to Israel, worked at the Liaison Bureau headquarters in Tel Aviv, and was then posted in the Israeli embassy in Washington to take charge of Jewish affairs — mainly lobbying among American politicians and officials on behalf of emigration from the Soviet Union. Efforts to keep in touch with Russian Jews became more difficult after the Soviets severed relations with Israel in 1967. The Israelis no longer had an embassy in Moscow to provide diplomatic cover.

As head of the Liaison Bureau in the 1970s, Levanon believed in quiet activity. In Israel and the Diaspora, however, various militant organizations rejected hidden methods and called instead for vociferous demands "to free Soviet Jewry." These groups forced the Israeli government to change its policy and go along with the public campaign.

At the same time, the United States and the Soviet Union started their pre-Gorbachev golden age of détente. Soviet party chief Leonid Brezhnev, under U.S. pressure, permitted around 250,000 Jews to leave his country. Two out of three moved to Israel.

The increased immigration forced the Liaison Bureau to expand. It began to appoint consuls to various Israeli embassies in Europe, and it sent liaison personnel to maintain ties with Jewish organizations throughout the world. Letters of support were sent to Soviet Jews, as were Hebrew books and packages of religious and other items rare in Russia.

Foreign Jews who traveled to the Soviet Union were offered briefings by the special Israeli diplomats, who gave detailed instructions on what to do and what not to do. They were told which Jews to meet and whom to avoid, and how to behave if detained by the authorities.[4]

Levanon and Mossad chief Hofi, working in close coordination on the great consensus project of immigration, were well aware that Israel's secret agents had always been involved in Jewish affairs. But they knew that Prime Minister Begin wanted more.

*

Israel regards itself as the national and natural home for the entire Jewish people, and as a refuge for each individual Jew wherever he or she may be. This is a matter of clear and unequivocal ideology, which has been cardinal to the Zionist movement since it was founded.

Behind the doctrine lies an element of national self-interest. Because of its demographic fears, surrounded by far more numerous Arabs, Israel needs new immigrants. They serve not only as a human reservoir, but also as justification for the state's existence.

Israel therefore feels an obligation to help every Jew or Jewish community in distress. The sense of responsibility most definitely extends to the secret agencies. When Israel believes that there are Jewish problems, its intelligence community becomes a "Jewish intelligence" service.

Israel's policy, enunciated publicly but not fully, holds that everything possible must be done to protect Jewish communities abroad, and also to bring them to the Jewish state as new immigrants. This should preferably, but not necessarily, be done by open and legal means. Where that has not been possible, Zionist organizations and Israel itself have rarely hesitated to use illegal means. That was the raison d'être of the Institute for Aliyah B and the basis for the massive wave of Jewish immigration from Yemen, Iraq, and the Soviet-bloc countries in Israel's first years.

Begin fully supported the Liaison Bureau's mission, but would have preferred a much more open and visible campaign rather than the silent tactics pursued by Levanon — already with a mark against him as a holdover from previous Labor governments. The new prime minister saw the need for massive rallies and petitions demanding freedom for Soviet Jewry. At that time, in the late 1970s, the number of Jews permitted to leave Russia was dropping sharply with a deterioration of relations between the United States and Leonid Brezhnev's Kremlin.

There were also some uncomfortable relations between Levanon's Liaison Bureau and foreign Jewish organizations that were working toward similar ends. An energetic young Israeli made the rounds of Jewish youth clubs in north London in 1980, asking for volunteers to travel to the Soviet Union. Around a hundred Britons between the ages of seventeen and twenty answered the call, and the mysterious Israeli directed them to a specific travel agency that provided them with discounted air tickets to Russia and Hebrew books, records, and cassettes to deliver there.

The parents of the adventurous British travelers were not at all happy to learn that their children were being turned into amateur secret agents. They angrily complained to the Israeli embassy in London, which put them in direct contact with Nehemiah Levanon. The head of the Liaison Bureau did not precisely explain his job, but he did tell the parents: "Don't get involved. This doesn't concern you. We know exactly what we are doing."

British organizations that campaigned on behalf of Soviet Jewry were similarly annoyed at the Israelis. They were all working toward the same goal, and everyone recognized that Israel had established a vital lifeline by collecting vast amounts of information about the Jews and their needs; but the non-Israeli groups felt they were being asked to finance trips without being told anything about them.[5]

After more than a decade as head of the Liaison Bureau, Levanon was replaced by Yehuda Lapidot. Begin was finally acceding to requests by his top advisers that he appoint a Likud party loyalist to the sensitive task of secret immigration. Lapidot did not have the "Jewish intelligence" experience of either Levanon or Avigur before him, but the new bureau chief had been a member of the hard-line Irgun militia that Begin led before Israel's independence. Lapidot was the number-two man in the April 1948 killing of some two hundred Arab civilians in the village of Deir Yassin near Jerusalem, condemned by the world as a massacre but justified by Begin as a necessary military operation. Instead of living in infamy, Lapidot went on to become famous as a talented biochemist at Hebrew University.

There were many in the diplomatic and intelligence communities who did not understand why the inexperienced Lapidot got the Liaison Bureau job. The new chief and Prime Minister Begin, however, understood each other perfectly. The bureau's work went much more smoothly, with Lapidot happily carrying out Begin's wishes by waging a highly public campaign for Soviet Jewry.

The bureau publicly bestowed the title "Prisoner of Zion" on any Soviet Jew who actively promoted the Zionist movement, Jewish culture, or both and was arrested for those activities. The Israelis drew a distinction between Jews who were simply dissidents fighting for Soviet human rights, and Jews who were active Zionists and were suffering because of their love for Israel.

If official Prisoners of Zion had relatives already outside Russia, they might be sent on extensive trips abroad to meet with foreign dignitaries and the international press — campaigning for free emigration from the Soviet Union. The Israeli government, through either the Liaison Bureau or the Public Council for Soviet Jewry, would pay all the expenses.

Anatoli (Natan) Shcharansky, the most famous of the Prisoners of Zion, did not even qualify for the label at first. He was imprisoned in Russia in the late 1970s on charges of spying for the CIA and was considered an activist on behalf of human rights in general. Only later did he throw the spotlight on himself as a Zionist and become a living symbol of the coordinated Israeli-Jewish fight for the right of Soviet Jews to emigrate. Shcharansky moved to Israel in 1986, when he was released from prison as part of a spy swap.

The struggle began to fade in 1985, with the emergence of Communist party chief Mikhail Gorbachev and his policy of *glasnost*. It is estimated that more than half a million Soviet Jews intend to move to Israel in the early 1990s, and Gorbachev is no longer stopping them.

Pressure by Arab countries and threats by Islamic terrorists prompted Israeli military censors to clamp a lid of secrecy on the exact numbers of immigrants and the routes they were taking. The Liaison Bureau, operating with the Israeli diplomats now permitted in Moscow, were involved in the planning. Shin Bet helped arrange security at the European transit points.

These new immigration waves rekindled the problem that Shin Bet had had to deal with in the early 1950s: fear that the Soviet Union was exploiting the opportunity to plant secret agents in Israel, and might use the flood of Jews as a springboard for launching Communist agents into the West.

The use of such techniques was confirmed by Ilya Grigorovich Dzhirkvelov, a senior KGB officer who defected to the West. He told British interrogators in 1981 that the Soviet secret police examined the lists of all Jews who asked to emigrate, looking for a few who might spy for Mother Russia. Some were recruited and ordered to start sending information back to Moscow immediately. Others were planted as "sleepers" who would do nothing for a few years and then be "reawakened" by Soviet controllers. The KGB set up a special department to recruit Jewish agents, to train them, and to run them.[6] However, the Kremlin found that many, once in Israel, refused to serve the KGB and filed no reports at all.

Further confirmation of the extent of Soviet efforts to penetrate

Israel came in London in 1982 with the espionage trial of Hugh George Hambleton, a Canadian economics professor who spied for the KGB. His case was in the British newspaper headlines as the tale of a man who worked in a NATO alliance office while secretly employed by the Kremlin. It seemed to have nothing to do with Israel. The connection was noticed only by coincidence.

Just minutes before Hambleton was brought into Court Number One in London's historic Old Bailey courthouse, a trial that was intensively covered by Israeli journalists ended in the conviction of Rhona Ritchie. She was a tall and attractive British diplomat whose career was shattered by disgrace while she was posted in Tel Aviv.

Ritchie joined the British Foreign Office in August 1979, having found the ideal job for a Scotswoman who knew several languages. She was trained in London in the art of diplomacy, and her first foreign posting came in July 1981 when she was assigned to the British embassy in Tel Aviv as press attaché. Three weeks later, Ritchie was invited to a diplomatic cocktail party at the Egyptian embassy, which opened after the 1979 peace treaty with Israel.

A simple handshake with a dark, handsome, young man put Ritchie's career onto a slippery slope downward to disgrace. She fell in love at first sight with Rifaat al-Ansari, second secretary of the Egyptian consulate. Israeli intelligence did not have to exert any great effort to uncover the ties between them. The two lovers did not even attempt to hide their relationship. They were seen at dozens of diplomatic receptions, or stealing kisses by candlelight in the small restaurants on Yirmiyahu Street in north Tel Aviv.

Perhaps the hot and humid Mediterranean summer and the heady feeling of liberation, so far from the dreary climate of Scotland, robbed the British diplomat of her good sense. She not only acceded to her Egyptian lover's advances, but also to his requests for information on secret telex messages that were sent to her embassy from London.

At the end of November, she handed Ansari a top secret document that gave details of the forthcoming visit of the British foreign secretary, Lord Peter Carrington, to the Middle East. If this information reached the wrong hands, such as a terrorist group, it could endanger Carrington's life.

Shin Bet had been watching and decided to put an end to the dangerous romance before it was too late. The Israelis furnished the British with a detailed report. Ritchie was then summoned to London on some supposed business, and she was arrested.

She admitted her guilt, expressed contrition, and cooperated with her interrogators. After her trial in the Old Bailey, she was given only a suspended sentence on November 29, 1982. The prosecutor, Sir Michael Havers, said, "I must admit that the behavior of the accused was more foolish than evil. She permitted herself to be so carried away by her involvement that she laid open to him secret telegrams."

Ritchie's world collapsed completely when she found out that her lover had a wife and children who had remained behind in Cairo. In truth, as the Israelis informed their British counterparts, Ansari was a professional intelligence officer using his good looks for his secret ends. Britain's sensationalist press had a field day, with headlines such as VIRGIN DIPLOMAT CHEATED BY ROMEO OF CAIRO and DON JUAN OF THE NILE.[7]

Israeli reporters in London, fascinated by the spicy mix of sex and espionage, avidly attended and reported on Ritchie's trial. By coincidence, as she left the courtroom, they saw another traitor brought to the dock. The reporters stayed to listen for a while, and they were glad they did. It was extremely rare for two cases in succession in Britain's highest criminal court to have an Israeli connection, but it turned out that Hugh Hambleton had also been spying in the Jewish state.

The KGB had recruited the professor, who held both Canadian and British citizenship, in the late 1940s. He turned out to be especially valuable to the Soviets when he got a job as an economist for NATO in Paris. British prosecutors said the professor caused "exceptionally grave damage" to the interests of the West.

As evidence of how much the Russians valued Hambleton, Yuri Andropov, the head of the KGB, who would later become leader of the Soviet Union, personally invited him to Moscow. At a festive banquet, they discussed Western defenses and specific assignments the professor had undertaken — notably, in Israel.

Hambleton broke down under questioning in the Old Bailey, changed his plea to guilty, and was sentenced to ten years in prison. He admitted that he visited Israel three times, in 1970, 1975, and 1978, entirely at Soviet expense. He did some legitimate economics research, but he had a lot of extra homework assigned by his KGB masters. During his first visit, Hambleton was assigned by his Soviet case officer in Austria, known only as "Paul," to find out whether Israel had produced atomic bombs and to investigate the extent of Israel's relations with South Africa.

Hambleton was also asked to prepare reports dealing with his field of expertise, economics. "Paul" asked him for details on the costs incurred by a Jewish immigrant in Israel: education, setting up a new business, acquiring a new home, and other specific questions researched by Hambleton. As the captured spy told his British MI5 interrogators, it was clear to him that he had been paving the way for the planting of Soviet agents in Israel.[8]

It is difficult to know to what extent Hambleton's report on how to plant an agent influenced the KGB, but on January 10, 1988, it became clear that a Soviet agent had been operating in the Jewish state since his arrival as an immigrant from Russia. The man in the mold of Israel Beer, who had been caught in 1961, was Shabtai Kalmanovitch — charged that January day in Tel Aviv District Court with spying for the Russians. He had been arrested by Shin Bet three weeks earlier, on his return from a visit to Eastern Europe.

When Kalmanovitch first left the Soviet Union for Israel in 1971, he was twenty-three years old and had already been recruited by the KGB. His case officers ordered him to become fully immersed in Israeli society, to build himself a strong economic base, and to befriend political and military leaders. Using Soviet funds, he acquired a reputation as a world-class businessman. His financial interests extended from Monte Carlo to Africa.

The seductive powers of wealth attracted friends with great influence in the Israeli army and government. One of them was Brigadier General Dov Tamari. Kalmanovitch invited Tamari, a former commander of a top sayeret unit, to visit Sierra Leone at the young Russian-Israeli's expense for some consulting work on security.

Kalmanovitch also fostered other ties with high-ranking politicians. At first he served as an adviser to eccentric parliamentarian Samuel Flatto-Sharon, who was a refugee from criminal charges in France. The job secured a valuable Knesset pass for the immigrant from Russia. He then helped Flatto-Sharon and New York congressman Benjamin Gilman when they worked with East Berlin lawyer Wolfgang Vogel to arrange a bizarre international prisoner exchange involving an American in East Germany, an Israeli in Mozambique, and a Russian in Pennsylvania.

Developing an appetite for bigger fish to befriend, Kalmanovitch invited cabinet ministers to lavish parties and business receptions at his ostentatious villa in a suburb of Tel Aviv. Many of his neighbors, intentionally or not, were senior men in the intelligence community. He even boasted that Golda Meir's door was open to him.

Kalmanovitch worked for a short time for the East European department of Israel's Labor party. He was assigned to ensure that new immigrants from the Soviet Union showed their gratitude to their new homeland by supporting Labor.

As a rule, the intelligence community sidestepped Israeli politics, but a few significant pockets of partisan bias remained in the mid-1970s. One of them was the Liaison Bureau. The Jewish immigration unit was considered an important political fortress, as it brought in new citizens who were sized up by all the parties to judge their electoral potential. Until Begin put Yehuda Lapidot in charge of the Liaison Bureau, Nehemiah Levanon had it in the Labor camp.

Especially when Labor was in power, until 1977, Kalmanovitch was in all the right places. During Begin's six years and afterward, the rich and influential Russian Jew continued to flutter around the edges of Israeli power centers until Shin Bet spotted him delivering secrets to known Communist agents in Europe in late 1987. On December 15, 1988, after a trial behind closed doors in Tel Aviv, Kalmanovitch was sentenced to nine years in prison.

Kalmanovitch's top-level connections and his ability to make friends in high places posed serious questions about Shin Bet's failure to spot him earlier. The damage he caused, however, was not severe. He was not able to gain access to secret defense installations, scientific institutes, or army bases.[9] He could tell his Russian masters what leading members of the Israeli establishment were thinking, but with very few details of what Israel was doing to protect itself.

By contrast, another Soviet spy who was planted as an immigrant was far more successful. Marcus Klingberg arrived in Israel much earlier and managed to burrow deep into the defense infrastructure of Israel.

Klingberg reached the newborn state's shore as an immigrant from Eastern Europe in 1948, when he was twenty years old. He studied the natural sciences, and at the end of the 1960s he was appointed deputy director of the government's high-security Biological Institute in the town of Nes Ziona, about ten miles south of Tel Aviv. As he seemed to be sickly, Klingberg would often travel to Switzerland for "therapy."

In 1983, Klingberg suddenly disappeared. Mysterious men came to the institute and took everything in his files. Shin Bet had discovered that the Swiss trips were visits to a Russian spymaster. With absolutely no publicity, he was charged with espionage, convicted in a secret trial, and sentenced to life in prison.

Klingberg caused serious damage because he had been one of the top men working on top secret projects at Nes Ziona. As early as 1973, the institute there was linked by foreign researchers to "topics related to chemical and biological warfare." United States intelligence analysts concluded that Israel, at the very least, was developing defensive measures against the poison gases believed to have been stockpiled by several Arab countries. There were even more frightening reports that Iraq in the 1980s was working on possible germ warfare. Israel would want to have stocks of vaccines and the means to monitor air and water against potential chemical or biological aggression.[10]

Penetration by Soviet spies was damaging, but Prime Minister Begin was willing to take other risks for the strategic goal of acting for the good of the Jews. For instance, he forged links with unsavory regimes around the world. In South America, Israel sold weapons and military know-how to Chile and Argentina, where the military juntas barely concealed their anti-Semitism. In return, the Israelis obtained pledges from the dictators in Santiago and Buenos Aires that they would protect the Jews and permit them to leave — with their cash and property.

A similar policy was adopted with Romania, the only Soviet-bloc state that preserved its diplomatic relations with Israel after all the other Communist countries severed theirs following the 1967 war. A key figure in the clandestine and special relationship with Romania's president, Nicolae Ceausescu, was a white-haired, elderly Israeli named Yeshayahu (Shaike) Trachtenberg-Dan.

In World War II Shaike Dan volunteered for the British army and parachuted, together with other young Palestinian Jews organized by Reuven Shiloah, behind the Nazi lines in the Balkans. He was one of the survivors who returned to Israel and joined the Liaison Bureau under Avigur and Levanon.[11]

Dan's secret activities made him a target for several Eastern European espionage services, but an American named Charles Jordan paid the price.

Jordan was a senior officer of the American Joint Distribution

Committee, a Jewish welfare organization known as "the Joint." He arrived in Prague, the Czechoslovak capital, on August 14, 1967. Two days later, he left his hotel and disappeared. When he failed to return, his wife reported his disappearance to the police. Four days after that, his body was lifted out of the Moldau River. The Communist authorities said that Jordan must have somehow fallen into the water and might even have committed suicide.

The secret services of the Soviet bloc always suspected that the Joint representatives were nothing but CIA operatives, and they were aware of the ties between the Joint and Israel's government. Jordan attracted quite a bit of attention from Communist intelligence operatives, especially as he had arrived in Prague from Jerusalem.

It can now be stated with near certainty that Charles Jordan was murdered — in a case of mistaken identity — by Communist agents. They believed that their victim was Israel's Shaike Dan.[12]

Undeterred, Dan continued to operate in Eastern Europe and he won President Ceausescu's agreement to permit the departure of Romania's Jewish citizens. In return, Israeli experts serviced Romanian tanks and other military equipment, and the Jewish state imported far more Romanian goods than it truly needed — as there is a limit to how much prune jam a country can use. With the help of Jewish welfare organizations in the West, Israel specifically agreed to pay three thousand dollars for each Jew permitted to leave. Officials said Romania was simply being compensated for the cost of educating its citizens, but it was clear to all sides that this was ransom being paid. Dan used to fly to Bucharest with a suitcase full of cash to make the payments. Israel also endorsed Romania's request for "most favored nation" trading status with the United States.

The only condition set by Ceausescu, which Israel accepted, was that these agreements not be publicized. This was not simply to protect his friendships with his sister Communist states or the Arab countries. Romania's president feared that other minority groups, especially those of German ethnicity, would press similar emigration demands upon his government. Ceausescu and his family received around half of the sixty million dollars in cash paid, over the years, by Israel until his downfall and execution in 1989.

The financial quid pro quo remained secret. In obvious contrast to the noisy policy adopted by Israel in demanding the freedom of emigration for Soviet Jews, Jerusalem maintained a low profile and absolute silence with regard to the Romanian Jews. Different circumstances call for different methods. The departures for Israel were therefore described officially in Bucharest as "reunification of families," and not as emigration.

Shaike Dan became a leading Western conduit to the Romanian leadership. He advised the U.S. government, and as an intelligence-community expert on the status of the Eastern European Jewish "family," Dan gave briefings to every Israeli leader from Golda Meir through Menachem Begin.[13]

In Begin's eyes, the Jewish family knew no borders and had to be reunified whenever and wherever opportunities could be found. Under him, the intelligence community became equally family-minded.

Ethiopia's Jews, while considered unique because their skins were dark, had the same strong desire as their Jewish brethren in Morocco, Romania, and the rest of the Arab world and Eastern Europe. The Jews of Ethiopia never stopped dreaming of the Bible's Promised Land. They called themselves *Beta Israel,* "the House of Israel," even though their non-Jewish neighbors labeled them with the derogatory term *Falashas,* which means "strangers" in the worst sense of the word — akin to "bastards" who belong nowhere.

In the distant past, they had been a mighty tribe of fighters with their own kingdom in the northern Ethiopian mountains. Gradually, after a series of setbacks in battles with other tribes, Beta Israel's power dwindled. By the middle of the twentieth century they numbered around twenty thousand people, concentrated primarily in Gondar and other districts. The Christian Ethiopians who controlled the surrounding regions prohibited purchases of land by "Falashas," and as a result the Jews became artisans and sharecroppers in a country where owning your own field gives the only real chance of having enough to eat.

In the early 1950s a handful of young Ethiopian Jews managed to reach Israel, and they applied pressure on the Israeli government to bring the rest of the Jews out. Despite excellent secret ties with Israel, the government of then emperor Haile Selassie refused to allow the Jews to emigrate. It was a matter of national pride: A respected emperor could not be seen to be losing his subjects.

The Labor-dominated Israeli government, on the other hand, did not go out of its way to help Ethiopian Jewry. Reuven Merhav, who worked in the Mossad station in Addis Ababa, recalls: "The Jews banged on the doors of our embassy. Their leaders begged us to get them out. But we sent them away crestfallen."[14]

The Israelis feared that merely bringing up the issue could ruin the strategic ties with Ethiopia — one of the key countries in the "peripheral" strategy of diplomatically outmaneuvering the Arab countries.

It was also significant that the Orthodox religious authorities in Israel declared their refusal to recognize the "black Jews," and that added to Israel's reluctance to help. The Ethiopian Jews continued to wait for a sign from Zion, but the sign was delayed. Only when Menachem Begin and his Likud won the 1977 election was there a dramatic change in Israel's approach, and for a few months it appeared that the Ethiopian Jews would realize their dream.

After speaking emotionally at the White House in Washington in July about the sufferings of the little-known Beta Israel, Begin brought up the specific points that had interested Ethiopia's Colonel Mengistu. President Carter refused, however, to change allegiances in the Horn of Africa so as to supply Ethiopia, rather than its hostile neighbor Somalia, with arms. In the U.S. administration's view, Colonel Mengistu's regime was tyrannical, Marxist, and unworthy of American support.

Begin's letter from Jerusalem to Addis Ababa, worded by his adviser Hurwitz, informed the colonel that Israel itself would supply the military aid. The result was two strange coalitions in northeastern Africa that can be explained only by the aphorism "Politics makes strange bedfellows." It could be added that international politics makes even stranger ones. Marxist Ethiopia was supported in 1977 by the Soviet Union, East Germany, and Israel, while Somalia had the support of the United States, Saudi Arabia, and Egypt.

In return, the Ethiopian government agreed to permit the departure of small numbers of Jews. Up until February 1978 two groups, totaling 220 Jews, were flown directly from Addis Ababa to Israel in Israeli cargo planes that had secretly brought weapons to Ethiopia.

Foreign Minister Dayan inexplicably uttered a careless remark that cut short the honeymoon between Ethiopia and Israel. Dayan admitted, in a news conference, that Israel was furnishing military supplies to the Ethiopian army. He quickly said that he meant uniforms, but it was clear that he meant weapons, and the revelation was enough to prompt Mengistu to cut the covert relations. His Jewish citizens would no longer be allowed to leave.

Begin, while angry at his foreign minister, was at least slightly comforted by Mossad chief Hofi's enthusiasm about finding alternative routes. While Hofi worked on his plans, Begin protected the security of the operation with his silence. He even had to tolerate, without responding, abuse being heaped upon him by international Jewish organizations. They complained that Israel was doing nothing in the face of reports that Ethiopia's Jews were being persecuted by their government, rebel groups, and gangs of robbers. The critics suggested that Israel might be apathetic because of the black skin of the "Falashas."

"Mr. Begin, you have to respond," Yehiel Kadishai begged the prime minister, as Kadishai could not stand seeing the attacks on the leader he revered. Begin, however, refused to budge. He was absolutely unwilling to reveal that action was, in fact, being taken.[15]

The Israeli prime minister knew in 1979 that the rescue operation was already in full swing. Young Ethiopians who had moved to Israel earlier were recruited to work for the Jewish state. Just as young Moroccan Jews had been sent on assignment to their own native land twenty years earlier, the Ethiopian Jews underwent a brief training period and were sent back where they had come from — now as secret agents of Israel.

The inexperienced Israeli operatives traveled to Jewish communities and proposed that whoever was able to leave should make their way, by a long and dangerous route, to neighboring Sudan. The Ethiopian-Israelis briefed the leaders of the Jewish villages and in some cases accompanied them on the perilous journey. Entire villages began to trek along unmarked trails. In many instances they were caught, tortured, and forced back to their villages.

Thousands died along the way, but those who managed to reach southern Sudan were lodged in a camp established twenty miles from the border. It was a cesspool of humanity — overcrowded, with insufficient food and no clean drinking water — administered, as best they could, by personnel of the United Nations High Commission for Refugees.

The only consolation for these Ethiopian Jews was that their condition was still better than that of other refugees in the camp. In their case, at least, there were often Israeli agents on hand to ensure that the

Jews received the best possible treatment. The clandestine envoys who were black mixed in with the Ethiopians, but there were also white Israelis who assumed various cover identities — as relief workers from Europe, for instance.

The next objective was to gain the clandestine cooperation of Sudan. The U.S. government helped apply pressure on President Gaafar Numeiri, a member of the Arab League and officially hostile to Israel, by offering financial assistance. Inevitably, this was little more than bribes paid into his personal bank accounts. Egypt also helped because Anwar Sadat was a personal friend of Numeiri and, at Begin's request, urged Sudan to help the Ethiopian Jews escape. Begin had thus found a valuable side benefit to his peace treaty with Egypt.

General Numeiri promised to turn a blind eye to the transport of Jews, so long as everything was kept secret. In order to work out the details, the Mossad sent a senior operative to Khartoum at the beginning of 1980, and he coordinated the operation with Abu Tayeb, the head of the Sudanese security services. The most convenient and effective method was to transfer the Jewish refugees by the shortest possible route — by sea to the port of Eilat — but Numeiri did not want his own shoreline to be used and demanded that, in any event, the Jews be moved via a third country and not directly from Sudan to Israel.

The Mossad and Sudan finally hammered out an arrangement whereby the Ethiopian Jews were moved through camps in southern Sudan, in coordination with UN field workers, and across the border into Kenya. The Kenyans were, of course, old allies of Israel and were parties to the secret agreement. This escape route was closed, however, after a small private airplane belonging to an American charity crossed the border from Sudan and had to make an emergency landing in Kenya. The occupants, including five Ethiopian Jews as the smuggled cargo, were arrested and a Nairobi newspaper published details of the clandestine operation — including information on the Mossad station in Kenya. The Nairobi government insisted on shutting down the flow of "Falashas" rather than risk the hostility of Arab and other African nations.

With no alternative immediately available the Mossad was forced, once more, to use its talent for improvisation. The agency again needed some foreign assistance, however, and this time Israel's operatives turned to the United States. The chief Mossad representative in Washington asked the CIA to help liberate Ethiopia's Jews, and the Americans agreed with surprising alacrity. With the new Reagan administration in office, the military and intelligence ties between the United States and Israel were at their strongest.

The Mossad and the CIA established a dummy corporation named Navco, which leased land by the Red Sea in Sudan with the stated intention of constructing a holiday village for undersea divers. Indeed, foreign divers did soon arrive in the area, but not the amateur variety who enjoyed looking at coral reefs. These were members of Israel's naval commando force.

The frogmen received Ethiopian Jews who were sent to the Navco village by Mossad operatives inland, and under the cover of nighttime darkness they took the refugees in small boats to Israeli vessels anchored offshore. The ships then sailed the Red Sea to Sharm esh-Sheikh, the southern tip of the Sinai Peninsula, then still occupied by Israel. The Ethiopians, soon to be Israelis, were then flown in cargo airplanes to air force bases in central Israel.

The Mossad assigned a team of photographers to record for posterity the final stages of the exodus. These films and videotapes were intended only for the archives of the secret agency, and they were considered extremely sensitive. An Israeli government cabinet meeting, however, was treated to a private showing, and several ministers — including Begin — could barely hold back their tears as the amazing saga unfolded on the screen. It made no difference that these Jews were dark-skinned. The sufferings and struggles which they had survived were clear, as was the joy they felt when finally reaching the soil of Israel.

Some of the ministers recalled the daring operations in which Jewish refugees from Nazi-ravaged Europe managed to reach the shores of pre-Israel Palestine. Now that the Jewish people had their own state, it seemed absurd that the techniques of illegal immigration had to be used again. But when no one wanted to go on record as aiding the Jews to escape the horrors of Ethiopia, the State of Israel had to resort to clandestine methods. The Red Sea route, through the bogus holiday village on the Sudanese coast, brought some two thousand Ethiopian Jews to Israel.

The operation's planners were concerned that the pace could not be stepped up. Thousands more Jewish refugees, having crossed the desert from Ethiopia despite difficulties of biblical proportions, were waiting for their chance to reach the Promised Land. Sudan's President Numeiri, meantime, knew that the Mossad and the CIA were using his country as a conduit, and he became increasingly concerned that the operation might be exposed. Numeiri could never explain to the anti-Zionist, fervently Moslem majority of Sudan why he was helping Israel. He was also afraid that radical Arab regimes, especially his neighbor and enemy, Libya, would discover his involvement with the Israelis and would brand him a traitor.

The Sudanese president thus took a firmer stand, insisting that the exodus between Ethiopia and Israel be thinned to a trickle. Unfortunately, this was just when the number of Jews leaving their villages and risking their lives to walk to Sudan increased tremendously into a mighty wave. Prime Minister Begin and Mossad chief Hofi knew that time was running out. They decided on a grandiose operation which they hoped would bring twenty thousand Jewish refugees to Israel in a very short period of time. It would be called Operation Moses.

The first step was to refurbish an old runway near the Sudanese town of Shubak. Then, one night in March 1984, two Hercules transport planes landed, speedily took on board two hundred Jews who had been brought by truck, and took off into the invisibility of the night sky. The operation, using unmarked aircraft belonging to Israel's air force, was repeated a number of times that month. The Mossad made sure not to leave anything on the ground that might indicate Israel's involvement, not even an empty cigarette pack or a matchbook.

A few Ethiopian Jews were flown out of Khartoum airport on commercial flights to Europe, to catch connections to Israel. The Mossad wanted to make more use of the airport, knowing it was far safer than the desert landing strip being used by Israeli crews, but President Numeiri would have to agree. His own troops would have to guard the airport and to keep curious onlookers away whenever special, unscheduled flights were about to leave.

At Israel's request, the United States promised further economic aid, $200 million, to Sudan in return for a promise by Numeiri that he would allow Jews to fly out of Khartoum. The key negotiator was George Weber of the U.S. embassy in Khartoum, working under the title "refugee coordinator."

To grease the wheels and to ensure Numeiri's final approval, the

Mossad deposited $60 million in European banks, primarily in Switzerland and London, to the accounts of Numeiri and a number of his aides, including Abu Tayeb. Much of the money was specially collected by Jewish fund raisers worldwide, who knew only that it was to "help the Falashas."

The Mossad also persuaded George Mittelman, a Belgian millionaire who was also a religious Jew, to help the secret project. Mittelman was ideal, simply because he owned an airline — the little-known Trans Europe Airlines. Even better, TEA pilots and crews had plenty of experience with Khartoum airport as they regularly flew devout Moslems from Sudan to Mecca, Saudi Arabia, during the annual *hajj* pilgrimage. Mittelman agreed to place his airplanes at Israel's disposal, and to keep his mouth shut. He did consult Belgium's Prime Minister Wilfried Martens and Justice Minister Jean Gol, who was responsible for the Belgian secret service and just happened to be Jewish. They both gave Mittelman the nod to help the Israelis.

From November 21, 1984, until the first week of 1985, thirty-five flights left from Khartoum's international airport, carrying seven thousand immigrants to Brussels. After a two-hour refueling stop at TEA's home base, the airplanes headed back toward the southeast — but this time to Israel. The operation worked with the precision of a Swiss watch, and it always took a day off on Saturdays because the Ethiopian Jews devoutly honored the Jewish Sabbath.

Even though hundreds of people in Israel and abroad knew about Operation Moses, the secret leaked no further. The editors of the Israeli newspapers agreed not to publish any reports that Ethiopian Jews were arriving, and even the foreign correspondents based in Israel who heard about it displayed sufficient responsibility not to file any dispatches that might jeopardize the operation.

Instead, it was an Israeli official who was unable to hold his tongue. Operation Moses met a premature death because of the indiscretion of Yehuda Dominitz, a senior official of the Jewish Agency. His office had become an active participant in the arrival and accommodation of the Ethiopian Jews, and in worldwide fund raising. At the beginning of January 1985, Dominitz was interviewed by an obscure Hebrew-language journal, *Nekudah,* or "Point," published by Jewish settlers in the occupied West Bank. They had high hopes that Ethiopians would come and help expand the controversial settlements. Dominitz unnecessarily gave details of the amazing project to rescue

Ethiopian Jewry, and the four hundred foreign correspondents in Israel saw this as a signal to quote the journal and report fully on the entire operation.

The cat had leapt out of its bag, and there was nothing for Israel's leaders to do but celebrate the success — so far — of their formerly secret project in Africa. The new prime minister, Shimon Peres, had been in his job for only three months. He hurriedly convened a press conference and answered any and all questions on how Israel had brought some ten thousand Ethiopian Jews to their "historic homeland." Peres, the Labor party leader, apparently wanted to take credit for an operation that had begun at the initiative of Begin and his Likud.

The story was important news throughout the world. As President Numeiri had feared, the Arab states and the PLO's Yasser Arafat condemned him as a "traitor" for having helped the "Zionists" recruit added manpower for their army. On January 5, two days after Peres's press conference, the Sudanese government informed Washington that the exodus of the Ethiopians through Khartoum would have to stop at once. Ethiopia followed suit, by closing its border with Sudan and accusing both Numeiri and the Israelis of "kidnapping" Ethiopian citizens.

In Sudan itself, there still remained over a thousand so-called Falashas, mainly young people, because Israel's policy had been to evacuate the sick, the old, and the women first. Under further pressure from the United States, with the personal intervention of then vice president George Bush, Numeiri agreed that six U.S. Air Force Hercules planes could land on a deserted airfield near one of the refugee camps on March 28, 1985. There the Americans picked up the remaining Jews and flew them directly to Israel.

Numeiri's days were numbered. A short while later, he was deposed by a military coup. In a twist of historical irony, the new prime minister was Sidki el-Mahdi, the same Sudanese politician who initiated secret contacts with Israel in London in 1954. Numeiri and other government leaders, including secret service chief Abu Tayeb, were tried in absentia. They were accused of corruption, accepting bribes from the Mossad and the CIA, and collaborating with the Israeli enemy. Numeiri found asylum in Cairo, by courtesy of his friend Hosni Mubarak, successor of the slain Sadat. The worst part of the matter was that nearly ten thousand Jews still remained in Ethiopia. They continued to suffer there, along with nearly all the people of that arid land.[16]

An interim summary of this amazing operation, possibly the most remarkable epic in the history of Israel's "Jewish intelligence" — in many ways a greater achievement than Iraq, Yemen, and Morocco combined — can be given in a single sentence: Begin initiated, Sadat mediated, Dayan botched, Hofi rectified, Reagan paid, Peres talked, and Numeiri was ruined.[17]

The tragic and unexpected end of Operation Moses exposed, for the first time, clandestine links that had remained happily hidden for years. Israelis were displeased by the exposure and the fact that thousands of Jews were still stranded in Africa. However, much that was positive had been accomplished. Begin had achieved his twin goals of securing his place in history books as a peacemaker and ensuring that Israel would act for the good of the Jews. But he also embarked on a third path, and this was the start of a new period in the history of Israeli intelligence: the era of adventurism and of major failures.

TWELVE

The Age of Adventurism

THE STILLNESS OF THE HOT MORNING was shattered in the West Bank by three explosions before eight o'clock on June 2, 1980, and so were the bodies of three Palestinian mayors. The fiery and popular Bassam Shaka of Nablus, the elegant English-style gentleman Karim Khalaf of Ramallah, and the quiet Muhammad Tawil of El-Bireh barely survived bombs planted in their cars outside their homes.

Outrage and sympathy were expressed around the world for the politicians, who lost limbs and did not conceal their "feeling" that the Israeli authorities were responsible. The army, meantime, launched an investigation and Prime Minister Begin denied any official complicity in the attacks. Many Israelis suggested that the mayors were attacked by fellow Palestinians, and there certainly were many precedents for radical factions killing Arabs who were considered too moderate or too close to the Israelis.

Behind the scenes, however, Shin Bet director Avraham Ahituv believed that the attackers were most likely Jews. If investigators pursued the trail, it would probably lead to the controversial Jewish settlements in the West Bank. Ultranationalist settlers had the means and the motive to terrorize the Arab mayors. Based on the sophistication of the car bombs and the absence of fingerprints and other physical clues, there was also reason to believe that the underground group responsible had to be taken very seriously — as a law enforcement challenge, without regard to political considerations.

Ahituv met with Begin and asked for permission to plant Shin Bet agents as spies among the Jewish settlers. In the 1950s, 1960s, and 1970s, networks of wiretaps and informants had been used effectively against extreme left-wing Jews in Israel. Senior Shin Bet officers always believed that the Left was susceptible to subversion from outside, whether by Soviet intelligence or by Arab interests.

In the years after the 1967 war, however, the extreme Right became a growing source of concern. This Jewish fringe group developed a Messianic complex, religious fanaticism, extreme nationalism, and implacable hatred of the Palestinians.

Shin Bet was granted a free hand in surveillance of one of the right-wing organizations, Rabbi Meir Kahane's Kach party. An Israeli successor to the Jewish Defense League founded by Kahane in the United States, Kach had a political platform calling for the expulsion of all Arabs from Israel and the occupied territories. Shin Bet agents infiltrated Kahane's party, filing full reports on what was happening within so there would be advance warning if a maniacal member were to embark on a campaign of murder or mayhem. Kach activists were arrested from time to time, based on tips received from informers.[1]

Over the years a number of other Israelis belonging to tiny, naive, mentally unstable, or ephemeral groups were arrested for planning to attack Arab civilians or even to blow up the sacred mosques on the Temple Mount in Jerusalem. Many devout Jews believed that the Moslem places of worship would have to be flattened before the Messiah could come and save the world, for he would build a third Holy Temple for the Jews in place of the gold and silver domes of the Omar and el-Aqsa mosques and would then proceed to save the world.

Shin Bet was effective against the so-called nut cases but had a much more delicate task when it came to West Bank settlers. Most of them were widely considered to be hard-working patriots, and they had excellent and obvious ties to Begin and his Likud establishment.

As Ahituv had feared, the prime minister rejected his request to plant spies among the settlers. Begin put aside the professionalism required for security and intelligence, in favor of emotional and political considerations that dictated doing nothing.

This was a different Begin from the one who took office in 1977. After securing his role as a peacemaker by making compromises to achieve a peace treaty with Egypt, the "real" Menachem Begin — the highly nationalistic demagogue, as depicted by his opponents — was yearning to break out of his moderate shell. By 1980, a year after making history with Egypt's charismatic president Anwar Sadat, Begin began to fall under the spell of General Ariel Sharon.

Known to friends and foes alike as "Arik," Sharon also had plenty of charisma. He was born in 1928 as Ariel Scheinerman on a farm north of Tel Aviv and was raised on socialist dogma. Later choosing the Hebrew name Sharon, he remained in the embrace of Zionism's dominant Labor movement.

He showed great courage and skill during his obligatory military service and decided to make the army his career. Sharon was wounded in the 1948 war, but in 1953 he helped set up Israel's special forces as head of a famous and feared commando platoon known as Unit 101 — the forerunner of the élite sayeret forces introduced later. A response to Palestinian terrorist attacks, Unit 101 had only forty-five men and existed for only a short while. In Sharon's words, they were "five months that were to have a fundamental impact on the country's effort to rid itself of terrorism."[2]

"We had a group that was ready to strike back," added Sharon, who led his men across the borders into Arab countries on retaliation raids. The soldiers of Unit 101 were rough, tough, and bedazzled by Sharon. Their most notorious attack was against a Jordanian village, Kibbiya, on the night of October 14, 1953. Responding to the murder of an Israeli woman and her two children, Unit 101 and some support troops entered Kibbiya with a huge quantity of explosives. Most of the fifteen hundred residents fled, before the Israelis flattened nearly fifty houses. The explosions killed sixty-nine men, women, and children who had been hiding in their homes. Years after the international furor that ensued, Sharon said it was an inadvertent "tragedy" that civilians had lost their lives.[3]

Condemnations from the United Nations and elsewhere prompted Israel's army to dissolve Unit 101, making it part of the paratroop corps. Sharon's reputation soared, however, as he was promoted to commander of the paratroops and was a definite candidate to become army chief of staff.

His paratroops did far more than jump out of airplanes. Sharon called them "anti-terror guerrillas, unconventional fighters" who in 1971 took on the task of eliminating terrorism from the occupied Gaza Strip. The Israelis regularly dressed as Arabs and even posed as guerrillas in order to infiltrate enemy cells. In seven months, by the general's own count, his men killed 104 Palestinians and arrested 742 others.[4]

Sharon never did make it to the army's top job. While he certainly commanded the respect and loyalty of a legion of lifelong friends, he also rubbed many other people the wrong way. Disappointed, Sharon resigned from the army — by coincidence a mere three months before the Yom Kippur War of 1973.

He immediately returned to duty to help reverse Israel's early setbacks in the war, daringly driving west of the Suez Canal into the Egyptian mainland to force a cease-fire. Sharon then channeled his ambitions and tactical genius into politics. The Labor party already had plenty of generals in starring roles, and he decided he could do better in a political party where he could play first fiddle. Sharon thus found his way to the Liberal party, which despite its name was a right-wing group.

With his limitless energy, Sharon quickly managed to persuade several parties in what was then a fragmented right-wing opposition to merge under the roof of a single umbrella organization that named itself Likud, Hebrew for "consolidation" or "unity." In less than four years, Sharon would see his creation win the voters' mandate to rule the nation.

After Likud's election victory in 1977, Sharon plotted tactics on the battlefield of government bureaucracy. With his military background, he understood the importance of controlling and supervising the intelligence community. Intelligence means information, and information means power. The retired general perceived Israeli intelligence as a state within a state — conducting its own foreign policy and influencing defense and domestic policies. Sharon took a keen interest in such autonomy.

Knowing that Begin was planning to bestow the defense ministry on General Ezer Weizman, the former air force commander who masterminded the Likud election campaign, Sharon nominated himself to head a new ministry of intelligence. Similar suggestions had been made a dozen years earlier, in 1966, when another general — Yigal Allon — had been considered for such a post, but it was never created. In Sharon's vision, the ministry would be in charge of all the intelligence agencies and could even take Aman away from the defense ministry.

Begin rejected Sharon's proposal and instead gave him the agriculture ministry. The war hero used the post to launch his own offensive: allocating budgets for the construction in the occupied territories of Jewish settlements, which he called "facts on the ground," as though defying the outside world to remove the Jews from the land they had captured. While waiting for greater opportunities to arise, Sharon closely monitored the quarrel between the prime minister and Shin Bet chief Ahituv over the 1980 car bombings.

Ahituv was thinking of resigning. Begin was stonewalling his demand for a tougher investigation of the apparent outbreak of Jewish terrorism. The Shin Bet chief knew, however, that his sudden departure would severely jolt the domestic security agency and whip up a huge political storm that would benefit no one. He decided to swallow his professional pride, toiling on for another year.

When Ahituv finally left Shin Bet in 1981, intelligence-community insiders who were asked to deliver a critique said that he had made a mistake by requesting Begin's permission to spy on the settlers. If the Shin Bet chief believed there was subversion and violence in Israeli society, they said, then he should have used his own judgment and authority to plant a network of informers among the Jews of the West Bank.

In the absence of any solid information on the car bombers, Shin Bet and the army were unable to stop the "Jewish underground" from continuing along the path of violence. Several West Bank settlers were dressed as Arabs when they burst into the courtyard of the Islamic University in Hebron in July 1983, spraying the students with bullets and killing three Palestinians. That crime, too, remained unsolved until May 1984.

There was a turning point in that month of May, when Israeli police in Jerusalem discovered twelve bombs attached to Arab buses in East Jerusalem, carrying passengers including children. A bloodbath was narrowly averted, and this time Shin Bet was able to pounce. The explosives were of the type used by Israel's army, indicating that soldiers or reservists had pilfered them from military arsenals.

Shin Bet knew exactly whom to arrest, because by 1984 it did have agents planted in the Jewish underground. Begin had resigned the previous year, and the new Shin Bet chief — Avraham Shalom, who had been Ahituv's deputy — took it upon himself to crack the case no matter what was required. The terrorist cell, it was found, consisted of around twenty Jewish settlers dedicated to killing and intimidating Palestinians. The Jews were treated somewhat more gently by Shin Bet than are Arab terrorists, but still the suspects confessed all and were tried, convicted, and imprisoned.

*

While Begin, as prime minister, could be criticized for hesitating when law and order were challenged by the Jewish underground, he certainly showed no patience or mercy toward threats from abroad. Peace with Egypt did not mean he had gone soft, as Begin proved with a bold decision in 1981. On June 4, fourteen F-16 and F-15 fighter-bombers of the Israeli air force destroyed the Iraqi nuclear reactor in Baghdad. Militarily, it was a singularly successful operation that showed great accuracy and exceptional intelligence over an unprecedented distance from Israel.

The background to the attack shows the key role of the intelligence community in Begin's fearless foreign policy. The Mossad and Aman had been watching and waiting from the first moment that Iraq's intention to purchase a nuclear reactor from France became known. The possibility that any Arab state — especially radical Iraq — would obtain nuclear weapons that could threaten the Jewish state kept Israeli leaders awake at night.

It was in November 1975 that France formally agreed to supply Iraq with two nuclear reactors, a small one for research and a larger one with a capacity of 70 megawatts. The Iraqis dubbed the project Tammuz, based on the name of a Canaanite god and referring to the Arabic month in which the Ba'ath socialist party came to power in 1968.[5]

Until Begin became prime minister in 1977, the Israeli government had used quiet diplomacy in attempts to dissuade France and other countries, such as Italy and Brazil, from supplying Iraq with the equipment, uranium, and technical know-how which they had agreed to furnish for Project Tammuz. Israel also asked the United States to intervene, hoping that President Carter's campaign to prevent the proliferation of nuclear weapons might influence France. The quiet approaches were fruitless, however. The construction of the nuclear reactors at a secret location near Baghdad continued apace.

Begin decided to adopt an entirely new policy. He called in his intelligence chiefs and declared that henceforth the destruction of the larger, potentially weapons-producing Iraqi reactor would be considered one of Israel's supreme national goals. Begin ordered them to make every possible effort to obtain information on the Tammuz One reactor: how quickly it was being built and the extent of cooperation between Iraq and other nations.

More than any other Israeli leader, Begin was haunted by the Nazi

Holocaust. He regarded the extermination of six million European Jews not only as a terrible event in history, but as a clear warning of present dangers. The prime minister, as a result, established a new doctrine: Israel would not permit any Arab state to develop an offensive nuclear capability.

Begin's secret battalions went quickly into action. A team of agents arrived in Toulon, France, by various routes in the first week of April 1979. Their objective was a large storehouse in the seaside town of La Seyne-sur-Mer, where two cores for the Tammuz nuclear reactors were awaiting shipment to Iraq. French authorities later said it was an extremely professional job: explosives attached to the cores themselves, timers set for 3:00 A.M., and not a trace of the attackers when the blast occurred.

A French ecology group claimed responsibility for the bombing, but this was not taken seriously. France's SDECE intelligence agency quickly concluded that the destruction of the nuclear components was an act on behalf of Israel, almost certainly committed by the Mossad.[6]

Begin and the Israeli intelligence community hoped that France would use the explosion as an excuse to terminate its aid to Iraq, but within a very short time their hopes were dashed. The French government announced that it would honor its agreements with Iraq and would supply it with new cores.

Begin turned to what he considered Israel's last remaining course of action: the military option against Iraq itself. In coordination with chief of staff Raful Eitan, Begin ordered the Mossad and Aman to investigate the possibility of a direct attack by ground forces — whether army sayeret commandos or some sort of irregulars — on the Iraqi reactor. Explosives primed and placed by people were more likely to be accurate than an attack from the air. But General Eitan also ordered the air force to build a full-scale model of the reactor, based on espionage reports, and to practice bombing it.[7]

As the preparations for an attack began, major differences emerged among Israeli decision makers. A raid on Baghdad, the longest ever attempted by the air force, was being considered and planned with a general election on the horizon. With just a few weeks to go before polling on June 7, 1981, opposition leader Shimon Peres and former army generals in his Labor party learned of the plans from friends and ex-colleagues in the military and intelligence establishments.

Peres approached Begin to urge that Iraq not be attacked. Privately, Labor leaders feared that a raid on the reactor would enhance the popularity of the Likud and Begin among voters.

Some of the most influential voices in the intelligence community also opposed the overt military option. Mossad chief Yitzhak Hofi and Shlomo Gazit, head of Aman until Yehoshua Saguy replaced him in February 1979, believed that there was still a long time before the Iraqi reactor would be "hot," the operational stage at which it could begin to pose a real danger. These intelligence men, perhaps even representing a majority, suggested mounting a firmer diplomatic initiative. They warned that bombing Baghdad might prompt Iraq and Iran to call off their Gulf War and unite against Israel — just when the war that began in 1980 seemed to be serving Israel's interests — and would certainly trigger a tidal wave of international condemnation.[8]

On the other hand, a strong coalition of Likud cabinet members led by Ariel Sharon rallied around General Eitan in supporting the raid. Prime Minister Begin was certainly sold on the idea, and Aman commander Saguy planned the operation with enthusiasm and efficiency. The attack was executed to perfection only three days before election day. The Likud bloc triumphed at the polls, too, and Begin won a second term as prime minister.

It turned out that the Begin-Sharon-Eitan view of the international repercussions was also correct. The woeful warnings from Peres, Hofi, Gazit, and others in intelligence proved wrong. Israel suffered little diplomatic damage, largely because the Americans and Soviets were tacitly relieved that Iraq's nuclear Tower of Babylon was flattened. The superpowers said little. More importantly, the new socialist president of France, François Mitterrand, this time used the attack as an excuse to scale down nuclear cooperation with Iraq. France decided not to replace the reactor which Israel had demolished.

The attack on Baghdad was the launching pad for the Begin government's new approach to problems on the foreign front after Likud's reelection in 1981. The prime minister was aggressive and adventurous when he felt it was necessary in the defense of Israel, and some of his own cabinet colleagues were astounded by his willingness to take great risks.

A clear expression of the second-term policy tone was the appointment of Sharon as minister of defense. For more than a year, Begin had stubbornly confined Sharon to the agriculture portfolio in the cabinet. Rather than give Sharon the job he fervently wanted, Begin had even served as defense minister himself, after Ezer Weizman resigned as a protest against the new, militant approach. Continuing to resist, Begin remarked — only half in jest — that "the day that Sharon is appointed minister of defense, he will surround the prime minister's office with tanks."[9]

Sharon's conquest of the defense ministry was, for him, the realization of a cherished dream. It was also not enough for him. In one way or another, he still wished to take control of the intelligence community.

He had already persuaded Begin to appoint Rafi Eitan, an old Sharon crony, as counterterrorism adviser to the prime minister. Not to be confused with the army chief of staff, Raful Eitan, Rafi Eitan was the seasoned intelligence man who scored his greatest coup in the kidnap team which captured Adolf Eichmann in 1960.

Eitan is known in the intelligence community as Rafi ha-Masriach, "Rafi the Smelly," not because of any unsavory activities but because he had to wade through sewage while on a pre-1948 sabotage mission for the Palmach against the British in Palestine. He was born in 1926 on Kibbutz Ein Harod, in Israel's Jezreel valley. After going to the movies once with his mother, he told her: "I want to be a spy like Mata Hari." Decades later, he might have more aptly named James Bond as his role model. Eitan turned his childhood fantasies into childhood reality, because he was undertaking secret missions for the Haganah from the age of twelve.

He was wounded on the day of Israel's statehood, May 15, 1948, and then joined an intelligence unit of the army. After the War of Independence, he was recruited by Isser Harel and served in the joint operations department of Shin Bet and the Mossad. Formally in Shin Bet from 1950 to 1953, then transferring to the Mossad where he became chief of operations, Eitan was involved in practically every spectacular staged by the intelligence community. When Eichmann was hanged in 1961, Eitan was a witness in the prison. The Nazi war criminal's last words, "I hope soon you will follow me," were directed at Eitan.[10]

The veteran senior operative felt compelled to resign in 1972 when he learned that he had no chance of being chosen to replace Mossad chief Zvi Zamir. Eitan had sharp operational and personal disagreements with Zamir and later with his successor, Hofi, when Eitan was called upon as a consultant. Eitan began to share his friend Sharon's view that the Mossad needed to be reformed, tamed, and even weakened.

At age forty-six in 1972, Eitan tried his hand at various businesses from raising tropical fish to dealing in West Bank land. But, as many others before him who had attempted to exchange their cloak and dagger for civilian clothes, Eitan was unable to make a success of it. Sharon saved his old friend from sinking into further boredom and returned him to government service in 1978 as the official counterterrorism expert: a coordinating job with little authority, on the edge of the intelligence community.

Sharon also discovered, within the defense ministry, the intelligence treasure known as Lakam — the Science Liaison Bureau — the existence of which was known to very few people. A systematic and thorough man, Sharon studied Lakam's history in the secret files of the ministry, noting how the agency had transformed itself from protector of the Dimona reactor's security to a wider role in actively procuring materials needed for Israel's defense.

Many within the defense and intelligence apparatus considered Lakam director Binyamin Blumberg a genius, although his duties and activities were not precisely known. Sharon was not pleased, however, to note that Lakam had become a private fiefdom that did almost anything it wished to, without feeling accountable to anyone.

When the leading lights of the intelligence community had periodically asked for a report on Lakam's actions, Blumberg simply had ignored them. Defense Minister Dayan gave the supersecret "science liaison" agency his full support, but without ever wanting to know exactly what it was up to. He delegated responsibility for Lakam to his assistant, General Zvi Zur. The general, who had been army chief of staff in the early 1960s, gave Blumberg a free hand. The liberal attitude extended even further when Shimon Peres returned to the defense ministry in 1974, after an absence of eleven years — this time as minister of defense who replaced Dayan after the humiliation of the Yom Kippur War.

Among the few Israelis who knew of Lakam there were some who complained that Blumberg was far too partial to his friends, giving them information and freelance assignments that helped make them rich. There were even nasty rumors that the Lakam chief was profiting personally, although few people doubted his ascetic probity and modest lifestyle. Still, defense ministry authorities felt they had to look into the complaints about questionable management of Lakam.

After Menachem Begin and his right-wing Likud bloc took office in May 1977, the efforts to dismiss Blumberg intensified. In the eyes of the new administration, he was linked to the old Labor party establishment.

Likud's deputy minister of defense, Brigadier General Mordecai Zippori, suspected that some of Lakam's operations involved laundering money for the Labor Party. He tried to persuade his boss, Ezer Weizman, to fire Blumberg in 1979 on the grounds that there were no controls over him. Defense Minister Weizman convened a meeting and secured Blumberg's agreement to report more fully and more frequently to him.

Sharon read Lakam's history, heard even more from various advisers, and then took the complaints against Blumberg more seriously than had his predecessor Weizman. More than grievances, these were charges of wrongdoing from employees of Lakam who offered evidence that the agency had been laundering ill-earned money.

As far as Sharon was concerned, he did not need specifics to dismiss Blumberg. The new defense minister had planned to put his own, anti-Labor man in anyway, but now he had an excuse. The complaints spread as rumors and grew into slander, and while they were mostly without foundation they made it easier to fire Blumberg. After his three decades in the intelligence community, including more than twenty years as head of Lakam, there was naturally a tremendous storm about his departure in 1981 — but only within the community; there was not one mention in the Israeli press.

To impose order and his own will, Sharon quickly put his friend Rafi Eitan in charge of Lakam. For the first time since the days of Reuven Shiloah and the nine months of Meir Amit's overlapping jobs, a senior official in the intelligence community not only wore two hats but was subordinate to two bosses. Holding the position of counterterrorism adviser to the prime minister, Eitan was under Begin; whereas as head of Lakam, he was under Sharon.

The coup in Lakam was an important step in Sharon's efforts to become the dominant figure in Israel's security-intelligence establishment. Two independent organizations stood in his way, however: Shin Bet and the Mossad. Sharon knew that no prime minister would agree to forgo his direct ministerial supervision over these two agencies, but he did hope to persuade Begin to replace their two chiefs. He was especially interested in removing Yitzhak Hofi from the Mossad.

The enmity between Sharon and Hofi stemmed not only from basic differences in their views of politics, defense, and the role of intelligence. It also included an undercurrent of mutual hostility extending back many years. Following the Suez campaign in 1956, four battalion commanders in the paratroops brigade "rebelled" against their brigadier, Colonel Ariel Sharon. The head of the "rebels" was his deputy, Lieutenant Colonel Yitzhak Hofi. Suggesting that their commander was a coward, they said that Sharon had not led his men into battle, as he always preached was a commander's duty. Instead, they alleged, he had preferred to remain in the rear.

Sharon and the rebels turned to two neutral officers to settle their dispute, but the arbitrators reached conflicting conclusions and could not agree on a ruling. This strange episode had been kept secret for many years, but Sharon is credited with having the memory of an elephant and did not forget Hofi's mutiny.[11]

Sharon intended to seize his once-in-a-lifetime chance to settle his old score with Hofi. The long-range destruction of the Iraqi nuclear reactor in June 1981 increased his chances of doing so. Hofi had displeased Begin by counseling against the raid on Baghdad.

The Mossad chief was not, however, cowed in any way by Sharon. Hofi was aware that within twelve months, he would be completing eight years in the Mossad, the longest that any person had remained at the helm since Isser Harel. The time to retire was approaching. In any event, rather than assume a bureaucratically defensive posture, Hofi embarked on a vehement and unprecedented attack.

On June 18, 1981, without seeking Begin's permission, Hofi was interviewed by the Israeli newspaper *Ha'aretz* — as the anonymous "chief of the Mossad" — and warned that politicians should stop talking too much to take credit for the air raid on the Iraqi reactor.

While he could not be named, under Israeli law, Hofi's statements still marked the first time that the head of the Mossad had been interviewed on the record. He claimed that, because of numerous leaks to the media about the Baghdad bombing, "tremendous damage is being caused, and it is liable to affect sources of information and ties with parties outside Israel."[12]

By the nature of things, this interview invited interpretations and guesses as to whom exactly the Mossad chief had in mind. A number of journalists who were close friends of Hofi gave the answer: they said that he had been referring to Sharon and newspaper columnist Uri Dan, one of the controversial minister's closest friends.

As could be expected, Sharon responded to Hofi in kind. Dan himself published a vitriolic attack on the unnamed Mossad chief in the afternoon newspaper *Ma'ariv,* claiming that the interview had supplied the Labor opposition with ammunition and that the intelligence chief had intended that precise goal: to serve the Labor party that had appointed him to his position.

Dan also claimed that Hofi was in constant contact with the leaders of the opposition, had leaked secrets to them, and had misled the prime minister by not supplying him with accurate information on the Iraqi nuclear reactor. The *Ma'ariv* columnist explicitly called upon Begin to dismiss the Mossad chief.[13]

The prime minister refused to respond to Dan's call, even though it was well known that the power behind the article was Sharon and even though Begin himself had been angered by Hofi's unauthorized interview.[14] Dan's column was considered too angry, too biased, and too politically divisive. The editors of *Ma'ariv* were displeased, and Dan quit the newspaper in favor of a new job: media adviser to Sharon and spokesman for the defense ministry.

Hofi, however, was still the head of the Mossad. As an experienced military tactician, Sharon could see that his objectives were not being reached by a frontal attack and changed his approach in favor of an indirect strategy. He helped set up various "forums," mostly unofficial think tanks comprising government officials and private citizens. Political opponents referred to these meetings in the defense minister's office in Tel Aviv as "the war room" or "Arik's court."

The participants in what rapidly became an influential tool included Rafi Eitan; another former Mossad operative, Rehaviah Vardi, whom Sharon had appointed as the government's "coordinator" in the occupied territories; Major General Avraham Tamir, the minister's assistant for planning and strategy; private arms merchant and Aman veteran Yaakov Nimrodi; and, from time to time, David Kimche, the veteran operative in Africa who had risen to the number-two job in the Mossad before leaving to become director general of the foreign ministry.

For a quarter of a century, from the day that he joined the Mossad as a British-born academic in 1953, Kimche dreamed of heading the agency. At the end of the 1970s Kimche believed that he had an excellent chance, because Begin apparently considered him Hofi's natural successor. Hofi was not going to allow it, however, as he strongly resented Kimche for acting as though he were a one-man organization — frequently vanishing on mysterious missions that no one else, including the agency chief, knew about. In the Mossad, the globe-trotting Kimche was known as "the man with the suitcase." Hofi also accused his deputy of wasting money. Kimche denied all the charges but finally was unwilling to remain where he was clearly unwanted. He resigned from the Mossad in 1980.

Kimche accepted a job offer from his former Mossad colleague and respected elder, Foreign Minister Yitzhak Shamir. Kimche became director general of the foreign ministry, although without giving up his ambition to be the Mossad chief one day. He maintained contact with his old colleagues and continued to keep up to date with what was happening within the agency.

Rafi Eitan, the Mossad veteran with similar ambitions, began to expand the activities of Lakam, the Science Liaison Bureau given to him by his friend Sharon. The shadowy agency's concerns did not simply stop at scientific liaison, and Eitan achieved a tenfold increase in what intelligence professionals call "productivity." If the Lakam people had laid their hands on two hundred documents a year in the old days of Binyamin Blumberg, the annual figure under Eitan reached two thousand.

Lakam began to enter gray areas overseas, an operational no-man's land which should have been the sole province of the Mossad. Eitan also found himself in incessant confrontations and disputes with the Mossad, when acting in his other capacity as counterterrorism adviser to the prime minister.

Hofi strongly resented Eitan's independent operations, and the head of the Mossad complained both to Begin and to his fellow secret service chiefs in the Varash committee.

There was more good news for Sharon from the intelligence community when Avraham Ahituv was replaced as head of Shin Bet by Avraham Shalom, who was previously named Bendor. He was an old friend of Rafi Eitan and worked with him on field operations including the Argentine kidnap of Eichmann in 1960. Sharon and Shalom were on the same wavelength on many issues.

Sharon was also pleased by the likelihood that another of his allies would take over at the Mossad. Major General Yekutiel (Kuti) Adam, a military man who had worked on joint projects with the espionage agency, was Begin's firm favorite to succeed Yitzhak Hofi. Adam and Sharon were paratroopers together in the 1950s.

Sharon's self-confidence kept growing, and he did not shy away from efforts to reformulate Israel's foreign and defense policies. In December 1981, the new defense minister delivered a wide-ranging speech which declared that Israel's security interests extended beyond the region of its direct confrontation with the Arab states and included also Pakistan, the North African states, and even more distant parts of Africa.[15]

Sharon did not limit himself to words. Faithful to his views, he attempted to implement them through a variety of political, strategic, and intelligence projects.

The Mossad soon found itself confronted by the independent activities of Sharon's friends: former Mossad agent Nimrodi, and Nimrodi's business partner Al Schwimmer, former chief executive of Israel Aircraft Industries. Their wheeling and dealing often brought them into contact with Arab merchants and politicians, and their policy adviser and conduit to Israeli power centers was Sharon.

Nimrodi, who had lost millions of dollars when Ayatollah Khomeini's Islamic legions overthrew the Shah of Iran, continued to lobby on behalf of Western contacts with Teheran. As an acknowledged expert, he hoped to lead the West back into the potential market of 45 million Iranians. In part, he hoped to regain his lost investments. He considered himself a supreme patriot, but the line that separated Nimrodi's own interests from those of the State of Israel was often blurred.

Nimrodi and Schwimmer met Saudi billionaire Adnan Khashoggi, cooperated in a few business ventures, and enjoyed trading ideas which they thought could lead to peace in the Middle East. The three men believed in coexistence through capitalist cooperation. The Khashoggi connection helped Nimrodi obtain a secret political document drawn up by the crown prince and heir apparent to the Saudi throne, Prince Fahd. It was quite a coup for Nimrodi and that naturally rankled the Mossad, which accused him of "running around underfoot" and disturbing their work.[16]

The document, known as the "Fahd Plan," spoke for the first time of Saudi recognition of the Jewish state. Nimrodi brought it to Israel even before it was published in Riyadh. He was excited about it and liked the idea that all the Saudis wanted, in exchange for working for peace and mutual recognition between Israel and the Arab world, was the right to fly the Saudi flag over the Moslem holy places in East Jerusalem as a symbol of guardianship over those shrines as well as those in Mecca and Medina.

Prime Minister Begin was, however, angry at Nimrodi for even attempting to portray the document as moderate. Begin would not consider any whittling away of Israeli sovereignty over all of Jerusalem, and he did not wish to examine the details of the document. In Begin's view Fahd's words were a mere reformulation of the old Arab extremism, reflecting an attempt to force Israel to surrender what Begin considered the soil of the Jewish homeland.

The Saudi affair was nothing, however, compared with the almost mind-boggling plans cooked up during a series of secret trips in late 1981 and 1982. The clandestine network of contacts could be summarized as an Iranian-Sudanese affair linking Israel and Saudi Arabia, and the web began to be spun in North Africa.

Nimrodi and Schwimmer, as Khashoggi's guests aboard his luxurious DC-8, flew from Europe to Morocco for discussions with senior Iranian army officers living in exile since the shah was toppled. They also met there with the late shah's son, Prince Reza Pahlavi — known to insiders as the "Baby Shah." He was a weak character, but Western intelligence agencies were interested in Reza as someone they could influence. The CIA helped him broadcast clandestine radio and television messages to Iran, where his words fell with a dull thud.

The Baby Shah had taken up residence in Morocco, with a coterie of servants and military men, plotting an almost impossible return to power in Teheran. They told Nimrodi, Schwimmer, and Khashoggi that all that was required was financial support to buy arms and pay the salaries of a mercenary force that could overthrow the ayatollahs.

The two Israelis seriously believed such a coup could succeed, and they hurried home to tell Sharon. The Baby Shah's dreams seemed to fit in conveniently with Sharon's wider geostrategic aspirations, and the defense minister's friends were excited. After a series of nearly breathless international telephone calls and meetings, a larger group of plotters came together in Africa.

There they were, one of the most incongruous assemblies imaginable, standing on the green and manicured lawns of the Mount Kenya Safari Club. It was May 13, 1982. In the welcome seclusion of the exclusive safari resort owned by Khashoggi — near the Tanzanian border, separated from Nairobi by some one hundred miles of grazing land where the wildlife runs free — six Israelis, two Sudanese, and a Saudi shook hands among the flowers and fruit-laden trees.

The gathering was intended always to remain a secret, but it was so relaxed that one of the group even took snapshots of the others as they chatted. There was Arik Sharon with his wife, Lily — whom he took on almost all his secret missions — laying on the charm with foreigners who were officially his enemies.

The business they discussed was deeply serious, however. The Sudanese were President Gaafar Numeiri and his intelligence chief, Abu Tayeb. Sharon recalls: "I was surprised to find the Sudanese president soft-spoken and extremely polite."[17]

Numeiri was also "knowledgeable and perceptive," agreeing with Sharon that their common foe was Libya. The Sudanese leader was willing to consider far more than the cooperation, which had already begun, with Israeli intelligence's project to rescue Ethiopian Jewry. Now the Israelis — in the persons of Sharon and his "court" — had bigger plans for Numeiri and his territory.

The defense minister was there with Nimrodi, Schwimmer, Kimche, and Tamir, and their master plan was to turn Sudan into a gigantic arms cache for "special projects." Saudi Arabia would provide the finance: Khashoggi told his guests that he had won King Fahd's agreement to sign checks up to $800 million — "and if necessary," he said with a smile, "perhaps even one billion dollars!" Israel would come up with the weapons, either home-produced or captured surplus. The arsenal would contain much more than rifles, mortars, and bullets. It would also include tanks, airplanes, and missiles.

The carrot for Numeiri was the money to be paid both to his country and into the president's own pocket. As middlemen, Nimrodi, Schwimmer, and Khashoggi would be instrumental in buying and selling the weapons, profiting from the usual commissions paid to intermediaries.

For Sharon there was the opportunity to win a sizable export order, which could easily include arms captured from PLO guerrillas and Arab armies over the years. The plan to build up an arsenal in Sudan offered the welcome irony that the Saudis could be made to pay Israel for guns and ammunition that were originally purchased by the PLO and Arab states using Saudi financial aid.

For whom was all this firepower intended? Iran was high on the agenda, and the Baby Shah and his exiled generals would have received the weapons they wanted to launch a coup against Ayatollah Khomeini. Instead of the insignificant opposition they had become, Reza and his followers could suddenly pose a genuine threat to the Islamic Republic and bring Iran back into the arms of the West.

Weapons would also be supplied from the depot in northeast Africa to guerrilla forces that were fighting governments inimical to Israel, to Sudan, and to Western interests. These civil wars could be waged in Africa, Asia, or even in the Arab world. For such a project, the sky was the limit. Numeiri and the Israelis agreed to meet again in Alexandria, Egypt, in July 1982 for more detailed discussions.

The Mossad was excluded from the Mount Kenya meeting but insisted on receiving a full report. Kimche, after returning to his office at the foreign ministry, informed the Mossad that President Numeiri had agreed to permit it to open a permanent station in Khartoum. The report also said Sharon had ensured that Numeiri would continue to cooperate in the exodus of Ethiopian Jews.

Yitzhak Hofi was naturally pleased to have a new Mossad station in an Arab capital, but he resented being left out of the meeting with Numeiri. The Israelis who had established close links with Adnan Khashoggi were embarking on a major covert operation without the Mossad, when the agency had never liked or trusted the Saudi tycoon. "Arik's court" was threatening to encroach into Hofi's territory.

In addition to considerations of internal politics and bureaucratic territoriality, the Mossad's analysts had genuine concerns about the Iranian-Sudanese project. When it came to Iran, the Mossad believed that the Baby Shah and his powerless generals were men whose days had passed. A small-scale invasion of Iran, which was then successfully holding back the huge army of Iraq, would be extremely unlikely to triumph. It would more likely lead to a huge embarrassment and, perhaps, exposure of the plotters behind the coup.

As for the wider, geostrategic goals of the proposed Sudanese arsenal, Hofi and the Mossad believed that Sharon was overstretching the abilities and interests of the State of Israel. There was the further objection that the Mossad had concluded, in this and other cases, that it was not a good idea to trust Arabs — certainly not to the extent of putting Israeli lives, limbs, money, and prestige at risk based on the cooperation and goodwill of nations such as Saudi Arabia and Sudan.

Foreign Minister Shamir, a Mossad veteran, was also inculcated in the faith of not having too much faith in Arab partners. In assessing the Sudan project, he sided with the Mossad and was not swayed by the director general of his ministry, Kimche. Prime Minister Begin did not take a definite stand, telling Sharon and his friends that they would have to present more convincing evidence that a coup in Iran could succeed — as a first step in the wider, more ambitious plan.

The Mossad was not about to let the plan proceed even one step further. Hofi considered it a bad idea for Israel, and clearly bad for the Mossad. He sent one of his top deputies on a secret flight to Morocco, by way of Europe, to see the Baby Shah. The senior Israeli spy made his identity, aside from his real name, quite clear to Reza and told the young prince: "I am authorized by the highest circles in Israel to tell you that the Israelis with whom you have met are not our authorized representatives. They would only draw you into trouble. Please coordinate directly with us in the future, although this plan involving Sudan does not interest us."[18]

The Mossad envoy flew back to Tel Aviv, again careful to disguise himself on his transit through Europe. His mission was accomplished. The colossal project developed by Sharon, Nimrodi, Kimche, and the Arabs was dead. It was an extraordinary way of conducting government business. The American parallel would be for the Pentagon to embark on a policy initiative behind the State Department's back, only to have the CIA step in and sabotage the plan. The Israeli intelligence community had slipped into bureaucratic jealousies and infighting.

The Sudanese-Iranian plan was the beginning of the end of the grand strategy developed by Sharon during his years as defense minister. While involved in many complex schemes, he devoted most of his attention to a strategic goal much closer to home: creating a new Lebanon, just to the north of Israel.

He was determined to destroy the PLO's military infrastructure in southern Lebanon — "a terrorist state within a state," in the words of Israeli policy makers. After a series of painful guerrilla raids and rocket attacks against Israeli towns and farms in the northern Galilee region, followed by Israeli retaliation in the form of air raids or artillery barrages, Begin had reluctantly agreed in July 1981 to an American-sponsored cease-fire with the PLO. It was clear, however, that this was a temporary and weak accord. Palestinian splinter groups continued to attack Israeli troops, and the army and air force were itching to retaliate.

Begin and Sharon both felt a visceral hatred for the PLO, which they regarded as a group of murderers out to destroy Israel. The prime minister openly likened Yasser Arafat to Adolf Hitler. It was clearly only a matter of time until Israel attacked the Palestinian strongholds in Lebanon. The only questions were when the Israelis would strike, and how large and ambitious their operation would be.

In an attempt to clarify the possibilities, Sharon and his aide, General Tamir, met secretly in Geneva in January 1982 with Syria's General Rifa'at Assad, the brother of his nation's president. The meeting proved that in the world of Middle Eastern clandestine diplomacy, anything is possible. After all, there was Israel's most militant government minister holding a civilized conversation with a senior representative of Israel's most threatening and belligerent foe.

Rifa'at Assad was a colorful, cruel, and controversial military man who was also a hedonist pursuing wealth and women. In addition, he was a realist who might publicly refuse to recognize Israel but privately respected its power. He knew that Israel and Syria, in spite of their hostility, had at least two common interests: to weaken the PLO and to stabilize Lebanon by partitioning it.

Merely holding the Geneva meeting was an achievement; but nothing, not even a tacit understanding, emerged from it. It is not clear whether the Syrian met with his Israeli enemies with the approval of his brother, President Hafez el-Assad, but it is very likely.

Israel's efforts to further its interests in Lebanon consistently involved secret diplomacy. The Mossad and Aman had kept in close contact with Lebanon's Christian militias — the Phalangists — for eight years. The first contacts had been made in 1974, when the Christian leaders feared they were losing the dominance they enjoyed in their country. Their Moslem rivals formed a coalition with the many Palestinian refugees in Lebanon, increasing their power and influence while demanding a greater piece of the political pie. Christian politicians, however, stubbornly rejected any reforms in a system that had suited them nicely.

It was Jordan's King Hussein, himself involved in secret diplomacy with Israel, who persuaded the Christian militia chiefs of Lebanon, Camille Chamoun and Pierre Gemayel, to enter into contacts with the Jewish state. Chamoun, a former Lebanese president, and Gemayel, a government minister, held long discussions with Israel's Prime Minister Rabin. It was agreed that Israel would help the Phalangist militia, which ironically had begun as an admiring model of Nazis and other European Fascists in the 1930s.

On the Israeli side, the Mossad had responsibility for contacts with the Phalangists and took an especially keen interest in Pierre Gemayel's son Bashir. The young Gemayel was a lawyer, but in a country of lawlessness he was known to be bold, sly, and murderous. He showed no hesitation in killing his Christian "allies" — members of the Chamoun and Franjieh families — so as to be sole ruler of the militias.

As part of his education in the 1970s, Bashir Gemayel worked for a law firm in Washington, D.C. He was approached there by the Central Intelligence Agency, and the son of the Christian militia leader agreed to be a paid informer for the CIA. The Americans paid Gemayel thousands of dollars and were proved to have chosen well when, despite being the youngest of Pierre's six children, Bashir was promoted ahead of all his siblings to take charge of the country's largest Christian militia in 1976.[19]

After helping the Christian Phalangists survive the Lebanese civil war of 1975–76, the Mossad was permitted to open a new "station," including a powerful radio transmitter, in the port of Jounieh. The Christians were embattled by hostile Moslems and Palestinians in the rest of Lebanon, but Gemayel and his clan had absolute control in the port just north of Beirut. In addition to Mossad operatives, Israeli army officers traveled to Jounieh and set up a formal liaison system with Gemayel's Phalangists much stronger than anything Israel was able to achieve in other Arab countries.

At the same time, the Israelis formed their own Lebanese militia in southern Lebanon to combat the growing PLO presence in the area and to help protect Israel's northern border. The force was called the South Lebanese Army and was dominated by local Christians in and around the town of Marjayoun. The SLA men wore what were quite clearly Israeli uniforms, with the Israel Defense Forces markings simply stripped off, and drove tanks and jeeps that did not even have all their Hebrew labels removed.

Aman was responsible for training, equipping, financing, and clothing the SLA. Phalangist combatants from northern Lebanon also underwent training by the Israeli army, as well as by Mossad and Shin Bet experts when it came to intelligence and interrogation methods. The head of the small security and intelligence service which the Phalangists had established with Israeli help was Eli Hobeika.

Aman and the Mossad wholeheartedly supported the contacts with the Phalangists, believing that they gave Israel important advantages. They enabled Israel to set up a broad network of informers that supplied up-to-date information on Palestinian guerrilla groups, the Syrian army, and political developments in that part of the Arab world. The secret links with Lebanon also fit into the traditional "peripheral" concept of Israeli policy. The Christians of Lebanon could naturally be friends of Israel, because they were the enemies of the Moslems.

Until 1981, Israel went no further with the Phalangists than helping them to help themselves. David Kimche, then in charge of the Mossad's activities in Lebanon, said the Israeli liaison officers in Jounieh always made it clear to the Christians that Israel would not fight their battles for them. Begin, when reelected, ordered Hofi to expand and deepen the contacts with the Phalangists. Sharon took them even further.

The Christian leaders, who were aware of Begin's moral vulnerabilities, began to apply pressure on him to increase Israeli aid to them. They bawled that they were in danger of annihilation by the Syrians, and they cunningly staged provocations and issued false reports to back up their version of reality. Begin, sympathetic to oppressed minorities — especially when Moslem Arabs were the oppressors — tended to believe the Phalangists.

Sharon knew the truth and had no real fear that the Christians of Lebanon would be wiped out. But he believed that Bashir Gemayel was a man after his own heart, who would be willing and perhaps able to implement the Sharon strategy to bring about a new order in the Middle East.

On the night of January 12, 1982, a small but powerful group of Israelis gathered at a military airport near Tel Aviv. They included Ariel Sharon, General Tamir, representatives of the Mossad, Aman chief General Yehoshua Saguy, and other senior army officers. They were given a short briefing on how to behave should anything go wrong, and how they might escape from enemy territory if necessary. They then took off in a military helicopter.

It was a strange flight into the unknown for these men who were entrusted with the security of Israel. They looked down on the blackness of the Mediterranean and then the blinking lights of the Lebanese shoreline, trying to identify the places they were flying over, until they saw the brighter lights of Beirut. The helicopter proceeded northward to a landing strip in Jounieh, where Sharon and his colleagues were met by the local Mossad station chief.

Bashir Gemayel had only been told that "a senior Israeli official" planned to come, but he had already guessed who it would be. Smiling at the sight of the burly Sharon, the young Phalangist leader said, "I knew that you would come. We waited for you."

Over a string of sumptuous meals, interspersed with tours of various parts of Beirut, the two sides worked intensively to reach a broad and basic understanding. When he returned to Israel, Sharon crowed to his friends: "I have finalized the plan with the Christians. Now we can carry it out. I tied their feet."[20]

Exactly five weeks later, the cooperation agreements were confirmed when Gemayel was flown to Jerusalem to meet with Prime Minister Begin. Sharon wanted Begin to be convinced in person.[21]

The defense minister's claim of a convincing and all-encompassing alliance with the Phalangists triggered a fierce debate in Israel's intelligence community. Aman insisted vehemently that Israel could not trust the Christians enough so as to base any troop movement on their support. Military intelligence had reports that Gemayel also had ties with the Syrian leadership and to some extent with the PLO.

The Aman analysts wondered how the Phalangists could be considered trustworthy when some of the arms they had received from Israel later found their way to the PLO. Some of the Christian leaders allegedly engaged in private deals involving arms and drugs. Aman also opposed embarking on a military venture that would bring the Israeli army into confrontation with the Syrian forces in Lebanon.

Sharon was adamant, however, that the time had come to carry out his plan to change the course of history. To everyone's surprise he found an ally in the Mossad, an organization which he generally treated with extreme suspicion.

Hofi, in effect, said the Sharon plan could work. The Mossad behaved as though it had forgotten one of the most sacred rules of intelligence: Never become too intimate with your sources. All the lavish dinners enjoyed by Mossad men in Beirut, and all the fruitful return trips by Phalangists clandestinely visiting Israel, had effectively sealed an alliance that left little room for questions or doubts. Gemayel and his men always made a point of agreeing with everything the Israelis said, while going even further to underline the Lebanese Christians' hatred of the PLO.[22]

Knowing he had lost the internal bureaucratic struggle, Aman's General Saguy agreed to be the one to inform Israel's all-important American allies. Visiting Washington at the end of January 1982, the chief of military intelligence warned U.S. secretary of state Alexander Haig that if Palestinian provocations continued Israel would have no choice but to invade Lebanon — all the way to the outskirts of Beirut. Sharon flew to Washington a few months later to repeat the warning.[23]

From June 2 to 4, the defense minister was on a clandestine mission — arranged by the Mossad — in Romania. Under the cover of a family visit, Sharon was offering "technological cooperation" to the only Communist government that maintained diplomatic relations with Israel. Experts from Israel Military Industries and Israel Aircraft Industries accompanied Sharon.[24]

On June 3, Israel's ambassador in London, Shlomo Argov, was shot and crippled for life by Palestinians who ambushed him after a diplomatic party. The gunmen were from the renegade Abu Nidal faction rather than the PLO mainstream, but in any event Sharon considered the attempted assassination "merely the match that ignited the fuse."[25] Israel was now certain to invade Lebanon, looking to the Lebanese Christians to help wipe out the PLO.

On June 6, Sharon sent his troops across the border. It was only the second war ever initiated by Israel — the first having been the Suez campaign of 1956. It turned out to be Sharon's Waterloo. Just as Aman had warned Sharon, the Christian forces did not abide by their word. They did not help the Israelis fight the PLO, and Gemayel later refused to sign a fully fledged peace treaty with Israel. Sharon sank deep into the Lebanese quagmire.

The declared aim was to eliminate Palestinian artillery and rocket positions that were threatening civilians in northern Israel. The invasion was officially named "Operation Peace for Galilee."

Israel's leaders had broader hopes that a thundering PLO defeat would undermine the allegiance to the organization felt by the Palestinians of the West Bank and Gaza Strip. Begin wished to strengthen Israel's hold on the occupied territories, while offering the Arab residents a form of "autonomy" as promised in the peace treaty with Egypt. The PLO absolutely rejected autonomy, insisting on winning outright statehood. Begin wished to encourage alternative Palestinian leaders who would be willing to work with the Israelis.

Sharon's aspirations were even more ambitious. He ordered his tanks to keep rolling, fighting, and advancing to Beirut's suburbs. There they would link up with Lebanese Christian forces and help them impose their own law and order in Lebanon. The plan would include the election of Bashir Gemayel as president. He would then expel the Syrians from Lebanon and would sign a formal peace treaty with Israel. Gemayel would certainly force all the Palestinian fighters to leave, whether on ships to other parts of the Middle East or by road to Syria.

On the fifth day of the war, Sharon's aspirations concerning the Israeli intelligence community were dealt a severe blow. His close friend General "Kuti" Adam was killed in battle on June 10. The top candidate to be chief of the Mossad was dead.

Adam was gone, but after eight years it still was time to replace Yitzhak Hofi. Begin turned to Hofi himself for advice, and on June 27 the prime minister recommended to the full cabinet that Hofi's deputy, Nahum Admoni, be appointed head of the Mossad.

It was the first time that the man chosen to lead the agency in Israel's secret battles was himself a career officer in the Mossad. In keeping with traditional security restrictions, Admoni was not publicly named. Insiders described him, however, as a "nondescript" and "average" man, a "manager," a bureaucrat without any sparkle, but one who was stable and deliberate. Fifty-three years old, he was American-educated and had spent twenty-eight years as a secret operative at various foreign outposts. Admoni had worked his way up through the ranks.

He was born in Jerusalem in 1929 to a family that had moved to Palestine from Poland a few years earlier and changed its name from

Rotbaum to Admoni. His father was the architect of Jerusalem's parks, and the Admonis lived in the exclusive Rehavia neighborhood — not far from the luxurious King David Hotel. A high proportion of Jewish leaders before Israel's independence in 1948 and since then have come from Rehavia: government officials, cabinet ministers, university professors, army officers, and intelligence operatives.

As a teenager, Nahum Admoni served in the Haganah and its intelligence branch, Shai. Shortly after the 1948 war, he went to America to study international relations at the University of California at Berkeley. Admoni worked in a Jewish Sunday school, in a synagogue as a caretaker, and in a factory that produced uniforms for the U.S. armed forces. He met and married his wife in California, and they never had a better time than they did in those five years on the West Coast. It was the only period in his adult life when Admoni could escape the pressures of the undercover war against Israel's enemies.

Admoni hoped to become a diplomat, but upon returning to Israel he took a job as an instructor in the intelligence community's special academy in Jerusalem. David Kimche, who would later become his rival for the Mossad's top job, was also teaching in the academy.

It was only natural for the Mossad to recruit Admoni from the ranks of teachers into the legions of doers. In stations ranging from Washington to Ethiopia, Admoni spent three decades in the secret agency's political and liaison department. He was involved in all cooperative projects with the CIA for years, and he was an expert in the Mossad's alternative diplomacy on behalf of Israel. But when it came to clandestine actions against the Jewish state's enemies, Admoni had relatively little operational experience in the field. He was not an adventurer; he was not a killer; but he was solid and was respected for his diligent work.

As the Lebanese war unfolded along bloodier and increasingly unpleasant lines, Sharon's initial promises of a rapid blitzkrieg gave way to the reality of an occupied territory stretching between Israel's northern border and Beirut. It was an area full of refugees and turmoil, and it had to be controlled.

Avraham Shalom's Shin Bet was given the unsavory assignment of deploying in Lebanon to find friends and fight enemies. Shiite Moslem villages, which at first welcomed the advancing Israeli troops because the hated PLO was being forced out, now became centers of anti-Israeli terrorism — inspired by the image, and by some active agents, of Iran's Ayatollah Khomeini. Suicide truck bombers, whose compatriots killed more than 250 U.S. Marines and French troops in Beirut in 1983, started by attacking Israeli units in the south. Fanatical Shiites willingly drove and detonated vehicles packed with explosives, entering Heaven's gates by pushing the Jews back to their border.

Shin Bet was in no way ready for this type of confrontation. Shalom and his operatives had experience with Palestinians in the West Bank and Gaza who may not have been happy living under Israeli occupation since 1967, but they never volunteered to blow themselves up to make their point.

In the summer of 1982 Israeli army units guarded positions around Beirut. Israel's air force dominated the skies to prevent any attempts by Syrian warplanes and missiles to interfere, and Shin Bet started to set up systems of law and order in southern Lebanon. Meantime, a bureaucratic battlefront appeared when Shin Bet agents came across a rival Israeli — Rafi Eitan — driving around the area and checking on their work in his role as the prime minister's adviser on terrorism. Eitan was there, in part, because Sharon depended on his loyal friend to keep an eye on Shin Bet.

His less reliable friend, Bashir Gemayel, did complete one facet of the plan by being elected Lebanon's new president on August 23. The president-elect secretly visited Nahariya, Israel, a few days later to meet with Prime Minister Begin, and on September 12 Sharon visited Gemayel's home near Beirut. They agreed that on September 15 Sharon would return with Foreign Minister Yitzhak Shamir.[26]

Instead, Sharon's plans for Lebanon were blown to bits on September 14. The two-way radio in the defense minister's car crackled with an urgent message to contact the head of the Mossad immediately. Being driven at the time to his farm in southern Israel, Sharon told his chauffeur to turn off the road at an army base so he could telephone Tel Aviv.

Yitzhak Hofi, still in his office during the transition to Admoni, coldly informed Sharon that Gemayel had been killed by a powerful bomb at his party headquarters in Beirut. First indications were that Syrian agents were responsible. It was an embarrassing and frustrating event for Hofi, retiring from the intelligence community with ambiguity rather than victory, and it was absolutely terrible news for

Sharon. The process which the defense minister had counted on, the establishment of normal relations between Israel and Lebanon, could have vindicated the controversial war. Now it had reached an explosive end. Gemayel was assassinated only a few days before he was to have been sworn in as president.

The next morning, September 15, Sharon was flown by helicopter to Lebanon. With him, to pay respects to the bereaved Gemayel family, was a dazzling hierarchy of Israeli intelligence: Aman's commander General Saguy, Shin Bet chief Avraham Shalom, and Mossad deputy director Menahem (Nahik) Navot. That day, they all barely escaped with their lives.

The man who endangered nearly all of Israel's defense chiefs was an Aman colonel who met their helicopter and was to drive them to the Gemayel dynastic estate. The colonel, who was in Beirut as liaison to the Phalangists, got lost. He drove Sharon, Saguy, Shalom, and Navot directly toward PLO positions in Moslem-dominated West Beirut. They were lucky that a Christian policeman flagged them down and urgently advised them to turn around and get out of there. "I don't know who that policeman was," Sharon recalls, "but I have no doubt that he saved my life along with those of the various high-ranking intelligence and security people with me, including the colonel whose idea this shortcut was."[27]

Somehow arriving safely at the Gemayel mansion, Sharon expressed his condolences to Bashir's father, the veteran militia leader Pierre Gemayel. Navot acted as note taker in the conversation, which took on a surprisingly formal character. The meeting, in short, was important — even vital to the next turn of events — and Navot's handwritten minutes have been preserved in the Mossad's high-security archives. Those minutes later became a key factor in a huge defamation trial in New York, when Sharon sued *Time* magazine for falsely reporting that he had suggested to the Gemayels that they exact revenge on the Palestinians remaining in Beirut. Sharon won the case.

In any event, the Phalangist leaders were busy the next day, on September 16. They decided that Amin Gemayel, Bashir's brother, would be their candidate for president, and they sent their gunmen on a vengeance mission into the Palestinian refugee camps of Sabra and Chatila in Beirut's southern suburbs. The units that entered were commanded by Eli Hobeika, no stranger to the Israelis, and the heavily armed Phalangists simply walked past the Israeli army units which surrounded the camps. Hobeika's aim was to "clean out" the Palestinian guerrillas.

The militiamen instead engaged in a nonstop, twenty-four-hour orgy of bloodletting that cut down children, mothers, and elderly people. The PLO's fighting men had already fled. Responding with murderous hysteria to the murder of their beloved Bashir, the Phalangist attackers shot and stabbed to death over seven hundred unarmed Palestinians. It all happened under the noses of Israeli enlisted men and officers, who manned their observation posts just outside the camps but did not seem to care what was happening.

Television brought the pictures of the pathetic piles of bodies into homes all over the world. The subtle detail that the Phalangists, and not the Israelis, were the killers was lost on most foreign audiences. The world saw the Sabra and Chatila massacre as the final word on Israel's invasion of Lebanon. It had been a disaster.

Begin tried to say that the massacre was a case of Arabs killing Arabs and had nothing to do with Israel. Foreigners did not accept that, however, and neither did thousands of Israelis who protested their own government's actions in Lebanon. Begin agreed to appoint a special commission of inquiry, chaired by former supreme court justice Yitzhak Kahan, to establish whether there was any Israeli involvement in the Sabra and Chatila atrocity.

While waiting for the Kahan Commission verdict, Sharon continued to press on with his strategic projects elsewhere. He saw an opportunity in Africa to deliver a punch in the nose to Libya's Colonel Qaddafi, self-styled Islamic warrior against Zionism. The Libyans were actively involved in a civil war in Chad, their southeastern neighbor. Qaddafi backed the antigovernment rebels. Just to the east of Chad, Sudan's President Numeiri feared Libya and did his best to help Chad's pro-Western President Hassan Habre. The United States and France, the former colonial ruler of Chad, were also on Habre's side.

The Israelis were particularly annoyed at Qaddafi because he was blocking their energetic efforts in the early 1980s to restore their influence in Africa. The Libyan revolutionary threatened, blackmailed, and bribed fellow African leaders not to restore diplomatic relations with the Jewish state. The fact that he supported the most fanatical and violent terrorist groups in Europe and the Arab world only heightened the importance of the goal shared by Israel and the United States: to weaken the Libyan leader wherever possible, in the hope that he might eventually be overthrown.

Sharon had his senior aide, General Tamir, explore the possibilities of anti-Libyan action in person. In November 1982 Tamir vanished from Israel, as was his frequent habit as a clandestine envoy. He flew to Paris for a meeting with a senior Chadian minister. They discussed the conflict in northern Africa and the threat of direct intervention by the Libyan army. The Chadian was optimistic that Habre's forces could defeat the rebels, but he feared a full-scale battle with Qaddafi's troops. Chad was pressing France for a commitment to send in the French army, if the Libyans were to move in from the north.

Tamir's conclusion, based on all he heard, was that Israel should establish a small military presence in Chad. He was seeking the best of all worlds: that France would bear the burden of saving Habre's government, while Israel could take at least partial credit for dealing Qaddafi a setback. Tamir and the Chadian minister agreed in Paris that the Israeli should visit N'Djamena, the capital of Chad, and they finalized details of a secret communications link with Israel.

Two weeks later, the awaited signal from Chad was received and Tamir donned civilian clothes for a flight to Paris. From there he took a long, tiring flight to N'Djamena, a city of half a million people scarred by the devastation of a truly vicious war. Many houses in the capital had been destroyed, the roads were pitted, and debris littered the entire town.

The word *n'djamena* means "the city where one rests" in one of the local dialects, but the Israeli general was given no rest. Immediately after arriving, he was rushed to the presidential palace to meet with Habre. Their talks lasted all night, and in the morning the general was taken for a tour of the front lines out in the northern desert. Both sides agreed that Israel would send military experts to Chad to help its army in both the civil war and the battle against Libya. Tamir returned to Israel, by way of Paris, and reported to Sharon.

Next, it was Sharon's turn to travel. In late January and on February 4, 1983, he visited a number of African countries to propose that they renew diplomatic relations with Israel in exchange for military assistance. Dozens of nations had abided by a decision of the Organization of African Unity in late 1973 to cut their ties with Israel, as a reaction to the Yom Kippur War and the consequent oil embargo, which made Arab petrodollars more valuable than ever. While visiting Zaire, Sharon met not only that nation's President Mobutu Sese Seko, but also Chad's President Habre. They established a meeting of the minds on the need to confront Libyan subversion. As an immediate gesture to Chad, Sharon gave Habre a cargo of light weapons flown especially from Israel. Within a very short time, the Israeli army sent a delegation of fifteen advisers to N'Djamena from a secret contingent already posted in Zaire.

When the Mossad found out about Tamir's secret mission and Sharon's personal diplomacy, Nahum Admoni was furious. Africa had traditionally been the Mossad's turf, not the defense ministry's. But the entire operation had been carried out behind the Mossad's back, and Sharon showed no apparent intention to inform the Mossad. Admoni complained to Prime Minister Begin, pointing out that it was highly perilous to station Israeli army officers in a country with an unstable regime, where rebels could gain the upper hand at any time. The dangers were even greater, because Israel's military advisers in Chad might be taken prisoner by the front-line troops of Libya.

Sharon and Tamir defended their diplomatic foray, stressing to Begin the advantages of helping moderate Africans and moderate Arabs such as Sudan's Numeiri in a bid to defeat Colonel Qaddafi. The prime minister decided, however, that Admoni was correct about both the dangers and the bureaucratic etiquette of including the Mossad in matters of clandestine diplomacy. The fifteen Israeli officers were ordered to return home from Chad.[28]

The moment of truth was near in Israel, as the Kahan Commission published its report on the Sabra and Chatila massacre in Beirut. On February 8, 1983, retired judge Kahan decreed that Israel would have to accept "indirect responsibility" for the mass slaughter. His report also specifically recommended that Ariel Sharon be "excluded" from the post of defense minister. Sharon reluctantly resigned on February 14.[29]

The invasion of Lebanon, which had been launched the previous June but still had Israeli forces mired in hostile territory, was seen by Israelis as regrettable at best, and as a ghastly mistake in the eyes of many. The warfare unleashed by the Israelis in an already violent country killed thousands of Lebanese and Palestinians, both civilians and combatants, and the Israeli casualties were far greater than the army had anticipated: more than six hundred soldiers killed and thousands wounded.

The goals of Operation Peace for Galilee were unattained. The Syrians were not expelled from Lebanon. Lebanon did not sign a peace treaty with Israel. The PLO was still alive and fairly well, although expelled from Beirut and southern Lebanon. Despite Prime Minister Begin's hopes, the Palestinians of the West Bank and Gaza continued to pledge allegiance to Yasser Arafat, as Israel tried in vain to cultivate an alternative Arab leadership in the occupied territories.

Within Israel's defense establishment, the intelligence community was considered to have done very badly. The Mossad failed in its most basic function of evaluation by placing its bets on the benefits of an alliance with the Phalangists, now seen worldwide as a gang of bloodthirsty murderers.

Word also leaked out that the Mossad and Aman, although asked repeatedly by Begin and Sharon, had been unable to furnish precise details of Arafat's movements. Several attempts by Israeli forces to kill the PLO leader, during the war, took many other lives instead. The booby-trapped cars and precision air raids simply missed Arafat, the man whom Begin had dubbed "a beast on two legs."

When an Israeli sniper finally had a chance to fire on the Palestinian leader, during the ceremonial evacuation of Beirut by his guerrillas, it was deemed politically unwise to shoot Arafat since he had been humiliated anyway by apparent defeat. In any event, assassinating the head of the PLO in front of American and other diplomats supervising the withdrawal, as well as the world's camera crews, would have been very stupid. The sniper held his fire.

In October 1983, eight months after Sharon's departure from the defense ministry, Prime Minister Begin astonished his cabinet by declaring "I have no more strength" and submitting his resignation. The death of his wife, Aliza, had visibly depressed him, and a vigil by Israeli antiwar protesters across from his official residence also seemed to drive Begin into an introspective silence.

Foreign Minister Shamir became the new prime minister, as Begin withdrew into almost total seclusion in his modest home on Zemach Street in Jerusalem. Although he was one of Israel's great historical figures, Begin refused to explain his motives for either war or peace. His few confidants said that he was tortured by the feeling that he had been led astray by Sharon and chief of staff Raful Eitan, and in place of the jubilation of victory that was promised he had the deaths of hundreds of young Israelis in Lebanon on his conscience.

Nine months after Begin's dramatic departure from the political stage, a new Israeli government was formed from the deadlocked result of a national election that deeply divided the country. After months of wrangling between Likud and Labor in the summer of 1984, party leaders Shamir and Peres decided to share power in a unique government of national unity. The cabinet was made up of both major political blocs, and after Peres served as prime minister for the first twenty-five months he would hand the job back to Shamir in an unprecedented "rotation" for the second half of the government's term.

There were great hopes for change in many facets of Israeli life. The reluctant coalition managed to agree on an economic plan that reined in the galloping three-digit inflation. Israeli forces withdrew from almost all of Lebanon, patrolling only a "security belt" near the border alongside their surrogates in the South Lebanese Army.

Sharon was merely the minister for trade and industry in the coalition government, but he continued to cast an influential shadow on the nation's strategic outlook. Meantime, his friends in and around the intelligence community — Shalom, Eitan, and Nimrodi — would stir up some amazing trouble in the next few years.

THIRTEEN

Killings and Coverups

"MR. PRIME MINISTER," one of Yitzhak Shamir's bodyguards whispered to him, "there is an urgent message for you to contact the head of Shin Bet."

Anything but that, Shamir thought to himself as he quickened his pace, his bodyguards at his heels, to a side room in the international convention center in north Tel Aviv. Short and solidly built, with bushy eyebrows as his trademark, Shamir glanced at his watch.

It was 7:30 P.M. on April 13, 1984, and in a few hours the results of the internal elections of his Likud bloc would be known. Shamir had been preoccupied for weeks by the battle of the titans that had been raging in Likud for the top posts on the list of Knesset candidates. More than half a year after Menachem Begin's dramatic resignation bequeathed the premiership to Shamir, party rivals David Levy and Arik Sharon refused to recognize him as the leader of Likud. Shamir was aware that the results of the internal elections would decide the struggle.

The prime minister knew the most likely subject of Avraham Shalom's call. Shin Bet was on the verge of solving one of the most important mysteries in Israel in recent years: exposing the Jewish terrorist organization that had killed Palestinian students and attempted to murder the three West Bank mayors.

Unlike his predecessor, Shamir did permit Shin Bet to plant informers among the Jewish settlers in the occupied territories, and at the last briefing he had been given by Shalom the prime minister had been told that more than twenty suspects would be arrested in the near future, all of them settlers.

Shamir did not attempt to intervene in the investigation, but privately he dreaded the inevitable findings. He hoped that the indictments would come after the internal Likud voting — even better, after the general election due a month later. Arresting Jewish settlers would place Shamir and his party under tremendous pressure from extreme right-wing and nationalist parties, which would accuse the Likud of being unpatriotic and would attract some of Likud's traditional voters.

"Mr. Prime Minister, I have already spoken to the head of Shin Bet," Colonel Azriel Nevo, the prime minister's military aide, said as Shamir entered the room. "He reported that Arab terrorists have hijacked a bus along the Number 300 line, after it left the central bus station of Tel Aviv on its way to Ashkelon. Military and police forces are on alert, and orders have been given to stop the bus. There is fear that the terrorists will try to cross into Egypt and take the passengers along as hostages. We have no further information, not even regarding casualties."

In spite of the seriousness of the incident and his natural concern for the bus passengers, Shamir felt a certain sense of relief. He was confident that the security forces — the army and Shin Bet — would defeat the terrorists, and the political fallout would favor Likud. The incident would dramatize Shamir's belief that concessions should not be made to Israel's Arab neighbors and certainly not to the PLO, because this would only give encouragement to terrorism. Most opinion polls had Shimon Peres's Labor party in the lead, but Shamir could portray Peres as soft on the Arabs.

The military censor prohibited any news reports on the hostage drama, but the fact that a bus had been hijacked could not be kept secret for long. Rumors began to fly among the thousands of delegates at the Likud conference, and then on to the scores of reporters and photographers covering the political gathering. Most of the newsmen made a mad dash for their cars and began driving southward in search of a story even hotter than the Sharon-Levy struggle for influence in Likud.

Soldiers at a roadblock, meantime, had managed to shoot out the tires of the bus and brought it to a halt in the Gaza Strip, less than six miles from the Egyptian border. The bus was surrounded by large numbers of police, army, and Shin Bet personnel. Avraham Shalom himself arrived on the scene.

Shalom had joined Shin Bet after short stints as a kibbutz member and as a soldier. He had always wanted to belong to Israel's cream of the crop — the elite pioneers whose lives were so intertwined with power, politics, and voluntarism that they identified completely with the State of Israel and its struggles. They could not live without their homeland, and it seemed that Israel could not exist without them.

He was born in 1929 as Avraham Bendor to parents who moved to Palestine from Germany after Hitler's rise to power. In Tel Aviv, as in Berlin, his parents attempted to give him a bourgeois education that would befit a prosperous German-Jewish businessman. But Avraham Bendor/Shalom preferred socialist values and joined a kibbutz.

The 1948 war brought him into the army, where Isser Harel noticed him and recruited him into Shin Bet. Shalom had the soul of a dedicated soldier and was known for putting his all into any mission — even training exercises. Among his valuable talents, he spoke English and German. He was also quiet, ascetic, and cold. Always appearing angry or upset, he never gave a hint as to why.

In three and a half decades with Shin Bet, Shalom participated in most of its major operations, including the joint mission with the Mossad to kidnap Adolf Eichmann in Argentina. Shalom was always a field and operations man. He developed a close working relationship with Yehuda Arbel, and together they conducted many secret attacks against Palestinian terrorists. This remained Shalom's focus after he was appointed head of Shin Bet in 1981, replacing Avraham Ahituv.[1]

Watching the motionless Bus 300 on the road near Gaza, Shalom knew that the army and police had units specially trained to storm all types of hijacked vehicles and rescue hostages. Shin Bet's job would be to interrogate the Arab attackers and discover their accomplices, sources of arms, and paymasters.

The sandy terrain alongside the road in Gaza was a beehive of antiterrorist activity. Giant searchlights turned the nighttime into day, as armed soldiers mingled with uniformed police and Shin Bet men in their civilian clothes. Walkie-talkies echoed back and forth, and dozens of press photographers provided even more light with their flashes. A short distance away stood the Israeli bus, under the control of four Palestinian gunmen.

Shalom, senior army officers, and Defense Minister Moshe Arens were on the scene in the predawn hours of tension, but they could not dispel the feeling that there was a lack of order and control. It was typical of any major event in Israel: there were clearly too many people milling around for the job at hand, and while there was great confidence and even bravado it seemed that the authorities would improvise their way to success rather than follow an organized plan.

Amid the gossiping crowd of officials and operatives who had come as much out of curiosity as their desire to help, antiterrorist specialists were gathering as much precise information as possible about the hijackers, the weapons they had, and the locations of any explosives on board the bus.

Not for an instant was there any intention of knuckling under to the terrorists' demands. The hijackers wanted fellow Palestinian guerrillas released from Israeli prisons; but they would not succeed. Once all the necessary data had been assembled with the aid of night-vision and audio eavesdropping equipment, the Israeli forces knew that the hijackers had only light sidearms — not even a machine gun. They were amateurs.

Israel's professional army commandos were ready, and the signal was given for the rescue assault to begin. Soldiers of the top sayeret, who had practiced the technique hundreds of times, smashed several windows and were inside the bus in seconds. They opened fire immediately, killing two of the terrorists and wounding the other two. The hostages were free, although a twenty-year-old woman was killed in her seat and other passengers were slightly wounded.

The men of the sayeret quickly returned to their base, maintaining the invisibility that is part of their mystique, after handing over the two wounded terrorists to another army unit and to Shin Bet interrogators. Israel's soldiers had swiftly accomplished yet another dazzling rescue — after some two dozen similar feats since 1967 — making it look easy to do what other nations could hardly ever manage.

"But that can't be," Alex Libak, a photographer for the new tabloid newspaper *Hadashot,* said when he heard the army's announcements on the radio a few hours later. The official spokesman first declared that two terrorists had been killed and two wounded. An hour later the announcement was corrected, now saying that all four bus hijackers had been killed in the army assault.

Libak was puzzled because he had witnessed the shootout and vividly remembered the charred bodies of two hijackers — the bus had caught fire in the gunfight — but had also seen how soldiers and men in civilian clothes were pummeling two wounded terrorists with their fists and rifle butts. He even remembered the terrified eyes of the Palestinians, as he hurried to the *Hadashot* photograph laboratory to develop his rolls of film. Libak did not have to make much of an effort to find the picture he was looking for. It clearly showed security men leading away one of the hijackers for questioning.[2]

"You're sure?" said Yossi Klein, the newspaper's young editor. He was amazed when Libak showed him the photo and told him what he had seen.

"Yes, a thousand percent," the photographer answered.

What was odd was that the defense ministry itself seemed unsure of what precisely had happened on the night between April 13 and 14. Arens appointed an internal commission of inquiry, headed by Major General Meir Zorea of the army reserves, an honorable man with an impeccable record.

Arens's spokesman, Nahman Shai, called the military censors' office and asked them to prevent the publication of any reports on the controversy. The censors and Shai himself contacted all the newspapers and many foreign reporters in Israel to say that any article on Bus 300 would have to be submitted for censorship. The implication was clear: Any article, report, or radio or television dispatch would be banned. The reason given for this decision was that any publication, even a mere hint, that the two terrorists had been caught alive and subsequently killed while in captivity could cause the deaths of Israeli prisoners held by Palestinian guerrilla groups.

Klein suspected that behind the stated reason there were other factors at play, meant to deprive the Israeli public of the truth. In direct violation of the military censors' ban, he splashed Libak's dramatic photo across *Hadashot*'s front page, with a brief news item that the defense ministry had established a commission of inquiry to examine the circumstances surrounding the incident.

Following *Hadashot,* which was motivated in part by its appetite for a sensational scoop and added sales, the other newspapers soon published details of the case. Defense Minister Arens reacted vigorously, using his legal authority to punish *Hadashot* by closing it down for four days. Excluding administrative actions against Arab newspapers in East Jerusalem and the occupied West Bank, this was the first time a Hebrew newspaper had been ordered shut since the Communist party's *Kol Ha'am* in 1952. The stern reaction against *Hadashot* strengthened suspicions that its story was accurate.

The next month, on May 24, 1984, the Zorea Commission submitted its report to the defense minister, stating clearly that two of the terrorists had been taken alive off the bus. It was now necessary to investigate, to find out who had killed them. The Zorea report was classified and was not released to the press; but it was sent to the police, Attorney General Yitzhak Zamir and the state prosecutors, and the military police for further attention.

Political battles continued as always, with Shamir retaining the Likud reins. The general election in June 1984 produced a stalemate: a dead heat between Likud and Labor, and neither able to woo enough small parties into a coalition. The two political behemoths were forced to create a strange new creature, the government of national unity with its peculiar "rotation" of prime ministers.

Shimon Peres had first crack at leading the unwieldy coalition, which immediately immersed itself in quarrels over his efforts to halt the galloping inflation rate, which had jumped the 600 percent hurdle, and his insistence that Israel's troops be brought home from their disastrous adventure in Lebanon. Nothing was being said about the hijacking of the bus the previous April.

Only a small minority of Israelis would care about the death of two Palestinians who were, after all, terrorists. Even as Bus 300 faded from public memory, a battle royal was being waged behind the scenes.

Shin Bet's men had testified to the Zorea Commission that they had received the two terrorists from the army so badly beaten up that they had not even been able to interrogate them. This Shin Bet version said that the two hijackers died a short time later from the blows previously inflicted on them — obviously pointing the finger of blame at the army.

The investigative team working for the state prosecutor, Yona Blatman, was inclined to go along with Shin Bet's story. In July 1985, Blatman charged Brigadier General Yitzhak Mordecai, who was the commander in charge of the army's rescue operation, with responsibility for the two deaths.

General Mordecai was court-martialed and did not deny that he had hit the terrorists with the butt of his revolver, but he explained that he had done so "for the needs of operational intelligence" — to find out immediately whether bombs had been planted aboard the bus. In any event, he added in his defense, "when I received them, they were already in bad shape."[3] The military court accepted his claim that by the time the hijackers were forcibly taken off the bus they had practically died from their wounds. The general was acquitted of all charges.

Based on all the testimony available, Blatman and Attorney General Zamir recommended that two Shin Bet operatives be tried for having beaten the terrorists. These two Israelis were also acquitted — but they had faced only an internal Shin Bet court. The agency always has its own disciplinary court, consisting of three members: one from Shin Bet, one from the Mossad, and a district court judge who is president of the special secret tribunal. The court is convened when a Shin Bet operative is accused of violating orders or the agency's code of conduct.[4]

The internal court is known for the severity with which it treats even the most minor infractions. Shin Bet personnel who are caught exploiting their position for private purposes are dismissed. For example, operatives who used their official missions abroad as an excuse to smuggle a television or videotape recorder into Israel were tried and dismissed, forfeiting all their rights to severance pay or a pension. Those found lying or not giving full reports to their superiors were also dismissed. Only rarely was a violator given a second chance.

The aim was to create — and in this it was successful — labor relations based on mutual trust and accurate reports. The reports would not always be pleasant, and everyone in Shin Bet knew that the agency had to be involved in questionable endeavors and dirty tricks. How else could the state be protected, considering the challenges and dangers of the Middle East? But Shin Bet chiefs always explained to their personnel that regardless of how serious or disturbing the circumstances, they had to give a complete and factual account to headquarters. Shin Bet wished to adopt as sacrosanct the principle that, while the nature of the work would often entail lying to the outside world, operatives would speak only the truth to their superiors.

The bus case proved that this was an impossible expectation. Sooner or later, a person who has been given permission to lie in certain circumstances will permit himself to lie in other circumstances as well. So it was with three of the highest-ranking men in Shin Bet: Reuven Hazak, Shalom's deputy; Peleg Radai, head of the security branch; and Rafi Malka.[5] Even though they were in their forties, while Shalom was in his fifties, all four were considered "the Arbel kids" who acted in the spirit of Yehuda Arbel's daring operations against terrorism. After so many outrages by Arab attackers and so many successes in combating the terrorists, the "kids" broke apart completely over a single bus hijack.

Hazak, Radai, and Malka traded notes and found that they had all been ordered by Shalom to present false testimony and forged memoranda to the agency's internal court. They were willing to do anything for Shin Bet, including lying, fabricating documents, and concealing evidence, but this deliberate deception of Shin Bet's own disciplinary tribunal proved too much for them. They had done it, but now they wanted to come clean.

The three men went to Shalom and demanded a full explanation of why they had been ordered to act as they did. When Shalom's explanations failed to satisfy them, they urged him to resign.

Shalom refused to quit, but he permitted Reuven Hazak to meet with Prime Minister Peres. The meeting was short and frosty. Peres did not want to believe what he was hearing from Hazak. The prime minister had heard beforehand from Shalom that Hazak was making a power play for the job of Shin Bet chief.

Peres was also concerned about the political implications. After all, this was a case that related to the period when Yitzhak Shamir had been prime minister and Moshe Arens defense minister. Now, when all were together in the national unity government, a decision by Peres to side with Hazak could blow the coalition apart. Shin Bet's Shalom could imaginably have been acting with Shamir's knowledge all along. Political infighting based on intelligence scandals, such as the Lavon Affair in Egypt three decades earlier, had never benefited any of the politicians involved. These matters were best left secret.

For a variety of reasons, Peres accepted Shalom's claim that Hazak had a hidden agenda — to stage an internal revolt in Shin Bet. Bolstered by the prime minister's backing, Shalom felt sufficiently strong to suspend all three of his opponents. He was kicking out his former protégés.

If Shalom thought that he was thus closing the lid of Pandora's box, he was deeply mistaken. The three Shin Bet officers pressed forward with their struggle. Even though the agency chief specifically forbade them to do so, they went to Attorney General Zamir at the end of 1985 and gave him further, hair-raising details of alleged perjury and coverups.

Shin Bet was immediately split into two camps: those who supported Shalom, and others who backed the three rebels. It was impossible to remain aloof from a struggle that touched nearly everyone in the secret agency. Clashes between morals and expedience, between emotion and logic, and between loyalty and a higher patriotism were coming to the surface.

Rafi Malka filed a lawsuit in Israel's supreme court, charging that Shalom had wrongly suspended him and demanding that he be reinstated. At Shin Bet headquarters in Tel Aviv, all that everyone discussed — the secretaries who typed the reports, the technicians who invented the counterintelligence equipment, the mechanics who maintained the counterterrorism systems, the operatives checking in from their posts in the occupied territories, and even the heads of departments — was "the case," as if they had no other work to do.

All manner of wild rumors flew around, with the most absurd accusations being made. All the resentments and grudges bottled up for years were being voiced, even to journalists who could not possibly publish them because of press censorship.

Among other tales, it was hinted that behind the extraordinary mushrooming of the scandal stood a woman. It was claimed that one of the three rebels was on intimate terms with a senior Israeli attorney, and that she had pushed them into complaining to the attorney general. This was not merely a debate on how to treat hijackers once they were captured. It was an argument over leadership, morality, and trust. Shin Bet had never known an internal war of such ferocity.

Yitzhak Zamir, who had been dean of the law faculty at Jerusalem's Hebrew University before being appointed in 1981 as attorney general and "legal adviser" to the government, was deeply shaken by the seriousness of the accusations being made. He went to Prime Minister Peres and told him everything he had heard. Zamir said he intended to hand all the evidence, hearsay and documentary, to the police for a formal investigation.

Peres was shocked — not by the evidence he heard, but by the attorney general's plans to pursue it in the way of all perjury and coverup allegations. The prime minister tried to explain to Zamir that a police investigation of Shin Bet would seriously harm national security.

Zamir suggested, as a compromise, that Shalom resign immediately. Shalom and Peres rejected the proposal out of hand. Peres then convened an urgent meeting with Shamir, formally deputy premier, and Defense Minister Yitzhak Rabin. These three men, known collectively as "the prime ministers' club" because all had experience in the top job, decided to do whatever they could to stop Zamir.

Whether Labor or Likud, no one in the major parties wanted to see Shin Bet torn apart even more. In the conflict between democracy and national security, Israel's leaders chose to defend their domestic security agency rather than democratic values.

The three "club" members knew that the attorney general had already asked, months earlier, to be relieved of his position. With no connection at all to Bus 300 and the Shin Bet mess, Zamir had been hoping to retire from government. Peres, Shamir, and Rabin concluded that they should make Zamir's resignation immediate, with a minimum of fuss. They could then have an attorney general and legal adviser who would be more amenable.

The club, accustomed to acting almost as a government within the government — three politicians, making all the toughest decisions on their own — was not going to have its way so easily this time. It was simply too late to stop a scandal that had already begun.

Zamir preferred to postpone his intended departure so he could pursue the Shin Bet case. He saw no contradiction between the democratic rule of law and national security. On the contrary: in his view, an attempt to cover up and obscure matters could only harm Israel.

On May 18, 1986, Zamir lodged a formal complaint with the police, compelling them to investigate the charges and countercharges within Shin Bet. By now, in private talks and even in the public media, the subtle, censored hints had changed from "the Bus 300 case" to "the Shin Bet affair."

A few days after the police launched their probe, Israel's state-owned television news broadcast a brief report of an investigation affecting Shin Bet. Because of the censorship system operated by Aman, the TV newscast was not able to name the intelligence officers concerned. Instead, it referred to "a senior official" and to "the case," which brought to mind the Lavon Affair of the 1950s. Once again, only Israelis who already knew about the scandal could understand what the news media were trying to say. The general public was left in the semidark.

The cork finally flew out of the bottle when the censorship system proved how ineffective it had become. An American television network violated censorship by naming Avraham Shalom as the "senior official." ABC News reported that he was suspected of having ordered the killings of the two bus hijackers, and that the government was trying to cover up the entire case despite the stand adopted by its attorney general. Because the American people had been told rather more about the case, the censor now had to permit the Israeli newspapers to repeat what had been broadcast in the United States. At the very least, Shalom's name was out in the open. A Shin Bet chief had been unmasked in public.

The investigation took shape at an increasingly dizzy pace. The police reluctantly questioned the Shin Bet personnel involved, including Shalom, plus the ministers in power at the time of the hijack, Shamir and Arens.

Shalom, who had decided to defend himself, hinted that he had been acting "with the authority" of Prime Minister Shamir. But once he saw that the evidence was mounting against him and that there were real chances of his being charged with murder or manslaughter, Shalom engineered a clandestine, late-night meeting of the entire cabinet on June 23. On the recommendation of the prime ministers' club, the government passed an unprecedented resolution: The head of Shin Bet and his three rebellious operatives would all be dismissed, and as part of the deal a total of eleven members of Shin Bet would be granted a blanket pardon — so that they could not be brought to trial. The cabinet also appointed a commission of inquiry of three government attorneys, headed by Yehudit Karp, to investigate the Shin Bet case in detail.

Shalom and the others had their immunity from prosecution, which was fortunate for them considering the illegalities exposed by the Karp Commission. Publishing its report at the end of December 1986, the panel praised Hazak, Radai, and Malka for testifying, and it stated its firm conclusion that the three rebels had told the truth. The commission said that the head of Shin Bet had lied, had ordered his aides to lie, and had altogether pulled the wool over the eyes of three prior investigations — by Zorea, by Blatman, and by the Shin Bet disciplinary court.

Karp and her panel also ruled that Hazak, Radai, and Malka had known of Shalom's decision to lie to the Zorea and Blatman commissions. As part of the coverup, the Shin Bet chief had managed to place one of his own men on the Zorea inquiry panel. Only when the Karp

Commission issued its report did the true intent of Shalom's demand become clear.

The Karp report revealed that the Shin Bet representative on the Zorea Commission, Yossi Ginossar, had been Shalom's Trojan horse, informing his boss of the direction being taken by the investigation and influencing the commission to reach conclusions that favored the Shin Bet chief.

Ginossar carried out his task with complete loyalty to Shalom. He changed some evidence, suppressed other statements and documents, and did everything possible to be sure that the coverup would be complete. Before each session of the commission, he met the Shin Bet operatives who were due to appear before the panel. Ginossar would brief them, and he would make sure that their testimony did not conflict with that of others. He hoped that Shalom would help him become the next head of Shin Bet.

Guided gently but surely by Ginossar, the Zorea Commission placed the blame for the killing of the two Arab terrorists on General Mordecai. Whitewashing Shalom's role thus involved blackening the name of a prestigious military officer. The Shin Bet chief was willing to see Mordecai convicted, when the person who had given the orders to kill the terrorists was none other than Shalom himself.

The truth, as it emerged through Karp's report, was that the two wounded bus hijackers were transferred to Shin Bet for interrogation and then killed. The security agency's staff attorneys, who were involved in the coverup, rationalized their behavior by claiming that they had attempted to protect what they called "one of Shin Bet's biggest secrets." The Karp Commission condemned the in-house lawyers.

In his defense, Shalom continued to claim that he had simply acted on the basis of authority granted to him by the prime minister. According to Shalom, he had had a meeting with Yitzhak Shamir in November 1983—five months before the bus hijack—in which the question of how to deal with captured terrorists was dealt with in a general manner, without referring to any specific event. More particularly, Shalom claimed, Defense Minister Arens had authorized the killing of the two terrorists. Arens denied this completely, and while Shamir admitted to having had such a conversation with Shalom, Shamir denied that he had ordered the Shin Bet chief "not to take prisoners."

The Karp Commission chose to believe the prime minister and the defense minister, and not the head of Shin Bet. The commission also stated clearly that on the night of the bus hijack itself, the Shin Bet chief had not received any orders from the prime minister as to how to treat the terrorists.[6]

As a result of the report, it was decided that the practice at the time of Prime Ministers Golda Meir and Yitzhak Rabin would be revived, whereby there would be a note taker present at any meeting between the prime minister and the heads of the secret services. No one had attended the Shamir-Shalom talk in 1983, so there were no memoranda or minutes.

The Karp report left the Israeli public shaken, and even more so its confidence in the intelligence community. After so many years of hearing nothing about Shin Bet and trusting in its proper behavior, many citizens felt that the security chief of their democratic country had acted in a manner characteristic of the worst of dictatorships. According to the reports appearing in the Israeli press, he had behaved as if he were above the law. In the eyes of many Israelis, Shalom could have been forgiven if he had "only" been guilty of killing two Palestinian terrorists. But the coverup, as described in newspapers, went beyond acceptable limits.

As in Israel's Lavon Affair and America's Watergate scandal, the true dynamite was not in the deed itself but in the coverup that followed. As understood by the general population, it seemed that the top people in Shin Bet — the most sensitive branch in the intelligence community, because its actions can affect every Israeli citizen — had conspired against their political superiors and the public they were meant to serve.

Had any one of the central characters in the case stood up at any stage and admitted, "I gave the order," there would have been a chance to contain the fire. But everyone involved in the Shin Bet scandal seemed to try to pass the blame on to others.

The chief of the agency, Avraham Shalom, had to start a new life as a private citizen. Prime Minister Peres helped him get a job with Shaul Eisenberg, an Israel-based international merchant of aircraft, arms, and goods and services of almost all sorts. Shalom was sent to New York, but to avoid the glare of unfavorable publicity he went under his old name, Avraham Bendor.

In the United States, Shalom/Bendor made good use of his professional experience to procure defense-related contracts for Eisenberg. He had always appeared to be an unhappy man, but now he genuinely seemed displeased with his lot. New York was exile for him, and the work was far from fascinating. He even had to take care of the kind of business details which he had delegated to his Shin Bet subordinates for many years.

He had few alternatives. The Shin Bet killings and coverup were too fresh, too embarrassing, and too painful for anyone to give him a decent job in Israel. Shalom/Bendor's homeland had rejected him.

He also found it hard to act freely abroad, however. The Port Authority of New York and New Jersey canceled a $75,000 contract with an Israeli company called Atwell Security when it learned that the firm's president was Bendor and who he really was. The Port Authority said simply it was "no longer satisfied with the agreement" it had signed for security advice at the New York–area airports from the Eisenberg-owned firm of consultants.[7]

In the absence of an explanation by Shalom himself for the killing by interrogators of the two bus hijackers, his friends in and around Shin Bet came up with their own justifications. One claimed that it was a cold-blooded and "professional" move — quite right in terrorist warfare, because the hijackers were amateurs who acted on their own initiative and could not provide any intelligence on any enemy organization. Unable to supply information, they represented no value to Shin Bet. Even a trial, in this view, would be too good for them.

There were others who could explain the decision based on the cumulative influence of Shin Bet's involvement in Lebanon between 1982 and 1985, until the national unity government withdrew the Israeli troops. Lebanon was Shin Bet's Wild West. Press reports spoke of Yossi Ginossar traveling around like a sheriff. There were cases of smuggling and other breaches of army and secret-agency regulations, and reports to Shin Bet headquarters were incomplete at best. The agency's operatives knew that while certain norms and rules of behavior were in effect in the West Bank and Gaza, there was nothing but barely controlled anarchy in Lebanon. The misbehavior learned there spread to the occupied territories.[8]

Everything that was published about Shin Bet and its problems in 1987 was read avidly, and nowhere more than in one of the cells of a military prison in central Israel. As he sat engrossed in his thoughts and longing for his family in Kafr Kama, the afternoon papers arrived in Izat Nafsu's cell, just as they had been arriving for the previous seven years.

He was suddenly overcome by emotion and turned pale. In one of the newspapers, he saw a photograph of Ginossar — one of the Shin Bet officers who had just been pardoned by President Chaim Herzog, as part of the cabinet's decision to end the scandal. The news was that Ginossar had now been given a job in Ariel Sharon's ministry of trade and industry.

"That's the man who interrogated me and set me up!" Nafsu exclaimed, and he hurriedly scribbled a letter to his lawyer. "I said to myself that even if a hundred years pass, I will not forget Ginossar's smile, a mocking smile, and how he told me to strip, spat at me, and afterward, when I was on the floor, stomped on me and pulled out my hair."[9]

That was the beginning of a new case, no less severe than the bus hijack, in which Shin Bet's once-good name was sullied. This one was related to Lebanon.

No one could have expected a security scandal to emerge from a clean and prosperous town such as Kafr Kama, in the rural hills near the Sea of Galilee. Most of the members of Israel's tiniest minority live there: a few thousand Circassians, non-Arab Moslems whose origins are in the Caucasus Mountains of the Soviet Union.

Like almost all the other young men of his community, Nafsu volunteered to serve in the Israeli army, and he was proud that he had attained the rank of lieutenant. In 1976, well before the Israeli invasions of Lebanon in 1978 and 1982, he was sent to serve in the south of that country — a mere thirty miles from his home in Kafr Kama, but across the border from Israeli territory.

"I did not have a specific assignment," Nafsu wrote in his diary. "It was in the first days of Israel's involvement in the region. I was involved in all types of intelligence assignments, without being given any type of real briefing. I was not given specialized training or warned of any specific precautions to take. My assignment required me to live among the Lebanese, many of whom were informers."

Nafsu used the word *shtinker* in his diary, a Hebrew borrowing of the English word "stinker," to describe relatively unimportant collaborators and informers whom Israeli intelligence employed from among the Arabs in Israel and outside the nation's borders. The young lieutenant wrote that his job was to provide arms, ammunition, and medical supplies to Christian and Shiite Moslem Lebanese who would oppose the Palestinians.

Obviously sensitive to the complex historical and religious enmities in Lebanon, Nafsu called it "a place which destroys souls." He wrote: "It was easier for me to liquidate a person there than it is for the Mafia in New York. All around me, the cruelty of jungle law prevailed. Everywhere we looked, we saw events taking place which, in our terms, were utterly appalling — murder, revenge. Human life was cheap."

The diary records many incidents of Israeli soldiers and operatives becoming rich by smuggling cigarettes, watches, televisions, and even drugs into Israel. "For me," Nafsu added, "Abu Kassem was the symbol of all these things. He was a *shtinker* who worked for all sides. He was the Zorba of southern Lebanon. He was as sly as a snake. He was the Lord of Survival, and it was he who decreed my fate."[10]

On the rainy night of January 4, 1980, according to the diary, a knock on his door in Kafr Kama awakened him. Nafsu was still three quarters asleep when he blindly asked in the Circassian language, "Who's there?" There was no reply. Only when he repeated the question in Hebrew did he receive an answer and he opened the door to find one of his friends, Danny Snir — an officer in his army unit. Snir told Nafsu to accompany him immediately on a secret mission into Lebanon, promising that he could return home in a day or two.

Nafsu agreed immediately. He went up to the second floor, took a bundle of clothes he kept ready, kissed his wife, Siahm, whom he had married only three weeks earlier, and accompanied Snir. The next time Nafsu saw his home was seven and a half years later.

Rather than being taken to his military unit Nafsu was brought to a hotel suite in the port city of Haifa, and that is where he first made the acquaintance of Yossi Ginossar. Nafsu did not know the man's real name at the time, but as Nafsu was being treated so well he believed that Shin Bet was out to recruit him.

As the conversation continued, however, he realized that he was under investigation. The anonymous questioner kept asking about a certain PLO man who, according to Shin Bet, had been in contact with Nafsu. Only then did the Circassian officer begin to be afraid.

The Shin Bet man said, "Confess that you were a double agent of the PLO. You can't play around with us; we know everything. We have been following you for months." Nafsu denied all the charges vehemently and he continued to do so after being transferred to Kishon prison in Haifa, where Shin Bet maintains its own cells.

"Days and nights of investigation, threats, and intimidation began," Nafsu wrote, adding that the then anonymous Ginossar had a superior who called himself only "Pashosh."

"Once 'Pashosh' came into the room and claimed that he was the deputy head of Shin Bet and head of its investigations branch. He threatened to send me to a facility used to investigate terrorists, and that they would inject me with a substance which would render me impotent. This threat of an injection was repeated constantly throughout the investigation. Someone would open a drawer, as if he were taking out the hypodermic."

Nafsu's diary says the Shin Bet interrogators also threatened to detain his wife and strip her naked. "They would sometimes bring *Playboy* magazine with its pictures of nude women, so that I would get the message. They also threatened to bring my wife and tell her that I had had homosexual relations with Abu Kassem, and that they would spread rumors in my village that I was a 'homo.' "[11]

Nafsu understood that the material against him was based on Abu Kassem's testimony, and that the alleged motive for his working with the PLO was sexual blackmail. Ginossar claimed that he had witnesses, including Abu Kassem, who had seen Nafsu go to bed with a PLO man and with a Lebanese Christian man. After the threats, other Shin Bet investigators came to Nafsu's cell and played the role of the good guys. They promised him that if he cooperated and told everything he knew, they would give him a furlough so he could visit his wife.

The specialty of any intelligence agency, and Israel's Shin Bet is especially talented in this area, is discovering the weaknesses of the people it contacts. In the case of Nafsu, his weak points were his wife and his masculinity. As a member of the Circassian community, with its clearly defined status for the male, he was afraid of the humiliation that he would suffer if the interrogators' innuendos were circulated.

After forty days of continuous interrogation, he finally broke. He confessed to all the crimes attributed to him, including treason and espionage against Israel through contacts with the PLO.

But when the trial began before a military tribunal, Nafsu retracted his confession and claimed that it had been obtained through pressure and threats. The Shin Bet investigators denied this, of course, and the judge — as in most cases regarding the security agency — believed them.

The trial was conducted behind closed doors, and even the accused's family was denied access to the courtroom. After hearings and deliberations that dragged on for two years, Nafsu was convicted. At the end of 1982, he was sentenced to eighteen years in prison and demotion to the rank of private.

Only Nafsu, his family, and his lawyer — who had previously been Israel's chief military prosecutor — continued to believe in his innocence. Even after his judicial appeals were rejected Nafsu refused to entertain suggestions, from Shin Bet among others, that he request a pardon. "I wanted an acquittal, not a pardon," he explained.

Nafsu got what he wanted — but after long suffering — on May 24, 1987, when the Israeli supreme court acquitted him of espionage and treason charges and annulled his eighteen-year sentence. Nafsu was freed, was promoted to the rank of sergeant, and was paid all the salary due since his arrest. The justices did sentence him to two years in prison, time already served, for failure to report meetings with PLO members in Lebanon. The focus of the ruling, however, was harsh criticism of Shin Bet, its interrogators, and the methods they used to extract confessions.

The secret agency's actions were merely part of a wider, hostile environment. Shin Bet was like the bogey man with whom parents would threaten their children if they did not behave. So it was in the case of Daniel Shoshan. He was a private in the Israeli army, sentenced in October 1986 to ten years in prison for "transferring information to the enemy." As an army mail courier, he allegedly handed documents to an Arab in the West Bank who had PLO connections. The military police interrogators intimidated Shoshan by warning him that if he did not confess to the charges, they would turn him over to Shin Bet — and that would, no doubt, be much worse for him. Based on what he had heard about Shin Bet, he succumbed to the pressure and confessed to a crime he did not commit.

Two years later, after a retrial, Shoshan was completely cleared. The appeals judges ruled that the military police had used physical force and other coercion to obtain the young soldier's confession, and that they had concealed evidence from the court.[12]

The Israeli public became accustomed to a new, negative reality. Barely a decade earlier, it had been practically forbidden to utter the name of Shin Bet and absolutely unacceptable to criticize the secret services. Now, within less than a year, the veil of secrecy had been lifted twice to show Shin Bet sullied by its two worst scandals: the killing of the bus hijackers, and the improper prosecution of Nafsu. The agency's judgment, piety of purpose, and modus operandi were now under widespread suspicion. The people of Israel were seeing their domestic security agency for the first time, and they did not like what they saw.

President Herzog, who had consented to the deal whereby he pardoned the senior officers of Shin Bet, now declared that the Nafsu case had made him feel "ashamed." The new attorney general, Yosef Harish, defied the wishes of the prime ministers' club and of Shin Bet itself by ordering an investigation of Nafsu's interrogators. The official intention was to press criminal charges, even though it was clear that Ginossar could not be touched because of the blanket pardon he had received.

Following pressure by public opinion, as represented by Israel's newspapers and magazines, the government appointed a commission of inquiry on May 31, 1987, just a week after Nafsu was set free by the supreme court. The newest inquiry into the intelligence community and its methods would be headed by Justice Moshe Landau, who had retired from the supreme court. The other two investigators were former Mossad chief Yitzhak Hofi and the state comptroller, Yaakov Maltz. For half a year, the Landau Commission heard testimony from prime ministers, heads of Shin Bet, its operatives and legal advisers, those who had been interrogated, representatives of the Israeli Association for Civil Rights, and even foreign attorneys from Amnesty International.

In the meantime, yet another disturbing case came to light. Awad Hamdan, a twenty-three-year-old resident of a small village near the town of Tulkarem on the West Bank, was arrested on July 19, 1987, by Shin Bet men. He was suspected of membership in a Palestinian terrorist organization. Two days later, he died in his cell. His interrogators claimed that he had died of a heart attack, but his family stated that his corpse showed signs of physical brutality.[13]

Suspicions of torture swirled about the Hamdan affair and they tainted even the government's pathological institute, where forensic experts were in charge of determining the cause of death of all who expired under suspicious circumstances in Israel.

Until the Landau Commission report in late November 1987, the institute had the reputation of being reliable, professional, and trustworthy. It then became clear that, in the interests of "security," a number of the doctors there had distorted the facts. They readily determined the cause of death of the two terrorists killed in the Bus 300 affair — in Shin Bet's favor as far as was possible — and agreed to state that Hamdan had died as the result of a heart attack.[14]

The Landau report was simply devastating: a printed record of how deeply the rot had penetrated inside Shin Bet. It said that as early as 1971, the then chief of the agency, Yosef Harmelin, had agreed to have his men lie in court. The report noted that Harmelin did not order his men to lie, but simply accepted this as a fact of life.

Landau, Hofi, and Maltz unanimously revealed that Shin Bet operatives lied to Israeli courts as a matter of course and habit, even though Israeli law imposes a penalty of seven years in prison for perjury. Shin Bet employees placed themselves above the law.

The decision to lie stemmed from the drastic upsurge in terrorist acts that followed Israel's capture of the West Bank and Gaza Strip. As the terrorism increased, Shin Bet investigators felt they had to use psychological pressures and some forms of torture — "physical pressure," in the words of the commission — to extract confessions from the guilty.

Shin Bet took on the assignment of obtaining preventive intelligence, to give the earliest possible warning of Palestinian attacks. Its methods, however, went beyond Israeli law. Hundreds of terrorist trials were little more than summary court martials, in which military prosecutors would simply read aloud the confessions obtained by Shin Bet. When defendants claimed that they had been tortured or otherwise coerced into making false statements, the military judges — without any jury in the process — accepted Shin Bet's denials.

A pattern of perjury continued for sixteen years, spanning the terms of Avraham Ahituv and Avraham Shalom at the top of the agency. The Landau report said that Shalom "found a norm based on false testimony, so we were told, which 'was transferred from one generation to the next.'

" 'When I think of the war against terrorists,' so he told us, 'I do not think in the context of the Israeli court.' He did not even understand that there is something wrong with this norm. The commission regards him as one of those responsible for the existence of this defective method."

The report deplored the entire Shin Bet leadership, "which failed in not understanding that no security consideration, important or vital as it may be, can place those involved above the law. The leadership did not understand that it had been entrusted with an essential mission which might possibly justify certain means, but not all means, and certainly not that of giving false testimony."

Landau's conclusions were written with more crystal clarity than most government documents when he noted that within Shin Bet, it was mandatory that operatives tell the truth. "Whoever was found not to have reported the truth within the service was punished in the most severe fashion, and there were even cases of dismissal from the service. This approach created a type of 'double bookkeeping': insistence on truth within the service on the one hand, and false testimony in court on the other. This dual message evidently did not disturb anyone for sixteen years."

At the same time, because the commission stressed the complexity of Shin Bet's struggle against terrorism, it explicitly stated that the agency's interrogators have the right to use a certain degree of "pressure" on people — meaning Arabs — being questioned, without defining what the limits should be. The report cautioned, however, that each Shin Bet operative should not "make his own rules for himself, arbitrarily, in applying pressure upon the person being interrogated." The report continued:

> In such circumstances, Israel's image as a law-abiding state, which observes civil rights, might be irreparably destroyed, and it might come to resemble those regimes which grant their security services unlimited powers. In order to prevent this danger, one may not use excessive pressure upon a person being interrogated. The pressure may not reach the stage of physical affliction or of brutality against the person under investigation, or of any serious infringement of his honor which denies his dignity as a human being.

Hoping to offer some sort of guideline, Landau wrote: "The degree to which these means are employed must be weighed against the degree of expected danger. The means of physical and psychological pressure must be defined and limited in advance. Every departure from the permissible must be met by a reaction from the commanders which is forceful and unhesitating."[15]

The commission thus chose a middle course between the view that the law must be supreme, regardless of the terrorist threat, and the opinion that fighting terrorism requires departures from the strict rule of law. But even while Justice Landau and his colleagues were concerned about a Shin Bet running wild, they did not attempt to uproot overnight the unlawful norms to which the agency had become accustomed.

Even before the ink on the report had dried, it became clear that three Shin Bet interrogators had lied to the Landau Commission. As soon as the new head of Shin Bet found out about the false testimony, he suspended all three. The irony was that the new agency chief was none other than Yosef Harmelin — coaxed out of retirement for a second term twelve years after leaving Shin Bet, and seven years after flying aboard a United States evacuation aircraft out of Teheran, where he was Israel's unofficial ambassador until the Islamic revolution in 1979.

It was during Harmelin's original Shin Bet term, from 1964 to 1974, that the habit of lying to the courts had developed. Harmelin was an established and respected veteran, however, and was welcomed in 1986 as an interim Shin Bet chief to fill in at a time of crisis. His assignment was to reintroduce order, trust, and hope in the agency, which had been torn apart by the various scandals and inquiries.

There was grave fear that Shin Bet's efficiency would be seriously impaired. Morale was certainly terrible. After the Karp and Landau reports, many Shin Bet operatives felt that they had been abandoned, as usual, by the politicians who expected the secret services to take care of the dirty work in the cruel war against terror.

In Shin Bet, the signs of discontent continued to grow. Operatives barely concealed their disgust with investigators and journalists who seemed to expect a pure, ultraclean form of warfare against terrorism. The Shin Bet people blamed politicians for failing to make long-range decisions on the status of the occupied West Bank and Gaza Strip and law enforcement there. "We are the scapegoats of the occupation," was how many in Shin Bet felt. More than thirty-five years after the original revolt of the spies who abhorred the formation of the Mossad, it appeared that another minirevolt might break out inside the Israeli intelligence community.

Harmelin, in his quiet way, managed to stabilize the Shin Bet ranks and to calm down his employees. He was unable, however, to rectify the damage caused to the reputation of Shin Bet and of the entire intelligence community. For the first time in Israel's history, the secret services ceased to be sacred cows which need not face questions about their methods of operation.

The kinds of questions that rocked the CIA in the 1970s confronted Israel's intelligence community in the 1980s with unprecedented doubts and painful truths. Having lost a large measure of public confidence at home, Israel's spymasters were also facing a crisis with their best friends abroad.

FOURTEEN

A Spy in America

WHEN JONATHAN JAY POLLARD burst into the Israeli embassy compound in Washington, D.C., on November 21, 1985, it was the final act in a covert operation that threatened the Jewish state's lifelong relationship of trust with its most vital ally, the United States, one of the key sources of Israeli strength.

Jay Pollard was sitting in his five-year-old Ford Mustang that Thursday morning, sweating profusely. He was at the wheel; his wife, Anne Henderson-Pollard, sat on his right; they had their birth certificates, marriage certificate, family photographs, their cat, and their cat's vaccination papers with them. The Pollards were ready to flee America. They were just outside the gates of the embassy compound, near Connecticut Avenue and Van Ness Street in Northwest Washington, and their engine was running.

The heavy steel doors swung open to let another car in. Pollard stepped down on the accelerator, swerving around the other vehicle, to bring his Mustang into the parking lot at the front of the embassy building, which was new, but built in an ancient style of Jerusalem stone and arched windows. An Israeli security guard was about to pull a gun out of his concealed shoulder holster, when the pudgy, balding thirty-one-year-old driver blurted out something about being a Jew seeking asylum. "The FBI is on to me, I need help," he told the puzzled Israelis.

Within moments, FBI agents who had followed Pollard were telling the Israeli security team, through the intercom at the gate, that the man who had just entered the compound in a Mustang was wanted for questioning. Armed with diplomatic immunity, the Israelis could have done almost anything — although sheltering a fugitive would surely lead to a damaging diplomatic incident. The front gate made a quick internal telephone call to the top floor of the six-story building, where Israel's intelligence agencies had their Washington representatives.

The embassy's chief security officer had heard from Pollard himself the previous day, reciting the names of Rafi Eitan and other handlers and demanding help. In a second phone call, the security man told the American to come to the embassy if he could "shake" the FBI. But here was the FBI right behind the Pollards, who were still waiting in the parking lot out front, surrounded by Israeli plainclothes guards.

"Sorry," the two Americans seeking refuge were told, as the Israeli security men escorted them back out the front gate. The FBI men arrested Pollard, and they drove his wife home to 1733 20th Street, N.W. Jonathan Jay Pollard was on his way to a life in prison.

Pollard was a civilian who had worked for the U.S. Navy for six years, most of that time in various intelligence and counterterrorism units. Lest that sound too swashbuckling, Pollard was only a desk man. But he was a man whose desk included a computer with access to almost every secret collected and stored by America's huge intelligence network. And while he considered himself a loyal American, he was also a fervent supporter of Israel.

Pollard was born on August 7, 1954, to a Jewish family in Galveston, Texas, and he spent most of his youth in South Bend, Indiana. These were not America's strongest centers of Jewish culture or pro-Israel activism, but Pollard was a loner anyway. He developed his Zionist zealotry on his own.

Pollard studied at Stanford University, one of the nation's finest, where his international relations professors found he had an overactive imagination. He claimed to be a colonel in the Israeli army, although at other times he said he was a captain, and he even told acquaintances that the Mossad was grooming him to be a spy within the U.S. government.[1]

Pollard's dorm neighbors considered him "very troubled and shadowy," and he once was so agitated about a group of Israelis supposedly trying to kill him that he showed friends a revolver and locked himself in his room. He also told them that once, on guard duty on a kibbutz, he had killed an Arab.[2]

Pollard's stories always involved Israel, and he left some people with the impression that the Mossad was paying his tuition fees.

While the tales did not all seem to be credible, they were told with such conviction that it was hard to believe they were totally false. They were.

After receiving a bachelor's degree from Stanford in 1976, Pollard crossed the country to the Fletcher School of Law and Diplomacy at Tufts University, near Boston. His graduate courses did not yield a degree, but the United States Navy hired him as a civilian intelligence analyst in the fall of 1979. His Washington-area navy jobs were in agencies with names such as the Naval Operational Surveillance and Intelligence Center, the Naval Intelligence Support Center, and the Naval Investigative Service (NIS).

He was one of the chosen few brought into the new Anti-Terrorism Alert Center in NIS headquarters in Suitland, Maryland, when all the American armed forces greatly expanded their effort to detect early signs of a terrorist threat. That was in June 1984, in reaction to the suicide truck bombing that killed 241 U.S. servicemen in Beirut the previous October. A serious attempt to bring together all available facts, clues, and rumors in this shadowy field necessarily involves access to a wide range of sources and reports: on likely targets, potential attackers, the identity of groups and individuals aiding terrorists, and what other countries are doing about it.

In this age of terrorism, hardly any specific area in government service and defense work could be quite so multidisciplinary. In other words, Pollard enjoyed access to almost everything. Not only did he have a computer that could reach into memory banks throughout the federal intelligence system; not only did he have permission to see top secret papers; he had the even higher level of clearance known as SCI, or Sensitive Compartmented Information. And he had D.C.'s most valuable library card — a "courier card" that permitted him to visit high-security archives and carry documents back to his office for analysis.

The nightmare of why his American employers failed to detect his erratic personality traits in school, his exaggerated boasts and his outright lies, would go on to haunt security officers in Washington for years. Pollard applied to the CIA for employment in 1977 but was rejected. When the Pentagon's Defense Investigative Service (DIS) performed the standard background check on Pollard as an applicant for a navy intelligence job two years later, they interviewed Pollard's father and a few fellow students at Fletcher. But the CIA reportedly did not provide the DIS with the Agency's assessment of Pollard as "a fanciful liar, a closet spy, a Zionist zealot, and a drug abuser."[3]

In 1981 the navy did strip Pollard of his security clearance for a short while, because of unspecified emotional problems described as "bizarre behavior." Pollard even claimed to be a close friend of a senior South African intelligence man, but when that official visited the United States, Pollard's bosses quickly discovered that his claims had been false. They suggested that he seek psychiatric counseling, but Pollard battled through the bureaucracy for about six months, filing a formal grievance and winning a reversal of the decision — if only because the U.S. military could not prove that there was anything wrong with its peculiar civilian employee.

Jay Pollard, the American intelligence analyst who dreamed of spying for Israel, set out to live his fantasies. He took his first real step into the realm of treason in May 1984, when he met the man who would make him a spy. Through a New York businessman he knew, Pollard was introduced to an Israeli air force colonel named Aviem Sella.

It was conspiracy at first sight. Pollard told the colonel that he had positive proof that the United States was not sharing all the intelligence data it should with Israel, and Pollard said he was angry about it. Sella, one of Israel's finest pilots, who had taken part in the raid on the Iraqi nuclear reactor in 1981, listened with interest.

Sella dutifully reported through the chain of command, all the way back to air force headquarters in Tel Aviv. From there, his report about a frustrated U.S. intelligence man interested in helping Israel was passed to Rafi Eitan, the frustrated Israeli intelligence man now associated with the defense ministry as head of the technological espionage agency Lakam.

Israel was already obtaining valuable technology of the most sensitive kind from at least one source in the United States. Among the go-betweens was an Israeli entrepreneur in Hollywood who introduced his country's defense officials to a corporation named Milco of California, owned by Richard Smyth. An American Jew, Smyth was charged by a federal grand jury in May 1985 with smuggling 810 krytrons to Israel. Krytrons are electronic devices that can be used as detonators in nuclear bombs. A special license was required to export them, but had Smyth applied for a permit the U.S. government would have refused on the grounds that Israel had not signed the international Nuclear Non-Proliferation Treaty.

FBI investigators found that 80 percent of Milco's business, dating back to 1973, was with Israel. Smyth was freed on one hundred thousand dollars bail, but three months later he did not appear for his trial. He disappeared, but sightings of Smyth were reported in Britain and in Israel.

Israel apologized to the United States after the case hit the headlines, stating that the krytrons were meant for medical purposes and had not been used in its nuclear program. As the Americans demanded, all "unused" detonators were returned.[4]

A number of other incidents were reported in 1985 in which Israeli government corporations, such as Israel Military Industries, were allegedly involved in shady deals with American corporations. Some of the Americans were even put on trial. Government officials, especially in the U.S. Customs Service and the FBI, did not hide their outrage at Israel's conduct.

Still, the loudest and clearest message from Washington, especially after Ronald Reagan became president in 1981, was that Israel would never suffer long for anything it did. The golden era of the undeclared but vigorous U.S.-Israeli alliance had finally reached full fruition.

There was no formal pledge, as in the case of NATO and other military pacts, that an attack on one nation would be considered an attack on both. But Israel had good reason to feel itself just as close to and more protected by the United States than the official Western allies such as Britain could feel.

Reagan went further than any U.S. president had done to make the Israelis feel secure. There was no real U.S. government protest at the invasion of Lebanon in 1982. The State Department railed against the construction of Jewish settlements in the occupied territories but did nothing about it. Most importantly, the White House gave enthusiastic backing to a formal memorandum on strategic cooperation with Israel.

Much of the memorandum was kept secret, but visible effects included an increase in port visits to Haifa by America's Sixth Fleet. Military equipment and medical supplies were prepositioned in Israel by the U.S. armed forces, and joint training exercises were far more common than ever. The invisible effects included heightened cooperation between the intelligence communities — including the fight against terrorism, in which the United States was almost totally dependent on the Israelis for information on Arab terrorist groups.

CIA veterans with long years of service in the Middle East concluded that the Israelis could get away with anything and certainly knew it. One American spy even told a Mossad contact, only half jokingly, that Israel was lucky it never became the fifty-first state. "Why are we so lucky?" the Israeli intelligence man wondered.

"Because then," said the CIA agent, "you would only have two U.S. senators, and this way you have at least sixty."

The Reagan administration, with the enthusiastic endorsement of the pro-Israeli Congress, was giving the Jewish state around three billion dollars a year in aid, two thirds of it in military support. The well of generosity appeared almost bottomless, and the fountain of forgiveness for the occasional transgression never ran dry.

Still, the intelligence communities of both countries knew enough to be suspicious of each other. The FBI was especially wary of the wide range of Israeli activities in the United States, convinced that much of it amounted to spying, and it was always on the lookout for violations of law in Israel's aggressive acquisition of technology.

The fact that there had been a few prosecutions and even more leaks to the press by angry American officials served as a warning to Eitan and the rest of Israel's military-industrial establishment that covert action always carries the danger of being caught. This was no new revelation to Eitan, a seasoned professional who had been directing complex plots and running agents for decades in the Mossad and Shin Bet. When he read Colonel Sella's report from New York, Eitan was both intrigued and dubious about the appearance of Pollard as a "walk-in" volunteer. It could be a "sting" operation by the U.S. authorities or a trap of another sort, and a spymaster such as Eitan knows to be cautious about anyone who seems overly eager.

Eitan also knew, however, that the young American could be very valuable. Despite the formal exchange agreements, Israel's intelligence community always assumed that the United States was not sharing everything. Pollard could fill the gaps. Only with a spy on the inside could the Israelis know what they were missing.

Pollard also represented Eitan's chance to out-Mossad the Mossad, as part of his efforts to expand Lakam into new territory — to show that only he could obtain more from Washington than the CIA and the Pentagon were providing.

Mossad chief Admoni refused to have his agency formally run a spy in the heart of the American intelligence community, in light of the 1951 cooperation agreement with the CIA and successive updates of the accord. There were daily contacts, including computer links, plus formal meetings twice a year to consider new plans for cooperation and to review the world with a view toward joint opportunities. It would be embarrassing and even destructive to the relationship for the Mossad to plant an agent among its friends; even worse, to be caught.

While spying covertly, dishonestly, and directly on each other's intelligence communities was officially considered out of bounds, wily espionage plotters on both sides knew that it could be done if the utmost caution and professional spycraft were used. The first priority, according to Americans and Israelis who clearly have carried out such operations, would be to mask who was really running the show. In theory, if the CIA found an agent it could recruit within Israeli intelligence, the ideal technique would require that the agent not know he was being hired by the United States. He should be "false-flagged," meaning he would be told it was Switzerland or West Germany or somebody else offering him money in exchange for information.

If the agent does know for whom he is working and indeed insists that he only wishes to serve the United States, then at the very least he should not be run through the local CIA station in Tel Aviv. There should be no traces of American involvement, and meetings should be held in third countries. The operation should be directed from some other CIA station.

Even better, alternative agencies should be used. The CIA should not be involved formally in running spies within Israel and should hand over such responsibility to another part of the U.S. intelligence community. Similarly, when presented with an espionage opportunity in the United States the Mossad could elect to leave the job to another agency such as Lakam.

In fact, there is no indication that American intelligence penetrated Israel's secret services. However, the United States has sent spies into Israel on specific missions to learn about military, economic, and scientific projects — including the nuclear program. Defense Minister Yitzhak Rabin remarked immediately after Pollard's arrest that Israel had discovered five American spies in the late 1970s and early 1980s in sensitive nuclear and industrial facilities. One had been gathering information within the state-owned arms development company Rafael in Haifa. Another was an American scientist working as part of an exchange program in the Nahal Sorek nuclear research reactor that had been given to Israel by the Eisenhower administration. The American spies were questioned, but Israel's less rigid legal system made it possible for the government to release and expel them for the sake of avoiding embarrassment and conflict with the United States.

In these operations, considered highly sensitive and never officially confirmed by Washington, the above recipe was scrupulously used. The American operatives came from third-country bases. The CIA station chief in Tel Aviv was never told, so he could totally avoid compromising his function as liaison with the Mossad. And if an Israeli agent had to be paid for information or "research," it was preferable that he never know that the American dollars he received were, in every sense, U.S. dollars. When the Pollard case came to light, Senate Intelligence Committee member David Durenberger let it slip that American intelligence had run at least one Israeli soldier as a paid agent during the 1982 invasion of Lebanon.

CIA headquarters staff in Langley was always tempted to look for potential agents among the hundreds of thousands of Americans who have moved to Israel. However, because they are almost all Jews who became immigrants for the sake of religion or Zionism, the CIA felt their ultimate loyalty would more likely be to Israel rather than to their native United States. While Israeli intelligence always believed that Soviet-bloc espionage agencies were planting spies among Jewish immigrants heading to their biblical homeland, they never seriously suspected that the CIA was doing so. Shin Bet officials found almost anything conceivable, but did not believe there were any longtime American moles among the waves of new Israelis.

On the other hand, American intelligence took it for granted that there were spies among the Israelis who moved to the United States or visited for work or study. How could a country considering itself at war, even a friendly nation, not send secret agents wherever there was useful information and material to be found?

Israeli covert activities in the United States were, indeed, widespread, but not nearly so structured or ominous as FBI officials and other xenophobes might have supposed. Israelis traveling abroad, even to America, were sometimes asked to keep their eyes open — especially if they were scientists taking part in projects of interest to

Israeli defense. But they would not be formally hired or even paid by the Mossad or Aman. Information that could help Israel ought to be sent home for patriotic reasons, many of the travelers felt. Most Israelis in America, of course, never did anything of the sort and never saw anything of espionage interest anyway. But from the few who did help, Israeli intelligence — sometimes getting the information through institutes and businesses with employees abroad — benefited.

Whatever the clandestine activity in the United States, the Mossad avoided using its local station in Washington — just as the Americans did in Israel. When an Israeli spy was sent to America on a specific mission, the Mossad people in Washington were not told. Also similar to the CIA recipe, if Israeli intelligence felt it had to pay an American for information, every effort would be made to use the "false flag" of another nation or, even better, to make it appear like a little harmless industrial espionage by a U.S. company.

Jonathan Pollard was truly an unusual case. He was a walk-in; he was working in naval intelligence with access to documents; and he was Jewish, offering to work only for his beloved Israel. Eitan knew of the dangers of using local Jews as secret agents inside their own home countries — along the pattern of Egypt and Iraq in the 1950s. But the information that Pollard could obtain was irresistible.

With the consent of the chief of staff and the air force commander, Eitan was allowed to use Colonel Sella for the unique mission. The two top military generals, Moshe Levy and Amos Lapidot, were not to know the precise details of what Sella, the veteran flier now studying computer science at New York University, would be doing for his country.

Eitan directed Sella to inform Pollard that the Jewish state was prepared to give him a try. The colonel had several guarded conversations with the American intelligence analyst, using public telephone booths in New York and Washington to minimize the chances of an FBI wiretap.

Sella commuted to Washington on shuttle flights from New York several times in the summer of 1984, to meet with Pollard and pick up documents. Sella was assisted by Eitan's Lakam attachés in both American cities, but unlike them Sella was not protected by diplomatic immunity. If he were arrested and tried for receiving secret papers, Sella himself, the air force, and the State of Israel would be severely embarrassed and probably much worse. The young colonel, although trained in combat flying rather than espionage, was willing to take the risk.

The first documents given to Sella were from the Naval Intelligence Service, mainly computer printouts from Pollard's terminal. They were rushed to Tel Aviv by diplomatic pouch, and they were astounding — by far exceeding Eitan's expectations.

Pollard had only recently joined the Anti-Terrorism Alert Center in Suitland, Maryland, yet he was immediately giving Sella information on subjects ranging far beyond his work at the ATAC. There were tantalizing details — not the full story, but filling in some of the gaps in Israel's own knowledge — on Syria's development of a chemical arsenal and Iraq's efforts to revive its nuclear program.

There was information on some of the newest weapons systems obtained by Israel's Arab neighbors. There were even lists and descriptions of arms recently purchased by Egypt, Jordan, and Saudi Arabia, and because those three Arab states were seen as pro-American moderates the United States had always refused to share its intelligence about them with Israel. Now, Eitan realized, Israel could have a window onto those countries.

Pollard's enthusiasm was overwhelming, especially after he was promoted within the ATAC in October 1984. His security clearance was elevated and, he told the Israelis, almost any document in the American intelligence network would be within his reach.

He could even borrow reconnaissance photographs taken by American spy satellites, but because these could not be reproduced by his computer terminal he would have to borrow the photos for a day or two.

Sella was thrilled. He knew how valuable the spy-in-the-sky could be. Just over three years earlier, before leading his squadron of fighter-bombers in the raid on the Baghdad reactor, Sella had studied U.S. satellite photos that pinpointed the target. Such access was rare, however. Only infrequently did CIA director William Casey share such gems with Israel as part of the strategic cooperation accords. Meantime, Sella completed his computer courses in New York and returned to Israel. Pollard waited for a new case officer.

Eitan was so pleased with the results so far that he decided to launch a new phase. Pollard and Anne Henderson, then his fiancée, were flown to Paris at Lakam's expense in November 1984. There, a little surprise awaited them. Avi Sella was again on the scene, and he wined them in the City of Light. Pollard was puzzled as to why they had been brought to France for a pleasant reunion. The mystery was cleared up when Sella introduced him to Yossi Yagur, his new case officer.

Yagur was Lakam's science consul at the Israeli consulate in New York. His official, but vague, résumé speaks of several unspecified jobs earlier in the defense ministry. In case the worst should happen, Yagur was protected by diplomatic immunity.

As consul since 1980, Yagur was accustomed to attending academic conferences, forging friendships with American scientists in the defense and other industries, and sending huge files of clippings from newspapers and professional journals to Lakam's analysts in Tel Aviv.

As a further surprise, Pollard got to meet the legendary Rafi Eitan, whose exploits such as kidnapping Eichmann were outlined to the young American to impress him. Eitan was introduced as director of the entire operation, and he and Yagur sat down with Pollard to discuss their next moves, including specific documents required for Israel's defense.[5]

In more relaxed moments, Sella encouraged Jay and Anne to admire the windows of some of the French capital's most elegant jewelry stores. When she fell in love with a large sapphire and diamond ring, Sella said, "Go ahead and buy it." He would pay, on condition that they make it their engagement ring.

It cost around ten thousand dollars, and in many ways it was the tangible mark of the Pollards' engagement by Israel. Sella even gave them a handwritten note that spoke of the jewelry as a gift from "Uncle Joe," just in case someone in Washington should ask them how they could afford such a thing. Jay and Anne would marry the following August in Venice and spend a three-week honeymoon there — which was not only paid for by Israel, but included a detour to Tel Aviv to meet Eitan again.

In compensation for necessary expenses and as a token of their appreciation, the Israelis told Pollard, he would be paid fifteen hundred dollars a month. In addition to Anne's ring, Pollard was immediately given ten thousand dollars in cash, and Eitan told him that a Swiss bank account had been opened for him. His fees would be deposited directly, for Pollard's use in ten years. By then, the American replied, he would hope to live in Israel. Yagur responded to that by showing him an Israeli passport already prepared for Pollard with his photograph and the false name "Danny Cohen." The Lakam team had not chosen just any old Jewish name. Their American agent had expressed great admiration for the Israeli master spy who was hanged in Damascus, Eli Cohen. So to butter up Pollard, Eitan and Yagur offered him the same family name on a passport. He would be welcome in Israel at any time, as an unheard and unseen hero.

What Eitan did not tell Pollard was that the diamond ring and the cash were part of a classic technique to ensnare a secret agent and keep him. The spy who tells his controllers he is acting voluntarily, out of ideological affection for the country he is helping — or disgruntled hatred of the nation he is betraying — can easily be overcome by fear or change his mind. Being a volunteer, he feels he can withdraw at any time.

A paid agent cannot. He feels obliged to deliver, and in the background lies the threat of blackmail. The recruiters could always get the agent in trouble with documentary proof of money handed over. By establishing this implied contract, the employer can feel certain of having hired a loyal agent.

Pollard's motivation was a combination of Zionism and excitement. The thrill of being a spy was enhanced by exotic trips and secret payments. But as a zealot, he doubtless got his greatest pleasure from knowing that he helped Israel defend itself.

As soon as he returned home from Europe, Pollard got right to work. He brought an entire suitcase full of documents — and the fabled satellite photographs of the Middle East — to a house in Maryland where he met Yagur. The case officer taught Pollard some codewords to be used in case communication or cancellation of an expected meeting was absolutely necessary. Yagur told Pollard that he would be expected and most welcome, every other Friday, at a special photocopying facility being prepared in a Washington apartment building where Irit Erb resided. She worked as a secretary for a Lakam man in the Israeli embassy.

An apartment filled with photocopying equipment had been purchased by Harold Katz, an American Jew working as a lawyer in Israel who apparently did not know how his Washington residence was to be used by the defense ministry. There was so much high-speed and high-quality copying hardware that a special electronic defense system was installed to prevent any electromagnetic interference that could be noticed on the television sets of neighbors.[6]

The Israeli handlers knew how to keep Pollard interested in his work: they stroked his ego. Yagur frequently told Pollard that he was extremely valuable, and that various parts of Israel's intelligence and defense communities were using the information he had provided. Because Pollard was in the business of analyzing such matters, he was not satisfied by generous but general platitudes. He insisted that Yagur find out, line by line, agency by agency, who in Israel was using the secret documents from Washington and how.

The various agency chiefs in Tel Aviv must have known that Eitan's scoops were coming from Washington. After all, only an American source could have provided satellite photographs. No one asked Eitan who his agent was. A military man? A Jew? An Israeli planted in the U.S. armed forces or secret agencies? Men such as Admoni of the Mossad and the new Aman chief, Ehud Barak, must have wondered. The quality of the "product" was so good that the nature and risks of the espionage operation should not have been ignored.

It is inherent in the system, however, that such questions are never asked about another agency's operation. Revealing details would violate compartmentalization. Their internal rivalries also would have stopped them from insisting that their counterparts reveal their sources.

Pollard was bringing huge piles of files to Irit Erb in fortnightly installments. At first, he did the selecting. But Yagur then made it a habit to choose certain documents in advance — as though he were ordering from a menu, in this case, apparently, a catalog of documents compiled by the Pentagon's Defense Intelligence Agency, the DIA. How could such a catalog, itself a classified document, fall into the hands of foreigners? American investigators saw this as prima facie evidence of another Israeli spy, probably more important than Pollard.

Theoretically, Israel could have obtained the catalog from an agent or a source in a NATO country, which might have gotten it from the United States. On the other hand, the Israeli embassy in Washington has a huge number of friends in the Pentagon, even when the secretary of defense is antagonistic toward Israel, as was Caspar Weinberger during Pollard's illicit activities.

Using his "courier card" — the most valuable library card in the Washington area — Pollard was able to borrow secret documents from six restricted archives: the CIA, the FBI, the State Department, the

DIA, his own NIS, and even the National Security Agency with its tight controls.[7] If it involved the Middle East, even peripherally, Pollard believed that Israel should know about it. He felt strongly that Secretary Weinberger and the U.S. intelligence community were not sharing with Israel everything they knew about potential threats to the Jewish state.

Thanks to their eccentric but effective spy, the Israelis received CIA analyses, copies of messages exchanged among American facilities in the region, details of Soviet arms shipments to Syria and other allies as spotted by U.S. secret agents or spy-in-the-sky satellites, and actual photographs from those satellites.

While much in the way of raw data and polished analysis was regularly shared between Washington and Tel Aviv, satellite photos had always been a particular problem. Out of a purported fear that information on the methods and capabilities of U.S. "technical" reconnaissance would leak out, the Americans usually rejected Israeli requests for specific photographs — or sometimes considered the pleas for so many days that they were no longer relevant. The United States had delayed indefinitely a reply on a more ambitious request by Israel: that it be given its own ground station and satellite receiving dish to receive and decode the photographs taken from orbit.

The photographs and analyses provided by Pollard allowed the Israelis, for nearly a year until he was caught, to monitor in detail the movement of various navies' vessels in the Mediterranean. There was a CIA file on Pakistan's efforts to build a nuclear weapon, an "Islamic bomb" project, which was of concern to Israel as the greatest such threat after destroying Iraq's reactor in 1981. There were details on chemical weapons stockpiled by Iraq and Syria, two of Israel's implacable enemies, where information was difficult to obtain.

Pollard's own reflections in prison, shared with journalist Wolf Blitzer, are significant in assessing why Eitan found him so valuable. Pollard said he found that Israeli intelligence is "by no means an all-knowing giant straddling the Middle East." The Israelis were devoting "their best human and technical assets against Syria, which represents the most immediate threat to their survival." Pollard said he concentrated on "their outer ring of enemies: namely, Libya, Algeria, Iraq, and Pakistan."[8]

The most valuable pieces of purloined intelligence, in terms of enabling the Israelis to carry out a specific mission, were the aerial photographs of PLO headquarters in Tunis. There were also reports on the air defense systems of the North African states on the way to Tunisia, including Colonel Qaddafi's Libya. Israel's air force bombed the PLO complex on October 1, 1985, in the most distant Israeli bombing raid ever. It flattened much of Yasser Arafat's base, and Pollard took pleasure in knowing that he had helped make it happen.

In Washington, Pollard was driving himself too hard. His overenthusiasm gave way to fatigue, and the navy's Anti-Terrorism Alert Center noted that his job performance markedly declined. He was doing a full-time job analyzing data and computerized intelligence reports for the navy, and then another full-time job as a spy obtaining many more documents for his Israeli handlers.

Pollard began to deliver thousands of pages dealing with terrorist threats, Soviet arms shipments, electronic communications intercepts, and weapons systems in the Arab countries. Eitan and the few analysts at his disposal in Lakam could barely keep up. One of Pollard's Stanford professors had felt that he "tended to overdo things; if you gave him an assignment to write a paper, it would come in elegantly, but much longer" than was assigned.[9] Now Pollard was behaving similarly, not as a student but as a sort of instructor to the Israelis.

America's intelligence community should have known Pollard was unreliable, based on his background and quirky behavior. His boss at ATAC was Commander Jerry Agee, who began to have doubts about Pollard's reliability after catching him lying twice about some trivial matters. Agee kept his eyes open and noticed "huge stacks" of top secret material on Pollard's desk that were not related to his assigned tasks. On Friday afternoon, October 25, a colleague reported that Pollard left work with a large package of material in computer center wrapping. The authorities found that he had just "accessed" Middle East message traffic.

Agee checked again on the following two Fridays, November 1 and 8, and noted that Pollard was collecting additional top secret data. Unable to sleep, Agee went to the office at 4:30 one morning and found even more Middle East material in Pollard's work space. The navy commander said to himself: "I've got a fucking spy!"[10]

Agee could not persuade the FBI to put Pollard under surveillance, because the agency already had its hands full with a rash of foreign espionage rings. But naval counterintelligence did plant hidden TV cameras around Pollard's work space. They watched him, and they felt certain that he was amassing his own personal intelligence library. He was detained for questioning on November 18.

Naval intelligence agents questioned Pollard for three days, on and off, but they did not hold him incommunicado. Experienced at telling tales of fantasy rather than fact, he told the agents that he would help them uncover a multinational espionage plot of which he was aware.

They were too lax, and even during the first session the interrogators permitted Pollard to call his wife. While ostensibly explaining that he would be coming home late that evening, he also told Anne to "take the cactus to friends." It was a code they had developed earlier, indicating that he was in trouble and any secret documents at home should be removed at once.

Ironically the Pollards were scheduled to have dinner that evening, the eighteenth, with Aviem Sella, who was on a visit to the United States. Sella had told the Pollards that the air force had promoted him to brigadier general, and they ought to go out to celebrate. Instead, as Anne left for the dinner date she was in a state of panic.

On her way out she tried to get rid of a suitcase that, for the Pollards, was as explosive as dynamite. It contained a fifteen-inch-thick stack of secret U.S. documents; it was in their apartment; and it was the "cactus" to which Jay had referred. Anne frantically turned to their friendly neighbors, the Esfandiaris, for help. She asked Christine Esfandiari to take the suitcase, which she said was filled with documents from Jay's work, and to deliver it to her at Washington's Four Seasons Hotel. She was extremely nervous and also gave Mrs. Esfandiari the Pollards' wedding album for safekeeping.

The Pollards had been good to the Esfandiaris, even lending them their Mustang on occasion, but a request to smuggle a suitcase out of the apartment building seemed too weird to Christine. She happened to be the daughter of a U.S. Navy career officer, and the next morning she telephoned the Naval Investigative Service and said, "I have some classified information that may be of help to you."

Mrs. Esfandiari later recalled: "It was very hard because we cared so much about them, but in good conscience we couldn't let something like that go. I couldn't believe that was our Anne and Jay. I was mad. I was hurt. I felt deceived and betrayed."[11]

Asking a neighbor for a favor was certainly not a professionally planned way to get rid of incriminating evidence. Among other things, the suitcase had Pollard's name on it. Even if it had made its way to the D.C. dump, it could have landed him into trouble.

Anne had a nervous dinner at a Chinese restaurant on K Street with Sella. "Jay is in trouble," she said. Sella sensed severe danger and nervously told Anne not to admit they had ever met. They never saw each other again.[12]

Anne Henderson-Pollard returned home and found that Jay was back from his first questioning session. Both were extremely agitated — Pollard telling his wife of the horrors of being questioned — and they decided to call their case officer. Pollard got through to Yagur and demanded asylum and transport to Israel.

Yagur, to warn Pollard but also to calm him, replied, "You're probably being followed. If you shake your surveillance, come in and we'll try to help." The remark was unexpectedly amateurish for an espionage handler: If Yagur believed that his agent was being followed, he should have known Pollard's telephone was being wiretapped, too.

Israel and the Pollards would all pay for their lack of professionalism in this most delicate and dangerous operation. The Israelis were in an unseemly race to see who could flee fastest. Within three days, Yagur and Sella flew home from New York; Irit Erb and her boss, deputy Lakam attaché at the Washington embassy Ilan Ravid, left for Israel from the capital. The news that an American had been arrested for espionage had broken — although with much confusion and only moderate impact.

When Pollard's handlers arrived in Israel, intelligence officials and politicians there already knew that media reports of his being brought from the embassy gates to FBI headquarters would be bound to harm Israel's relations with the United States — more specifically, with the CIA and the defense establishment.

When Israel first admitted the possibility of involvement with Pollard — a full three days after his arrest — there was general shock that Israeli intelligence would have been so stupid as to have allowed an agent to be arrested at Israel's embassy. With foreign espionage activities always believed to be in the Mossad's purview, the public was surprised that the Mossad could be so amateurish and foolish.

Within a few days, it was revealed that Lakam — its existence never even mentioned before — was responsible. But this did not offer much comfort to the people of Israel.

There was puzzlement on the American side, too. Ronald Reagan first heard of Pollard's arrest when the president was flying back to Washington from his first summit with Soviet leader Mikhail Gorbachev in Geneva. Of the Israelis, whom he had nourished with juicy financial and military aid, promoting them into major allies of the

United States, Reagan said, "I don't understand why they are doing it."[13]

On the other hand, the Americans should have known better. The CIA, for one, always assumed that Israeli spies were active in the United States. A secret study by the agency declared that after gathering intelligence on its Arab neighbors, the second and third priorities of Israeli intelligence were the "collection of information on secret U.S. policy or decisions, if any, concerning Israel," and the "collection of scientific intelligence in the United States and other developed countries."[14]

They also should have known more about Pollard and his unstable history, as it unfolded during his interrogation. It became clear that he should never have been in the intelligence community. The CIA had rejected Pollard, but the agency did not advise naval intelligence when he started working there.

Anne Henderson-Pollard was also arrested, because she knew of her husband's espionage activities and helped him whenever she could. She also succumbed to temptation by using some documents he obtained for her public relations work.

Federal prosecutors insisted on prosecuting Henderson-Pollard, but they were especially harsh in preparing a strikingly strong case against her husband. The prosecutors told U.S. District Court Judge Aubrey Robinson that "this defendant has admitted that he sold to Israel a volume of classified documents, ten feet by six feet by six feet" if all gathered into one huge pile.

Defense Secretary Caspar Weinberger wrote his own letter to Judge Robinson: "It is difficult for me to conceive of a greater harm to national security than that caused by the defendant." Weinberger said privately that Pollard deserved to be hanged or shot, adding that repairing the damage he caused could cost the United States a billion dollars.

On March 4, 1987, nine months after pleading guilty in a bargain that was supposed to mean he would not have to spend the rest of his days in prison, Pollard was given a life sentence anyway. Weinberger's letter had swayed the judge.

Pollard was thirty-two years old. His wife, at age twenty-six, had pleaded guilty to lesser charges of handling classified documents and was sentenced to five years in prison. Anne fell to the floor of Courtroom Eight in the federal courthouse in Washington and screamed, "No! No!" She nearly tore at the oak-paneled walls in grief and anger.

When more composed, she said, "I pray to God every single day I'll be reunited with my husband. That's all I live for."[15] Because of a gastrointestinal disorder, Anne would suffer terrible pain and severe weight loss during almost three years of imprisonment.

Pollard had made the mistake of boasting that he had been "quite literally, Israel's eyes and ears over an immense geographic area stretching from the Atlantic to the Indian Ocean." His memo to the judge also offered the opinion that the information he gave to Israel "was so unique" that the country's political leaders must "have known about the existence of an agent working in the American intelligence establishment." The way the Israeli handlers had "tasked" him, he said, indicated "a highly coordinated effort between the naval, army, and air force intelligence services."[16]

True as the assessment may have been, inflating the importance of his undercover work could hardly strengthen Pollard's case before Judge Robinson. But the spy felt abandoned by his spymasters, and implicating top Israelis was his bit of revenge.

U.S. investigators rushed to Tel Aviv to test the Israeli government's assertion that the Pollard affair had been merely "a rogue operation" — that the Jewish state's leaders had not known they had a spy in American intelligence.

To show their goodwill, the Israelis set up a liaison team to give U.S. investigators all possible assistance. Shin Bet chief Avraham Shalom was put in charge of the liaison effort, largely because the Americans would consider him a man of integrity. The Israeli public would soon learn that he was a master of coverups, as Shalom was publicly accused of lying to his own government and others as part of the scandal surrounding the killing of the two bus hijackers in 1984.

Apparently receiving full cooperation from Shalom, American prosecutor Joseph DiGenova and State Department lawyer Abraham Sofaer believed they were questioning all the Israelis involved in running Pollard. However, they were not told about Aviem Sella. Israel would not say precisely who had recruited Lakam's spy in Washington.

When, on top of that, the Americans were told that every single document provided by Pollard was being returned to them, they flew home to Washington and found that they had received only 163 out of over one thousand separate items they had expected. The sleight of hand angered the U.S. investigators, even though the point was purely symbolic: the Israelis obviously could keep copies of their photocopies, and Pollard had never given them any original documents or photographs to keep.[17]

FBI director William Webster was openly critical of the Israelis, accusing them of giving only "selective cooperation." Webster's attitude, as an antagonized and frustrated crime solver, would haunt Israel's intelligence community for a long time to come, because barely a year later Webster would become the Director of Central Intelligence, the head of the CIA.

With their eyes on the American practice of setting up investigative commissions, the Israelis reluctantly formed two inquiry bodies. One probe would be by the Knesset's foreign affairs and defense committee, chaired by Abba Eban. The other would be handled by a two-man commission appointed by the cabinet, but this effort ran into early trouble when a former chief justice of the supreme court, Moshe Landau, refused to serve. Landau was seventy-four years old, and after an honorable career on the judicial bench he did not want to be used as part of a coverup. He had insisted that he be given the power to compel witnesses to testify, and he had wanted the panel's findings to be binding. Another year and a half would pass before Landau would be persuaded to investigate the Shin Bet scandal.

The government did find two men with solid establishment connections who were willing to look into Lakam's use of an American spy: attorney Yehoshua Rotenstreich, who was a legal consultant to the intelligence community, and former army chief of staff Zvi Zur — who two decades earlier had supervised Lakam with an extremely light touch, when the secret agency was led by Binyamin Blumberg.

Israel's national unity government agreed that the two parallel investigations should look into everything, including the role of top politicians in the Pollard affair. The cabinet's leading trio played a concerted tune. Shimon Peres as prime minister, his foreign minister, Yitzhak Shamir, and the defense minister, Yitzhak Rabin, promised to cooperate with Eban's Knesset committee.

As long as the investigators dealt with the operational side — how Pollard was run, rather than who was behind it — they were on safe ground. Both inquiries agreed that Pollard worked for Rafi Eitan's Lakam, and that Aviem Sella played the role of middleman and seducer with the consent of his military superiors. Sella's name emerged in public only because Pollard gave American interrogators the name of his recruiter.

Where the two committees differed was on the question of political responsibility. The cabinet-appointed commission did not find — or at least did not mention — any connection with Israeli politicians. It considered the Pollard affair only as an intelligence operation in isolation. The parliamentary panel, before disintegrating because of divisions between Likud and Labor members, simply dropped a few hints that political leaders deserved some of the blame.

Pollard was recruited when Moshe Arens was defense minister, responsible for Lakam, and Shamir was prime minister. The American spy continued to provide information when Rabin replaced Arens, and Peres replaced Shamir. The four politicians concerned did concede that they had received some of the data provided by Pollard, but in keeping with normal practice they had never asked the identity of the source. If they had known, they claimed, they would immediately have canceled the operation.

Rafi Eitan, on the other hand, told the committees that his conscience was completely clear. "All my actions, including Pollard, were done with the knowledge of those in charge. I do not intend to be used as a scapegoat to cover up the knowledge and responsibility of others."[18]

The veteran spymaster seemed to be suggesting that the political leaders knew more than they were admitting. It would be no surprise that they did not know the name of Jonathan Jay Pollard and his specific job, but some appreciation of where the intelligence "product" must have come from could be expected from politicians who had long experience in military and clandestine affairs: Rabin as a former chief of staff, Shamir as a senior Mossad operative, Peres as the deputy defense minister who created Lakam, and even Arens with his military aeronautical engineering background.

If the U.S. administration and the American people were astonished by the lack of accountability in democratic Israel, they were further flummoxed when the Israeli culprits not only escaped punishment, but enjoyed promotions.

Shortly after returning from the United States, Brigadier General Sella was put in command of Tel Nof air base, the biggest in Israel. American military attachés were often there, south of Tel Aviv, debriefing Israeli pilots on their missions in U.S.-made warplanes as part of the bilateral defense and intelligence cooperation.[19]

The other shoe dropped when Sella became the third and last person — after the Pollards — to be indicted on criminal charges in the conspiracy. For the first time, a high-ranking military or civilian official of a U.S. ally was formally accused of espionage against the United States.[20]

When American officials learned that the air base commander had been the case officer who recruited Israel's spy in America, Washington decreed that no U.S. official would set foot inside Tel Nof so long as Sella was in charge of the facility. George Bush, then vice president, refused to visit Sella's base while visiting Israel in 1986.[21] The pressure worked. Israel's political and defense leaders sacrificed the young general on the altar of Israeli-American relations. Sella resigned his command.

The same Israeli leaders found it more difficult to remove Eitan. As minister for trade and industry, Ariel Sharon once again rushed to the rescue of his old protégé. Just as other intelligence veterans had discovered shelter in Sharon's fiefdom, Eitan was given the chairmanship of Israel Chemicals, the largest state-owned industrial company.

In some ways business continued as usual for Israel. The nation's complex military-industrial requirements could not change simply because Pollard had been caught. The state still needs its spies in Lakam's fields of science, technology, and industry. This, after all, was always one of the specialties of the Israeli intelligence community.

The Israeli government adhered to its public promise, soon after Pollard was arrested, to disband the "rogue" unit that ran him as a spy. However, the intelligence community continued in various ways to obtain all that seemed vital for national security. The community adjusted its division of labor and managed to get along without Lakam. The American authorities were not greatly bothered by this, it being so natural that Israel still had to meet its defense needs by technological espionage. But the United States insisted that Israel pledge never again to employ an agent within American intelligence.

As for Pollard himself, he felt abandoned by the Israelis to his life sentence in the federal prison system. He was bitter but still fervently supported the Jewish state and its defense. Israel's government, however, did nothing to defend him. While the cooperation with the U.S. prosecutors had been far from complete, the obstruction was meant to protect Avi Sella and the other Israelis who ran Pollard — not the American they ran.

There was some secret backing from the intelligence community, however, for a private group of Israeli lawyers and public relations people who collected money to help pay the Pollards' legal expenses. There were even some unofficial attempts by lawyers and relatives to explore the possibilities of a spy swap, with suggestions that Israel might be willing to release one or more of the Soviet moles it had captured — such as Shabtai Kalmanovitch and Marcus Klingberg — in exchange for Pollard. It was unclear, however, how the United States could benefit from such a deal. There was a confidential report in early 1990 that a Western spy imprisoned in Czechoslovakia could be part of a multisided swap. Many Israeli officials were reluctant, in any event, to have Pollard free and living in Israel as a reminder of a great embarrassment.

The most lasting damage caused by the Pollard affair was the creation of an uncomfortable rift between Israel and American Jewry. The Israeli intelligence community, for many years, had been careful not to confront Jews in other lands with the painful question of dual loyalty. Recruiting Pollard and taking advantage of his own divided allegiances shattered that pattern, and the U.S. Jewish community was deeply disturbed that its Gentile neighbors might believe that American Jews loved Israel more than the United States.

So why did Israel confront the six million Jews of America with this dilemma by using Pollard? Stupidity? Arrogance? Carelessness?

These were not the only questions left unanswered. A former CIA director says, "I've never understood why the Israelis ran Pollard. They get everything for free here in the U.S. The Israelis based at their embassy in Washington aren't just strumming their guitars. They're out there, doing legwork, meeting people. But they don't have to steal much, because ninety percent of what they get, they are purposely given by friendly and cooperative Americans."[22]

The shadow of distrust cast by the Pollard affair between U.S. and Israeli intelligence would never quite be lifted, but hurt feelings almost always give way to strategic realities and national interests. When the two nations needed each other in the mid-1980s, in coping with sensitive issues such as Iran and hostages, they found new, unorthodox channels for cooperation.

FIFTEEN

The Chaos of Irangate

THE IRANIAN PRIME MINISTER'S VOICE could be heard from the other end of the Swiss hotel suite. Mir Hossein Musavi in Teheran, was shouting down the telephone line at his intelligence chief, Mohsen Kangarlu. Kangarlu, in turn, glared at the Israeli who was with him in the elegant room. The Mossad, the Iranian thought, had just played a nasty trick.

Kangarlu, an important behind-the-scenes figure in Iran but hardly known in the West, was in Geneva's Noga Hilton Hotel with part-time Iranian intelligence operative and weapons dealer Manucher Ghorbanifar and an Israeli who was selling arms in the hope of liberating American hostages held by pro-Iranian Shiite Moslems in Lebanon. The Israeli was Yaakov Nimrodi, and the Iranians felt certain that he was a Mossad agent. Nimrodi was, in fact, only a former Israeli intelligence operative. Disturbingly, from the point of view of Israel's intelligence community, the Mossad knew nothing about what was going on.

It was November 25, 1985, only four days after Jonathan Jay Pollard's arrest in Washington triggered a dangerous loss of faith between the United States and Israel. Yet here was Nimrodi, authorized by Prime Minister Shimon Peres to join two other Israelis in cooperating closely with U.S. officials in the effort to trade arms for hostages.

Exposure would ruin the deal and sentence the Westerners in Lebanon to further years of miserable captivity. For both Israel and the United States, it was vital that the contacts with Iran be kept secret. The Israelis and Americans who were involved deceived even the Mossad and the CIA.

The Iranian prime minister certainly felt deceived that day, because he was at Teheran airport with senior military men examining ground-to-air missiles that had arrived on a clandestine flight from

Israel. Musavi dialed Kangarlu's suite and screamed, "Who is trying to treat us as fools? I am standing here with the Hawk missile expert of our army, and he sees that these are old Hawks — totally out of date and worthless to us!"

The Iranian officer had a list of military specification numbers — U.S. "milspecs" — and could see that the antiaircraft missiles were manufactured before the United States improved the Hawk's speed and accuracy.

Nimrodi, who had worked for decades in Iran for Aliyah B, for Aman, and finally for himself, sensed that something was seriously wrong. He had not been trying to fool the Iranians. They had already paid him nearly $24 million for eighty Hawk missiles, and the Americans had helped to arrange the delivery from Israel and a promised replenishment from U.S. stocks. It all made sense. It was a good deal for Israeli military exports. It would help establish contact with the relative moderates in Iran's radical hierarchy. And perhaps five more Americans, in addition to the one U.S. hostage already released in exchange for armaments, would soon be free as a pleasant dividend.

From his long experience, Nimrodi knew that Iranians were unsurpassed in their ability to invent difficulties, but he had a feeling that the "milspecs" dispute was a genuine problem and that its source could well be in Israel.

Nimrodi tiptoed down the hall to his own hotel room and telephoned his close friend and business partner, Adolph (Al) Schwimmer. He was at home in Tel Aviv, and he was exhausted. He could scarcely believe what he had gone through to get those Hawk missiles flown out of Israel. Nimrodi was now phoning from Geneva, but not to say that the Iranians were delighted and an American hostage was on his way to freedom. Instead, Nimrodi said the Iranians were livid and the crew of the chartered airliner was now held prisoner in Teheran.

Schwimmer had suffered the ordeal, the previous night, of finding a fistful of cash for the West German captain of the Boeing 707 that was about to leave Israel's Ben-Gurion airport with the Hawk missiles on board. Schwimmer was muttering curses all day at "those American crooks," because Lieutenant Colonel Oliver North of the U.S. National Security Council had sent an airplane but no money for aviation fuel. The Israeli had only around five hundred dollars in his pocket, and he quickly drove to the homes of wealthy friends to borrow the rest of the nine thousand dollars the pilot said he needed to refuel.

North was the main White House operative in the attempt to win freedom for half a dozen American hostages held in Lebanon. The Vietnam war veteran was fond of complicated covert operations. Now he was President Reagan's most active operative, in the most secret project of the administration — to barter arms for hostages despite Reagan's public stand against making deals with terrorists.

Why did Colonel North have to deal with two private Israeli businessmen in a clandestine mission, involving a third country and delicate national interests? And why were the Mossad and its intelligence soulmate, the CIA, not running the show — as might have been expected?

Like President Reagan, Israel's Prime Minister Peres had reached the conclusion that this operation could be run more smoothly through new channels rather than the traditional ones. Peres hoped that the use of private Israelis would not only free hostages, but would help the Jewish state profit from arms sales to its traditional market in Iran. The complex deal could also repair the damage in U.S.-Israeli relations caused by the Pollard affair.

But who were these Israelis, these three musketeers?

The first was Al Schwimmer, who was born in 1917 in the United States and decided in his youth to learn all there was to know about aviation. He mastered the field, from piloting small aircraft to selling airplane parts to small nations. He worked as an engineer for Lockheed and for Trans World Airways, served in the U.S. Air Force, and after World War II rediscovered his Jewish roots when he met Holocaust survivors in Europe. Schwimmer became a secret agent of sorts in Czechoslovakia, where he amassed arms sold by Western dealers and from the Soviet bloc. His own cargo airline transported the guns and ammunition to Israel before and after statehood in 1948.

An unknown hero who was helping the newborn state win its War of Independence, Schwimmer was commissioned as an officer in the Israeli air force. He returned to the United States in 1949, hoping to help his new Jewish homeland from afar, but first the American authorities charged him with illegally exporting airplanes and spare parts to Israel, Czechoslovakia, Italy, and Panama. Schwimmer and his company, Service Airways, were convicted in federal court in Los

Angeles in 1950 and fined ten thousand dollars. The FBI believed that in exchange for using the Czech airfield at Zatek, Schwimmer supplied the Communist government there with a training plane and a miniature radar unit.[1]

His next project was Intercontinental Airways, which did not transport passengers but instead served as a renovation and repair center in the United States for airplanes of the Israeli air force and El Al Israel Airlines. Prime Minister Ben-Gurion and his young defense aide, Peres, persuaded Schwimmer to return to Israel in 1951 and set up a modern manufacturer known first as Bedek and later as Israel Aircraft Industries.[2] It was a proud moment in 1975 when Schwimmer presented the air force with the Kfir fighter jet, based on the plans Lakam obtained from its Swiss agent Frauenknecht.

After his retirement from the state-owned aircraft manufacturer, Schwimmer became a special adviser to Peres and a partner in various businesses with Nimrodi. From 1984 to 1987, Schwimmer drew a symbolic salary from the prime minister's office of one shekel a year — less than one dollar.

The second Israeli was Yaakov Nimrodi, who was born in Iraq in 1926 but was brought up in Jerusalem, one of ten children of a poor family. His intelligence career began just before Israel's statehood in 1948 when Nimrodi joined the Palmach. After the War of Independence, he was a junior field officer in Aman.

In 1956 he was sent to Teheran on behalf of Israeli intelligence, working for both Aman and the Mossad in the early stages of the developing "peripheral" strategy. In the formal role of military attaché, Colonel Nimrodi spent most of the 1960s doing what he could to make Iran dependent on Israel.

He was instrumental and efficient in selling $250 million a year of Israeli defense equipment to Iran. He arranged demonstrations there of new Israeli weapons, and he always made sure that Farsi-speaking Israelis were used as military trainers. Years later, hundreds of Iranian officers who were secretly trained in Israel were still serving in Iran's army. Nimrodi can also take credit for building Iran's military intelligence corps into a respectable body.

Seeking his reward within the Israeli defense system in 1969, Nimrodi returned home and lobbied for the job of military commander in the West Bank, which had been captured from Jordan only two years earlier. He was rejected, however, and left the army.

After a short time in Israel, he returned to what he knew best: selling goods in Iran. He became a private merchant of arms and other Israeli products, acting as a "Mr. Fix-It" to arrange exports to the large Iranian market. Nimrodi, with his wife, Rivka, and their young children, returned to Teheran. All the sales of Israeli goods which he had arranged as part of his low-salary job as an Aman man he now handled as a private import-export agent. The commissions were huge — millions of dollars in some years.

In the unique way that flamboyant, wealthy men exhibit mutual attraction, Nimrodi met the Saudi tycoon Adnan Khashoggi. They enjoyed making plans together in both business and clandestine diplomacy.

Nimrodi, Schwimmer, and Khashoggi invested millions in the shah's Iran, but it was all swept away in the 1979 Islamic revolution. Nimrodi, having banked wisely in Europe, did save enough to settle in London with old Iranian friends as neighbors in exile.

The third Israeli was David Kimche. He was not a private operator; he was director general of Israel's foreign ministry. A veteran of clandestine diplomacy in Africa, Lebanon, and elsewhere, he was to represent his government officially in the secret deals with Iran. Longing to return to the action he loved in his Mossad days, Kimche did not find that the methods — including convoluted air transport arrangements — were at all strange.

On that long night of November 24, Nimrodi, Schwimmer, and Kimche were struggling to score an arms-for-hostages triumph by keeping the Boeing 707 on its flight path from Tel Aviv, via Cyprus, to Teheran. An Israeli army crew had barely managed to squeeze the first eighteen of eighty Hawk missiles aboard. Then, six hours after the airplane's 9:00 P.M. departure — with the refueling funds Schwimmer had scurried to collect — he was awakened by another telephone call. A man, obviously speaking from abroad, said he was the owner of the Boeing and was phoning from Brazil.

A bleary-eyed Schwimmer asked, "What, money again?"

"No," said the chartered aircraft owner, "our pilot has been arrested after arriving on Cyprus, because of irregular documents."

It was sheer luck that the Cypriot authorities had not opened the packing crates for inspection. Within hours they might do so, and in any event the press — Middle East correspondents from the world's leading media were based on Cyprus — would quickly learn of the mystery jet standing in a corner of Larnaca airport with its pilot under arrest.

Schwimmer telephoned Colonel North in Washington, where it was still Sunday evening, and North then partially lifted the veil of ignorance he had placed on the CIA by asking the Agency for assistance. At North's request, a CIA agent on Cyprus pulled some strings with the local authorities to have the pilot released quietly. The Boeing took off again, now refueled, at six o'clock Monday morning.

Obviously too excited to sleep, North called Schwimmer a few hours later to say that the airplane had landed in Teheran. Fully convinced that one or more American hostages would now be freed by Iran's friends in Lebanon, Colonel North told the Israeli, "God bless you."

When Schwimmer then heard from Nimrodi that the Iranian prime minister himself was at Teheran airport and furious about having been sent the wrong goods, Schwimmer immediately telephoned the deputy director general of the defense ministry in Tel Aviv, Chaim Carmon, who was in charge of loading the missiles and said, "Don't worry. Tell them the Hawks were modified in Israel and are better than the original missiles."

This reassuring message was passed from Tel Aviv to Teheran, by way of Geneva, where the telephone soon rang again. This time it was the Iranian colonel who was, with Prime Minister Musavi, bending over the crates filled with Hawks. The officer said he and a technician were examining the missiles, and he demanded to know, "What modifications?"

By now Ghorbanifar was staring at Nimrodi with hurt in his eyes, as though the Israelis who had always seemed so serious and sincere had now betrayed him at the climax of their seven-month relationship. Kangarlu was agitated and insisted that Nimrodi get the answers for the colonel in Teheran "at once!"

An urgent question was put by telephone from Geneva to Tel Aviv: "What modifications?" Nimrodi asked Schwimmer, who in turn telephoned his defense ministry contact. Carmon said he would check and call back. Within minutes he was speaking slowly and calmly as he finally told Schwimmer the truth: "Listen. Those missiles did not undergo modification."

Schwimmer realized that a seemingly well controlled operation had become quite absurd. He called Nimrodi with the bad news: "They're right. They are the old Hawks."

Nimrodi told Kangarlu just as the Iranian's boss, Prime Minister Musavi, came on the line again from Teheran. Kangarlu stuttered nervously as he told Musavi that Iran had indeed received an obsolete model of missile.

Musavi yelled on, and Kangarlu turned white as a sheet and fell to the floor. He had fainted from the pressure. His bodyguards feared it was a heart attack and began pounding Kangarlu's chest.

Nimrodi, meantime, fearing that the entire project was disintegrating before his eyes, grabbed the telephone and picked up the conversation with Musavi in the Iranian's own language, Farsi.

Nimrodi explained to Musavi, knowing not to offend the Iranian leader by identifying himself as an Israeli, that Kangarlu had just collapsed and that there had to be a calm, reasonable way to settle the "misunderstanding." Musavi kept on shouting, threatening to keep the transport airplane and put the chartered crew on trial, until Nimrodi offered to return to Iran the bulk of the payment already made.

The precise arrangements were made through Ghorbanifar, even as an ambulance took Kangarlu to a Swiss hospital, and the next morning Nimrodi was accompanied by burly Iranian bodyguards to a branch of Credit Suisse to transfer $18 million back to Iran's account.

The Hawk missile incident was a disaster for the arms-for-hostages deal, as engineered by Nimrodi and his small Israeli team. Nearly a year more would pass before the existence of the complex, three-sided negotiations would become public knowledge. At that time, U.S. officials would say they entered into the transaction because they trusted "the Israelis" and their superior knowledge of Iran.

The ultimate failure and the embarrassment caused to the White House by the Irangate scandal were due to the mind-boggling link between Iran and Central America. Colonel North tied the Iran operation to his secret program for sending aid to the anti-Communist Contra rebels of Nicaragua — hiding the Reagan administration's actions from Congress and the public, while skimming off profits from the ayatollah's money to pay for bullets in America's backyard.

David Kimche had little interest in the Contras but great interest in Israel's front yard, Iran. He was one of the great advocates of the "peripheral" strategy, both when he was in the Mossad and when he surfaced from the black hole of a clandestine career and joined the foreign ministry. He never abandoned the idea that Israel should collaborate with the Iranians. Despite the takeover by the ayatollahs in 1979, he believed that there must be a core of moderates — either in the army or elsewhere in society — who would be willing to cooperate with Israel and the West.

Within two years of starting his second, public career, Kimche did not stop short at mere dreaming. He was well aware that Israel was selling arms to Iran to expand its exports, to help the Jews of Iran, and to maintain a link with Teheran. In 1982, he took part in the complex planning of an anti-ayatollah coup with Nimrodi, Schwimmer, and Khashoggi in Morocco, Kenya, and Sudan.

Kimche was so confident that he permitted himself to go on the record, as the British-style gentleman on British television in February 1982, publicly urging that Israel and the West should encourage a coup in Iran. It was no coincidence that Nimrodi appeared on the same BBC program, filling the screen with his round face and plumes of cigar smoke, saying in heavily accented English that a coup could be a simple matter and was quite essential.[3]

In many ways, the earlier plot was a preview of Irangate. The difference was that in 1982, by sending its special emissary to the Baby Shah in Morocco, the Mossad was able to kill the conspiracy.

It would not therefore have been surprising if, in 1985, secret service veterans Nimrodi and Kimche had decided to ignore the Mossad completely when Khashoggi proposed a new initiative toward Iran. It was still important, however, to adhere to the bare minimum of intelligence-community etiquette. The Mossad was given a chance to express its opinion.

Khashoggi contacted Nimrodi and Schwimmer at the beginning of April 1985 and invited them to come urgently to London to meet him and several Iranians "who are worth meeting." Khashoggi added to the importance by indicating that King Fahd of Saudi Arabia himself had approved the plan he was about to propose.

Schwimmer, officially employed by Peres, told his old friend about the invitation and received the prime minister's permission to see what was on offer in London. Thus it was that the Irangate scandal began.

In a six-hundred-dollar-a-night suite in London's Hyde Park Hotel,

Khashoggi introduced Nimrodi and Schwimmer to an Iranian named Cyrus Hashemi. The Saudi said that Hashemi was a man of influence and a cousin of Ali Akbar Hashemi Rafsanjani, the speaker of the Iranian parliament, who was second only to Ayatollah Khomeini in political power in Teheran. Rafsanjani would become number-one ruler in 1989, after the ayatollah's death.

In a stunning turnabout, instead of suggesting the overthrow of the Khomeini regime, as he had done three years earlier in Kenya, Khashoggi was recommending that the Israelis join in making friendly overtures to specific elements of that regime.

Hashemi said he was authorized by senior Iranian government officials to look into the possibility of renewing contacts with the West. He said his aim was to restore contacts between Washington and Teheran, cut off nearly six years earlier when the U.S. embassy was seized by Iranian radicals, but Khashoggi had advised him to begin with the Israelis. What did Iran want? A renewal, Hashemi said, of the arms sales that Israel had stopped — at America's demand — and that Iran needed in the prolonged Gulf War against Iraq.

A short while later, Khashoggi similarly introduced Nimrodi and Schwimmer to Manucher Ghorbanifar, whom he identified as a Hamburg-based Iranian businessman authorized by Iran's prime minister to pursue better relations with the West — again, through Israel.

Intrigued, Schwimmer persuaded Peres to permit brief visits to Israel by Hashemi and Ghorbanifar to be "tested." In the course of April, using false passports which they themselves provided, the two Iranians separately flew from Europe to Tel Aviv.

"Ghorba," as he was immediately dubbed by the Israelis, traveled in the guise of Greek citizen "Nicholas Kralis." To avoid the border police at Ben-Gurion airport, who are excellent at spotting forged documents, the two Iranian but nominally non-Iranian gentlemen were escorted by Israeli agents through Passport Control without questions or visa stamps.

Peres was also intrigued at the possibility of renewing relations with Iran. Instead of protesting secret Israeli arms sales to Iran, this time the Americans might endorse them. The prime minister ordered the Mossad to interview Hashemi and Ghorbanifar carefully and issue a quick and full report. Mossad involvement was quite natural, and

Kimche and his fellow musketeers gave the agency a chance to take part.

Hashemi was simply full of talk, obviously willing to make some deals to arm Iran and line his own pockets, but lacking any political sophistication that might impress his Israeli hosts. The Mossad also checked its computerized files and found that Hashemi had a bad reputation for selling himself and his information to the highest bidder, without regard for any particular strategy. All the European security services, East and West, had used Cyrus Hashemi. The Mossad did not want him at all.

The Mossad was not enamored of "Ghorba," either, but all the Israelis who met him had to admit he was interesting. Both the Mossad and Aman interviewed him, as did the foreign and defense ministries. He told an impressive tale of having gone to Riyadh, the Saudi capital, and — in an audience arranged by Khashoggi — having warned King Fahd of Iranian plots to attack the sacred Moslem shrines in Mecca.

While the jury was out and the Mossad reserved judgment on Ghorbanifar, the defense ministry was delighted to say yes to a relatively simple deal suggested by him. It would be a further test of the Iranian's credibility, and an easy $40 million of revenue for Israel. Ghorbanifar telephoned Teheran from Israel and drew up a shopping list of artillery pieces, mortars, and ammunition which the Israeli ministry experts considered "old junk."

Within days that April, the Israelis chartered a cargo ship and prepared it to sail from Eilat to Bandar Abbas, Iran. The arms were loaded aboard, and Ghorbanifar seemed to prove himself again when a lieutenant colonel from Iran's army flew into Tel Aviv — out of uniform and also on a false passport — to sail home aboard the ship.

In the meantime, however, another telephone call from Ghorbanifar to Prime Minister Musavi's office in Teheran produced a totally different shopping list. The Iranians canceled the $40 million purchase and began to demand tube-launched, optically tracked, wire-guided (TOW) missiles their troops could use to destroy Iraqi tanks during a Gulf War offensive expected soon. Iran needed TOWs, and that was all it wanted from the Israelis. The ship never sailed. The lieutenant colonel flew home.

That, in a nutshell, was the problem with Ghorbanifar and whoever his contacts might be in Iran. Agreements might not be honored, and Israel could be sucked in ever deeper until it was providing the Iranians with whatever they wanted while receiving nothing in return except — at best — money. This problem made the Mossad more reluctant to participate, but the agency was still in the picture.

Ghorbanifar's new request was for hundreds of TOW missiles. The price of around ten thousand dollars apiece was attractive to Israel's vendors, but the fact that TOWs are strictly "Made in the U.S.A." and would have to be resupplied from there presented many problems.

On a second visit to Israel, Ghorbanifar could see that his new, simple, but lucrative shopping list was being met by doubt and hesitation. He stepped up the pressure — and the possible rewards for Israeli intelligence — by sitting down in a large Mossad guest house near Tel Aviv, and writing a long report on the political scene inside Iran.

It was dated May 2, 1985, and Ghorbanifar marked it "Strictly Confidential — For Your Eyes Only." It was highly professional from an intelligence man's point of view, and it revealed a well-organized mind. It impressed the musketeers, who had found Ghorbanifar to be so calculating and confusing that conversing with him was "a real challenge."[4]

His report was written for the Mossad but was surely designed by Ghorbanifar to be passed on to Washington. The United States, at that point, was completely out of the picture. He had tried several times to develop links with the CIA, offering information and various deals, but the Americans put him through lie detector tests and concluded that he was unreliable.

Ghorbanifar's detailed study of Iran began with the obvious. Intelligence professionals learn not to exclude the facts which "everybody knows," because they could be inadvertently forgotten in a final analysis. Therefore the Iranian visitor in Tel Aviv wrote: "The Imam Khomeini is Iran's sole ruler," adding that the most powerful politicians and Shiite mullahs at any particular moment were those who had Ayatollah Khomeini's support.

Ghorbanifar's secret report introduced the notion of three "lines" of politicians and clerics standing in the wings, competing for power below the supreme ayatollah's exalted level and awaiting his death. This was the kind of detailed analysis which both the U.S. and Israel knew they had been missing without good sources inside Iran.

Line One, Ghorbanifar wrote, was "Rightist," finding its strength in the army, the police, the parliament (known as the Majlis), most merchants, and even some Revolutionary Guards. They favored free trade and were strongly anti-Soviet. They opposed exporting the Shiite revolution by force, and they wanted friendly relations with both the West and other Moslem countries.

Line Two, he wrote, was "Leftist" and included both Prime Minister Musavi and President Ali Khamenei. Ghorbanifar described this group as "hardline at home and abroad," supporting terrorism and the export of an armed Shiite revolution. He blamed Line Two for the 1979–81 ordeal of the fifty-two American hostages in their Teheran embassy.

Line Three was described by Ghorbanifar as a "middle, balancing line" with great strength in the Majlis, in the supreme court, and scattered among revolutionary foundations.

He was able to name names — dozens of Iranians, some prominent and others hardly known in 1985 — and he placed them neatly into the three political lines. He quoted Khomeini as saying: "Stop the line-playing." But Ghorbanifar also predicted that after the ayatollah's death, one of the political groupings would win the struggle and "eliminate the other two."

His advice to his Israeli and, he hoped, American readers was: "We must support Line One, eliminate Line Two, and absorb Line Three."[5]

It was politics by numbers, and Kimche now felt he had something to tell the Americans about. The three musketeers had always intended to bring the United States into their scheme, and now they believed they held the bait to bring the huge fish into the net. The best possible bait would be the hostages in Lebanon, and the Israelis knew how desperate Reagan and his White House were to liberate their countrymen. Kimche's team would dearly love to free the hostages and informed Washington that there was an attractive contact, well worth examining.

Even before receiving Ghorbanifar's three-line analysis, President Reagan's national security adviser, Robert (Bud) McFarlane, reacted to what he heard from his old friend Kimche. McFarlane sent a part-time consultant on terrorism and the Middle East, Michael Ledeen, to Israel to discuss the possibilities of joint, covert efforts to gain contacts in Iran. Ledeen met with Prime Minister Peres, whom he knew from meetings of labor movement leaders in the Socialist International.

When Peres discreetly mentioned the possibility of selling weapons to moderate elements in Iran, it was only natural for Ledeen to take this as a mere rationalization for previous Israeli arms sales. These, he knew, were mostly intended to help fearful Jews flee from Iran without hindrance. Mossad operatives had helped smuggle Jewish Iranians across the border into Pakistan and Turkey, with Iran's authorities looking the other way.

After the Ghorbanifar report, there was the more complex and attractive motivation of attempting to help one political line emerge victorious from Iran's inevitable power struggle.

Peres decided to proceed in league with the three musketeers. He ignored the Mossad, which finally — at the delicate stage of drawing in the Americans — decided not to take part. The Mossad did not believe in the entire scheme and saw no real opportunities in radical Iran.

The situation was truly abnormal. In other times if the Mossad said no, a proposal would be canceled. Now, after thirty years of dominating covert operations on Israel's foreign horizons, the Mossad was completely locked out from a covert project abroad.

More puzzling is the fact that the Mossad was excluded by Peres — a prime minister not usually known for breaking with long-standing operational traditions. He was not Begin in his era of adventurism, or Sharon, who sought major reforms in the Mossad.

Nahum Admoni, however, was not able to protect the primacy of his agency. He was not nearly so strong a Mossad chief as Yitzhak Hofi had been in 1982 when he stamped out the Sharon-Nimrodi proposal to stage a coup in Iran from Sudanese bases. In 1985, Admoni merely registered his objection but retreated in the face of the prime minister's wishes.

Peres was strongly in favor of the Iran project. When the Mossad advised scrapping the plan he preferred to press on with an ex-Mossad official and two businessmen, rather than cancel a project with potential political benefits that could include President Reagan's lasting gratitude.

The prime minister did make a minimal effort to put an intelligence professional in charge of the threesome. He asked former Aman chief Shlomo Gazit to oversee the musketeers, but Gazit quit within weeks "because the Mossad is not completely in the picture" and he refused to take orders from arms dealers whose political actions could have a profit motive.[6]

The prime minister sent Kimche to Washington to supplement what McFarlane had already heard from his adviser, Ledeen. It was automatic, almost a reflex by both Americans and Israelis, to connect the word "Iran" with the thought of "hostages." And Ghorbanifar was dangling the possibility of freeing William Buckley, the CIA station chief in Beirut who had been kidnapped by pro-Iranian Lebanese Shiites and was under severe torture. The notion of swapping arms for hostages was off and running.

The musketeers loosely organized themselves along professional divisions of duty. Kimche was liaison officer with the Americans, Nimrodi was in Geneva and London as financier, and Schwimmer was the operations officer who had to solve transportation problems.

On the American side, the circle of people who knew about the secret deals widened. Defense Secretary Weinberger did not like the operation, but was brought into the picture when the Pentagon had to replenish the Israeli arsenals missile for missile after every Israeli shipment to Iran. That had been the price demanded by Defense Minister Rabin for his cooperation.

A jet chartered by Schwimmer brought 508 TOW missiles to Iran — which paid $5 million — in two flights, in August and September 1985. The Reverend Benjamin Weir was released, after sixteen months in captivity, and the trade in weapons for human beings was in full gear, with great expectations.

Kimche would be back in the thick of covert operations, in search of peripheral alliances. Nimrodi would put his old stomping ground, Iran, back near the top of Israel's agenda and would also turn a profit. Schwimmer would be fulfilling his view of serving Zionism, while exercising his abilities to maneuver airplanes. Peres would be a key statesman who pulled off a clandestine coup. All of them would be thanked by President Reagan for bringing back his beloved U.S. citizens.

All the aspirations of the Israeli musketeers were crushed by the ill-fated flight of the Hawks in November. The Iranians were furious, but more important, the Americans lost all confidence in the three Israelis. The project itself, however, was too tempting to be abandoned. The Americans wanted to keep going, and Peres was equally eager. Rabin was insisting, however, that someone else be put in charge of the Israeli side. But the Mossad was angrier than ever about the entire affair and refused to lift a finger.

A new conduit through the darkness had to be found. Peres, as a master politician, did not hesitate to ditch the musketeers — even his old friend Schwimmer. The light at the end of the tunnel would now be Amiram Nir.

At the age of thirty-five, Nir may have looked too young for such worldwide wheeling and dealing, but his ambitions knew no borders. As the prime minister's adviser on counterterrorism, he represented a new generation of Israeli operatives. He was born as Amiram Nisker in 1950, after the State of Israel was established, so he did not have the traditional background as a prestate underground fighter.

Unfortunately for Nir, he did not even have a combat background. He served his country's cause as a reporter for the Israel Defense Forces' radio station and had the misfortune of losing an eye in a car accident. For a while, he wore a Moshe Dayan–type black eye patch before a false eye was inserted.

Nir excelled as a journalist and became a well-informed defense correspondent for Israeli television. The golden boy also married one of the daughters of the Moses family, the country's leading newspaper proprietors.

Feeling keenly his lack of military experience in a nation of warriors, Nir volunteered for a one-year hitch in the army and became a lieutenant colonel in a reserve tank battalion. Now satisfied, he turned his career in a new direction and became an aide to Shimon Peres when he was opposition leader.

While researching for his Ph.D. at the strategic studies center at Tel Aviv University, he was swept into the prime minister's office — as the expert on terrorism — when Peres led the new national unity government formed in 1984.

The intelligence community rejected Nir, however. He was an outsider and lacked the right background. Espionage men never liked journalists, anyway. The secret services also were resentful that Peres ousted veteran spy Rafi Eitan in favor of Nir.

The new counterterrorism adviser tried his best to convince the intelligence chiefs that he was a man to be trusted. As a first step, he hoped to acquire Eitan's other hat — as chief of Lakam — not knowing Eitan was busy running Jonathan Jay Pollard in the United States. Nir was also interested in the top job at Shin Bet, once Yosef Harmelin completed his postscandal interim term; and Nir's long-term ambitions extended to the Mossad. First, to be taken seriously, Nir settled into the dark shadows of the job he had just landed.

The prime minister's adviser on counterterrorism was a position created when Golda Meir wanted her own close counsel during the post-Olympics revenge killings of Palestinian terrorists, and endorsed a year later in the wake of the 1973 war and the Mechdal intelligence failure.

The adviser was to give the prime minister the tools for improved decision making in the war against terrorism. Nir, with his analytical mind, took easily to coordinating the activities of the intelligence and security agencies. He pointed to an attempted terrorist attack in 1985 as the model to prove that his work was needed.

An Arab ship, with Palestinian guerrillas aboard, left Yemen. Detecting and tracking a vessel near an Arab country was Aman's responsibility.

When the ship approached Israel's territorial waters, it entered the jurisdiction of the Israeli navy.

The terrorists planned to land on the beach in Tel Aviv. That would be a job for the police.

The attackers then hoped to break their way into the Kirya compound, containing the headquarters of the general staff. The army would have to prevent that.

Next to the headquarters is the defense ministry itself, with Yitzhak Rabin on the second floor. The Palestinians planned to take him hostage. Protecting a minister is Shin Bet's business.

Someone in authority had to prevent such an assault from falling through the bureaucratic cracks. In this particular case the navy stopped the terrorists before they reached the beach, torpedoing the Arab vessel and taking several Palestinian prisoners. Nir showed the intelligence community that his organizational role was vital.

The final proof that he could be a leader among intelligence men — a prince of the covert community — was that Nir abandoned his old talkative habits as a journalist. The media veteran ignored his friends in the media.

When Nir was given the chance to exercise his coordination capabilities in the Iran affair, he sensed a once-in-a-lifetime opportunity to expand his one-man counterterrorism bureau into a new, secret intelligence unit. He found a soulmate in Oliver North. North and Nir were both lieutenant colonels, and they were both great fans of secrecy and good organization. They got to know each other — by scrambled telephone connections — when the Israelis assisted the United States in tracking the hijacked *Achille Lauro* cruise liner in October 1985.

It was Nir, as counterterrorism coordinator, who informed the Americans that Israel was intercepting and recording every word spoken by radio between the Palestinian hijackers and their PLO controller, Abul Abbas, on shore in Egypt. Aman chief Ehud Barak, whose agency intercepted the conversations, went on American television — targeting the U.S. audience, even before talking to Israeli TV — to play some of the tapes on a small recorder held in his hand.

Confident that he had the backing of the prime ministers' club of Peres, Shamir, and Rabin, Nir felt he could start laying plans with North for an around-the-world crusade against international terrorism. His first assignment, in December 1985, was to revive the Iran affair.

Nir had little trouble gaining the confidence of the White House — North being his biggest booster in Washington. Elbowing his way into the Iranians' hearts, however, required more finesse and a few gimmicks. One such stunt was a meeting in a London casino which had two objects: to prove that the three musketeers were ousted from the scene, and to impress the Iranians that Nir was now Peres's man.

Nir originally planned to use his leader's visit to Britain's Prime Minister Margaret Thatcher in January 1986 as an opportunity to introduce Peres himself to North and Ghorbanifar. The Iranian, however, leaked word of the plan to his old buddy Nimrodi. Nimrodi informed Schwimmer, who immediately flew from Tel Aviv to London to confront Peres and demand to know why they had been replaced by Nir. The prime minister denied he was planning a meeting, and he did not see Ghorbanifar.

To demonstrate his close relationship with Israel's leader, Nir instead tricked Peres's senior aide, Colonel Azriel Nevo, into accompanying him to the casino. There, he drew Ghorbanifar's attention to the photograph in that day's newspaper which showed Nevo standing alongside Peres. If Peres was with Nevo, and Nevo was now with Nir, it stood to reason that Nir was the prime minister's personal delegate.

North was also in London, confirming that Ledeen — in an American parallel of the Israeli manipulations — had been ousted. North would now work directly with Nir. If Nimrodi and company had been out to out-Mossad the Mossad, Nir had just out-Nimrodi'd Nimrodi.

Nir also managed to persuade the White House to renew the arms deliveries to Teheran. He even joined McFarlane, North, and a team of American intelligence men — all on false Irish passports — on a secret visit to Teheran in May 1986 for talks that were not only fruitless, but completely ridiculous. Trying to rescue U.S. hostages, they could all have been taken hostage by Revolutionary Guards. Nir and the Americans were tempting fate, in the lion's den.

Two more hostages, Father Lawrence Jenco and David Jacobsen, were freed by Iran's allies in Lebanon. Even as they were received in America and at the White House with all of Reagan's favorite hoopla, the seeds of failure planted in Teheran were yielding fruit. The story of the McFarlane-Nir trip was leaked to the world press by domestic foes of the Iranians who had spoken to "the Great Satan" — killing the arms-for-hostages deal in November 1986.

As a scandal, it was not dead. The secret and illegal actions of McFarlane, North, and their National Security Council unraveled in public, and the trail led to the Oval Office. The American press and public demanded to know about President Reagan's involvement. Did he authorize trading arms for hostages? Did he permit North to violate the Congressional ban on aid to the Contras, by using Israeli arms dealers and their Swiss bank accounts to divert the profits made off the Iranians? The media and official investigators could find only that Reagan had delegated responsibility to a host of aides, who were forced to resign.

One man who survived all the questions, the probe by Senator John Tower's commission, and the Congressional hearings was Vice President George Bush. Refusing to reveal what he had known, thought, felt, or done during the Iran affair, Bush was elected president in November 1988.

The only person who might conceivably have been able to damage Bush politically died in an airplane crash three weeks after the election. Amiram Nir perished, just short of his thirty-eighth birthday, in a small Cessna T-210 bound for Mexico City from a tiny airport in

Uruapan. It crashed in bad weather 110 miles west of the capital.

Two and a half years earlier, in the plush and traditional surroundings of the King David Hotel in Jerusalem, Nir had met with Bush and had given him a briefing on the ongoing deal with Iran. The new president would never talk about it.

The chaos of Irangate put a halt to Nir's promising career. He remained in the prime minister's office for some eighteen months, but as an embarrassment, assigned no real duties. Upon resigning in the spring of 1988, he moved to London with the total silence that had become his adopted trademark. No one knew the precise nature of his work; there were only some hints that he might have been preparing his cover for a new espionage mission.

The Mexican police said the Israeli whose body they found had rented the Cessna under the name "Pat Weber." It was Nir, but the only explanation offered for his presence in Mexico was a sudden interest in purchasing avocados for export.[7]

Amiram Nir took to his grave, in Israel, the remaining secrets of Irangate.[8]

SIXTEEN

Business at All Costs

"WHEN WE DEMONSTRATED our Galil rifle in the Philippines," said an Israeli arms dealer at the end of the summer of 1982, "we brought over the rifle's designer. First, he dropped it in a tank of water. Then he rubbed it in the dirt. Then he started firing it. The Filipinos were greatly impressed."[1]

They did not, however, buy any of the guns — standard army issue and Israeli made, based on the Soviet Kalashnikov. The buyers could not overcome their reluctance to deal with Israel, target of a concerted Arab campaign to brand the Jewish state a "pariah state." The Galil is only one of the many Israeli weapons that are considered among the best in the world, but the drive for foreign sales constantly runs into political brick walls as it did in the Philippines.

Israel is therefore forced to search actively for lucrative markets and to sell its military hardware to regimes with dubious reputations such as South Africa, Iran, and dictatorships in Latin America.

Exporting arms is considered by Israel to be a vital national interest. It is not only a source of foreign currency and a useful means of projecting influence overseas; there is a more basic business logic. To have its own defense industry — which Israel is convinced it requires to avoid dependence on the kindness of other nations — it must achieve economies of scale. The Israeli arms industry must manufacture far more guns, bullets, shells, uniforms, tanks, missile boats, and more sophisticated equipment than Israel itself can use. Foreign sales defray the price of research and development, and the costs of having military industries can be met by revenues from abroad.

It is no wonder, then, that the intelligence community is involved in protecting this vital interest by promoting the products. Mossad operatives, when abroad on missions as unofficial ambassadors, and Shin Bet men, acting as clandestine counterterrorism advisers, spread the word about the excellence of Israeli products. The guns and other matériel become part of a package deal: good advice from the Israelis goes hand-in-hand with battle-proved weapons.

This is a relatively new phenomenon, which began after the 1973 war. Earlier arms exports were handled more directly by Sibat, a Hebrew acronym for *Siyua Bitchoni,* "Security Assistance," a small department in the defense ministry in Tel Aviv. Negotiations were handled discreetly, and when selling to countries which were anxious to conceal their business links with Israel, Sibat made sure that the arms source was kept secret.

Sibat was set up because of public uproar in the mid-1960s when the international media exposed the first secret arms deal between Israel and South Africa. It was a new and jarring embarrassment for the Jewish state, hailed worldwide as a shelter for Holocaust survivors, to be linked with the reviled racist regime in Pretoria. The defense ministry established the new foreign sales unit, not to prevent similar deals in the future but to conceal them.

Under Sibat's sponsorship, secret defense ties flourished. Israeli advisers taught the South African Defense Force — its very name echoing that of Israel's army — how to combat African National Congress and Swapo guerrillas along the same lines used in fighting Palestinian terrorists. Israel sold guns and larger weapons systems to the South Africans, but even more helpfully granted them licenses to make their own versions of Israeli armaments.

Armscor and other South African companies produced a missile boat identical to Israel's Reshef, itself modeled on the ships the Israelis seized from Cherbourg; the Cheetah, nearly the same as the Kfir fighter-bomber, which was based on the stolen Mirage plans obtained by Lakam; and Scorpion, a sea-to-sea missile indiscernible from Israel's Gabriel.

The naval cooperation was dramatically exposed in early 1982 with the arrest of Ruth and Dieter Gerhardt. He was a captain in South Africa's navy and commander of the highly strategic Simonstown naval base near Cape Town. South African counterintelligence, tipped off by a friendly Western espionage service, established that the Gerhardts were long-serving spies for the Soviet Union.

Their trial was secret, but part of the charge sheet was leaked. It revealed that among the many tasks assigned by Soviet intelligence to the South African couple was to spy on their country's secret military and defense relationship with Israel. Like John Hadden and others in the CIA fifteen years earlier, the Soviets had also detected signs that Israel was working on submarine-based nuclear warheads. They instructed the Gerhardts to find out whether the Scorpion-Gabriel missiles could be or would be or were already armed with warheads that would give the Israelis a nuclear launch option in addition to their ground-based rockets and attack bombers.

It was from the Simonstown base in September 1979 that a group of South African ships set out toward the southwest in a highly secret operation. A few days later, a Vela satellite run by the U.S. National Security Agency detected a bright flash over the South Atlantic — matching the signature of a nuclear explosion. The Carter administration suspected that it was the test of a South African bomb, presumably with Israeli involvement, and scientists said it appeared to have been a compact device — impressively "clean," they said, with hardly any radioactive fallout and therefore difficult to detect after the detonation.[2]

Ten years later, Israel and South Africa were again reported to be cooperating in nuclear research and in the development of Jericho ground-to-ground missiles. The South Africans announced in July 1989 that they had test fired a booster rocket for a ballistic missile, and Bush administration officials said that equipment seen by American intelligence looked just like the Israeli setup for missile tests.[3] It appeared to be a further extension of a top secret program that grew from the sales originally coordinated by Sibat.

The agency did not engage in pure intelligence work, and Sibat's director did not take part in the Varash committee of security-agency chiefs, but he was usually a retired senior military officer whose recommendations carried great weight in the alternative diplomacy practiced by Israel's intelligence community.

Sibat occasionally employed middlemen, mainly for the purpose of concealing Israeli involvement in the transaction, but government-to-government arms deals were generally well controlled by the relevant state agencies. Weapons sales from Israel were never unauthorized or "accidental." They were, however, sensitive — as in the American-approved sale of old Skyhawk jets from the Israeli air force to Indonesia, a Moslem nation that was overtly hostile to the Jewish state and therefore insisted on absolute secrecy.[4]

Until the Yom Kippur War, Israel's arms exports amounted to about $50 million a year. The defense industry then stepped up its efforts to produce domestically manufactured armaments, and military sales expanded into a second phase. Israeli middlemen started to take the initiative, actively knocking on doors and opening them for Sibat and the growing military-industrial complex. Within fifteen years Israel's arms exports grew, although the figures are not published officially, to over one billion dollars a year.[5]

These were the golden years for Yaakov Nimrodi, as an Israeli sales agent during his Iran days. When the Iranian market was shut down by Ayatollah Khomeini's takeover in 1979, Israel was anxious to find another buyer for its products and discovered China. The explorer who made it possible was Shaul Eisenberg.

Israel's wealthiest businessman, Eisenberg was born in Europe and found refuge during World War II in the Far East. He settled in Japan, where he married a Japanese woman and made his fortune selling war surplus and scrap metal.

Eisenberg quickly established himself as one of the leading middlemen in the region. He never lost his awareness of being a Jew, however, and his emotional ties led him to set up businesses in Israel and then to move his family there. He kept his interests in the Far East and in the late 1970s was able to pave a pathway to Beijing for Israeli military exports.

His most formidable tool was his private jet, on which he could ignore the official hostility between the two nations and fly high-level Israelis directly to China. Eisenberg made dozens of trips, carrying Sibat officials, army advisers, financiers, and military salesmen for what the Israelis described as their "toughest negotiations ever."

After making a solid initial contact, Eisenberg would leave the coordination of hidden deals and shipments to the Mossad, which acted in its traditional role as Israel's secret alternative foreign ministry. He was eligible for hefty commissions from Sibat and from Israeli defense contractors who would actually make the sale.

Israeli defense exports to China in the 1980s were estimated to total nearly three billion dollars for the entire decade.[6]

With the mushrooming exports, the Israeli arms industry reached its third stage. Israeli middlemen started not just knocking on doors, but actively pulling and dragging their government into doorways which they claimed to have opened. There was an abrupt change: the middlemen were attempting to dictate Israeli foreign policy, based on their own financial expectations. Nimrodi's behavior in the Irangate episode was no longer unique.

Israel has an entire new class of Mossad, Shin Bet, and senior army veterans working to persuade their own country to sell while convincing foreigners to buy. These former intelligence and military men are part of a social network — which can be called the "formers" — as self-centered and protective of its members as any aristocracy in the world. Their family backgrounds, education, and lifestyles might vary, but they have one desire in common: to do business at all costs.

The environment was right in many ways for these men to put profit before everything else. Israeli society underwent a transformation in the 1970s and 1980s. In part, there was the fatigue brought about by war after war. The idealism and pioneering spirit of Israel's first quarter century had to compete with self-interest and materialism.

In the early days, people were ashamed to discuss money and it was considered "coarse" to concentrate on making it. It was almost frowned on to profit from business deals, especially when they involved national interests. In today's Israel, however, making money has become a Golden Calf, before which much of the society — including its intelligence and military circles — kneels.

The "formers" find that their careers end early and that their pensions are no higher than the paltry civil-service average of twelve thousand dollars a year. They feel they have few marketable talents after working even harder than their international counterparts, and they particularly envy CIA agents for their fat salaries and generous pensions. The same comparison could be made, however, for any professions in low-wage Israel.

As soon as they leave their intelligence or army work, and sometimes while they are still employed by the state, many Israelis make connections which they will find useful for making a living — often a very nice living — in private life.

Some are genuine heroes. Others will leave you with that impression, and who can check with their former employers? They exploit the reputation which the Israelis have built up in counterterrorism, military expertise, airline and office security, and personal protection.

Countries such as Iran, when it was at war with Iraq, and some of the Latin American juntas became utterly convinced that Israelis could provide them with anything and everything. Israel sold complete weapons systems to South Africa and licensed companies there to manufacture the Israeli-designed Kfir fighter jet as the renamed

Cheetah, as well as Reshef missile boats and sea-to-sea Gabriel missiles under new names.

Ostensibly private Israeli arms dealers have occasionally been used by their government to sidestep political barriers — even when the obstacles are put up by Israel's chief benefactor, the United States. Although forbidden by Washington, Israel permitted a former official dealer, Norman Shkolnick, to negotiate the sale of a dozen American-made Skyhawk bombers to Argentina's navy. This was in the spring of 1982, just as Great Britain was sending its naval task force to recapture the Falkland Islands from the Argentines. The Reagan administration clamped an arms embargo on Argentina and sternly told the Israelis to stop the Shkolnick deal. The sale of the warplanes was canceled, but U.S. officials remained suspicious of both Sibat and "private" Israeli merchants.

On the other hand, some of the private brokers who happen to come from Israel are only bluffing when they suggest that they represent their government. It was that impression of omnipotence that retired brigadier general Avraham Bar-Am tried to convey.

Bar-Am, a thirty-year army veteran in the infantry and armored brigades, left the army in 1978. He had been disciplined for providing guns to alleged Israeli underworld figures. As an unemployed veteran, he looked around him and saw how well a number of his good friends were doing in private business.

Former senior officers of the air force including its commander in the 1973 war, Major General Mordecai Hod, had set up sales agencies that represented large Israeli suppliers and giant American manufacturers. The officers, who had dealt with these corporations during their military careers, in essence continued to maintain these ties after leaving the military and entering civilian life. Bar-Am was especially impressed with the wealth amassed by Nimrodi in Iran and figured that he could do the same.

Along with about a thousand other retired senior officers, Bar-Am applied for, and was issued, an apparently routine defense ministry document authorizing the holder to go forth and prospect for sales of Israeli arms. The permit, however, specifically banned participation in actual negotiations.

At the end of April 1986 General Bar-Am, two other Israeli businessmen, and fourteen other men were arrested by American customs officers. All were the victims of a four-month sting operation, in which Iranian arms dealer Cyrus Hashemi — who had visited Israel the previous year, in the first act of the Irangate drama — acted as a United States government informant. All seventeen defendants were indicted in New York for involvement in an alleged conspiracy to sell Phantom fighter planes, tanks, missiles, and an array of other sophisticated weapons to the Iranians.

The shopping list was sheer megalomania, and it was difficult to believe that Bar-Am and his colleagues would be able to obtain so much to sell to Iran. Hashemi, however, had been in Israel with Nimrodi, had even met CIA director William Casey on his own in 1985 to suggest a huge arms-for-hostages deal, and was able to persuade Bar-Am that the entire package would be welcomed by all governments concerned.

Hashemi's true motives were blurred, once the customs service used him to frame Bar-Am and the others. Even the White House was left confused. In a discussion with President Reagan in November 1986, his closest advisers wondered whether Israel had an official role in the Bar-Am arms-dealing ring.

Vice President George Bush asked, at that meeting, "Is that case a private or public endeavor to sell arms for Israel?"

One of the aides, not identified in official White House notes, replied, "Probably private with government knowledge."

Bush felt that the arrests could lead to further problems. "Israel may try to squeeze us," he said.[7]

The Israeli government emphatically denied that it was involved in the alleged scheme, but Bar-Am phoned the Israeli military attaché in Washington after his arrest and insisted that friends in the Mossad had checked out the participants in the arms deal.[8]

By 1988, amid the embarrassment of Irangate and the revelation of U.S. weapons sales to the ayatollahs, the American authorities dropped their criminal charges against Bar-Am. He was one of those defense and intelligence veterans who, while perfectly patriotic when in official service, ignored Israel's interests once their income depended on supply-and-demand market realities. When an opportunity arose to sell some jeeps, rifles, ammunition, mortars, spare parts, and other "small junk" that Israel did not want anyway, the privateers had few hesitations. They did not even check whether Jerusalem might object.

Sibat claimed in 1989 that it was tightening up its system of oversight, now requiring anyone selling Israeli military equipment to apply for permission regarding every nut, bolt, and bullet. Many of the privateers seemed undeterred, however. In the world of covert operations, these former operatives had had drilled into them that many missions are not worthwhile because of the damage which might result from exposure. But after becoming private businessmen, they hardly seemed to care about such niceties. When they made mistakes, the Jewish state was invariably blamed.

Worse still, some of the intelligence veterans believed that everything they did do automatically became Israel's national interest. The self-righteousness was at times stunning, and the gray areas were blinding. Did they lobby for a particular political step because it would be good for Israel? Or was that just an excuse, when their only concern was the good of their bank balances?

Israel occasionally ended up involved with some of the ugliest regimes in the world. A private intelligence veteran might find a business opportunity, say, in an African dictatorship such as Idi Amin's Uganda or Mobutu's Zaire, and before long other former operatives and army veterans were training the security services of these countries.

The defense ministry in Tel Aviv generally applauded, although privately, profitable export deals initiated by the "formers." Word often leaked out through diplomats and journalists. Inevitably, Israel's unfortunate image as a pariah state in league with other international untouchables was strengthened.

Mike Harari, one of the Mossad men who retaliated against Arab terrorists after the 1972 Olympics massacre, was among the former operatives with friends in high places. The son of a customs official, Harari was born in Tel Aviv in 1927. His career was similar to that of many of his generation in Israeli intelligence. He served in the Palmach and Shai, and when the state was proclaimed he joined its intelligence community.

His Shin Bet job in the 1950s was as security officer for the foreign ministry, and he then spent the next twenty years in the anonymity of the Mossad. He was always a field operative on special missions, with a reputation for extreme thoroughness. In 1972 and 1973 he was in charge of the assassination squads hunting Palestinian terrorists in Western Europe, until the Lillehammer fiasco. Only Harari, his girlfriend Tamar, who served as his female assistant, and the two gunmen managed to leave Norway. The other members of the hit team were arrested.

Harari was able to remain in the Mossad, despite his involvement in the most serious blunder in the history of Israel's secret services up until that time. In Israel of the 1970s, even after Lillehammer, no one dared to voice public criticism of the intelligence community or to demand a public inquiry or dismissals.

The veteran operations man was given a new assignment, far from the Mossad's head office. Harari was put in charge of the agency's major station in Mexico City. The station's duties are to track Palestinian activities in the Americas and to sell Israeli armaments. Harari made many rich and powerful friends, while flying around Latin America to promote Israel's interests. Among them were Panama's dictator, General Omar Torrijos, and his chief of military intelligence, Colonel Manuel Noriega. On a mission related to Mossad finance and shipping arrangements, Harari had met Torrijos in 1968. They were introduced by a member of Panama's large and prosperous Jewish community, and Harari was even called upon to mediate in the prickly relationship between the dictator and his Jewish father-in-law.

After more than thirty-five years of serving his nation, Harari went private in 1980. He launched a short career as an insurance man, and later he began to divide his time between Israel and Central America.

The Mossad at the time was still sufficiently powerful within the Israeli bureaucracy to carve up the world into fiefdoms for its favorite "formers." Even where the foreign ministry openly had an official embassy, much of the real business was done by ex-operatives. Panama was given to Mike Harari. You never truly retire from the intelligence community. You are always at its disposal.

Panama's leaders, with their penchant for playing both sides of the fence, had strong ties with the United States but also maintained good relations with Cuba's Fidel Castro. The Cuban revolutionary was an ardent supporter of the Palestinian cause and a jet-setter to radical gatherings worldwide, making Castro an interesting target for Israeli espionage. Through the filter of Harari and his Panamanian friends, Israel collected intelligence on Cuba's dealings with Palestinians. When Torrijos died in a mysterious airplane crash in 1981, Noriega inherited both the country and the friendship with Harari. The new Panamanian strongman had long cooperated with the CIA but began to incur U.S. wrath by becoming involved with alleged drug smuggling from South America to the United States.

Harari, meantime, became the indispensable right-hand man to Noriega. The Israeli persuaded the general to dismiss business tycoon Shaul Eisenberg from the post of honorary Panamanian consul in Tel Aviv. Harari took the honor for himself.

He hired Israeli bodyguards and also trained local men to protect General Noriega, whose mansion in Panama City benefited from the classic Israeli perimeter security of barbed wire and electronic sensors. Harari helped Noriega organize his soldiers into the Panama Defense Force, even named for Israel's army. Through Harari, Israel also sold light arms to the Panamanian national guard. Before long, all commercial deals between Israel and Panama, not only weapons, began to go through Harari's hands. His profit lay in the commissions.

Harari made no public pronouncements and was seemingly allergic to having his name appear in the press. Only twice was his photograph published in Israeli newspapers, when he accompanied General Noriega on an official visit to Israel in 1985. A third attempt to photograph him failed. That was in June 1988 at a large garden party in suburban Savyon to honor a professor on the publication of his new book.

As Harari feasted at the party, a young photographer from one of the Israeli dailies steadied her camera for a shot. Harari recoiled. He then strolled over to the photographer and politely demanded that she hand over her exposed film. He promised to develop all the prints and return them to her within a day or two — except for the picture she had taken of him.

When she refused, the mystery man grabbed the camera from her, pulled out the film, and burned it before the astounded eyes of hundreds of guests. "No one dares to photograph Mike Harari," he declared, and continued to mingle around the garden as if nothing had happened.

The line between national interest and personal greed became blurred, with huge sums of money floating around and ready to be plucked. In the United States, after Noriega was indicted for alleged drug smuggling in 1988, officials whispered about the mysterious Israeli who helped to protect the general. And when the United States invaded Panama in December 1989 and overthrew Noriega, the media wondered what had happened to the dictator's favorite Israeli.

In the fashion that typically surrounds any intelligence man, Harari's actions during the U.S. invasion were cloaked in contradictory disinformation. An American diplomat in Panama City told reporters that the former Mossad man had been arrested trying to escape, but the story was later retracted as a supposed case of mistaken identity. Another account suggested that Harari had been staying with Noriega's family — while the dictator himself was spending the night with a mistress — when two shadowy Israelis came to visit and warned him of the invasion, driving off with him to a safe escape only six hours before the paratroops landed.

On the other hand, American officials pointed out that while they had been out to capture Noriega they had no arrest warrant naming Harari. The Israeli had not been implicated in the narcotics charges against the Panamanian dictator in Miami's federal court.

The elusive Harari surfaced in Israel, granting the first interviews in his life but shedding no new light on his decade in Panama. In his surprisingly high and thin voice, the former Mossad officer complained that Palestinian killers might target him because of all the press attention.

"They say I wiped people out," Harari said. "Don't they realize that puts a death sentence on me? What did I ever do to the press?"

During his years as a privateer, Harari helped Israel with introductions to all the right people. And it seemed more than mere coincidence that when Colonel Oliver North, zealous servant of President Reagan, chose foreign allies to help him circumvent Congress by delivering arms to the anti-Communist Contras in Nicaragua, he turned to both Israel and Noriega.

With Reagan out of office, North convicted of an Irangate felony, and Noriega indicted as a drug runner, Israel found that its old operative Harari was an embarrassment.

The most logical explanation, however, is that Harari was not truly on Noriega's side once America and all the odds were stacked against the dictator. When the United States decided firmly to oppose and depose him, it is most unlikely that the Mossad took a contrary position and stubbornly clung to Noriega. He had been friendly to Israel and good to Panama's own Jews, but he was not all that valuable. In a business where interests always outweigh sentiments, the CIA had cooperation from the Mossad, which naturally would have used its loyal veteran Harari.

So while the general was jailed in Miami, facing drug charges, Harari was permitted by the Americans to slip out of Panama and by Israeli intelligence to return silently home without even a record of "M. Harari" having crossed the border checkpoints in either country.[9]

Pessach Ben-Or, too, would constantly be regarded as an "Israeli agent," even though he was just a young former sergeant who pursued personal profit and represented another type of Israeli arms merchant. Ben-Or did not have an illustrious military past or the old "formers" ties with the political and defense establishment.

Born in Lod in 1948 as Pessach Spiegler, he was an ambitious lad from his earliest days. After he completed his compulsory army service, he joined his father as an employee at Israel Aircraft Industries. There he met Marcus Katz, a Jewish arms dealer and middleman from Mexico who represented IAI in Latin America.

Spiegler/Ben-Or moved to Mexico as chauffeur and bodyguard to Katz. The young Israeli quickly learned all the tricks of the arms trade. Ben-Or waited for the right opportunity, and it came in 1980 when the United States imposed an arms embargo against Guatemala. That country's regime was also locked in a dispute with Katz, so Ben-Or made his move, elbowing his employer aside to fill the vacuum and become chief arms supplier to one of the most notorious juntas in the region. By selling to a government brutally suppressing human rights, he became a millionaire.[10]

Ben-Or purchased a luxurious home, as protected as a fortress, in a suburban area in central Israel and invested his money in restaurants. His name was mentioned in connection with various unconfirmed arms transactions in Latin America, including the sale of weapons to the Nicaraguan Contras.[11]

While Mexico City is an important station for the Mossad — and a headquarters for some Israeli privateers — there are also major stations in Rio de Janeiro and Buenos Aires. The Mossad monitors the safety of the Jewish communities of Brazil and Argentina, and it also watches cooperative projects between those two nations and the Arab world. Israeli sources accused Brazil in 1981 of helping Iraq in its nuclear program, and they did their best in 1988 to persuade Argentina to stop its participation in an Iraqi-Egyptian project to develop a new ground-to-ground missile called Condor.

The Israeli intelligence community has been much more permissive in Latin America than elsewhere in the world, when it comes to allowing "formers" to work for governments and private groups. Most regimes in the region feel threatened by neighboring states and by restive rebels at home. In short, they generally wish to be armed to the teeth. For Israel's weapons dealers, the opportunities for profit have been extraordinarily attractive.

Some of the governments have hired Israelis as "security" consultants, condemned by human rights activists and other foreign critics for giving "dirty" advice on how to suppress political opponents more efficiently. While official Israeli policy is rarely clear when it comes to civil conflicts in Central and South America, it is true that the privateers have offered "counterinsurgency" training to élite military units in the region.

Guatemala, El Salvador, and pre-Sandinista Nicaragua all turned enthusiastically to Israeli "defense" products after the United States responded to human-rights abuses by reducing military aid. Persistent reports in the American and the Israeli press suggested that the United States was covertly paying for some of the Israeli goods, so as to help anti-Communist Latin Americans beyond the limits set by Congress. Several leaders of the anti-Sandinista Nicaraguan Contras said they received arms from Israel — including weapons captured from the PLO.[12]

Computers were among the most successful Israeli exports to the secret police of several oppressive countries. Privateers who had export permits from Sibat sold filing systems, guerrilla-identification software, and electronic eavesdropping devices based on the antiterrorism systems developed by Shin Bet.

Israeli "formers" were seen training military units and police forces in Guatemala, Honduras, and El Salvador, and in Colombia a lucrative contract became a huge embarrassment. Lieutenant Colonel Yair Klein, a reserves officer who had commanded an antiterrorist paratroop unit in Israel, had gone on to open a private security firm called *Hod he-Hanit,* or "Spearhead." A videotape broadcast worldwide in August 1989 showed Klein and other Israelis training armed Colombians who were identified as assassination squads for the cocaine barons of Medellín.

Klein, at age forty-four, fled from Colombia before an arrest warrant was issued but then was threatened with prosecution in Israel for activities that he insisted were fully authorized. Spearhead had an export license from the defense ministry's Sibat unit. Israeli officials said the permit covered only contracts with governments, not criminal militia groups. Klein said, "I trained a group of farmers who defended themselves against terrorist organizations, mostly the group called M-19 which wants to turn Colombia into a Cuba or Nicaragua."[13]

Israel was humiliated by the public connection with drug smugglers. Orders were issued to Sibat to tighten up, yet again, the criteria by which export permits are issued to Israelis who sell arms or military expertise.

Israelis seem to be making secret deals everywhere. A visitor to one of the "formers" in Europe is likely to be met by the bizarre sight of a wealthy Saudi or other Arab sitting comfortably, drinking, laughing, and doing business with Israelis. Whether there or in Africa, Asia, or Latin America, the privateers have given Israel, its armed forces, and its intelligence community a bad name. Sometimes it seems that almost every nasty or mysterious event in the world is blamed by the press and even foreign government ministers on the Israeli secret services.

In courts around the world "Israeli intelligence" or "Mossad" was put forward as a defense, as though all would be forgiven by judges if they believed a criminal had been working for Israel. The reputation of Israel's intelligence community had sunk sufficiently low to be dragged through the mud by gunrunners, drug dealers, and kidnappers in courtrooms from the Caribbean islands to the capital cities of Europe.

One such case came to light in Britain, when customs officers became suspicious of some obviously nervous Nigerian embassy shipping clerks. At Stansted airport, north of London, the clerks were gingerly preparing to load two large wooden crates onto a Nigerian Airways plane that was shortly to take off for Africa. The uniformed Britons were familiar with the usual type of diplomatic bags sent home by the Nigerian embassy in London. This time, on the afternoon of July 5, 1984, the crates seemed odd and one of them smelled, somehow, like a hospital ward.

They asked what was inside and the Nigerians refused to say, immediately hiding behind their diplomatic immunity. Undeterred, the British officers grabbed a hammer and crowbars and pried open the boxes.

In one box sat two white men, looking hot and guilty, who did not put up a struggle when they were arrested by police who were summoned by the customs authorities. In the other crate, a white man who immediately shouted "I'm a doctor!" had an intravenous drip running into the arm of a black man in a business suit, who was unconscious and rolled into a ball at the bottom of the box.

A complicated kidnap plot later known as the Dikko affair was thus foiled at the airport. The victim was Umaru Dikko, a former senior minister in the government of Nigeria who was now at the top of the "Most Wanted" list there after a military coup. The new regime said he had fled to London with millions of dollars in public funds. The Nigerians wanted to get him to Lagos to be put on trial, and they found three Israelis to do the dirty work for them.

Alexander Barak was the brain, and he and his assistant, Felix Abutbul — sharing a box that day — came from similar backgrounds on the criminal edge of Netanya, Israel. After they left the country in the early 1980s, their precise whereabouts were difficult to trace.

The third man was Dr. Lev Shapira, a Soviet Jew who moved to Israel and earned an excellent reputation as an anesthesiologist in a small hospital near Tel Aviv. He was in the box with Dikko and had drugged him.

After their arrest, the three Israelis lodged the by now common claim that they had done it for Israel. Their English lawyers said the Mossad had issued the orders. Israel's government denied it completely.

Even after they were sentenced to prison terms ranging from ten to fourteen years, a cloud of mystery lingered over the Dikko affair. Few facts were definitely established. The Nigerian Security Organization, acting from its embassy in London, ran the operation. The Nigerians committed amateurish errors, such as introducing their ambassador to the kidnap team. The three Israelis, however, were quite professional and efficient, as were two other Israelis who fled from Britain after grabbing Dikko outside his home and stuffing him into a van.

Some links were found with Jewish and Israeli businessmen who had good connections with Israeli intelligence and had lost heavy investments in Nigeria after the 1983 coup d'état. For whom were the five Israeli kidnappers working? For the businessmen? For Nigerian intelligence? For the Mossad? For the Israeli foreign ministry? For a combination of them? One thing is certain: If the operation had been successful and the crate containing Dikko had not been opened until it arrived in Lagos, the Nigerian government would have owed a huge debt of thanks to someone in Israel — either to the five kidnappers, or to a higher power behind them.[14]

Possibly worse than the damage to Israel's image, there is reason to fear that Israel's essential interests and secrets are being leaked abroad and are even reaching its enemies.

Perhaps Israel could not have avoided the security breach in the case of Ulrich Wegener, a West German police officer who established his nation's special counterterrorism unit, GSG-9. He and his men gained instant fame when on October 17, 1979, they used stun grenades and machine pistols to assault a hijacked Lufthansa airliner on the ground at Mogadishu, Somalia — liberating ninety passengers and crew, killing three hijackers and wounding one in a mixed team of German and Arab terrorists. The Germans were using the tactics pioneered by the sayeret commando units of Israel in the Sabena hijack of 1972.

No wonder. Wegener learned his craft from the same teachers. He was trained in hostage-rescue techniques in Israel. In June 1988, however, Wegener took these professional secrets to Saudi Arabia, when he went there to train special forces.[15]

Israel could not stop the German from going to the Saudis, still officially at war with the Jewish state. But what should it do when its own security employees, such as Danny Yissacharov and Yitzhak Yefet, sell the know-how they acquired while working for the state?

Yissacharov was a senior officer in charge of security for El Al, the Israeli airline. After leaving government service, he joined with a number of other intelligence-community "formers" to set up their own company offering consultancy services in the field of security and antiterrorism. Do you want to protect your office? Your mansion? Your airport? Call the Israelis. Yissacharov and his colleagues gained some lucrative contracts, and what he used to do for El Al he now did for American airlines.

Yefet also held the post of chief security officer for El Al, and after taking early retirement he ran a worldwide security-consultancy empire from a luxury apartment in New Jersey looking across to Manhattan. Yissacharov, Yefet, and dozens of other "formers" are generally resented by their ex-employers but laugh all the way to the bank.[16]

If at one time the kibbutznik wearing the short pants and simple hat of a happy worker in the fields was the symbol of the young Israel, emblazoned on all its early exports, the new symbols for Israel in the international community have become the arms merchants and other "formers."

The leaking of secrets, the flood of information, and the presence of hundreds of Israeli freelancers throughout all five continents were part of a general deterioration of standards and values in Israeli society. The low point came with the emergence of a traitor from the most secret depths of the Jewish state.

SEVENTEEN

The Nuclear Traitor

THE WIRY AND PREMATURELY BALD MAN was walking through downtown London's Leicester Square, taking in the neon lights and movie theater marquees. It was Wednesday, September 24, 1986, and despite his fears he expected that the next week he would shake the world.

Mordecai Vanunu had worked for nearly ten years as a technician in the top secret nuclear installation at Dimona, in the Negev Desert. He knew that it was a bomb factory, and that Israel had amassed a formidable arsenal of nuclear weapons. Vanunu had told one of Britain's newspapers, and soon everyone would know. He wondered, looking at the crowds of people milling around the square, if their lives would be the same after hearing the frightening truth that the next Middle Eastern war could lead to the end of the world.

Around the edges of the square, outside one of the discotheques, he noticed a tall, somewhat heavyset, and thick-lipped blonde. Mordecai looked at her, and she glanced back. Lately lacking in female companionship, he took an immediate interest and the first step.

Vanunu, who was thirty-two and unmarried, introduced himself as "Mordy." That was what his friends in Australia had called him but at home in Israel, he said, he was Mordecai. She said she was Cindy, an American traveling alone in this age of the liberated woman. Talking and walking with her was by far the best pastime Vanunu had that evening.

Vanunu thought that, having responded favorably to his initial advance, she might be interested in sex. But the subject did not come up, and as they parted that night Vanunu gave her the telephone number of his hotel as they promised to see each other again soon.

*

Vanunu was born in Morocco in 1954, the second among seven children in a Jewish family that moved from Marakkech to Israel in the early 1960s when the Mossad arranged clandestine emigration to Israel. The family settled in a slum neighborhood in Beersheba, a place with a history dating back to the biblical days of Abraham but now a dusty town in the middle of the desert. Vanunu's father, Salumon, struggled to make ends meet, selling religious and sacramental implements in the Beersheba market, where the mixed population of Jews and Bedouin Arabs mingled in commerce and conversation.

Vanunu served in the Israeli army, where he was a corporal and a mediocre member of the engineering corps. He then flunked out of a first-year physics course at Tel Aviv University. At age twenty-one he saw a newspaper advertisement for "trainee technicians" and applied to Kamag, the acronym for *Kirya le-Mechkar Gar'ini,* the Nuclear Research Center in Dimona.

He was first interviewed by the center's security officers, who worked closely with Shin Bet to screen applicants. They questioned him about drug or alcohol abuse, whether he had a criminal record, and about his political preferences. He went on the payroll in November 1976 and the Dimona center sent him on accelerated courses in physics, chemistry, mathematics, and English.

He passed an exam two months later, as did thirty-nine out of the forty-five other candidates, and in early February 1977 he took the official Volvo bus — which daily transported employees to their secret jobs — from Beersheba to the Dimona complex for the first time. In a classroom building within the high-security gates, Vanunu was required to sign a pledge not to reveal any secrets under a law that specified a prison term of fifteen years for telling anyone — even his fellow employees — about his duties in Dimona.

There was another short course in nuclear physics and chemistry, including lessons on the plutonium and uranium with which the new recruits would be working. Vanunu and the other newcomers went through medical checkups, received security passes, and then were given ten weeks to become acquainted with the facility and its routine before starting work.

Vanunu quickly learned that he was now a special member of society, even if he would never be permitted to tell why. Like other Israeli men, Vanunu was called to the army for a month's reserve duty. But he was immediately sent home when his unit was informed that he was now employed in an unspecified, but sensitive, defense project.

There was one more oral test to pass at the Dimona compound before a panel of three examiners, and finally Vanunu reported on August 7, 1977, for his first full shift. He was a *menahel mishmeret,* or "shift manager," between 11:30 P.M. and 8:00 A.M.[1]

Vanunu could have remained in the darkness, diligently toiling deep in the bowels of the Dimona complex, as do all the other anonymous workers. Sudden changes in his personality, however, put him on a different track. The first was when he tore himself away from his religious upbringing: The product of an Orthodox home, Vanunu became completely secular and cut all links with his family.

The second and most dramatic change occurred after the bloody Israeli invasion of Lebanon in 1982. He had once been like most other Moroccan immigrants—a nationalistic Zionist who believed in Menachem Begin and his Likud, and in being tough on Arabs. But Vanunu had a political reawakening, and his ideology turned radically in the other direction.

He became an enthusiastic member of left-wing groups on the fringes of Beersheba University, where he enrolled in the philosophy department and befriended Arab students. Vanunu even applied for membership in the Israeli Communist party, although leaving the application blank where it inquired about his employment.

He joined the vociferous campaign for the freedom of one of his teachers who had been jailed for refusing to serve in the army in occupied Arab lands. "But even among us, the left-wingers on campus, he was exceptional," recalled Dr. Ze'ev Tzahor, political activist and history lecturer at Beersheba University. "He radiated a deep sense of deprivation."[2]

Vanunu also turned out to be a notorious eccentric. School chums photographed him doing a musical striptease at a campus party. He became a nude model for art students. More seriously, he held picket signs along with Palestinian students in various protests. The university newspaper quoted Vanunu as saying, "Stop oppressing the Arabs."[3]

All these extracurricular activities should have caught the eye of Shin Bet agents, who track groups they consider subversive. If the right and left hands of the security agency each knew what the other was doing, Vanunu would have to be judged a terrible candidate for clandestine defense-related work. For months, however, nothing happened. Vanunu kept riding the Volvo bus to Dimona, and his work continued as normal.

By late 1985, security officers at Dimona learned that one of their employees — instructed to be silent, or at least unobtrusive — was making a public, antiestablishment spectacle of himself. Vanunu was warned to stop. When he continued on his unorthodox path, the nuclear authorities decided to fire him. To avoid public fuss or scandal, they did not officially brand him a security risk. They paid Vanunu his severance pay and dismissed him along with 180 other workers in a cost-cutting move in November 1985.

Within a month Vanunu sold his old car and his small apartment and, like many other young Israelis, he set out on a long journey to the Far East. Unlike the others, who usually return after a few adventurous months in the exotic Orient, Vanunu found himself on a soul-searching excursion that led to his third change of life.

He arrived in Sydney, Australia, in May 1986, and one Friday evening — ironically, the Jewish Sabbath — he drifted toward the lights and open doors of St. John's Anglican church. The Reverend John McKnight was there and recalls: "Mordy came in, he looked around, talked to me, and we became friends."[4]

Two months later, Vanunu made the final leap away from his entire boyhood and background: He converted to Christianity. It was a total divorce from the Jewish state.

Almost like someone who refuses to return the wedding ring, however, Vanunu held a tiny bit of his past in his pocket. He had never told anyone, but after he became friends with an odd Colombian named Oscar Guerrero, Vanunu's secret was irretrievably out. Guerrero was a hyperactive freelance journalist who, because of unemployment, had put away his pen and notebook in favor of a painter's brush. Guerrero was painting the church fence when Vanunu met him. After several weeks of friendship, the Israeli revealed his secret.

He told Guerrero that he had been carrying two rolls of color film since he left Israel, unsure of what to do with them. Guerrero could scarcely believe it when Vanunu said they were photographs he had covertly snapped inside the Dimona nuclear center during his night shifts.

The Colombian, propelled into profit-seeking enthusiasm by his freelance instincts, did not bother to ask Vanunu how he had smuggled a camera into Dimona — or his films out of Israel — but instead marveled at Vanunu as a chicken about to lay golden eggs.

Guerrero persuaded the Israeli that his story could be sold — and for enough money to last a lifetime. The idea appealed to Vanunu, once he finished wrestling with his conscience, as he had reached the conclusion that Israel's secret nuclear project was immoral and should be unveiled.

Guerrero appointed himself Vanunu's "literary agent," and together they contacted several international publications to offer a sensational scoop. But wherever they told their story, no one was willing to believe that Vanunu was a former employee of the Jewish state's most secret installation. His tale was rejected by *Newsweek* magazine and even by local Australian newspapers, until the British *Sunday Times* decided to give him a try.

The free-spending newspaper, owned by the Australian-born press magnate Rupert Murdoch, sent investigative reporter Peter Hounam to Sydney to meet the Israeli and assess his fantastic tale. Vanunu and Guerrero suddenly found themselves lavishly treated in the city's finest restaurants, answering endless strings of questions until Hounam reached his verdict.

They especially impressed Hounam, who had a degree in physics, by showing him the photographs after processing the film at an ordinary sixty-minute developing lab. The British journalist decided that it was worth bringing Vanunu to Britain for further inquiries. Hounam offered about fifty thousand dollars for the exclusive rights to the story and the photos, including the eventual publication of a book.

But the *Sunday Times,* like any other business-minded publisher, wanted to cut out the middleman. Hounam did not like Guerrero's style and questionable credibility, so he was dropped.

On September 11, 1986, Mordy's Australian friends brought him to Sydney airport, and he promised them he would return within three weeks. Hounam and Vanunu landed in London the next day, not knowing that Guerrero — displaying an almost wild journalistic feeding frenzy — followed them on a separate flight. None of them knew that two Mossad men were also following.

A few weeks earlier, the Mossad had received a message from a counterpart, the Australian Security Intelligence Organization. The

ASIO sent a brief file about an Israeli engaged in a peculiar form of solicitation: trying to seduce the news media into buying a "secret" story. The ASIO thought the Mossad might like to know. When it learned that Vanunu was heading to London, the Australian agency also told Britain's MI5.

Israeli intelligence officials now knew that they had a problem and would have to take swift action. Two Shin Bet agents visited Vanunu's brother Albert at his carpentry workshop and asked him whether he had heard from Mordecai. Without telling Albert why, one of the agents said, "If you get a letter from your brother, bring it to us."

The *Sunday Times* editors may not have been aware they were under surveillance, but they must have known they were holding a live bomb in their hands: an Israeli traitor with a story never told before.

Vanunu gave them more than sixty photographs he had taken inside the grounds of the Dimona compound, and more spectacularly inside one of the buildings, which he named as Machon 2. *Machon* means "institute" or "facility," which suggests a place of learning or a production center.

Vanunu said he was one of only 150, out of a total of 2,700 Dimona employees, with security clearance for Machon 2, which he revealed to be an underground bomb factory — pure and simple. Beneath the surface of the desert, he disclosed, Israeli scientists and technicians extracted plutonium from uranium fuel rods after their use in the silver-domed nuclear reactor above. The plutonium, Vanunu said, was used to make bombs.

The world had long assumed that the reactor, occasionally photographed from a distance by foreign military attachés and journalists defying press censorship, was secretly used to produce a few, simple atomic bombs. Vanunu's photos, taken inside the high-security compound, offered close-up views of the famous dome and the first evidence suggesting Israel was manufacturing advanced, thermonuclear weapons, probably including neutron or hydrogen bombs — compact but incredibly powerful.

Vanunu offered a detailed sketch of six hitherto unknown, below-ground levels of Machon 2. Above ground, the building appeared to be a two-story, little-used, unimportant warehouse. It was actually, he said, the key to Israel's development of nuclear weapons.

His roving photographer's camera recorded a tour of the corridors, laboratories, storage rooms, and control panels. Above one set of dials, screens, and meters was a neat Hebrew sign identifying it as Yehida 95, or "Unit 95." Vanunu told the British reporters what many of the units did in the process of separating plutonium. The photos showed "radioactivity!" warning signs in Hebrew and chambers where large rubber gloves built into the thick glass walls were used to handle the contents. Some also showed metal spheres, which Vanunu said were models of bombs.

Vanunu said the only outsiders who ever visited were senior military men, defense ministry officials, and Israel's prime ministers. One inspection point was known within Dimona as "Golda's Balcony," after Israel's prime minister stood there and saw the "production hall" below.

Everything Vanunu had heard, while chatting with older colleagues who had worked at the nuclear facility for years, accorded with reports that France had built Dimona for the Israelis. The French had dug the pit that contained most of Machon 2, and they installed the bomb-making equipment.

The facts and figures he gave also indicated that the 26-megawatt reactor provided by the French in the late 1950s had been substantially upgraded by the Israelis — apparently to 150 megawatts. Vanunu's information supported the suspicions by foreign governments and their intelligence agencies, echoed in the world's media, that Israel had far more nuclear capacity than it admitted. The facility had been fed by the extra uranium obtained from Zalman Shapiro's Numec company in America and in the ship-switching "Plumbat" ruse on the Mediterranean in 1968.

The experts and physicists enlisted by the *Sunday Times* studied the pictures, spoke with Vanunu, and considered the "flow rates, measures, temperatures, and other scientific data" he had memorized. Their conclusion was that Israel could easily have made at least one hundred bombs during his decade in Machon 2.[5]

The newspaper team was convinced. Vanunu was genuine, and his would be a great story. They had not reckoned, however, on the obstructive plans of Guerrero.

Angry at both Vanunu and the *Sunday Times* for abandoning him, the Colombian went to a rival newspaper, the *Sunday Mirror,* with his own, slightly garbled version of the nuclear revelations. The *Sunday Mirror* did not believe in Guerrero at all, but used him and a handful of Vanunu's photos offered by the Colombian — buying his tale for a few thousand dollars — simply to publish a two-page barb poking fun at the *Sunday Times* for falling for Vanunu and this patent nonsense.[6]

Israel's nuclear potential was being used as a weapon in a circulation war of British press barons, raging between *Times* proprietor Murdoch and his arch rival, *Mirror* owner Robert Maxwell.

Vanunu was angry and afraid when he saw the *Sunday Mirror,* with his picture on the front page. He was furious at the *Sunday Times* for hesitating with the real story, and he now felt certain that Israeli agents were following him.

To defuse the tension and to protect him, the newspaper had been moving Vanunu from hotel to country house and back again, from the suburbs to the forests and into the center of town every few days. On the day of his inadvertent publicity, he was staying at the Mountbatten Hotel in London's theater district under an assumed name. Only two newspaper staffers knew his location. The journalists tried to calm him, but they also told him that for the sake of good news standards they would need to get an official Israeli reaction before publishing the story the following week. It would, they told him, only make his account more credible.

On September 23, the *Sunday Times* sought a response from the Israeli embassy in London by giving it an outline of the Vanunu story. The embassy issued a denial and also tried to portray Vanunu as a minor technician who would not know anything anyway.

Ambassador Yehuda Avner was extremely concerned, however, and so were his superiors in Jerusalem. They were on the verge of panic, realizing for the first time the breadth and scope of what the nuclear traitor had revealed.

Prime Minister Peres, shocked but unable to do much to control information once it leaked beyond Israel's borders, summoned a special meeting of a committee of newspaper editors within the country itself. He begged them to minimize — rather than emphasize — the story, once the British paper published its version. Abandoning pure news judgment for patriotism, as they often do, the editors agreed to cooperate.

The meeting was supposed to be confidential, but word of it reached London. Ironically, Peres's bid to minimize the story was the final push to give it maximum exposure. The *Sunday Times* editors assumed that his plea to Israel's newspaper bosses must mean that the story being prepared in London was truly important. If the prime minister was concerned, Vanunu must have revealed genuine secrets — notwithstanding the Israeli embassy's denials.

Peres, at the same time, consulted with Rabin and Shamir in the prime ministers' club and decided to order the Mossad to arrest Vanunu — wherever he might be — so that he could be tried in Israel. It would be a lesson to the rest of the population that no one could get away with treason.

Because Peres was well aware of Prime Minister Margaret Thatcher's sensitivity about British sovereignty, the Mossad was also ordered not to violate British law. He knew of the damage the Iron Lady's wrath could wreak on Israeli-British cooperation, which was one of Peres's pet diplomatic projects.

The mission was thus even more difficult than it would otherwise have been. To abduct a man in a foreign land was hard enough when he was alert to the danger, was under protection, and was being moved among secret locations. The prime minister's ban on illegality then made the assignment almost impossible, as it tied the kidnappers' own hands.

The Mossad, knew, however, that it could rely on two elements: the readiness of British intelligence to cooperate in locating Vanunu — or at least to turn a blind eye — and the certainty of finding, in any man, the human frailties that can be exploited.

A team of Mossad men and women was sent to London to search for the nuclear traitor. The Mossad even stationed two men with a professional video camera to look out for Vanunu at the high-security entrance gate of Times Newspapers in Wapping, near the docks of East London. It was a stroke of good fortune that the angry British printers' union had a constant picket line outside Murdoch's publishing fortress. The security guards were already accustomed to seeing many television crews covering the labor protesters for one or another TV news show. This particular video crew was itself videotaped, the *Sunday Times* saying its security camera recorded a six-foot-tall fellow who said he was covering the strike situation for a student union, with an unshaven partner who said nothing.[7]

The Israeli surveillance team spotted its quarry leaving Wapping in a taxi. Other Mossad teams picked up the trail, using cars and motorcycles, and had no trouble following Vanunu to his hotel. It was simple, then, for Israeli agents on foot to shadow Vanunu wherever he went in the coming days. When he was walking in Leicester Square on September 24, it was the perfect time to send "Cindy" on stage to play her role.

For Vanunu, she seemed to be a gift from heaven. His *Sunday Times* babysitters had found him to be extremely nervous, perhaps not surprisingly, but this expressed itself in sexual hunger. The Israeli repeatedly and shamelessly propositioned the female members of the reporting team.[8]

Hoping now that his desires would be satisfied, he was anxious to see the American blonde again after the first meeting. She did call, the very next day. But the newspaper telephoned, too, to arrange another round of interrogation. When Vanunu complained that he had a date, a *Sunday Times* reporter drove him to the appointed rendezvous, the Tate Gallery on the north bank of the Thames, so the Israeli could meet his girlfriend and cancel his date. The reporter noticed that the plump, bleached-blond woman, in high heels, was reluctant to approach the car.

It was the only time that anyone other than Vanunu came face to face with "Cindy." The Israeli, reluctant to talk about her, told the newspaperman that she was an American makeup artist on a tour of Europe. Obsessed with sex, Vanunu also remarked plaintively that Cindy was refusing to go to bed with him.[9]

They did have a few dates in the following days, and exploiting his sexual appetite, his disgust with the *Sunday Times* delays, and then the fright of the *Sunday Mirror* story which did appear, Cindy persuaded Vanunu to get away from it all. He ignored the advice his newspaper friends had given him time and again: not to leave the country, not to fly, and not to check into any hotel that required him to declare his identity by showing his passport.

Cindy was taking care of everything, however. She paid cash for two business-class tickets to Rome. Forgetting his fears of being followed by the Mossad, Vanunu accompanied her to London's Heathrow airport and onto British Airways flight 504 on September 30. Before leaving, he telephoned the *Sunday Times,* said he was "going to leave the city," and promised to return within three days. The newspaper never heard from him again.[10]

As in the seduction of the Iraqi pilot Munir Redfa twenty years earlier, Israel's female agent was promising Vanunu that once they got to a safe house — this time, in Rome — everything would be all right. He could expect to get what he desired. It was a "safe house," but only in the professional, espionage sense of a protected and anonymous shelter for the Mossad.

Vanunu simply vanished from the face of the earth for forty days and forty nights. Only on November 9 did Israel's cabinet secretary Elyakim Rubinstein announce: "Mordecai Vanunu is legally under arrest in Israel, in accordance with a court order following a hearing in which a lawyer of his choice was present."[11]

Why, after weeks of silence, did the prime ministers' club decide to confirm that Vanunu had been captured? First, his family had threatened to go to the Israeli supreme court to force the truth out of the government. Second, Israel was concerned that the growing speculation in the media — that Vanunu was kidnapped on British soil — would harm relations with London. British members of parliament were complaining, Scotland Yard was investigating, and the *Sunday Times* itself reported that Vanunu was abducted, packed into a crate as diplomatic baggage, and flown to Israel.

The Israeli government chose to take the high road, declaring that Vanunu was under arrest on normal legal grounds. To cover the tracks of the covert operation in Europe, official sources in Jerusalem leaked various versions of the nuclear traitor's capture. All the distorted leaks shared one vital element, meant to protect Israel's relations with Britain: that no kidnap had taken place on British soil and that he had legally and willingly left Britain.

To guard the venues and precise methods used, one leaked version had Vanunu stepping onto a yacht with a female Mossad agent in the South of France, being arrested only when the vessel reached international waters. Another said he had happily flown to Paris, where he was then drugged and carried onto an El Al flight from France to Israel.

The truth was left in shadow, although the veil was slightly lifted by the criminal himself. Vanunu showed that, even under arrest and the duress of interrogation, he still had enough spirit and nerve to shatter Shin Bet security. Arriving at Jerusalem district court for a pretrial hearing, he pressed his palm against the window of a police van in which he was being closely guarded.

There, before the eyes and lenses of the world's press, the ink he had scrawled on his flesh revealed the truth. Written on his palm was:

I WAS HIJACKED
IN ROME ITL
30.9.86 AT 21.00 CAME
TO ROME ON B.A. FLIGHT 504

Vanunu, having limited space on his palm, could not detail his entire odyssey. In further court appearances, he arrived with his arms restrained, the van's windows painted dark, and with a motorcyclist's helmet on his head so that the press could not hear any messages he might shout.[12] Even after Shin Bet took away his pens and pencils, Vanunu — in an added mystery — found other ways to tell family members how he had been captured.

His brother Meir saw him in his prison cell and then went abroad to fill in the missing links in the Vanunu arrest: that as soon as British Airways flight 504 touched down at Fiumicino airport in Rome, Cindy hailed a taxi that promptly drove the couple to an address she gave — her supposed love nest.

As soon as they entered an apartment there, Vanunu was pounced on by two Israeli men, who held him down while Cindy injected him with a powerful anesthetic. Meir Vanunu added that his brother was then chained, driven to an Italian port, and transported to Israel by sea. After a week on the Mediterranean he arrived on October 7, was tied to a stretcher when taken ashore at dawn, and then was thrown into a cell with no light and a bare mattress on the floor.

Only when interrogated by Shin Bet did Vanunu learn that the *Sunday Times* had finally published his story. He had been in chains, at sea, when the newspaper splashed a huge headline across its front page: REVEALED: THE SECRETS OF ISRAEL'S NUCLEAR ARSENAL, followed by Vanunu's inside story of the work conducted at Dimona and a detailed blueprint of the nuclear facility, produced by one of the newspaper's mapmakers based on Vanunu's description of the underground Machon 2.

What the defendant could not know, as he was about to face treason and espionage charges and his family suffered the harsh reaction of its neighbors, was that the *Sunday Times* was attempting to repay its debt to Vanunu by pursuing the story. Staff members felt guilty about their amateurish failure to protect their prized news source.

It could and should have been so easy to keep Vanunu safe and happy. All that was needed was the intimate company of a woman. A rich and powerful newspaper could certainly afford prostitutes, and the *Sunday Times* staff did discuss providing the Israeli with paid companionship. But it was decided that a rival newspaper might one day learn that the source of the big story had been rewarded with sexual favors, and this would embarrass the *Sunday Times.*

The newspaper's investigative reporters discovered that the Israeli embassy in Rome rented a van at the beginning of October, and that the number of kilometers clocked when it was returned precisely matched the distance to and from the port of La Spezia. An Israeli merchant vessel, the *Tappuz,* or "Orange," had been there at the same time — but only after being diverted from another sea route. The implication was that the ship had brought the chained prisoner home.[13]

The British newspaper came up with some more circumstantial evidence in its hunt for the unknown seductress who had entrapped Vanunu. The journalists discovered that a "C. Chanin" sat next to "M. Vanunu" at the front of the British airliner flying to Rome, and that a certain Cheryl Chanin Ben-Tov was a woman from America who lived in Israel and was married to a captain in military intelligence, Aman. Mrs. Ben-Tov, based on a wedding photograph obtained by the *Sunday Times,* appeared to fit "Cindy's" general description. Intriguingly, her sister-in-law in Florida was a cosmetician named Cynthia (Cindy) Chanin.[14]

It might appear — from the van rental, the ship diversion, and the borrowed identity of a relative — that the Mossad had left a sloppy, even unprofessional trail. But Israel's intelligence chiefs did not really care. Vanunu was in custody, and that was what mattered.

Gray, mundane Shin Bet, still licking its wounds from the Vanunu failure — permitting him to work at Dimona, failing to prevent his photography spree, letting him keep the film for a year before taking it abroad, and then watching helplessly as he told even more secrets while behind bars — was once again in the shadow of the glorious, globe-trotting Mossad, which basked in the glory of the successful mission of bringing Vanunu home for trial.

Acting on short notice, the Mossad had captured the fugitive while obeying its instructions to remain on the correct side of British law. Prime Minister Peres was able to telephone Prime Minister Thatcher to assure her that none of her country's statutes had been violated.

They exchanged pleasantries and seemed happy with the smooth outcome of the Vanunu affair, but neither leader knew that beneath the surface a bitter confrontation was brewing between their intelligence communities.

The unusual clash began in 1986 with the discovery of eight forged British passports in a telephone booth in West Germany. They had been left there by a careless Israeli intelligence courier whose shoulder bag was found to contain the bogus documents, a genuine Israeli passport, and other papers linking the bag to Israel's embassy in Bonn. The British government strongly protested and elicited an apology from Israel — a tacit admission that the Mossad's forgers choose the United Kingdom as one of the many fake nationalities with which to equip Israeli spies.

A year later, relations between the Mossad and British security agencies were rocked in the wake of a murder in broad daylight near London's Sloane Square, within sight of the punks and tourists rubbing elbows in the trend-setting boutiques of King's Road. These are the favorite shopping grounds both of yuppies, known locally as Sloane Rangers, and of visitors and exiles from throughout the Arab world. These were also the hunting grounds for gunmen stalking a fellow Palestinian, Ali al-Adhami.

He had moved, with his wife and five children, from the lawlessness of Lebanon to seemingly stable London only two years earlier — for the family's safety. Adhami was a cartoonist for a Kuwaiti newspaper in London, *al-Qabas,* and was known for his bitter caricatures of Yasser Arafat as a political schemer who had an Egyptian mistress and was enjoying the high life while his people starved in refugee camps. On July 22, 1987, at age forty-two, Adhami was gunned down outside the newspaper office.

Scotland Yard could not find the killer, even though the British and Arabic press guessed from the start that Arafat had ordered the slaying. A clearer picture emerged at a seemingly unrelated trial, ten months later.

Ismail Sowan, a twenty-eight-year-old Palestinian, was charged with the illegal possession of arms and explosives in his apartment in Hull, in the north of England. He had been in the country for four years, as a research assistant at a college. When the British police raided his home on an anonymous tip, they found an arms cache that included sixty-eight pounds of the devastating plastic explosive Semtex, made in Czechoslovakia and favored by terrorists because it was not detectable by the security devices used at the world's airports.

Sowan told police that he had no idea what was in the suitcases hidden in his bathroom, that he had been keeping them for his friend Abdel Rahim Mustapha. They had known each other for many years in Beirut, Paris, and lately in Britain.

Mustapha was thirty-seven and ran a gasoline station in Leigh-on-Sea, on the eastern fringe of London's commuter belt. Beneath his cover as a legitimate businessman, however, he was a major in the PLO's Force 17, the élite unit set up for Arafat's protection by Ali Hassan Salameh.

After Salameh was blown up by a Beirut car bomb in 1979 at the end of a long Mossad manhunt, Force 17 expanded its functions. No longer merely defensive, it became a special assault force that often attacked from the sea — almost a PLO version of an Israeli sayeret commando unit.

Trained as Arafat's bodyguard, Mustapha was sent by the guerrilla chairman to Britain to organize an underground cell. He already had some offensive, operational experience, having taken part in an attack on El Al passengers at Munich airport on February 10, 1970, killing one Israeli and wounding others. He and his colleagues were freed by the West German authorities seven months later, as part of the ransom for a hijacked Greek airliner — showing how important Mustapha was for Arafat.[15]

Mustapha showed his gratitude to his beloved leader by supervising the liquidation of the critical cartoonist. He was extremely persistent: Having been expelled as an undesirable alien by the British government in April 1987, he had the dedication and daring to return under a false name in July for the Adhami shooting. When he had left in April, he had handed his terrorist arsenal — in the suitcases — to his trusted friend Sowan.

Arrested in August and pressed by British interrogators who suggested he was involved in killing Adhami, Sowan first told them about Mustapha and then astonished them even more: He said he had been working, all along, for Israel.

Sowan said that for many years he had been receiving a monthly salary of around one thousand dollars from Israeli intelligence. Born in East Jerusalem, then under Jordanian jurisdiction, he fell under Israeli control with the rest of the city in 1967. As in the case of other Palestinians who see no prospects in the occupied West Bank, Sowan went to Lebanon to study. In Beirut, he was recruited by the PLO.

Back in Nablus, in the West Bank, for a family visit, he was picked up by Shin Bet. Rather than being charged with contact with a hostile guerrilla organization, he was instead "turned" to work for the Israelis in 1978. It was a typical pattern for the recruitment of Palestinian agents, whose families can enjoy some benefits in the occupied territories while the agent is allowed to travel and study abroad, receiving money as the final binding element.

When Sowan moved to England, the Israelis even paid his rent. In return he was sent by his intelligence controllers to Lebanon, where he befriended Mustapha, and to France. At one point Israeli intelligence gave him a small electronic device, which he kept in his pocket and pressed when he met a PLO contact so as to signal Israeli surveillance teams. He was one of many Arab informers in the Middle East and Europe, who were run in a joint operation by the Mossad and Shin Bet in their hit-and-run war against Palestinian terrorists.

Sowan told the British police that he had tried to cut his links with Israeli intelligence, but it was not the sort of job you can quit. That was no wonder, because he was an important asset who had managed to penetrate one of the closed circles closest to Arafat himself. Sowan had accomplished a feat that was always near and dear to the heart of Israeli intelligence.

When the cartoonist Adhami was shot in London, Sowan happened to be in Israel — on vacation, seeing his family as well as his Israeli handlers. He had been so valuable that the Israelis could not resist sending him back to Britain, despite his own warnings that the murder had made it too dangerous for him to be there. He even told his intelligence bosses about the suitcases that Mustapha had left in his Hull apartment, but the Israelis merely told him to wait patiently and someone would come to relieve him of the burden.

Sowan's handlers acted without due caution when they decided to press on with a mission that had most likely run its course. The Adhami killing changed everything, yet the Israelis acted as though Sowan could simply proceed as before. Worse still, they let him sit on the arms cache, which only got him into deep trouble. Israeli intelligence had learned little from its recent run of mistakes.

Now in the hands of the British police, Sowan sang to save his skin. He named all his Israeli case officers, who worked undercover at the Israeli embassy in London. Sowan assumed that his disclosures would help his case in British judicial eyes, but they did not. He was sentenced to eleven years in prison.[16]

His conviction was the trigger for firm British action against Israeli intelligence. On June 17, 1988, Her Majesty's Government carried out an unprecedented sweep against a friendly nation's spies — expelling Israeli embassy attaché Aryeh Regev and announcing that another diplomat, Yaakov Barad, could not reenter Britain from his vacation at home. Britain's Foreign Office, usually reluctant to discuss intelligence matters, pointedly named Regev and Barad as "Mossad men." Barad had been running another Palestinian agent, Bashir Samara, who also penetrated the London cell of the PLO's Force 17.

Soon afterward, Israel withdrew another three operatives from its embassy in London — either on its own delayed initiative to smooth ruffled feathers, or acting on strong MI5 hints that the entire Mossad station should be dismantled.

The British authorities were furious. Perhaps they hoped that Israel would have given them some warning that the Palestinian cartoonist was going to be murdered. Even if such expectations were too high, considering that the Israelis would have to "burn" their own agent inside Force 17, the British wished that the Mossad liaison in London had at least provided a full briefing after the killing of Adhami. Even failing that, the Israelis could at least have told the authorities about the arms cache in Sowan's apartment.

The Mossad and Shin Bet had been hoping instead to have their cake and eat it, too. They were not especially concerned about the cartoonist, deceased in any event, and instead hoped against hope that Mustapha — or another big PLO fish — would return one day for his very special suitcases. The Israelis wanted the best of all worlds, but everything turned sour.

Intelligence chiefs in Israel were extremely reluctant to examine the Sowan disaster and draw the necessary conclusions. They did not find any culprits, and they did not dismiss anyone. It was typical of Admoni's easygoing and relaxed administration of the Mossad, at times focusing primarily on minimizing internal disputes. As with the failure to detect and deter Vanunu's treason, Israeli intelligence behaved as though facing its own deficiencies would simply be too painful.

Israel lost its valuable inside agent, Sowan, near the top of the PLO leadership. It lost its complete infrastructure in London when the angry British publicly blew the whistle. The Israelis nearly obliterated all their friendly ties with British intelligence, already frayed by the suspicions surrounding the Dikko kidnap affair and the capture of Vanunu.

Above all, the mishandled operation destroyed the last vestige of prestige which the Mossad had worked so hard to restore, after the failures of the 1980s, by luring Vanunu into prison.

Vanunu was convicted of treason, espionage, and disclosing state secrets on March 24, 1988. The three judges rejected his claim that he had acted out of ideological concerns. But the judges were listening when he said, "I am not a traitor and did not intend to damage the State of Israel." They sentenced him to a relatively lenient eighteen years in prison.

The clouds of mystery were not lifted, however. Vanunu himself, shown the photograph of Cheryl Chanin Ben-Tov, waved it off with "That's not the Cindy I knew."[17]

Also puzzling were the conclusions of Italy's famous counterterrorism magistrate, Domenico Sica. After investigating whether the crime of kidnapping had been committed by Israelis in Rome, he published the surprising conclusion in September 1988 that Vanunu had not been kidnapped at all.

The investigating judge said that the English written on the Israeli's palm was too good to believe; and that the photographs of Dimona's bomb factory, which Sica borrowed from the *Sunday Times,* could only have been taken with official cooperation. The "tourist's presentation" through the corridors and laboratories with no people in sight seemed bizarre to Sica, who said such dials and instruments would have had to be watched around the clock.

The Italian findings convinced some newspapers and magazines that Vanunu had been pretending to be a traitor, and that Israel had arranged the entire charade — "a well-organized disinformation operation," in Sica's words.[18] His verdict was as dubious, however, as it was convenient. The Italian judiciary, rarely independent of political considerations, preferred to drop the entire incident because "no kidnap" meant no need to investigate.

The intelligence communities of Israel and Italy have a long record of close cooperation, dating back to the 1950s. Was it just a coincidence that the Mossad chose Rome as the place to capture Vanunu? While Prime Minister Peres was adamant that no British laws be broken, Israel's spies sensed impunity in Italy.

Sica's suppositions were taken seriously, however, by an international press which felt that Israeli intelligence must have been incredibly clever — not unforgivably stupid — to allow Vanunu's treason.

The media had trouble believing that the almighty Israeli secret services could be caught so off guard, and foreign publications assumed instead that Israel's spies had used Vanunu in a sophisticated plot to frighten the Arabs by revealing that Israel had a nuclear arsenal.

Only a highly conspiratorial mind could believe, however, that any organization — even the best intelligence agency in the world — could undertake such a long-term, complicated operation: to win the consent of the three top politicians in the prime ministers' club and coordinate the actions of all the secret-service and military chiefs; to recruit a poor Moroccan with no physics training and then plot his extreme political changes; to equip him with photographs; to send him to the farthest conceivable foreign country and arrange his conversion to Christianity; to sell the story to the press; to set up a meeting of the Israeli prime minister with newspaper editors; to arrange Vanunu's disappearance and stage a trial in such a way as to fool his judges; to let his family suffer; and, presumably, to make him languish in prison.

And what for? So that Israel could remind the world of its unassailable military superiority in the Middle East, without formally announcing the existence of the nuclear arsenal? The Arabs and the rest of the world have long taken it for granted that Israel has "the bomb" anyway. Reminding them does no good. Instead, it spurs an unconventional arms race, with the Syrians, Iraqis, and Libyans racing to develop chemical and even nuclear weapons.

The ironic outcome of the Vanunu affair was that Israel's most secret of secrets — its ultimate taboo topic, never discussed in any forum greater than ten persons — was suddenly on front pages around the world in full detail, exposed to public discussion at a time not of the government's choosing.

The Israeli public had little time or inclination to focus on the implications of the affair. Attention quickly turned to questions perceived as more closely relating to the existence of the Jewish state — matters that Vanunu claimed had motivated him: the continuing Israeli occupation of captured Arab territories, and the challenge posed by Palestinian nationalism.

EIGHTEEN

The Death of the Informers

IT WAS MUHAMMAD AL-AYAD'S last stand, and he was making a desperate show of it. Running from window to window of his old stone house, spraying bullets from his Uzi submachine gun at his fellow Palestinians outside, Ayad did not care whom he might hit. He just wanted a way out.

"Ayad! Ayad!" His wife shouted the family name down the telephone to one of the Arabic-speaking Israelis who were supposed to protect them. The Ayads had been cooperating with the Israelis from the time they conquered the West Bank of the Jordan nearly twenty-one years earlier.

It was February 24, 1988, the seventy-eighth day of the popular revolt that taught much of the world an Arabic word. The *intifada,* or uprising, was already the longest and most damaging challenge the Israeli occupation ever had to face. Inspired by their six-day victory in 1967, the Israelis had quickly spread tentacles of law and order through the West Bank, Gaza Strip, Golan Heights, and Sinai Peninsula. The octopus, with its brain at the center in a northern Tel Aviv suburb, was Shin Bet.

As Israel's FBI, Shin Bet is dedicated to fighting the state's enemies, whether foreign or domestic, within the borders of Israel and occasionally abroad. Since the Six-Day War, Shin Bet's borders include the occupied territories. Muhammad al-Ayad worked for Shin Bet.

His neighbors in Qabatiya, one of the northernmost towns in the part of the West Bank that biblically minded Israelis call Samaria, said Ayad had been coerced — "recruited" did not seem quite the right word — to serve as an informer when Shin Bet had him under arrest in the first months of the occupation. Ayad was only twenty years old then and had been accused of causing some trouble, although no one could remember what. What mattered was that to gain his freedom, and later to grease the administrative wheels that ensured the prosperity of his café, Ayad agreed to provide information to Shin Bet.

"It is nothing major," a Shin Bet operative typically says to a potential collaborator. "It is not even against the interests of your people. You all simply want to live in peace, right? So if you see some troublemakers, you just tell us and we'll do the rest. No one will have to know."

But in the small villages, where secrets are hard to mask, Shin Bet's informers often were known. There were thousands of them among the over one million Palestinians of the West Bank and Gaza. Ayad's fate, however, would make future recruitment almost impossible.

The intifada had taken on new vigor that week in February, as the latest clandestine leaflets from the United National Leadership of the Uprising called for a general strike and protest marches to coincide with the start of an American diplomatic initiative. The Palestinians felt they had been ignored too long. The rebellion had already prompted Secretary of State George Shultz to fly in with a United States plan for Middle Eastern peace negotiations. Now the protesters wanted to be sure that America would listen to them.

Protesters clashed with Israeli troops throughout the West Bank and Gaza, but in Qabatiya law and order gave way to lawlessness and disorder. The whole town seemed to have poured into the poorly paved streets, day after day giving up school, work, and the old normality to march in hastily arranged parades, shouting slogans as they passed Ayad's house.[1] He should have grown accustomed to hearing chants such as "With our bodies and our blood, we will destroy the traitors and liberate our land!" On Wednesday the twenty-fourth, however, Ayad panicked.

He was forty years old, and he had cracked under pressure only twice: once when he gave in to the Israelis and agreed to work for them; and an episode more uncourageous than uncontrolled, when he fired his Uzi at some young Arabs who were trying to sabotage his car. That was a few months before the intifada began, back when Ayad knew that he could shoot at fellow Palestinians without putting himself in mortal danger. The Israelis would protect him. After all they had given him the Uzi, a mark of impunity more powerful than any badge of office.

With his house surrounded and then stoned by the mob, Ayad

picked up the lightweight machine gun, first waving it threateningly and then firing bursts of bullets from the roof and out the windows. All the tensions built up since the Palestinian uprising began were released in this unexpected, fatal confrontation. He probably did not even notice that among the thirteen Qabatiyans he hit was a small boy, a four-year-old who died instantly.

The demonstrators knew immediately. The blood was all the evidence they needed of Ayad's treason, which they had always suspected. Where cooler heads might have retreated in the face of gunfire and a dead toddler, the crowd continued to throw rocks and bottles in a relentless assault on the traitor's home.

He, however, was defending his ground. Shooting as though the West Bank were the Wild West and running like a trapped rat, Ayad told his wife to telephone the Israeli military authorities in Jenin, an Arab town four miles away, to summon a rescue force.

The army was busy that day, controlling unrest elsewhere, and did not get to Qabatiya in time. Who was this Palestinian calling for help, anyway?

He was an informer, one of many lending their eyes and ears to Shin Bet in the minisociety which the Israelis could occupy but could not penetrate without the assistance of Arab collaborators. But when they needed help, Shin Bet could not protect them.

Admittedly, it was a difficult time for the domestic intelligence agency. Shin Bet was scrambling to identify the organizers of the rebellion; but even after hundreds and then thousands of Palestinians were arrested in the West Bank and Gaza, the underground leaflets continued to be distributed and the crowds of protesters continued to throw stones and chant angry slogans.

Shin Bet's chief Yosef Harmelin was preparing to leave his post at the end of March 1988. He had only served a year and a half, but he had previously directed the agency and was only brought out of retirement to be a temporary caretaker after the killings-and-coverup scandal that tore apart Shin Bet. The secret service interrogators who beat two bus hijackers to death in 1984 had tried to sidestep responsibility by blaming military officers. The army clearly did not owe Shin Bet any favors after that, and when the intifada began senior military officers engaged in private but potent criticism of the security agency.

Internal Israeli rivalries certainly did not help Ayad, and before any Israelis could come to save him, the informer ran out of bullets. The mob poured into his house and pinned him to the floor, and several of the angry young men used a wire to strangle him. Ayad's wife was allowed to escape, even as the frenzied crowd set fire to her home.

By the time the army did arrive, with several Shin Bet agents in an unmarked car, they found Ayad on public display: a brutally beaten body, hanging from an electricity pylon near Qabatiya's bus station. Up there, on the wire, covering the corpse, was the green, black, red, and white flag of Palestine, a country that existed only in the nationalistic longings of people who had lost all the Middle Eastern wars.

Ayad's body was a gory symbol of rebellion, and a message to Shin Bet that its twenty-year control of the territories had broken down. Ayad was the sixty-fifth Palestinian who died in the intifada. The boy he killed was the sixty-fourth.

In the first eighteen months of the uprising, more than seventy Arabs who had collaborated with Shin Bet were killed by fellow Palestinians. Another hundred were slain in the following year. There were weeks in which more Arabs were being murdered by Arabs than were killed by Israelis. Alleged collaborators became the main targets of the intifada, but the violence was getting out of hand as many personal scores were being settled by the blade and the bullet. Drug pushers, common criminals, and prostitutes were killed by gangs vowing to "purify Palestine." The United National Leadership's clandestine leaflets desperately tried to redirect attention onto the struggle for independence from Israel — urging West Bankers and Gazans not to kill their neighbors unless "intifada courts" sentenced them to death.

The uprising brought about social changes that could best be described as a general upheaval. It was not simply a protest against the continued Israeli occupation, but a long and stubborn campaign aimed at shaking off Israeli military rule. And that is literally what intifada means in Arabic: "shaking off." The protesters wished to create an alternative system of government run by the Arab residents, forming the infrastructure of a future Palestinian state.

The uprising was precisely what Shin Bet was meant to prevent. The agency's network of informers should have told the Israelis of any significant attempts to organize dissent. Several thousand informers ranged across Palestinian society, from factory workers to intellectuals. With their incomes supplemented by Shin Bet stipends ranging between fifty and two hundred dollars a month, they were supposed to keep the Israelis informed of activists who might try to turn social and professional organizations into political power centers.

Shin Bet concentrated, however, on the area in which it excelled: preventing Arab terrorism. Informers were paid especially handsome bonuses for tips pertaining to violent groups. Isolated terrorist crimes, such as a stabbing of a Jewish settler in the West Bank, were solved by Shin Bet with impressive speed — thanks to information from agents planted inside the guerrilla cells, purchased from informers on "the street," or obtained by physical or psychological coercion from the dozens of "suspects" who were usually arrested in sweeps of the area around the scene of an attack.

There was no truly dangerous terrorist threat within the occupied territories. The intelligence system had accomplished that in the first months after the Six-Day War, and then it grew fat and complacent. Shin Bet operatives, spreading the word that they should be addressed by Arabic names they invented such as Abu Ibrahim, seemed arrogant. And most of them were.

In the field, they knew they were hated. They also knew that the worst thing they could do to a political activist in a West Bank town was to pretend to be his friends. They might visit his house frequently and grin as they left, or they could shout familiar greetings from their car while driving past. Arresting a young hothead could make him a local hero. Making him appear to be a collaborator would surely ruin him.

Actual collaborators were provided with special identification cards by Shin Bet, making it easy for the cooperative Arabs to pass through Israeli army checkpoints without undergoing questioning or searches.

At its headquarters in a northern suburb of Tel Aviv, Shin Bet concentrated on gathering information rather than producing informed analysis. Reports of trouble brewing here or there would lead to detentions, interrogations, and more reports being filed suggesting names of people, villages, and refugee camps to be investigated. But the big picture was missed.

Hardly anyone, in the intelligence community or elsewhere in Israel, wanted to believe that the Palestinians would rise up in mass rebellion. That had been the fear in the first months of the occupation in 1967, but for two decades since then the territories had been governed peacefully. Most of their residents had been cooperative, most of the time, with the Israeli authorities so as to continue their normal lives with a minimum of disruption.

A few months before the intifada began, the Israeli official responsible for monitoring West Bank and Gaza affairs was overheard denying the possibility of such unrest. The "coordinator" of government activities in the occupied territories, Shmuel Goren, was asked, "Well, when will the rebellion in the territories begin?"

It was a somewhat aggressive conversational opening, but Israelis are not known for standing on polite formality, and in any event it was a military man who was asking. Goren seemed to be taken aback, however, and he snapped, "No rebellion! Not ever!"

The officer persisted: "Are you sure about what you're saying?"

Goren ended the exchange with "You want to bet?"

Goren was a senior operative with the Mossad until 1984, and he certainly should have known whatever the intelligence community knew. His heated conversation ironically took place at a party densely peopled by Israeli intelligence officers. It was a wedding reception in honor of Aman veteran Yaakov Nimrodi's daughter, Smadar. It was the party of the year in Israel, but it was not to be *the* Middle East event of the year 1987. That was to be the uprising that Goren claimed would never occur.

The intifada began as a loose collection of events that were later coordinated by the shadowy United National Leadership in its leaflets, underground radio broadcasts from Syria, and word-of-mouth instructions. It began on December 9, a week after the Arab leaders at their summit conference in Jordan ignored the Palestinians by focusing only on the dangers of the Iran-Iraq war, while President Ronald Reagan and Soviet leader Mikhail Gorbachev met at the same time in Washington but did not bother to discuss the Palestinian problem.

Why did the intifada start when it started? The immediate spark flashed in Gaza on Tuesday, December 8, when an Israeli truck driver on the main road through town lost control of his vehicle. The heavy truck struck a crowd of Palestinians, killing four and injuring seven others in what police later called an accident. To Gazans, however, it seemed to be murder, the last straw, the breaking point, the signal for an explosion of anger that had been building for over twenty years. They took to the streets the next morning, the protest movement spread to the West Bank, and it went on and on.

Members of the intelligence community, especially Shin Bet chiefs, have almost always played a moderating role in formulating Israel's defense policies. They have been more reluctant to use force than many of the country's trigger-happy politicians. And they opposed capital punishment, believing that the certainty of death would prompt Palestinian guerrillas to fight even harder with their backs to the wall — inflicting heavier casualties on the Israelis — when otherwise the Arab terrorist would surrender. Shin Bet's killing of the bus hijackers in the Gaza Strip was an exception, not a policy, and therefore eventually met a harsh response in Israeli terms.

Because captured terrorists were not put to death, Israel's prisons were filled with them. And from time to time, many were released in various prisoner swaps despite the official unyielding rhetoric opposing deals with terrorists. The result of an exchange with Ahmed Jibril's Popular Front for the Liberation of Palestine–General Command in 1985 was the agitating presence of six hundred hardened Palestinian guerrillas and political activists in the West Bank. Palestinians convicted of murder and other crimes, who felt no remorse and were still believers in the armed struggle against Israel, were walking the streets after years of indoctrination by their fellow inmates in prison. They had organized classes, which ranged from Marxism to counterinterrogation techniques, learning how to confront Shin Bet under the very nose of the agency.

Such explanations are purely technical and fall short of completing the big historical puzzle. The exact timing of the outbreak of major events such as the French Revolution or the changes in Eastern Europe is difficult to explain. There is no convincing explanation of why the intifada began in December 1987 and not earlier. It is clear, however, that the uprising began because the Palestinians were fed up with the Israeli occupation.

Shin Bet and the military governors of the occupied territories had failed to see the Palestinians as a political people. Their primary aim was to control the territories by a combination of incentives and threats, known in traditional colonial terms as a carrot-and-stick policy. The security forces were always so confident of keeping order, while tens of thousands of Arabs peacefully earned their living by traveling daily to work in pre-1967 Israel, that the Israelis had not learned the lines of influence within Gaza and the West Bank.

Among the most difficult groups to penetrate were the religious zealots. They were Sunni Moslems, rather than the fanatical Shiites who rule Iran, but still the Gaza faithful took some inspiration from Ayatollah Ruhollah Khomeini and his revolutionaries in far-off Teheran. Ironically, Shin Bet had at times encouraged fundamentalist groups, thinking they would be a useful alternative to the mainstream support of the Palestine Liberation Organization, the PLO. It was yet another classical method of colonialism, divide and rule, that proved futile. Those same mosques eventually turned against Shin Bet by calling on collaborators to turn themselves in and "repent," while a radical religious group called Hamas arose and then was outlawed by the Israelis.

Clashes between the Israeli army and Palestinian protesters, armed mainly with stones and bottles, led rapidly to over three hundred Arab deaths in 1988, the first full year of the intifada, and a similar number of deaths in 1989. A new page in the history of the Arab-Israeli conflict was turned, as the rebel movement became uncrushable. In the first years of the uprising, the Israelis arrested over twenty thousand Arabs and held as many as six thousand in detention at any one time. There still were many more taking part in the daily, even hourly, protest marches.

When the uprising began in December 1987, top Israeli defense and intelligence officials did not attach particular significance to the events. Defense Minister Yitzhak Rabin did not rush back from a visit to Washington. Prime Minister Shamir and the army chief of staff, General Dan Shomron, in the weekly cabinet meetings, dismissed the trouble in the occupied territories as unimportant and repeatedly promised the twenty-five ministers that the unrest could easily be suppressed.

It took two months for Israel's intelligence chiefs, conferring every week as the Varash committee, to reach the conclusion that Shin Bet and the army had failed to stop the uprising.

Shin Bet's Harmelin had to report that the agency's network of informers was crumbling, but there was no explanation for failing to predict the intifada other than the privately expressed views of some Shin Bet men that their many official functions did not include prophecy. Their agency, they said, did not have the tools to anticipate large-scale rebellion.

Shin Bet had been assigned to preventing threats to the State of

Israel and had done very well at that. Harmelin felt that his operatives should not become the scapegoats for the failure of Israeli politicians to find a long-range solution in the region. He did set up a new department in Shin Bet, however, with the mission of monitoring and analyzing political trends in the Palestinian community.

The Varash panel members knew that the worst short-term failure was the inability to foresee that the Palestinians would change their tactics. They had shifted from isolated terrorist attacks, involving very few individuals, to less violent but much more widespread action that could outmaneuver the massive military strength of Israel. The armed behemoth, even with its sophisticated weapons systems, was too clumsy to react appropriately. Israel's leaders knew that a democratic society does not have the option of bringing in tanks and artillery to suppress demonstrators who are throwing stones and burning tires — unlike dictatorial regimes in the Middle East, China, and elsewhere.

Shin Bet's chief could report that his agents were intensifying their efforts to cut off the trouble spots from each other and from outside incitement. Israeli intelligence knew that the intifada was locally initiated by people in the occupied territories, but there were indications that PLO leaders outside the territories were moving quickly to jump on the bandwagon. Mossad chief Nahum Admoni revealed that one of the first acts of solidarity, for incitement and propaganda purposes, would be a voyage at sea.

The PLO spent around $750,000 in February 1988 to buy an old Greek car ferry called the *Sol Phryne.* It was renamed *al-Awda,* the *"Return,"* and was to bring 131 Palestinian exiles to the shores of Israel to dramatize their demand for a homeland. This would be an Arab version of the *Exodus,* the freighter that brought over four thousand Jewish survivors of the Nazi concentration camps to British-ruled Palestine in 1947, only to be repulsed and forced back to Europe — to the eternal embarrassment of Britain.

Coincidentally, the *Sol Phryne* itself had been built in 1947, had sailed among the Greek islands, and later specialized in transporting Christian pilgrims from Greece to Israel. In 1982 it was one of many ships that carried Palestinian guerrilla fighters out of Beirut, after Israel's invasion of Lebanon.[2]

Now the PLO was planning to use the ferryboat to embarrass Israel. Britain's mandate over Palestine had survived only one more year after the suffering Jews aboard the *Exodus* had been turned away. Forty-one years later the PLO could only hope, however unrealistically, that Israel's rule over the West Bank and Gaza would suffer a similar fate. The imminent confrontation at sea could only be bad for Israel's image, which was already badly tarnished by the army's tough measures in attempting to suppress the intifada.

The threat of a PLO propaganda coup was a major subject of a Varash committee meeting in Tel Aviv in mid-February. The Mossad's Admoni was the chairman, as usual, reporting that his agents in Greece were watching the PLO as it organized the publicity-seeking "Voyage of Return." The passengers were being assembled in Athens, and it was publicly suggested that a ship in the nearby port of Piraeus would be chartered for the voyage.

Israeli operatives passed the word around local shipping circles that anyone providing a vessel to the PLO could expect to lose that ship. The Israelis also asked around and found out that the *Sol Phryne* had just been sold to Palestinians. It was not in Piraeus. It was anchored in the harbor of Limassol, Cyprus.

The men and women of Mossad compiled lists of the Palestinians who were planning to sail toward Israel, and these included PLO men with violent pasts. The ship was also, however, to carry dozens of journalists, television crews, and even a leftist member of the Knesset, Israel's parliament. They were the PLO's insurance policy, the guarantee that the Israeli navy — which was expected to try somehow to prevent the newly named *al-Awda* from landing — would not sink the ship.

Admoni had a brilliant idea. The joint intelligence committee discussed sabotaging the ship before it took any people on board. They would have to act quickly, the Mossad chief said, because the Palestinian spokesman Bassam Abu Sherif was telling daily news conferences in Athens that the voyage would begin "at any hour, any time now." The PLO's mouthpiece was a heavily scarred, half-blind man. Sherif had managed to survive the explosion of a Mossad parcel bomb in July 1972 at his Beirut home, but lost an eye and several fingers. Insisting he had put radicalism behind him and now sought peace, Sherif had not been linked with terrorist violence for many years and by 1988 the Mossad was no longer out to get him. It just wanted to sink his propaganda project.

The Mossad chief brought the plan to sabotage the PLO ship while it was still empty to Prime Minister Shamir. Based on his own experience in the Mossad's European operations, Shamir could see the elegant logic in stopping the voyage before it began. He did not ask for precise details of the operational plan, but he knew that explosives would be used. The prime minister was told that the aim would be to avoid loss of life, and given such a desire the mission would have been considered a failure — at least partially — if innocent passengers had been killed.

Shamir was also asked to approve a killing. The intelligence chiefs wanted the go-ahead to assassinate a senior PLO figure, described by Israeli intelligence analysts as a "clear, potent, and persistent danger." Mohammed Bassem Sultan Tamimi, a lieutenant colonel in the PLO's semiofficial army, had been closely watched by Mossad agents in Jordan, Lebanon, and Tunisia. They reported that Tamimi was an activist in Arafat's mainstream Fatah faction, more a man of action than a political planner. He was thirty-five years old, was better known by the nickname Hamdi, and worked in the Occupied Homelands Directorate of the PLO.

Hamdi signed his own death warrant by planning dozens of attacks by Palestinian guerrillas inside the occupied territories, while organizing a PLO branch called Jihad Islami, or "Islamic Holy War," which was meant to attract religious Moslems.

One example of Hamdi's handiwork had particularly enraged the Israelis: By the ancient Wailing Wall in Jerusalem, during an army swearing-in ceremony on October 15, 1986, hand grenades exploded among the recruits and their proud families. One Israeli was killed and seventy wounded. Whoever threw the grenades — apparently one of Hamdi's agents — got away. The Palestinian Jihad Islami claimed responsibility.

The Israelis were determined that Hamdi would not escape punishment.

Prime Minister Shamir approved both plans, the assassination and sabotaging the PLO ferry, in a simple oral statement to the Mossad director. No American-style "intelligence finding" had to be typed out, signed, and placed in the files. No parliamentary committee had to be informed of the covert action. This was war, after all. Even in public, Shamir had branded the PLO plan to sail a ship toward Israel "a declaration of war."

The Mossad must have had an agent remarkably close to Tamimi/

Hamdi, and there is no doubt that the PLO and its Occupied Homelands Directorate were thoroughly infiltrated by informers. The Israelis knew that the Palestinian colonel would be flying from Athens to Cyprus on February 13, 1988, and they knew that Cyprus was a relatively easy venue for killing. The island is divided into Greek and Turkish sectors and barely 150 miles from Israel and Lebanon; the police were hopeless at solving political crimes. There were simply too many incidents, and the Cypriot authorities had enough problems without making enemies among Israelis and Arabs.

The only potential difficulty was that Tamimi/Hamdi was at his most vulnerable precisely where the *Sol Phryne,* the PLO propaganda ship, was waiting for its passengers. Whether the voyage was stopped or not, the glare of worldwide media coverage would soon come to the island. It might not be the ideal venue for a political killing. Admoni checked with Shamir, to be sure that the prime minister did not see a problem in the proximity of the two cases which the Mossad had been told to handle. The approval was reaffirmed.

On Sunday, February 14, the Israelis went into action. They had received an excellent tip: that Lieutenant Colonel Tamimi, a.k.a. Hamdi, would be driving around Cyprus that day with Marwan Kayyali, a PLO colonel who was based in Limassol. Kayyali's job was to ship supplies to the Palestinians remaining in Lebanon, using his excellent contacts in Limassol harbor. He was also involved in arranging the voyage of the *Sol Phryne.*

From the Mossad's point of view, the two missions were coming together beautifully. Israeli agents had little trouble planting a powerful bomb in Kayyali's green Volkswagen.[3] The device could be detonated by remote control, and the operatives who held the radio transmitter watched the automobile as it approached Kayyali's home in a small apartment complex in Limassol.

The presence of a third man in the car made the Israelis hesitate. But they were able to identify him as Mohammed Hassan Buheis, also known as Abu Hassan, an activist in the PLO's Occupied Homelands Directorate. Exercising the latitude of decision making permitted to Israeli field operatives, they considered Abu Hassan a legitimate target, too. One of the Israelis pressed the button. The Volkswagen was destroyed by the explosion. All three Palestinians were dead.

Early the next morning, the port of Limassol was rocked by another explosion. This one punctured the hull of the ferryboat *Sol Phryne,* rendering it useless for the "Voyage of Return." The Palestinians correctly blamed Israel, but all that Defense Minister Yitzhak Rabin would say was "The State of Israel decided it was compelled not to let them achieve their purpose, and we do that in whatever ways seem suitable."

The Monday blast injured no one. Cypriot police said a limpet mine, a simple but effective weapon commonly used by frogmen during World War II, had been attached to the *Sol Phryne's* hull from beneath the surface of the Mediterranean. It was neat work, the explosion destroying any evidence that could trace the mine's origins, and there was no chance of catching the attackers.

Operatives of the Mossad station in Nicosia, the capital of Cyprus, must have had a busy time. They certainly were involved in preattack reconnaissance and served as lookouts. They also played host to Israeli bomb experts and navy frogmen who came to the island for the two explosive missions.

PLO spokesman Abu Sherif said in Athens that another ship would be found. But the intended passengers, already tired of waiting, left Greece. The world's press lost interest. The *Sol Phryne* was repaired, but no one again suggested using it as a pale imitation of the *Exodus.* Shamir and intelligence had their way.

The PLO prepared a violent response instead. It would be an act of almost personal revenge by Khalil el-Wazir, better known as Abu Jihad, the "Father of the Holy War" who was Yasser Arafat's right-hand man and military chief. Wazir had been working closely with the Occupied Homelands Directorate, plotting strategy for exploiting the intifada. Three of his men had just been killed by the Mossad in Cyprus, and Abu Jihad was out for blood.

He sent three guerrillas at the beginning of March 1988 to Egypt, where they armed themselves from a hidden PLO cache and headed across the Sinai Desert, which the Israelis had returned to Egypt in 1982 under the Camp David Accords of 1978 and the peace treaty that followed. The Fatah band had surprisingly little trouble crossing the border on March 7 from the Sinai into the Negev Desert on foot. Within hours they managed to shock Israel's defense establishment.

They may not even have known precisely what they were doing. The guerrillas hijacked a passenger bus in the desert that day, and it happened to be the shuttle service transporting employees, with their high-security clearances, from the Negev city of Beersheba to the ultrasecret nuclear reactor at Dimona. It was an indirect attack on Israel's most secure facility.

The hijacked bus was stopped at a roadblock, and after pretending to negotiate, an antiterrorist unit of Israel's police staged a lightning assault. All three hijackers were killed. Three of the Israeli nuclear workers also died, however, and the PLO declared the raid a victory. Yasser Arafat said the victims were connected with Israel's clandestine atomic bomb factory, "the most dangerous military target in the Middle East." The PLO attack was a contribution, of sorts, by the guerrilla fighters outside "Palestine" to the uprising by their brethren living under occupation.

That was on Monday. Defense Minister Rabin was enraged and insisted on striking at the root cause of the terrorist violence. The intifada was bad enough; infiltrations were intolerable. Rabin asked Mossad chief Admoni to explore the possibility of killing Abu Jihad.

On Thursday, March 10, Admoni told his fellow intelligence chiefs, Shin Bet's Harmelin and Aman's director, General Amnon Lipkin-Shahak, that with around thirty days' preparation, the Mossad and the army could together mount a pinpoint assassination mission. The Varash committee agreed that the planning should begin.

The plan, without specific operational details, was explained by Lipkin-Shahak to the inner cabinet, the ten senior ministers from among the large, unwieldy twenty-five-member full cabinet. The prime minister told the bipartisan inner group that the PLO had to be sent a clear message that its "military" side would not be allowed to gain any advantage from the unrest in the occupied territories. Liquidating Arafat's top aide would inject fear into the Palestinian leader's heart, just when he might think that the Israelis were running scared during the intifada.

Some ministers realized that behind the official explanation hid another motive. The assassination would be a "show-off" operation to boost the morale of the Israeli public, which had suffered because of the inability to suppress the Palestinian uprising.

Meeting so soon after the shock and anger of the bus hijacking, most of the government ministers readily agreed. Peres, who was deputy prime minister, did raise objections. While this was not strictly a party-line issue, the Labor party leader seemed concerned that an attack on the top leadership of the PLO — for the first time in nine years — could ruin diplomatic efforts for a solution to the Palestinian problem through negotiations with Egypt and Jordan.

The Labor side of Israel's coalition government believed in withdrawing from much of the occupied territories in exchange for peace treaties. Shamir and his Likud bloc did not. Peres constantly suspected that Shamir was out to crush any peace feelers. Also objecting to the assassination plan were two other Labor ministers, former air force chief Ezer Weizman and the former president of Israel, Education Minister Yitzhak Navon.

In terms of military experience, however, the two ministers on the Labor side who had the most operational experience agreed with Prime Minister Shamir in this case. Defense Minister Rabin and Police Minister Chaim Bar-Lev were both former army chiefs of staff, and they both believed that Israel's military and its intelligence community should jointly send the PLO a stern warning. Approving an air raid on a military target is, admittedly, more impersonal and easier. But Abu Jihad himself was a military target who had to be attacked with precision.

Shamir told his senior ministers that the Mossad would need the participation of élite army units. The PLO military commander would be killed in Tunis, nearly fifteen hundred miles from Tel Aviv. While the raid had not yet been planned in detail it would likely resemble the Aviv Ne'urim assault on Beirut in April 1973, when the Mossad helped sayeret commandos land in the Lebanese capital and kill fifteen Palestinian terrorist chiefs in their homes — including Abu Jihad's predecessor as PLO military commander, Muhammad Najjar.

The inner cabinet told the Mossad and the army to proceed with their planning. In charge were Israel's top general, chief of staff Shomron, and his deputy, General Ehud Barak. Barak had deep intelligence and commando experience and was involved in the raid on Beirut fifteen years earlier. Now he was to work with the intelligence men again, and their task would be to duplicate the success of 1973, even though the distance to be covered this time was fifteen times greater.

General Barak had plenty of cooperation from military intelligence, and Aman commander Shahak had himself been with the commando forces in Aviv Ne'urim. In 1973, Shahak was known as

Amnon Lipkin. When choosing a Hebrew name to replace his family's European Jewish name, "Shahak," or "pulverize," was a powerful choice. The challenge of the Tunis mission appealed to him.

The intricate planning for the attack on Abu Jihad would seem to any military strategist to be a tremendous amount of trouble for the sake of killing one man. But imagine what the Americans or British would have done in World War II to get rid of a senior German or Japanese general. And would not the Germans have felt they were crippling the morale of the Allies if they could have assassinated General Dwight Eisenhower?

Removing a senior commander from enemy ranks would not settle the Arab-Israeli conflict, but the Israelis badly needed some sort of victory four months into the intifada. In addition, the experience of the 1970s had taught the Mossad that assassinating top terrorist leaders caused severe disruption to the PLO and its splinter groups. It made them fear the Israelis; it made them hesitate in planning their violence; and it forced them into making mistakes. Perhaps even more than the Israelis needed a triumph, they believed that the Palestinian resistance movement was overdue for a setback.

The Mossad, Shin Bet, and occasionally Aman had been keeping a close eye on Abu Jihad for years. Agents and informers in Arab countries and inside the PLO itself reported to Tel Aviv frequently and fully on his movements. An Israeli handwriting expert, Aryeh Naftali, had been asked by the Mossad in 1983 to produce a psychological analysis based on a sample of Arabic writing. Only later did he learn that the report he prepared was about the notorious Khalil el-Wazir, whom he described as a highly intelligent man, a good organizer with a precise, analytical mind and great reserves of strength.[4]

Official Israeli files also noted that among PLO politicians, Wazir was a great conciliator. He helped hold the organization together, because both Yasser Arafat and his violent rivals would listen to Abu Jihad.

He was a strong believer, however, in achieving victory through "armed struggle." At the age of nineteen, in 1954, he was arrested by the Egyptian army for laying mines in the Gaza Strip. The Wazirs lived in Gaza, ruled by Egypt, after Khalil's father fled the original family home when the State of Israel was born in 1948. In 1955, the junior Wazir initiated himself as a guerrilla by attacking a water facility on the Israeli side of the border. A few years later, he met Arafat and other Palestinian university graduates, and in Kuwait in 1959 they formed Fatah, a small organization that managed eventually to take over the entire PLO. He remained at Arafat's side throughout, seeking support in the early years by touring all the Arab and Communist countries. He took the name Abu Jihad, and wherever the PLO found a temporary home he directed the guerrilla war while Arafat shaped his own image into that of a diplomat.

At Mossad headquarters in Tel Aviv, Admoni and his operations planners studied their files on the raid into Beirut. Looking at how Israeli agents had earlier been infiltrated into an Arab country, it appeared to be as easy in 1988 in Tunisia as it had been in 1973 in Lebanon. Six Mossad agents, using false British and Belgian passports to pose as tourists and businessmen, had flown to Beirut in order to acquaint themselves with the buildings to be attacked and to rent six roomy cars.

In Tunisia, there would be only one target. The Mossad would need only three agents, to rent three cars. This time, ironically, they used Lebanese passports and spoke perfect, Lebanese-accented Arabic. The two men and a woman flew in as tourists. They traveled separately, and they appeared as relaxed as the other two million tourists who visit Tunisia in an average year.

As in the Beirut raid, the Israeli navy — led by Shayetet 13, the navy's élite "Fleet 13" of frogmen — later brought the army commandos to the beach near their target. Unlike the brief cruise to the Lebanese coast, a missile boat had to leave Israel around the same time that the Mossad agents arrived in Tunis on Tuesday, April 12. The boat was then in position to deliver approximately thirty soldiers to the North African coast on Friday night, the 15th. The men were members of Sayeret Matkal, the reconnaissance unit of the general staff, the hand-picked commandos who served the army chief of staff and the intelligence community.

Copying the Beirut plan, the élite troops landed on a tourist beach near Tunis aboard rubber dinghies in the dead of night. As in 1973, the Mossad agents were waiting on the shore. They had rented two Volkswagen minibuses and a Peugeot station wagon. It was a short drive from the beach at Rouad to the Sidi Boussaid suburb where Abu Jihad lived with his wife, who was also a PLO activist, and two of their children: a daughter, fourteen, and a two-year-old son. Another two sons and a daughter were students in the United States.

The Israelis had the advantage of two technological improvements that gave the commando force more security than their counterparts had had in Beirut in 1973. The first was the use of an Israeli Boeing 707 jet, outfitted with military communications gear, flying over the Mediterranean barely thirty miles north of Tunisia. Because it stayed within a civilian air lane known as Blue 21, just south of Sicily, the Israeli pilots had to pose as an El Al charter flight when in radio contact with Italian air controllers. It was a bit unusual, but flight controllers do not have the time or inclination to ask about every extra flight ostensibly between Israel and Europe.

Having the Boeing above the clandestine mission made it seem that Generals Barak and Shahak were on the spot. They could make operational decisions without any delays, because they were both aboard the converted airliner in easy contact by two-way radio with the commandos.

The other technical development was a device that enabled the Israeli team on the ground to jam the telephones of the Sidi Boussaid neighborhood near Abu Jihad's villa. At around one o'clock on the morning of April 16, one of the minibuses and the station wagon parked around a block away from the house. They plugged their device, which caused an immediate short circuit, into a telephone junction box previously located by one of the Mossad agents. The two vehicles were packed with troops in civilian clothes, holding their Uzi submachine guns and pistols between their legs, and they simply waited. In Beirut, their counterparts had had to fight PLO units and the Lebanese Gendarmerie to protect the main mission. This time, if necessary, they would battle PLO security forces or even the Tunisian army.

Eight commandos, driven by the Mossad woman in the other Volkswagen minibus, pulled up in front of Wazir's home. In two task forces of four men each, they swiftly assaulted the house. They had practiced on a similar villa in Israel. Such rehearsals in models of the target, often specially built, are considered by the Israelis to be absolutely necessary before embarking on complex missions behind enemy lines.

One team was responsible for on-site security and shot dead Wazir's driver, who was sitting in the PLO leader's car after bringing him home around ninety minutes earlier, at midnight. Also using pistols fitted with silencers, the Israelis killed a Palestinian guard in the basement of the house. Their task was to eliminate anyone who might stand between them and their quarry.

The other team, assigned to the target himself, broke down the front door and began the search for Abu Jihad. They immediately used their silenced pistols to kill a Tunisian guard, and then they spotted Khalil el-Wazir at the top of the stairs.

Abu Jihad had a small pistol in his hand. He had grabbed it when he heard the unusual noises outside and downstairs. He had been up late that night, watching videotaped news coverage of the intifada which he was busily trying to coordinate from abroad. He did not have a chance to aim or fire his weapon. Four Israeli commandos pumped seventy bullets into him with startling rapidity. After traveling the huge distance from Israel, they were not going to take the chance that Wazir might survive. His right hand, which had clutched the gun, was nearly severed. At age fifty-two, Abu Jihad was dead.

There was no need for further killing. The guerrilla leader's wife, who called herself Umm Jihad, "Mother of the Holy War," said later that she fully expected to be shot. She even turned to the wall, preparing to be torn by bullets. Instead, one of the Israelis shouted to her daughter in Arabic, "Take care of your mother!"[5] And with that, the commando force ran to the minibus and drove off at high speed. Wazir's wife and daughter were not entirely certain, but they believed they saw a woman among the attackers, wielding not a gun but a video camera to record the assassination.

Israeli intelligence had once again proved its unrivaled excellence at carrying out a delicate and difficult mission. Once again, the Mossad–Sayeret Matkal combination had made it look easy. All that the Tunisian authorities could find were the three rental cars and footprints on the beach, ten miles from Wazir's house.

The PLO naturally blamed Israel, but the Israelis could have kept the entire matter secret. It would not then have had the desired deterrent effect, however, so official Israeli sources provided two American news outlets, NBC Television and the *Washington Post,* with fairly complete accounts of what the Mossad and the army had done. Ezer Weizman, the minister most strongly opposed to the assassination, publicly shook his head, telling reporters, "It does not contribute to the fight against terrorism. It distances the peace process and will bring greater hostility. It also makes us more vulnerable around the world."

The intelligence community felt it had nothing of which to be ashamed. Aman commander Shahak was quoted in that week's issue of the official army magazine *Ba-Machaneh, "In Camp."* In an extract from an interview conducted before the killing of Abu Jihad, he said, "Anyone directing terrorism is a suitable target for elimination."

Shahak was enunciating one side of what had been a long and heated debate behind the closed doors of the intelligence community: Are assassinations of Palestinian leaders worthwhile? If so, should the targets be at the very top of the terrorist groups? In the 1970s and early 1980s that was the prevailing dogma, and Israel either killed or tried to kill PLO chiefs. Several attempts were made on Yasser Arafat's life, including letter bombs, aerial bombings, and car bombs in Beirut when Israel laid siege to the city in the summer of 1982.

Later, a counterargument seemed to prevail: that it was better to confront the devil that Israel knew rather than the unknown PLO leaders who might take control once Arafat was gone. A new generation of guerrilla chiefs could be more radical, bloodthirsty, and unpredictable.

The compromise reached between those two conflicting views was expressed by Brigadier General Gideon Machanaymi, the prime minister's deputy adviser on counterterrorism, who in 1985 devised the philosophy that only leaders of small terrorist groups are appropriate targets. A prime example would be Sabri el-Banna, alias Abu Nidal, the "Father of Struggle" who was responsible for two hundred of the bloodiest attacks against Israeli, Jewish, British, and American civilian targets in more than twenty countries. General Machanaymi advocated that in cases of such small organizations, fully controlled by one man, once the leader is eliminated the organization ceases to exist. Then, an assassination accomplishes something.

The same reasoning lay behind the attempt by Israel a year later to capture an entire planeload of Palestinian terrorists — seeking economies of scale — by intercepting a Libyan executive jet on its way to Damascus. Israeli intelligence had learned that several leaders of extremist groups, far more radical than Arafat, had gathered for a terrorist summit in Tripoli, Libya, on February 4, 1986. Among them were Georges Habash, Nayef Hawatmeh, Ahmed Jibril, and even Abu Nidal — a veritable who's who of notorious killers. With the support of Libya's Colonel Qaddafi, they plotted against Arafat's relatively moderate policies and vowed "to intensify the struggle against the conspiracies of Zionism and American imperialism."

The Mossad and Aman located the terrorist chiefs and received a seemingly precise tip, from informers, as to what flight they would be taking back home to Syria. As the jet passed the Israeli coast, four F-16 jets forced the Gulfstream airliner to land at a military airport in the north of Israel. But as the passengers were led out of the plane with their hands up, the Israeli intelligence operatives found there were no wanted men among them: only Syrian officials, including a senior Ba'ath party man who was close to President Hafez el-Assad. Israel released the airplane and all its occupants.

Two months later, the Syrians sought revenge by way of a remarkable plot to blow up an Israeli airliner. Brigadier General Muhammad el-Khouli of Syrian air force intelligence recruited a freelance Palestinian terrorist, Nezar Hindawi, and instructed him to find a dupe who would carry a powerful bomb aboard an El Al flight. He met a naive Irishwoman in London, promised to marry her, even made her pregnant, and then sent her as a human bomb onto a Tel Aviv–bound airplane. Only the excellent vigilance of the El Al security staff, trained by Shin Bet experts, led to the discovery of a sophisticated bomb inside her handbag. The British authorities captured Hindawi and sentenced him to forty-five years in jail. At least something worked right, after the failed attempt to gain a significant advantage in the war against Palestinian terrorists by capturing all the chiefs in one aerial net.[6]

Was there some lasting gain to be accrued in 1988 from killing Abu Jihad? Most Israelis were in no state of mind, distracted and frustrated by the intifada, to ponder such questions. In general, there was praise for the intelligence community and Israel's soldiers. It was quickly realized, however, that the army and Shin Bet were still left to grapple with the day-to-day violence of the intifada. Abu Jihad's death made no difference.

In fact, the protests and the attempts by soldiers to suppress them were especially ugly just as Abu Jihad was being buried in Damascus, Syria. Palestinians marked the occasion with huge and unruly protests in the West Bank and Gaza. Five more were killed by Israeli army bullets that day.

The names of the dead and wounded were listed as martyrs and heroes in the leaflets of the United National Leadership of the Uprising, which called for general strikes and other protests. Added to sticks and stones, these words were especially maddening to the Shin

Bet men, who had never heard such language used in the day-to-day life of the West Bank and Gaza.

Identical messages were being heard on an AM radio station that popped up out of nowhere — Radio al-Quds, "the Holy," the Arabic name for Jerusalem. Aman's direction-finding equipment quickly told the Israelis that the station was in southern Syria and was operated, with the apparent approval of Damascus, by a radical splinter of the PLO. It was a puzzle as to how the broadcasters could see and quote from the leaflets so quickly, unless they were composed in Syria or Jordan overnight and sent by fax or smuggled into the West Bank by Palestinian travelers crossing the Jordan River bridges.

Shin Bet's countermeasures reflected the frustration that drives people to take drastic steps. Israeli intelligence published its own, forged leaflets signed by the "United National Leadership" — calling, in persuasive Arabic, for continued rebellion but altering the true details of the commercial strikes meant to shut shops and factories. The Israelis, hoping to fight harassment with harassment, were sowing confusion as to the location and times of the work stoppages in an effort to create tension between the underground command and the population.

On the streets of the Palestinian villages there were two sets of leaflets: the genuine instructions for the intifada and the deceptive instruments of disruption distributed by Shin Bet. One of these, in early July 1988, called for a continuous seven-day strike, much longer than any previous protest shutdown. It turned out to be a fake, in the hope that Arabs unwilling to give up their livelihood for an entire week would lose their faith in the uprising's organizers.

The security agents had already tried to eliminate the leaflets, by watching all the print shops in the West Bank and Gaza. Two Palestinians, found to have thousands of the propaganda pamphlets in their truck during a routine search at a roadblock, were closely questioned.

Amid triumphant publicity, Shin Bet sent the army to raid the al-Arz Printing Company on the Arab, eastern outskirts of Jerusalem. The soldiers seized the printing press and four Palestinians, three of whom were promptly expelled to Lebanon. Security chiefs triumphantly leaked the story to Israeli news reporters, who told the public that night that a severe blow had been dealt to the intifada.

Some Israelis felt that it was simply absurd to watch one of the most sophisticated armies in the world combine its strengths with the highly praised intelligence community and then celebrate the mere seizure of an aging printing press.

Not only that. The leaflets continued to appear, directing various stages of the growing campaign of resistance. In November 1988 they called on the Palestinians to pour into the streets to celebrate the declaration of their independent state — by a decision of the Palestine National Council in Algiers.

The Palestinian leaders hoped that by their declaration they could duplicate the spontaneous explosion of joy on the part of the Jews exactly forty-one years earlier, when the United Nations decided to create the State of Israel. The Arabs, too, wanted to dance in the streets.

Israel's security chiefs decided to stop any public celebrations, and they put a high priority on preventing nationalistic outbursts. Israel resorted to such steps as switching off the electricity in the entire West Bank and Gaza Strip. This was not a measure of collective punishment to stop the local populace from having hot water, cooked food, laundered clothes, or reading lights. The objective was simply to prevent them watching television, so they could not enjoy the sight of Arafat and his PLO politicians declaring the theoretical creation of their own state in the West Bank and Gaza.

A curfew was clamped down that night and Israeli soldiers found themselves chasing children who were waving the outlawed green, black, white, and red Palestinian flags, who threw firecrackers into the air, and who attempted to dance and sing until soldiers came along to disperse the revelers.

The leaflets that directed all these activities were distributed, with surprisingly little trouble, about once a week. They were well written and bore the hallmarks of organized backing for the uprising. Texts were often distributed by facsimile machines, with PLO headquarters in Tunis using telephones and technology to play a full part in the fax revolution.

In more than two decades of the occupation, Israel had tried to encourage Palestinians to create their own leadership as an alternative to the hated PLO. The Israelis tried many tactics, including the creation of quisling organizations called Village Leagues. These West Bank "leaders" failed to lead, and Israel then argued that there was no one with whom to negotiate peace.

In the intifada the Palestinians did create their own United National Leadership of the Uprising, although its secrecy made it impossible to judge whether it truly represented the general population. It successfully remained underground but appeared to have a hierarchical structure based on local committees in the various towns and villages of the West Bank and Gaza. Its aim was to consolidate the desire of the Palestinians under occupation to develop alternative institutions to those imposed by the Israelis.

The committees assigned specific tasks that included cleaning streets, fighting prostitution and drug trafficking, and even killing collaborators. Shin Bet had the urgent task of penetrating the committees and the United National Leadership, but the Israelis were unable to suppress it.

In a bid to repair the damage and make some headway, the intelligence community eventually devised new tactics including the timeworn but successful use of secret military units. Under codenames such as Shimshon and Duvdevan, Hebrew for "Samson" and "Cherry," the army formed special units of Arabic-speaking soldiers in civilian dress and sent them into the West Bank and Gaza Strip to mingle with the local Palestinians.[7]

It was a repeat performance of the army's efforts in the early 1970s to confront a terrorist reign of violence in Gaza. One day in the summer of 1970, a small fishing boat flying the flag of Lebanon arrived on the Gaza shore. Six people hurried onto the beach and vanished. Local Gazans found Lebanese newspapers, cigarettes, and groceries aboard ship. The Israeli army immediately sent squads of troops and helicopters to sweep the area, in what appeared to be a serious and thorough search for Arabs who had infiltrated from the sea. The chiefs of the Palestinian guerrilla cells in Gaza, highly impressed by how important these new arrivals from Lebanon must be, broke the usual underground rules of compartmentalization and secrecy to contact them.

The contacts and the supposed Israeli search continued for three days. Then, at a clandestine nighttime meeting with local guerrilla leaders the six newcomers pulled out guns and killed the Gazans.[8] The gunmen were actually Israeli army commandos on special assignment.

The tactics used earlier in Gaza to combat terrorism led journalists in 1988 to reach the conclusion that the new Samson and Cherry units had similar instructions. Based on claims by Palestinians, foreign correspondents in Israel reported that soldiers in civilian clothing were shooting intifada activists in cold blood. Israeli authorities strongly denied the stories.

Whatever the truth of the "death squad" claims, there is no doubt that the special army units were coordinated by Israeli intelligence and used unorthodox tactics. ABC News accused Shin Bet of sending agents masquerading as an ABC camera crew to pick up a Palestinian suspect named Nezar Dadouk. Shin Bet was apparently afraid that he might flee if identifiable Israeli authorities were seen entering the West Bank town of Salfit, twenty miles north of Jerusalem. Dadouk was wanted for allegedly throwing firebombs.

According to witnesses, two Israelis who said they were from ABC approached the young man and said they would like to interview him. He entered their car, which had signs saying ABC NEWS in its windows, and later the family was informed that Dadouk was under arrest. As punishment for his alleged crime, the army dispatched bulldozers to demolish his house.

A network official sent a telex to Prime Minister Shamir, which said: "I have been informed that security forces in Israel have impersonated ABC News personnel in order to arrest a Palestinian Arab. ABC News is deeply distressed by this and insists that an investigation be conducted immediately to ascertain who authorized such an action."

Undercover Israelis, from time to time, monitored events while driving in cars marked FOREIGN PRESS. In the West Bank and Gaza nearly free access to Arab villages was enjoyed by foreign correspondents, especially the American media representatives, who were courted by both Israelis and Palestinians. Each side wanted support and sympathy from the United States.

In August 1989, soldiers disguised as tourists, with cameras and civilian hiking knapsacks, opened fire on a group of Palestinians throwing stones in Bethlehem. One Arab was killed.

In September, troops posing as Arab activists in the intifada — complete with the checkered headdresses favored by PLO supporters — burst into the home of a wanted man in Tulkarm. Seven soldiers were carrying axes and knives, according to witnesses, who added that once the Palestinian militant realized they were Israelis he jumped out of a third-floor window to escape. He suffered multiple fractures and was in a coma, under arrest.[9]

The army came up with new tactics but had trouble replacing Shin Bet's shattered network of informants. Too many had been killed by the neighbors on whom they had spied. Only a few Palestinians were willing to hold the *Teudat Meshatef Peulah,* or "Collaborator ID" card, which permitted them to have guns, fast cars, and two-way radios but could also be their death warrant. Shin Bet, in the first years after the 1967 war, had convinced the local population that Israeli informants were everywhere. By 1990 it seemed that the Israelis were nowhere.

The intifada attracted huge and renewed interest in the Palestinian issue, and Israel found that its security services were under worldwide examination. As the rebellion took on the attributes of a permanent feature of Middle East politics, many hidden truths about the Israeli intelligence community were surfacing. Years of apparent successes and intentionally leaked tales of glory had blotted out occasional lapses into amateurism, arrogance, brutality, complacency, mistaken strategy, and rivalries between agencies. Only in the 1980s, however, had they come in such abundance in a concentrated period of time.

The Israeli public, Jews around the world, and others concerned with Israel's security began to wonder about the intelligence community's effectiveness. Disturbing facts were emerging, with official censorship failing to conceal the negative side of the story.

NINETEEN

A World Without Trust

THE AUTHORS OF THIS BOOK were recently in Mossad headquarters in Tel Aviv. Admittedly, our visit did not take in the part of the building that houses one of the world's most respected intelligence agencies. Let us say we were just next door.

We could give the address. We could describe the rather unremarkable premises. We could say, from experience, whether people get around by escalator, by elevator, or simply by climbing stairs. We could even report that most Mossad offices moved in 1989 to a location outside the seaside city. But giving too many details would be crossing the line into potential violations of Israeli law.

No one is entirely sure about the line, although journalists based in Israel usually know when they are speeding right through the gray area into unlawful activities. The trick, both foreign correspondents and Israeli reporters have found, is to coast along the gray area without crossing to the other side.

In our case, we declare quite honestly that the author who lives outside Israel learned the addresses of Mossad and Shin Bet headquarters, as well as the names of the current chiefs, from sources in Washington, D.C. It is generally assumed that the intelligence services of the Soviet Union and of most Arab countries possess the same information — although we certainly did not tell them.

Many well-informed Israelis, notably politicians and journalists, also know the secret names. It has become something of a game, at chic parties, to leap into conversations with "The Shin Bet chief told me the other day . . ." or "I met the head of the Mossad and he said . . ." and those who do not know the identities are simply not "in" enough.

One Israeli newspaperman, out to impress the élite among his audience while signaling Shin Bet that he knows what it knows, played a game of cat and mouse with the name of the new agency chief in 1988

— ironically appointed the same day that Mordecai Vanunu was convicted. The inside joke was in the headline over an article purportedly about American TV detective Perry Mason: WHAT WILL PERRY FOLLOW? At the risk of naming Shin Bet's director, the clue is somewhat bolder in Hebrew: AKHREI MA YAAKOV PERRY?[1]

What did the writer achieve? He was hinting at a name that is supposed to be secret; and yet he was flying on the safe side of Israel's secrecy border without giving the censor the ammunition to shoot him down. Perhaps the Shin Bet chief was lucky that the clever headline appeared in a small-circulation newspaper, but this did not prevent his telephoning the chief editor the next day to ask: "Why did you do this to me?" The officially anonymous intelligence chief called the editor directly, because he knew he could trust her. Newspaper editors usually know who is who, even if they cannot inform their readers.

The flurry seemed entirely absurd when, in February 1989, the unnamed Shin Bet director celebrated his forty-fifth birthday amid ridiculous publicity. Israeli newspapers told the nation and the world that the man was separated from his wife, and that his girlfriend was a popular socialite who organized a huge surprise party for him with the connivance of secretaries and others in Shin Bet.

The festivities were held in the Israel Museum cafeteria in Jerusalem, and the 150 guests included government ministers, Knesset parliamentarians, and even ladies and gentlemen of the press. The newspapers reported later that Shin Bet operatives were drunk, as their famous but anonymous chief played "Summertime" and other jazz favorites on his trumpet. His party went on until three o'clock in the morning.

Prime Minister Shamir, the austere former Mossad agent, did not attend and was livid when he heard of the exceedingly public celebration. Shamir knew that the newspaper accounts were a potential gold mine for hostile intelligence services seeking to compile a file on the Shin Bet chief. The prime minister called him onto the carpet and then permitted reports of the scolding to be leaked to the press.

The seemingly trivial event was a watershed in the four decades of the domestic security agency. The once secret brotherhood's activities — from torture to perjury to late-night parties — were now fully exposed. It was said half jokingly that confronted by a crowd of celebrants shouting "Surprise," previous Shin Bet chiefs would have reacted very differently: Isser Harel would have sent them letter bombs. Yosef Harmelin would have been shocked into uncomprehending silence. Avraham Ahituv would have fired them all, and Avraham Shalom might have had them beaten to death.

The fact that journalists were invited to the fete had its own implications. Any reporter so cozy with the clandestine authorities of his or her nation might someday be called upon to do a favor or two. Intelligence operatives do, on occasion, contact journalists directly to urge them not to pursue matters that could threaten Israel's security. The individual reporter must decide how to respond, but it is clear that in a small country it is far better to be on speaking terms with military and intelligence sources. If the personal pleas should fail, in any event, the officials do have enforcement power in the person of the censor.

Journalists and editors almost always play by the rules, and they receive background briefings from the prime ministers, defense ministers, and even from secret service chiefs. The authorities want the press to understand the facts that lie behind official decisions, but they trust that specific facts relating to national security will not be published. It is a unique system established in 1949, shortly after the War of Independence.

The first prime minister, David Ben-Gurion, could have kept using the old British Mandate's emergency regulations to restrain press and other freedoms. He preferred instead to play the democrat while still employing the powers of so-called emergencies when he felt it necessary. Ben-Gurion found the newspaper editors to be perfect partners, willing to be censored voluntarily. They signed a formal agreement, which had no legal force but great survival power.

Under the 1949 accord, the chief of staff and minister of defense appoint a military commander who has an intelligence background to the post of chief censor, with the rank of brigadier general. With the office, formally considered part of Aman, comes a staff of seventy army officers and civilian employees who work at two "bases" in Tel Aviv and Jerusalem.

The agreement also says that Israeli newspapers, radio and television stations, and foreign correspondents based in the country are honor-bound to submit their articles and news items to the censor. It is more than honor, as far as Brigadier General Yitzhak Shani, chief censor since 1977, is concerned. "It is the duty of every reporter to submit his material to the censor," he says. "He who fails to do this is a criminal!"[2]

The man who oversees the system recognizes that he is a unique feature among democratic nations, as Israel is the only one with continuous, institutionalized military censorship. He enjoys similar authority to that of his scissors-wielding British predecessor in the Palestine Mandate days. But there is a lot more voluntary cooperation these days.

If their publications or broadcasting stations are members of "the committee of editors," alleged violators of the censorship regulations are usually brought before a special tribunal with journalists and censors as the judges. The tribunal can impose fines or insist that the newspaper or magazine cease operation for a punishment period.

Even without the nicety of the tribunal, the censor and his staff can order that publications be shut down. They have done so in the cases of Hebrew newspapers in 1952 and in the Shin Bet scandal of 1984. Closure orders are far more frequent in the case of the Arab press in Jerusalem and the occupied territories — even more so since the intifada began in 1987.

There is an appeals tribunal, consisting of a senior army officer, a journalist, and a prominent lawyer or politician. Beyond that, appeals may be lodged with Israel's supreme court.

The courts have never questioned the censors' power to listen in on journalists' telephones, specifically overseas calls made by foreign correspondents. The censors can also read telex items as they are typed to the outside world. Direct computer links and facsimile machines caused problems for the censors for a while, but methods to intercept the more modern signals were also developed.

The purview of the censor extends beyond military secrets, which understandably include identifications of specific army units, codes, names of intelligence officers, troop movements, and sensitive topics such as nuclear weapons. The subjects that may also be censored include immigration to Israel, the construction of new roads, new Jewish settlements in the occupied territories, energy supplies and oil-storage facilities, and both trade and political links with countries that do not have diplomatic relations with Israel; in other words, anything that could be interpreted as the fortification of the state in its broadest sense.

The 1949 agreement has been modified on three occasions, each time narrowing the list of topics subject to censorship. But the list remains long and includes sixty-nine subjects.[3]

What does the press receive in return? Reasonableness. Editors and reporters can even negotiate with the censor, restoring controversial paragraphs so long as they are worded slightly differently. The censor usually acts sensibly, not overstepping his authority and — when not under heavy political pressure — only sniffing around when genuine military matters are concerned. But he is sometimes pressed to stick his nose into other issues, as almost a political censor. Retired politicians have found that their memoirs have been cut, apparently to prevent embarrassment to government and military officials.

A navigable path has been found through this minefield, and the participants in the game generally know where they stand. There is a tacit agreement that articles on issues such as highway construction and economics do not have to be submitted in advance to the censor, unless they touch upon sensitive topics such as the intelligence community.

If an Israeli or foreign correspondent wishes to name the secret service chiefs or include their addresses in a dispatch, he is supposed to know that the copy goes first to the military censor. The secret facts will then duly be excised. So why write them down in the first place? The threat of censorship often becomes self-censorship.

By the same token, when reporters and editors feel they can get away with a technical violation of censorship, they may well take the risk. In 1981, for instance, an Israeli journalist working for an American newspaper revealed that the head of Shin Bet was then Avraham Ahituv. The newsman's main aim was to tell the world that the secret service chief had clashed with Prime Minister Begin over security policy regarding West Bank settlers and their alleged involvement in bombings against Palestinians. The chief censor recommended that the journalist be put on trial, but the attorney general decided not to press charges.[4]

The censor did even less in similar circumstances in 1986, when an American television network exposed Avraham Shalom as the head of Shin Bet being investigated in connection with the killing of the two Palestinian bus hijackers.[5]

The Israeli system occasionally reaches the rock bottom of absurdity when it prevents local newspapers from publishing certain facts, even though the foreign press — beyond the reach of the censor — does publish the full story. The intelligence scandals of the 1980s were prime examples, when Israeli newspapers were only permitted to quote stories that had already appeared in foreign publications. The information had often come surreptitiously from Israeli sources whose lips were supposedly sealed by the censor.

Newspapers in America had already predicted, in the weeks before Nahum Admoni retired as Mossad chief in March 1989, that he would soon be replaced after nearly seven years as head of the agency and twenty-eight prior years of Mossad service. At least in the short term, the fact that Admoni was replaced by his deputy — and the name of the new Mossad chief — remained secret.

The authors of this book will not violate the censor's absolute ban as did some Israelis when they leaked Admoni's identity to Britain's *Sunday Times* within days of his promotion in September 1982. At least one intelligence "former," who did not agree with Prime Minister Begin's selection, spelled the new chief's name on a telephone line to London. It was pure luck that the journalist could not hear the letters clearly and published the name as Nahum Adnoni.

Quoting and even reprinting entire pages from English, French, or other foreign-language publications occurred on such a colossal scale that one editor quipped that he could probably fire all his reporters and replace them with translators.

The censor and other Israeli authorities seem to feel that the country's own newspapers are some sort of official mouthpieces. It is as though anything that appears in an Israeli publication will be seen abroad as more authoritative. Israeli newspapers can thus do more damage.

The censor apparently doubts that the Israeli papers are considered to be truly independent. Even if the local newspapers were to make mistakes and print inaccurate reports, the authorities fear that the errors or misquotes will be taken worldwide as facts. If it has to do with the military or intelligence, better that the Israeli media say little or nothing.

General Shani insists that he does not become involved unless secrets are revealed. "With the passage of time, faced with reality, Israel has more and more released its rigid censorship grip," he says, "Censorship has become more logical and more reasonable, dealing with issues which only affect the direct security of the State of Israel."

And, he adds, "when journalists are not accurate or when they exaggerate, or when in the course of a so-called analysis or commentary they reach conclusions which are way off-beam, I don't like it but it's not my job to interfere."[6]

The entire system is controversial, of course, in a country that proudly boasts of being the only democracy in the Middle East. Two principal reasons are given for maintaining the sometimes petty secrecy that goes hand in hand with Israeli censorship. One reason is mystical; the other is practical.

In a habit adopted from the British, who never publish the accurate names of the secret agencies known as MI5 and MI6 or the identities of the service chiefs, the Israelis preserve a similar mystique around their intelligence community. The intelligence community believes that the people of Israel sleep better at night knowing that they *are* protected, and not because they know precisely *who* is protecting them and *how.*

It is, at all times, an ingrained habit in the world of espionage — based on both convenience and tradition — not to tell anything, when silence can be maintained instead. In the words of secret service veteran Rafi Eitan: "The best thing an intelligence man can do is to keep out of the media." When it served his own interests in the Lakam and Pollard affair, however, Eitan was giving interviews and background briefings left and right.

As for the practical reason, defense officials justifiably point out that many small terrorist groups — whether Palestinians, Marxists, or simply anarchists — can actually be helped by details that may seem petty. If such terrorists, so the argument goes, were easily to obtain the names and addresses of intelligence agents and agencies, these would become potential targets for attack. Yes, the officials admit, the Russians, the Syrians, and probably the PLO know everything there is to know about the Mossad chief and his headquarters, but there is no reason that every little troublemaker in the world should know.

The mystical argument — silence for the sake of silence — meets with opposition, however. In the post-Watergate spirit of governmental openness that spread from the United States to other Western democracies, the blind faith that citizens had in their governments and defense establishments has worn thin. There are growing demands that politicians, civil servants, the military, and even intelligence agencies be more accountable to the public.

Israel, however, is different from the United States in its form of government. All executive power in Israel lies with the cabinet formed by the prime minister, whose authority is based on the majority he or she commands in parliament — reflecting the multiparty outcome of the last election. Checks and balances operate quite differently than they do in Washington.

Envious of the regular hearings held by committees of the U.S. Congress on subjects ranging from the defense budget to CIA assassination plots, vigorous democrats in the Israeli Knesset would dearly love to have the power to confirm or veto candidates for the directorships of the Mossad and Shin Bet.

They are not satisfied by the fact that the Knesset's foreign affairs and defense committee has a six-member subcommittee known as the Committee of the Services, which is supposed to oversee the secret agencies. Although the agency chiefs or their deputies do appear before this tiny panel, the investigative instincts of its members usually evaporate when they hear the spicy details of covert operations. The panel is bribed, in a sense, with the excitement of hearing "inside information." The subcommittee has no real powers, aside from using its ears to listen. Some members have complained that the intelligence agencies, which are supposed to brief them, instead bypass the panel and leak stories to foreign journalists when the spymasters think it will help Israel's image.

The legislature has never improved the vague legal basis for the intelligence community. The best the security agencies can do, in private, is point to Article 29 of the Basic Law of the State of Israel, which says: "The Government is authorized to carry out on behalf of the State, in accordance with any law, any act whose implementation is not lawfully entrusted to any other authority." In other words, the government can have its own agencies do anything that no specific agency is constitutionally required to do, so long as it is legal. But anything that is not specifically banned is considered legal, and so the intelligence community may function.

Domestic security, as protected by Shin Bet, does have the extra backing of various laws which ban both subversion and espionage conducted against Israel. These include measures known as the Penal Revision (State Security) Law of July 1957 and the Military Law of June 1955, but especially the Defense (Emergency) Regulations of 1945, which were brought in by the British to crack down on both Arabs and Jews in Palestine. These allowed the British army, and later the Israel Defense Forces, to arrest and deport alleged subversives and to designate "closed areas" that may not be entered by journalists or other visitors for hours, days, or years. The authority to wield such powers was transferred from the IDF to the police in 1966, but in truth it is Shin Bet that makes the relevant decisions.[7]

What harm could there be in making the intelligence officials accountable to parliament? Supporters of the present arrangement respond by pointing out that members of the Knesset leak information day and night — almost as the second oldest profession in the land of the Bible. No secrets could be shared with any sizable Knesset panel. The status quo's backers also point out that in a parliamentary system, it is the prime minister who is accountable for his entire ministry. He or she must bear the blame if the Mossad or Shin Bet commits an unacceptable act, and if necessary it is the prime minister who must resign.

In Israel, however, a noteworthy habit has developed among cabinet ministers: not to accept responsibility.

The only control mechanism that remains is a powerless civil servant — the state comptroller, usually a wise, elderly, and retired judge — who is charged with overseeing the intelligence agencies and, indeed, all government offices. They, in turn, all have one thing in common: They usually ignore his reports, which are full of dense language and statistics that envelop the harsh realities of wasted resources, stolen goods, and corruption where they exist.

In looking into the activities of the intelligence agencies, the state comptroller has access to the expense accounts and budgets of the Mossad and Shin Bet, but without knowledge of the covert operations that necessitated the expenditures. There is nothing he or she can meaningfully criticize, and the comptroller has little choice but to accept the explanations offered by the secret service chiefs.

Even when the agencies need a few million dollars more than originally apportioned, they can approach the budget committee of the Knesset with no more explanation than "It is for a vital mission," and the extra funds are always granted.

Israel is in an almost permanent state of war and has been since its birth in May 1948. It is surrounded by hostile nations and a constant terrorist threat, so the rules of defense and intelligence must differ from those that apply in America or other Western countries. Many secrets do have to be better kept than they are in other nations, because the slightest error or security lapse could cost lives in Israel.

Censorship is understandable when it concerns battles while they are raging, counterterrorism missions while the troops are still in motion, and details of security methods including names of intelligence operatives and informers whose lives would be endangered. But these arguments hold up only when they are not pursued to an exaggerated degree.

It seems ludicrous that Israel confirms nothing about its intelligence agencies, while often having something of which to be proud. It even took the authors several days to get an accurate reply from the prime minister's office when asking for the precise and full name of the Mossad.

We wanted the exact name, as used by the Mossad in its English-language correspondence. We know that the agency is not in the habit of writing official letters too often, but considering its liaison relationships with foreign espionage agencies, the Mossad must have a name to put atop its letterhead and by which to refer to itself.

Officials responded to our inquiry with various names. At one point, we were advised to see the annual report of the state comptroller. But no details of intelligence budgets are published, and in any event the report is in Hebrew and the names of the agencies can have varying translations.

Eventually, the prime minister's press spokesman returned with an answer and an explanation: "It took me a hell of a long time to check it. I eventually talked to the head of the Mossad, who was very suspicious and could not understand why I was demanding to know. But I got it for you. Here is the name."

And with the triumph of sharing exclusive information, he whispered, "The Israeli Secret Intelligence Service." The ISIS is a dour, British-style, pale shadow — for official foreigners only — of the legendary and proud name of the Mossad, or Institute for Intelligence and Special Tasks.

Asking who is the current director of the agency is somewhat easier, because the prime minister's spokesman will simply say, "You know I cannot tell you that."[8] This may seem ridiculous when the heads of foreign secret services know the name, when many former Mossad and Shin Bet operatives believe there would be no harm in revealing the names of those agency chiefs, and when the name of the commander of the most important agency to the nation's defense — Aman — is permissible to publish.

The only interested party kept firmly in the dark is the great Israeli public, the taxpayers who foot the bill. Some veterans have even proposed establishing a press office, at least for Shin Bet, as it is little more than a police force with the added spice of secrecy.

When journalists ask whether the Mossad was responsible for some adventure or exploit somewhere in the world, official responses may vary. Usually the reply is some form of "no comment," but spokesmen in Jerusalem will often say, *"LaHaDaM,"* a pronounceable Hebrew acronym for *Lo Hayu ha-Dvarim Mi-olam,* which means "These things never happened."

Long experience has shown that these answers have absolutely no value. To put it bluntly, Israeli officials are often lying. It is difficult to believe anything in the Middle East, a world without trust. When it comes to matters of life and death and high politics, the officials defend vehemently their right to lie. Journalists similarly point out their obligation to keep asking questions.

Problems arise when officials abuse their power and sidestep the censor, to leak a favorable interpretation of potentially embarrassing events. When Israeli leaders wished to give their own version of the Jonathan Pollard espionage affair to pacify an angry and hurt American public, they privately unveiled the whole story — or one side of it — to a major U.S. newspaper in November 1985. They even told the correspondent, through their assistants, that he would not have to submit his article to the censor; everything would pass.[9]

After nuclear traitor Mordecai Vanunu was spirited away from England, officials in October 1986 leaked various versions intended, above all, to emphasize that he was not kidnapped from British jurisdiction. The true details of the Mossad operation that brought Vanunu home for trial were still blurred, however. It was a case of revealing an inch while covering up a yard. The censor, knowing his political masters' wishes, took no action despite these obvious violations of the regulations.

It took sheer gall, then, for the censor to punish foreign correspondents who in April 1988 received a leaked account of the killing of the PLO's Abu Jihad in Tunis. Officials such as Prime Minister Shamir, who claimed to colleagues that he simply heard about it on the radio, feigned ignorance. But others in authority, knowing that one of the purposes of the slaying was to intimidate the Palestinian enemy, chose their conduits: correspondents for an American TV network and a leading U.S. newspaper. They duly published the story, and then they were stunned when the Government Press Office stripped them of their accreditations as foreign correspondents.[10]

One arm of government often seems ignorant of what the others are doing. Journalists in the Israeli democracy have to cope with not knowing when and what they will be able to publish. The same is true in the field of personal memoirs. The haphazard nature of secrecy and censorship yields different rules for different cases and different people.

Secret service veterans have to cope with the inequalities of the censor's judgment and have to guess when the climate is right for revelations. Several wasted their time writing books which the censor then refused to clear, but ex-Memuneh Isser Harel is a prolific author. He seems to know, without asking, how much he may reveal about intelligence operations such as the kidnapping of Eichmann.

Some veterans, to bypass the censoring authorities, turn their factual knowledge into extremely plausible fiction. Their urge to write yields novels. While these are obviously autobiographical at times, publishing no precise facts means no problem with the censor, and no violation of the pledge of lifelong secrecy signed by every intelligence operative.

Other Israelis who have left the secret agencies or special military units reveal secrets without publishing a word. They are to be found throughout the world, sharing their craft with foreigners who pay them for Israel's expertise in defense and security. The consultants obtained their knowledge while working for the Israeli government. Simply by doing — and teaching others how to do — they are revealing as many secrets as someone who produces the written word.

The censorship system targets only published and broadcast material, but Israel's enemies — Arab and other intelligence services — closely follow open, covert, and personal sources. True, a great deal of information in modern espionage comes from openly available material. But information obtained either secretly or indirectly is also important and has to be targeted as well. The Israeli censor's work seems predicated on the thought that a person who loses a coin in a dark alley will only be searching where the streetlight is shining.

Israel tries to stem the flow of news items in the media, while turning a blind eye to the flood of revelations coming from former operatives. If Israel is so concerned to stop the leak of classified information, why have a censor concerned only with publications? What about the activities of mercenaries, expert privateers, and other people holding secrets?

Perhaps it is a matter of convenience. It is far easier to keep track of the public media than it is to spy on what ex-spies are doing. Consider also that the people involved are former members of the defense and security "family," precisely the same sort of "old boys" still to be found in Jerusalem making the decisions. In fact, the team that is currently in government might expect in the future to be out there as consultants, too.

The worst damage has often been done by officials still serving in the government. Foreign Minister Moshe Dayan's statement in 1978, which confirmed the secret relationship with Ethiopia, did more harm than the mountain of ink and tiny bits of newsprint deleted by the small army of worker ants employed by the military censor. And when a Jewish Agency official revealed the clandestine exodus of the Ethiopian Jews in 1985, he ruined more lives than any journalist in the history of Israel.

News reporters are usually less dangerous, yet they are in many ways more accountable. The men and women of the media may be punished, by a variety of sanctions including prison terms, while politicians and other officials blithely survive their verbal misdemeanors.

In judicial proceedings, too, the Israeli authorities jealously preserve their right to pick and choose the times at which they will demand absolute secrecy or permit full disclosure. Espionage trials involving Israelis or foreigners who spied against the State of Israel are almost always totally secret. Even the name of the accused is banned from publication. More than one "Mr. X" has stood trial in a Jerusalem or Tel Aviv courtroom.

Mordecai Kedar, Avri El-Ad, Ze'ev Avni, and more recently Marcus Klingberg were tried in total secrecy and were even imprisoned as anonymous X's. In the cases of Mordecai Vanunu and Shabtai Kalmanovitch, it was officially announced that they were accused of serious crimes but no access at all to their trials was permitted.

It is a manipulative system in which the authorities use their powers, not necessarily to protect secrets regarding national defense, but to keep embarrassing failures under wraps. That was the motive in the enforced disappearance of the spies and other prisoners, just as it was in the totally unpublicized case of Peter Puhlman.

A German Jew born to parents who perished in the Holocaust, Puhlman was an engineer recruited by *Hauptverwaltung Aufklärung,* the East German "Central Office of Information." His Communist intelligence masters planted him in West Germany, where he married a young Israeli woman and moved to Tel Aviv. In November 1971 Israel Aircraft Industries hired him to work on aerodynamics, where he seemed to be displaying skill and professionalism until Shin Bet arrested him for espionage five months later.

As an East German spy, Puhlman had penetrated one of the most sensitive defense manufacturers in Israel. In strict secrecy, he was tried and then sentenced to fifteen years in prison. Nothing was published about his arrest, the charges, the trial, or his fate. He was released in 1982, and only a tiny item was printed by an Israeli news agency.[11]

How can a democracy, with a free press and full civil rights, conduct itself in such silence and secrecy? The intelligence agencies, the military censor, the government, and the judicial system walk a tightrope between protecting national security and preserving the primacy of law. The potential dangers are great: if people, both Israeli citizens and foreigners, can disappear — with even their families sometimes not informed — there is the possibility that people in all walks of life could have their rights infringed.

There are signs that government agencies are demanding wider powers and are trying to whittle down civil rights. The Knesset passed the Secret Eavesdropping Law in 1979 and modified it several times since, to set up the first orderly system of bugging by state agencies. Authorization was thus given, by statute for the first time, to the police, Shin Bet, and Aman to plant microphones and intercept telephone calls as their needs might require.

The police are to use such tools only to catch offenders and solve crimes, and then only with a warrant from a senior judge. Only one of the top commanders of the police is empowered to seek such a warrant.

The "security authorities," as the two intelligence agencies are defined in the law, have a far easier time. They are required to secure the approval of the government minister in charge of them: The prime minister in Shin Bet's case, or the defense minister in Aman's, would normally give written authority. But the law adds that if the secret agency needs to begin eavesdropping without delay, Shin Bet's chief himself can approve forty-eight hours of bugging without higher approval.

The Mossad asked for similar powers, but the legislative committee refused because the agency is not supposed to work domestically.

In the United States, even defense and espionage cases require judicial warrants for wiretapping. The CIA and the National Security Agency are permitted, but only with warrants, to mount surveillance within the United States on foreign citizens who are not protected by the Constitution — but not on U.S. citizens.

The Israeli intelligence community has few limitations in such activities. Targets for eavesdropping can be either Israelis or foreigners, and even the military Aman can wiretap them all. The law specifically permits intelligence agencies to keep the transcripts of eavesdropping sessions, even if the tapes themselves are destroyed.

The army chief of staff, General Raful Eitan, ordered Aman in the early 1980s to record his generals' telephone calls when he feared there were leaks to the press. A military chief has the authority to intercept the conversations of anyone, including civilians, using military telephones — even the prime minister and the defense minister who, in a democracy, are in charge of the army.

The Israeli twilight zone between security requirements and democratic values was further blurred in late 1989. Prime Minister Shamir in December accused Science Minister Ezer Weizman of secretly dealing with the PLO, not only violating government policy and law but "betraying" Israel. A former air force commander and defense minister, Weizman was stunned — especially when Shamir backed up his charges with classified information.

The prime minister, with his authority over Shin Bet and the Mossad, had been informed by them — as was proper — that one of his cabinet members was in contact with PLO officials. They had apparently provided him with transcripts of a meeting Weizman had in Geneva in July with a PLO diplomat and subsequent telephone conversations between the minister's home and PLO headquarters in Tunis. Weizman, once a military hawk but now a political dove, openly advocated negotiations with the Palestinians and was quietly advising the PLO to accept American mediation.

That Israeli intelligence monitored the incoming phone call from an Arab country, especially from Arafat's headquarters, was not surprising and a simple technological feat. But a cabinet minister's home telephone was involved, so it was politically sensitive.

More impressive was the fact that Israel's spies got their hands on a word-for-word record of what one of the PLO's top officials was doing in Europe. It is clear that Israeli intelligence had a valuable source near the highest echelons of the PLO.

Should Shamir, himself a former intelligence operative well acquainted with the rules of the game and their implications, have gone public with the material given him by his espionage chiefs? To underline his total refusal to deal with the PLO and to back up his accusations, the prime minister declared that he had evidence from security agencies.[12] For the sake of his political goals, Shamir violated a traditional taboo and endangered methods of intelligence gathering.

Simply by reading the Israeli press, the PLO's own security people could realize that the organization had been penetrated. Equally serious was the fact that Israel's prime minister dragged Shin Bet, for the first time since Ben-Gurion's day, into the embarrassing position in which it was used in a politically divisive battle.

The Weizman affair strengthened the impression that the system needed reform to prevent the manipulation of the intelligence community for partisan ends.

How can the public feel confident that politicians, generals, and secret agents, especially when some are exposed as having lied to their own superiors and government, will stick to a strict interpretation of the law on wiretaps?

The answer is that there can be no such confidence. There is a need for clearer regulation, without twilight areas on the fringes of legality. Dependence on goodwill often leaves the door open to bad intentions.

Similarly, a democracy cannot rely on voluntary censorship which is conducted on the basis of old accords from the days before computers, facsimile machines, and satellite communications. In a democracy at war, censorship may have its place but only if it is coherent and consistent.

Finally, the accountability of the intelligence community to the public — as represented by parliament — must be increased. The scandals of the 1980s showed that while individual missions can be accomplished with great success and aplomb, the agencies fail when they display misjudgments and dangerous abuses of power.

There need not be a contradiction, despite appearances, between the openness of democratic society and its defense by covert means. The light of life in a free country need not be blotted out by the sometimes dark security apparatus at its heart, so long as it is clear who is in charge: the public, through the government elected in the light of day.

The business of intelligence is too serious to be left to the intelligence agencies and a handful of politicians alone.

TWENTY

Into the Future

ISRAEL ENTERED THE SPACE AGE on September 19, 1988. A rocket blasted into the sky from a launch site near the Mediterranean coast south of Tel Aviv, a short distance from the research nuclear reactor at Nahal Sorek.

It was the public debut of Shavit, the comet launch rocket based on the Jericho developed as a possible delivery vehicle for Israel's secret nuclear bomb. Shavit carried a satellite named Ofek, "Horizon," and propelled it into orbit. The head of the space agency, celebrating its first successful launch, happened to be the veteran Aman technology wizard Yuval Ne'eman. He told reporters that Ofek was an experimental craft. It circled the earth for four months.

Proud statements from Ne'eman, Prime Minister Shamir, and other Israelis reflected the feeling that the Jewish state had just scored an important breakthrough. After joining the exclusive nuclear club in strict secrecy, Israel was openly declaring itself the eighth nation on earth to possess rockets capable of launching satellites.

By injecting Ofek into its intended orbit, an ellipse ranging from 155 miles to 620 miles above the earth, Israel's domestically produced Jericho/Shavit proved its ability to hit a precise target — in this case, a trajectory high in the sky and beyond. There is no longer any ambiguity as to which country is leading in the race to build ballistic missiles in the Middle East. Without risking the lives of air force pilots, Israel can accurately strike or retaliate against its enemies both near and distant.

More significant is the future potential for spying from space. Israel planned a series of satellites after the first Ofek, and the coming generation would have cameras and sophisticated communications. They would also be able to remain in orbit, passing over the Middle East every ninety minutes, for a lot longer than four months. Ofek-2 was successfully launched on April 3, 1990.

As Israel develops a permanent system of eyes in the sky, it will have more information than ever to ready itself for war with its Arab neighbors. Troop movements and other military preparations across the borders will easily be seen, far earlier than is presently possible.

As in other areas of technology, Israel wants to eliminate any and all dependence on favors from foreigners: begging the United States to provide satellite photographs, or sending agents such as Jonathan Pollard to steal them. Former Mossad chief Meir Amit said: "If you are fed from the crumbs of others according to their whim, this is very inconvenient and very difficult. If you have your own independent capability, you climb one level higher."[1]

The Israelis have a lot to keep their human and electronic eyes on. Syria is stockpiling mustard gas and other poisons that could be mounted on their Soviet-supplied missiles. Libya began manufacturing chemical weapons, and Colonel Qaddafi's air force purchased West German equipment for midair refueling on long-range flights.

The fastest-growing danger comes from Saddam Hussein, a dictator pursuing his goal of having Iraq become the Middle East's top superpower with chilling rationality. He used chemical weapons and long-range missiles in the Gulf War against Iran and threatened to unleash them to destroy "half of Israel." Iraqi arms smugglers were caught with nuclear technology, while Baghdad unveiled increasingly impressive missiles, including one in 1989 that could launch a satellite. Israeli intelligence concluded that Hussein could have a nuclear warhead in the 1990s.

Israel's strategic planners have had little choice but to settle on a two-pronged response. First, the intelligence community redoubled its efforts to discover everything possible about the Iraqi nuclear, chemical, biological, and missile programs. But the facilities in Iraq have been spread out and hardened. An air raid attempting to repeat the feat of 1981 would be far more difficult.

The second part of the secret strategy is a second-strike capability — surviving any Arab attack on Dimona and Israeli airfields. The Israelis are believed to have made significant progress in the work, detected by the CIA as early as the 1960s, to develop submarine-launched nuclear weapons: low-altitude Cruise missiles that could be fired from standard torpedo tubes and could fly the 600 miles to Baghdad.

Israel's three submarines, obtained from Britain in 1977, are nearing obsolescence. But in a little-noticed deal in 1990, Israel arranged to purchase two subs from West Germany, the half-billion-dollar price to be paid by the United States as part of military aid to Israel. The offshore, survivable nuclear deterrent could soon be reality.

Even as Israel reached its technological zenith, its intelligence community, ironically, was at a low ebb. Looking into the future, in many ways, was a welcome distraction from reviewing the past. At the end of the 1980s, the secret services had many problems and Israel might understandably look back in anger. The community could not simply shake off the memory and reality of failures and setbacks which had come in quick succession:

- The Mossad's misjudgments in Lebanon
- Shin Bet's killings and coverup
- Using Pollard to spy on Israel's best friends in America
- Intercepting a Libyan executive jet in the mistaken belief that Palestinian terrorists were aboard
- The disarray of the covert Iran-America connection
- Losing control over freelancers and "formers" around the world
- Allowing nuclear secrets to get out
- Being caught and expelled for running double agents in Britain
- Operating an outdated and irrelevant censorship system
- Misleading the government over the future of the occupied territories, just as a Palestinian uprising was beginning

The litany of blemishes in a distasteful decade was symptomatic of the diseases endemic among the secret agencies of other nations: internal rivalries, lack of control by politicians, a desire to expand beyond reasonable limits, poor coordination among agencies, overlapping duties, and duplicated efforts. Israel's intelligence community had suffered these in the early 1950s and early 1960s as childhood diseases, but had overcome them. In the 1980s, they surfaced again. Deep cracks shattered the mystique of Israeli intelligence as precise, professional, and even invincible.

Image is surprisingly important for seemingly faceless, secret agencies. The morale of Israeli operatives is closely linked to their perception among friends and enemies. In addition to the feelings of Israel's own operatives, there is also an impact on the readiness of other nations to cooperate with Israel's intelligence community.

Foreigners and Israelis alike marveled at the ability of the Jewish state's intelligence agencies — usually ascribing all the credit to the Mossad — to capture Eichmann in Argentina and to rescue hostages at Entebbe. Experts abroad also considered Israel the definite leader in preventive intelligence and the general fight against international terrorism.

In the quest to look good, Israeli politicians leaked some details of the Mossad's feat in persuading the Iraqi pilot Munir Redfa to defect to Israel with his MIG-21. Tears flowed freely when Israeli intelligence became Jewish intelligence to bring Ethiopian Jewry to the Promised Land; and the same had been done for the Jews of Iraq, Morocco, and other countries.

Israel has been wise enough to maintain total silence, however, about most of its clandestine activities. Occasionally publicizing a fantastic feat can be valuable, but precisely how Israel strengthens itself is nobody's business.

Entirely outside the publicity spotlight, Lakam helped build Israel's defenses by obtaining scientific and industrial secrets abroad. There was no intention of ever revealing the agency's existence until Pollard's arrest in 1985 left little choice. Israeli intelligence continues to pursue similar objectives, although in different forms and without directly employing American citizens.

The sometimes agonizing choice between total security to protect sources and modes of operation, and revealing secrets for the sake of scoring public relations points, arose in the wake of the terrorist bombing of an American civilian airliner. When Pan American World Airways flight 103 was destroyed by a bomb over Lockerbie, Scotland, at the end of 1988, Israel was unsure how much to say publicly. There was an unwillingness to be associated in any way with what was surely an intelligence failure. But Israel wanted to be certain that the world would blame Palestinians for the deaths of 259 passengers and crew and another 11 Scottish people on the ground. Israeli sources told selected news reporters to consider the Popular Front for the Liberation of Palestine–General Command the most likely suspect.

Even if Israel had not discreetly offered a few tips, investigators in Scotland and in West Germany — where flight 103 originated — would surely have acted on the circumstantial evidence already available to link the aerial mass murder to the PFLP-GC. Based in Damascus and founded in the late 1960s by former Syrian army captain Ahmed Jibril, the group had a history of attacking civilian airliners.

More significantly, a PFLP-GC cell was caught red-handed in West Germany with a bomb made of plastic explosives and barometric-triggered timers hidden in a Toshiba radio-cassette recorder. A similar device brought down the Pan Am jumbo jet.

Israeli intelligence, specifically Aman, knew quite a bit about the leader of the cell arrested in Germany. Hafez Kassem Dalkamoni had been in Ashkelon prison, on Israel's Mediterranean coast, for ten years after crossing the Jordan River in 1969 and attempting to blow up an electricity pylon. All Dalkamoni had managed to do was blow off his own leg. Given a life sentence for terrorism, the prisoner became an observant Moslem but also a leader of anti-Zionist sloganeering among fellow inmates.

Dalkamoni was set free in 1979, at the age of thirty-three, as part of an exchange of prisoners with the PFLP-GC. Many intelligence men had opposed — just as they did when an even larger prisoner swap was arranged in 1985 — the release of men considered to be highly dangerous. But Israeli politicians and army commanders would do almost anything to secure the freedom of soldiers captured by Palestinian guerrilla groups. It was part of Israeli military and intelligence tradition.

Yigal Carmon, adviser on counterterrorism to Prime Minister Yitzhak Shamir, called Dalkamoni "an exact replica of his master Jibril."[2] Dalkamoni's activities were monitored as he returned to the PFLP-GC, and an Israeli intelligence report named him as commander of "the Western sector, which is in fact an international terrorist apparatus." He used training bases in Syria and Lebanon, but his operations in Europe were based in several safe houses in West Germany.

The Israelis appear to have planted one or more agents in Dalkamoni's German network, because the Mossad's liaison officer in Bonn was able to warn West German intelligence of an imminent attack in October 1988. The target, it was believed, would be an Israeli handball team touring Europe.

West Germany's equivalent of Shin Bet mounted extensive surveillance and wiretapping of the PFLP-GC cell and its telephones. Speaking in code, the cell called Syria and Jordan to say that "the medication" had been "made stronger than before" and, on October 23, "things are almost ready." The Germans consulted with the Mossad's liaison man and then pounced.

Sixteen suspects were arrested on October 26, and along with the radio-recorder bomb and an arsenal of weapons the police found documents indicating that the sophisticated bomb was meant to bring down a Spanish airliner flying from Madrid to Tel Aviv: Iberian Airways flight 888 on October 29. Over a hundred passengers and crew were saved, because of a tip from Israel and action by the Germans — an excellent example of the "preventive intelligence" of which the Israelis are justly proud. However, within fifteen days the West German authorities released fourteen of the PFLP-GC suspects they had rounded up.

Barely six weeks after most of Dalkamoni's cell was let loose, ostensibly for lack of evidence, Pan Am flight 103 was blown up. Only Dalkamoni and an alleged accomplice were still in custody, and the media concluded that the Germans had made a serious mistake. Contradictory stories circulated about alleged double agents, double crosses, and supposed warnings that had been received but ignored.

Nearly all the tales were disinformation. The highly professional intelligence services of Israel, the United States, West Germany, Great Britain, and the other nations involved were obeying one of the primary imperatives of the craft: protect your sources.

The Pan Am disaster was an example of the complexity involved when security agencies try to deal with a unique and small pool of informers: free-lance terrorists who are utterly untrustworthy with their shifting loyalties.

After the tragedy had taken place and the lives of the 270 victims could not be saved, the immediate objective of intelligence agencies was to find the culprits but without compromising modes of operation and collection methods. It was clear that the Dalkamoni cell had been extensively penetrated, by Israeli and other security services. Most of the PFLP-GC men were released so as to protect the identities of the informers planted within.

There is the tantalizing fact, however, that Israel's army sent sayeret commandos on a rare mission to raid a PFLP-GC "operational headquarters" in Niameh, just south of Beirut, a mere ten days before the Lockerbie disaster. Ordinarily, the Israeli air force would have bombed the base from a safe and impersonal altitude. On December 11, based on information from their intelligence community, the Israelis felt it was worth putting their soldiers in grave danger to find something at the Niameh base.

This may have been an attempt to capture Ahmed Jibril himself. In any event, the operation became a messy one when Jibril's guerrillas fought back furiously. As part of the firefight, the Israelis sent in dogs with explosives wrapped around their bodies — detonated as unique canine bombs in crowded parts of the Palestinian base. One Israeli officer was killed, and dozens of soldiers had to be hurriedly evacuated by helicopter. Still, Israel mysteriously calls the Niameh raid a great success, leading to speculation that something important was learned about PFLP-GC operations — perhaps including the plans of the Dalkamoni cell in West Germany.

While the Israelis had inside information — in part from their mole or moles in the PFLP-GC and in part from the assault on Niameh — it was not sufficiently specific for the Mossad to issue an alert regarding Pan Am flight 103 on December 21. Even the best intelligence in the world can fail to prevent every single terrorist crime.

Usually, however, Israeli penetrations of the enemy are highly valuable. Yet, as a secret assessment written by the CIA in 1976 said:

> Military Intelligence [Aman] officers do have problems in handling Arab agents, who tend to exaggerate and often fail to report accurate details. Therefore, the Military Intelligence officers encourage their Arab agents to provide photographs, maps, and other corroborating documents. Military Intelligence officers also cross-check reports, often by using other agents in the same region.
>
> Despite Israeli warnings during training, Arab agents tend to tell other members of their family about their association with Military Intelligence. Occasionally an Arab agent may recruit all the members of his immediate family as subagents and try to get his case officer to pay them salaries. The Israelis refer to these family subagents as "nonfunctionalist." These subagents sometimes compromise a whole operation as a result of boasting about their activities.[3]

The CIA authors probably did not know how accurately their report reflected the behavior of one particular family, the Shaheens of Egypt. Despite the reluctance of the Israeli intelligence community and the censor, Israeli newspapers revealed in November 1989 how Aman recruited Ibrahim and Inshirah Shaheen, Palestinians living in Cairo. It was a standard recruitment operation by military intelligence — low-key and notable neither for its difficulty nor its immediate value. The Shaheens had been found in the Sinai town of El Arish after the 1967 war and, after moving to the Egyptian capital, began providing more interesting information to Aman.

They even sent some good tips about Egypt's preparations for the 1973 war, but the hints of war were ignored in the general Israeli complacency of the period. The Shaheens were eventually infected by the worst disease a spy can catch: carelessness, on their own part and that of their handlers. Ibrahim Shaheen was arrested by the Egyptians in 1974 and hanged three years later. His wife and their three children were imprisoned.

After peace negotiations between Egypt's President Sadat and Menachem Begin began, the family was quietly released and managed to slip across the border to Israel. The intelligence community helped them convert to Judaism, adopt the family name Ben-David, and start new lives. But the Shaheens suffered from typical post-espionage depression and complained publicly that they had not been sufficiently compensated and had been shabbily treated.

The Shaheen case sharpens a debate within the CIA over Israel's ability to run agents in Arab countries. Some CIA men say that Israel is severely handicapped by having no embassies in the Arab countries, except for Egypt, making it impossible to have spies at work under diplomatic cover. They also say the Mossad is weak "at acquiring highly placed assets inside the Arab establishment," including so-called walk-ins who volunteer their services — as Pollard did — for ideological reasons.[4] Other CIA men say the lack of embassies forced Israel's spies to sharpen their skills and develop more sophisticated, covert means of penetrating Arab society.

The ultimate walk-in was a fly-in. Muhammad Bassam Adel became the first known defector from Syria, Israel's harshest enemy, on October 11, 1989. A major in the Syrian air force, Adel was especially welcome because he brought his Soviet-made MIG-23 warplane with him. Thirty-four years old and single, he apparently risked being shot down both by fellow Syrians and by the Israelis when he piloted the jet to a small airstrip in northern Israel.

Defense Minister Rabin and his top military intelligence officers rushed to the scene to begin interrogating Adel. The Syrian later claimed, at a news conference organized by Aman, that he had acted totally on his own "because I wanted to live in a democratic country where people can freely express their views" and that he "had not contacted any Israeli" before his dramatic flight.

Syrian officials charged that Adel had been a Mossad spy for years and had simply stolen the jet. Israel behaved as though it were surprised by his arrival and embarrassed that antiaircraft defenses apparently could not stop a single MIG from crossing the border.

The truth appears to be more complicated. It is absurd that a Syrian pilot would risk being shot down by the famed air defenses of his country's most reviled enemy for the sake of freedom. He could have flown to Turkey or Cyprus instead, delighting the NATO alliance with the gift of his aircraft. It is likely that Adel was recruited in Syria by an Israeli spy, much as Munir Redfa had been lured to defect from Iraq in 1966. Adel similarly received a new identity and help in starting a new life.

As for the Israeli air force's announcement that a failure of the air defense system would be investigated, because the incoming MIG-23 had not been detected, it seems that the approaching blip on the radar screen had been wrongly interpreted. Israeli intelligence knew that Major Adel would be defecting but not precisely when. If he gave a prearranged signal, it was missed. That was the technical failure of air defense. It would have been even more disastrous if the Israelis had mistakenly shot down Adel and the intelligence bonanza he was flying.

However they actually obtained their prize, Aman experts were busy examining every piece of the MIG-23. The Russians had begun supplying the model to Syria in 1973, but the defector's airplane had some interesting electronic add-ons that told the Israelis a lot about the dogfighting and bombing capabilities of Soviet aircraft. Aman and the Mossad delightedly offered the information — and a full hands-on inspection — to the United States Air Force and the CIA, hoping this would further repair some of the damage done to strategic cooperation by the Pollard affair.

Intelligence exchanges are the secret backbone behind the warm friendship Israel has with the United States. This is vital for the Jewish state, and the Mossad — since the Pollard and Irangate scandals — jealously guards its leading role in clandestine relations with the Americans.

Turf fights have repeatedly flared between Israeli agencies. After the Mossad gave Panama to Mike Harari and other fiefdoms to intelligence veterans, in secret arrangements, an outright competition developed. The foreign ministry, feeling itself stepped on by the Mossad, started to show its muscle. It forced the espionage agency into a compromise in the mid-1980s, in which responsibility for renewing diplomatic relations with Kenya became a foreign ministry job, while Nigeria still remained a Mossad territory.

In Papua New Guinea, in the distant South Pacific, a request for Israeli aid in 1987 sparked another round of competition. The tiny country's leaders asked the Mossad to help them establish their own security service to monitor Indonesian expansionism. The Mossad, claiming it was short on manpower, wanted to give Papua New Guinea to one of its "formers" as yet another fiefdom. But the foreign ministry blocked the plan.

Acting widely as an alternative diplomatic service, the Mossad has opened doors and maintained relations with dozens of countries which prefer that these connections not be known. Digging beneath the surface, however, uncovers a basic question: What is so wonderful about having an intelligence agency doing something the foreign ministry would normally do? It could be argued that there is no great value in maintaining clandestine relations with countries that do not show the generosity or goodwill to have open diplomatic ties with Israel. The Mossad simply gives the other nations an easy way out — receiving military, medical, and agricultural advice from the overenthusiastic Israelis without risking economic or political boycotts by the Arab world.

Both the spy-diplomats and the official diplomats of Israel are thrilled, in fact, when a foreign nation does agree to establish open relations with the Jewish state. Ethiopia's decision to resume formal ties with Israel in November 1989 was the fruit of years of secret labor by Mossad envoys and brought several great benefits: the prospect that thousands of Ethiopian Jews, left behind when the secret exodus ran into difficulties, would soon be flying to Israel; the reestablishment of an Israeli intelligence listening post on the Red Sea coast, facing Saudi Arabia and monitoring maritime and radio traffic to and from Jordan, Sudan, and Egypt; and the reopening of Israel's embassy in Addis Ababa as a convenient Mossad station. In return, Israeli experts in farming and guerrilla warfare provided training to a government suffering both famine and provincial rebellions.

In most cases, however, Israel has to live with the reality that many foreign states insist on doing it the secret way. Fearing leaks to the press, they refuse to deal with Israel's foreign ministry. They do benefit from a bilateral relationship, however, and have developed complete confidence in the Mossad's ability to be the great guardian of secrecy. Among the countries concerned have been China, Indonesia, and Morocco.

Israel's defense needs have not changed, at their roots, in over four decades. The state is still surrounded by hostile nations, which are increasingly willing to accept the reality of Israel's existence but continue plotting and fighting to weaken it. Even as Arafat and the PLO embark on a new, diplomatic path, Israel is still faced with extremist Palestinian terrorists whom it must counter.

The demographic statistics looming over Israel will continue to demand Jewish immigration into Israel, so as not to be outnumbered by Arabs within Israeli territory, and this will require Jewish intelligence. In addition, Israel will need to research and develop its technological and industrial advantages, using inventiveness as well as the kind of espionage which was Lakam's specialty to keep ahead of the Arabs.

Israel has always been strong when it comes to facts and ideas. The intelligence community is extremely successful at obtaining them. It is also among the best in the world at executing specific missions, such as an assault against targets far from Israel's borders.

Israeli intelligence is not so good, however, at processing, analyzing, and evaluating the information it obtains. Problems of coordination persist in disseminating the data to the various "customers" in official Israeli circles. That caused the failure to see the 1973 war on the horizon.

Intelligence analysts did not realize, in 1967, that a long-term occupation of the West Bank and Gaza Strip would be harmful to Israel. They did not foresee the peace initiative of Egypt's President Anwar Sadat ten years later. They did not correctly evaluate the situation in Lebanon, when plotting the Israeli invasion of 1982. They did not predict war between Iran and Iraq in 1980, nor the end of the conflict in 1988. They did not detect that, in reaction to the Gulf War, Saudi Arabia was purchasing Chinese medium-range missiles that could reach Israel.

It has become fashionable in Israel, in a sharp departure from the once automatic praise for the intelligence agencies, to blame them for events taking unexpected or unwelcome turns. Once honored as princes, Israel's spies are uncomfortably — and usually unfairly — cast as selfish and confused has-beens. The Middle East defies simple predictions, but in the new critical spirit Israelis express disappointment when their secret services cannot wave a magic wand and solve all outstanding problems.

As the 1980s ended, Israel was unsure as to how it felt about its intelligence community. The public was told, briefly and without detail, that Shin Bet had a new director as of 1988 and the Mossad a new chief in 1989. Israelis could only hope that the new men would do better. Expectations were probably too high in the past, and so the failures of foresight were often exaggerated. What Israeli citizens should realize is that intelligence is simply an extension of their nation's policies. If the policies are faulty, even the best intelligence in the world cannot repair them.

It is doubtful that even if given all the proper warnings by Aman and the Mossad, Golda Meir and Moshe Dayan would have gone to war on Yom Kippur in 1973. They were still prisoners of "the Concept" that the Arabs were incapable of beating Israel. The government leaders of 1982, or at least Menachem Begin and Ariel Sharon, were determined to sweep the PLO out of Lebanon and nothing the Mossad could say would have stopped them.

Prime Minister Shamir seemed to give little weight to an intelligence assessment delivered by Aman in March 1989, warning that Israel had few alternatives but to negotiate with the PLO. First, Shamir said publicly that there was no such report, and then he condemned whoever it was who leaked it from the cabinet. In another context, Shamir revealed his affection for secrecy: "Events are usually known by those who should know," he said, "and whoever does not know should continue not knowing."[5]

A senior aide to the prime minister is said to have criticized Aman's assessment in a letter to agency chief General Amnon Shahak, adding that if the report was published it could be used by the United States to apply pressure on Israel to talk to the PLO.[6]

The danger of the intelligence community's becoming politicized continues to increase, as the unsolved Palestinian issue and the debate over contacts with the PLO divides Israeli society. As long as the problem persists and there is no consensus, the intelligence chiefs find it difficult to operate in a professional environment overshadowed by political concerns. If half of the country absolutely refuses to consider dealing with the PLO, as seen in the Weizman affair of 1989, the intelligence community's task of providing objective, emotionless assessments of one of the biggest issues facing Israel becomes nearly impossible.

Even if politicians do pay close heed to the advice, analysis, and wisdom of their intelligence chiefs, does it really help the decision-making process? Are the great energies and resources put into secret services absolutely necessary for Israel?

Israeli intelligence failed to predict the surprise attack by Egypt and Syria in 1973. As in the 1941 surprises of Adolf Hitler's invasion of Russia and the Japanese attack on Pearl Harbor, the individual facts that could have formed a composite picture of aggression on the horizon were available. They were simply not put together into a coherent and convincing whole, and the warning signs were ignored in each case by the leaders of the target countries.

These were intelligence failures of a strategic nature — blindness to grand questions of war and peace. Modern history has shown that intelligence communities usually do not have much say in formulating policies, but they do have a role in pursuing limited and specific goals set by their political masters. There is no doubt that intelligence can be useful on a tactical level.

In preparing for and fighting a war, advance information on the disposition of enemy troops and firepower is clearly a key element in achieving victory — so long as the information is analyzed and disseminated correctly. Similarly, preventive intelligence can save lives by providing advance word of an expected terrorist attack. Secret agents are also the ideal choice for executing well-defined assignments that often require pinpoint precision.

Israeli intelligence has done all that, but repeatedly has essayed a deeper and broader role in the nation's defense. By dwelling excessively on grand design and inflated ambitions, the secret agencies have betrayed their own true nature. The outer bounds of what can be accomplished should be recognized.

Israel should not expect its intelligence community to be more than it can be: an excellent example of what a small nation with meager resources can do by using them to the utmost. The community's history has demonstrated both the inescapable limitations and the maximal achievements of intelligence.

NOTES

Prologue

1. Meir Amit, in Zvi Ofer and Avi Kober, eds., *Intelligence and National Security* (Ma'arachot/Ministry of Defense: Tel Aviv, 1987), pp. 123–32.
2. Gazit, quoted in *Hadashot* [Tel Aviv], December 28, 1986.
3. Amit, in Ofer and Kober, *Intelligence and National Security,* pp. 123–32.
4. *Ha'ir* [Israeli weekly], October 10, 1986.
5. The *Independent* [London], August 26, 1989, p. 8.
6. *Koteret Rashit* [Israeli magazine], June 11, 1986.
7. *Ma'ariv* [Tel Aviv], May 9, 1989.
8. *Yediot Aharonot* [Tel Aviv], January 2, 9 and 16, 1987.
9. Central Intelligence Agency, *Israel: Foreign Intelligence and Security Services* (Washington: March 1976), classified "Secret," as published by Iranian Islamic militants who seized the U.S. embassy in Teheran in late 1979; p. 42.

1: First Steps

1. Hagai Eshed, *One-Man Mossad: Reuven Shiloah, Father of Israeli Intelligence* (Tel Aviv: Edanim/Yediot Aharonot, 1988), p. 120.
2. Ibid., p.31
3. Abba Eban, interviewed by the authors, August 27, 1988.
4. Eshed, *One-Man,* p. 42; also Tom Segev, *1949: The First Israelis* (Jerusalem: Domino Press, 1984), p. 34.
5. Eshed, *One-Man,* pp. 84–8.
6. Ibid., pp. 97–102.
7. Ibid., pp. 14–16.
8. Herzl Ehrlich, interviewed by the authors, September 19, 1988; Stewart Steven, *The Spymasters of Israel* (New York: Ballantine Books, 1980), p. 23; Ze'ev Schiff and Eitan Haber, *Israel, Army, and Defense: A Dictionary* (Tel Aviv: Zmora, Bitan, Modan, 1976), pp. 222–3.
9. Eshed, *One-Man,* p. 120; Michael Bar-Zohar, *Isser Harel and Israel's Security Services* (Jerusalem: Weidenfeld and Nicolson, 1970), pp. 32–5.
10. Bar-Zohar, *Isser Harel,* p. 40.
11. *Yediot Aharonot* [Israeli newspaper], April 7, 1988.
12. Schiff and Haber, *Israel, Army, and Defense,* p. 189.
13. Eshed, *One-Man,* p. 127; Bar-Zohar, *Isser Harel,* pp. 62–4; Steven, *Spymasters,* pp. 33–9.

14. Eshed, *One-Man,* pp. 127–9.
15. Isser Harel, *Security and Democracy* (Jerusalem: Edanim/Yediot Aharonot, 1989), pp. 170–5.
16. Steven, *Spymasters,* p. 39.
17. Eshed, *One-Man,* p. 136; and authors' interview with Asher Ben-Natan, December 12, 1988.
18. Yaakov Frank, interviewed by the authors, September 20, 1988; also *Ma'ariv* [Israeli newspaper], January 30, 1984.
19. Interview with Frank; Shlomo Hillel, *East Wind: On a Secret Mission to the Arab Lands* (Jerusalem: Edanim/Yediot Aharonot and Ministry of Defense, 1985).
20. Hillel, *Mission,* pp. 236–45; Howard M. Sachar, *A History of Israel* (New York: Alfred A. Knopf, 1985), pp. 398–9.
21. Sachar, *History,* p. 403.
22. Aryeh (Lova) Eliav, retired Israeli naval officer and Aliyah B operative, interviewed by the authors, April 9, 1989.
23. Segev, *1949: The First Israelis,* pp. 119–20
24. Eshed, *One-Man,* p. 137.

2: Childhood Development

1. *Al Hamishmar* [Israeli newspaper] weekend magazine, September 5, 1975; Harel, *Security and Democracy,* pp. 226–47.
2. Segev, *1949: The First Israelis,* pp. 292, 294.
3. Ibid., p. 264.
4. Bar-Zohar, *Isser Harel,* p. 264.
5. Ibid., p. 99.
6. Bar-Zohar, *Isser Harel,* pp. 106–8; Harel, *Security and Democracy,* pp. 199–215.
7. Harel, *Security and Democracy,* pp. 199–215.
8. Avri El-Ad, *Decline of Honor* (Chicago: Regency Books, 1976), pp. 282–4; Moshe Zak, *Israel and the Soviet Union: A Forty-Year Dialogue* (Tel Aviv: Ma'ariv Book Guild, 1988), pp. 301–2.
9. Yossi Melman, *The C.I.A. Report on the Intelligence Services of Israel* (Tel Aviv: Erez, 1982), pp. 61–3.
10. Ibid., p. 67; Stephen Green, *Taking Sides: America's Secret Relations with a Militant Israel* (New York: William Morrow, 1984), p. 19; Bar-Zohar, *Isser Harel,* pp. 1–32; Harel, *Security and Democracy,* pp. 41–69.
11. *Ha'ir* [Israeli newspaper], September 26, 1986.
12. According to former operative Eliyahu Ben-Elissar, interviewed on Israel Defense Forces Radio, 1986.
13. Interview with Avraham Dar in *Yediot Aharonot,* January 1, 1988.
14. El-Ad, *Decline of Honor,* pp. 60–2; see also Aviezer Golan, *Operation Susannah* (New York: Harper and Row, 1978).
15. Miles Copeland, *The Game Player: Confessions of the CIA's Original Political Operative* (London: Aurum, 1989), p. 61.
16. Interview with Jean Bennett and her daughter Michele, in *Ha'aretz* [Israeli newspaper], January 1, 1988; also *Davar* [Israeli newspaper], November 26, 1987.
17. Avraham Dar in *Yediot Aharonot,* January 1, 1988.

18. *Ha'aretz,* January 1, 1988.
19. Ibid.; *Davar,* November 26, 1987.
20. Harel, *Security and Democracy,* pp. 41–69.

3: Nuclear Maturity and Lakam

1. Article by Mordecai Bar-On, aide-de-camp to chief of staff Moshe Dayan, in *Yediot Aharonot,* October 24, 1986; also Ben-Natan interview.
2. *Ma'ariv* [Israeli newspaper], October 24, 1986.
3. Michael Bar-Zohar, *Bridge over the Mediterranean: Israeli-French Relations, 1947–1963* (Tel Aviv: Am Hasefer, 1965), referring to its title; Matti Golan, *The Road to Peace: A Biography of Shimon Peres* (New York: Warner Books, 1989), p. 43, reflecting Peres's view.
4. *Ma'ariv,* December 5, 1986.
5. *Davar,* December 29, 1986.
6. Green, *Taking Sides,* pp. 149–50.
7. Matti Golan, *Peres* (Tel Aviv: Schocken Books, 1982), p. 54.
8. Ibid., pp. 71–4; and Golan, *Road to Peace,* pp. 52–5.
9. Peter Pringle and James Spiegelman, *The Nuclear Barons: The Inside Story of How They Created Our Nuclear Nightmare* (London: Michael Joseph, 1982), pp. 295–6; Golan, *Road to Peace,* p. 51.
10. *Yediot Aharonot,* May 29, 1987.
11. Golan, *Road to Peace,* pp. 57–8.
12. Amos Perlmutter, Michael Handel, and Uri Bar-Joseph, *Two Minutes over Baghdad* (London: Vallentine Mitchell and Company, 1982), p. 26.
13. Harel, *Security and Democracy,* pp. 220–8; *Ma'ariv,* October 4, 1989.
14. Pringle and Spiegelman, *Nuclear Barons,* p. 296.
15. Authors' interview with the scientist, who remains anonymous for his own protection, January 1988.

4: Strategic Alliances

1. Eshed, pp. 164–5.
2. David C. Martin, *Wilderness of Mirrors* (New York: Harper and Row, 1980), p. 10–12.
3. Martin, *Wilderness,* p. 20.
4. Green, *Taking Sides,* p. 19, quoting a memorandum from acting Secretary of State Robert Lovett to Secretary of Defense James Forrestal; also Martin, *Wilderness,* p. 20.
5. Martin, *Wilderness,* p. 21; Eshed, *One-Man,* p. 163.
6. Harel, *Security and Democracy,* pp. 381–2.
7. Steven, *Spymasters,* p. 32.
8. See Yossi Melman and Dan Raviv, *Behind the Uprising: Israelis, Jordanians, and Palestinians* (Westport, Connecticut: Greenwood Press, 1989).
9. Avi Shlaim, *Collusion Across the Jordan* (Oxford: Oxford University Press, 1988), p. 423; Copeland, *Game Player,* pp. 93–101. The Israeli intelligence connection was revealed by scholars, including Professor Itamar Rabinovich, at a Tel Aviv University seminar in April 1989.
10. Aryeh (Lova) Eliav, *Rings of Testimony* (Tel Aviv: Am Oved, 1984), pp. 156–64.

11. Melman, *C.I.A. Report,* p. 57, quoting a classified report by the CIA dated 1976 and published in 1979 by the Islamic militants who seized the U.S. embassy in Teheran; also Eshed, *One-Man,* pp. 262–4; Bloch and Fitzgerald, *British,* p. 113; Richard Deacon, *"C": A Biography of Sir Maurice Oldfield, Head of MI6* (London: Futura Books, 1985), p. 113.
12. Samuel Segev, *The Iranian Triangle: The Secret Relations Between Israel-Iran-U.S.A.* (Tel Aviv: Ma'ariv Books, 1981), p. 88.
13. Melman, *C.I.A. Report,* pp. 59–60.
14. Harel, *Security and Democracy,* p. 392.
15. See Teresa Toronska, *Oni* (London: An-Eks, 1985).
16. Letter to Melman from Flora Lewis of the *New York Times,* May 9, 1989; and authors' interview with a senior *Ma'ariv* journalist who worked with Ben but demanded anonymity, April 1989.
17. Harel told the authors on June 28, 1989, that Israel obtained the document and passed it to the CIA by "normal channels." See also Eshed, *One-Man,* p. 164. A confidential senior source said Shin Bet achieved the feat, not the Mossad.
18. The *Guardian* [British newspaper], May 13, 1987.
19. William Colby and Peter Forbath, *Honorable Men: My Life in the CIA* (New York: Simon and Schuster, 1978), p. 365; quoted in John Ranelagh, *The Agency: The Rise and Decline of the CIA* (London: Weidenfeld and Nicolson, 1986), pp. 560–3.
20. Peter Wright, *Spycatcher: The Candid Autobiography of a Senior Intelligence Officer* (New York: Viking Penguin, 1987), pp. 346–7.
21. Ibid.
22. Martin, *Wilderness,* p. 57; Eshed, *One-Man, p. 160; Washington Post,* December 5, 1987.
23. *Ha'aretz,* May 13, 1988; also an interview with Harold (Kim) Philby in London's *Sunday Times,* May 22, 1988. See also Chapman Pincher, *Their Trade Is Treachery* (London: Sidgwick and Jackson, 1981), p. 14.
24. Pincher, *Their Trade Is Treachery,* p.186; and Deacon, *"C,"* pp. 29, 69, 80, 230, 250–5.
25. Deacon, *"C,"* p. 250.
26. Chapman Pincher, *Traitors: Labyrinths of Treason* (London: Sidgwick and Jackson, 1987), p. 93
27. William Colby, interviewed by the authors, January 1988.

5: Harel the Crusader

1. Bar-Zohar, *Isser Harel,* pp. 135–8.
2. Joshua Tadmor, *The Silent Warriors* (New York: Macmillan, 1970), pp. 93–5.
3. Bar-Zohar, *Isser Harel,* pp. 106–8, 148.
4. *Yediot Aharonot,* October 24, 1986.
5. Israel Beer, *Israel's Security: Yesterday, Today, Tomorrow* (Tel Aviv: Amikam, 1966); and Isser Harel, *Soviet Espionage: Communism in Israel* (Tel Aviv: Edanim/Yediot Aharonot, 1987), pp. 93–169.
6. Harel, *Soviet Espionage,* pp. 131–6.
7. Ibid., p. 20.
8. Ibid., p. 21.
9. Harel, *Soviet Espionage,* pp. 169–175; *Ma'ariv,* November 14, 1986.
10. *Ha'ir,* October 23, 1987; Harel, *Soviet,* p. 65; *Davar,* November 26, 1984.

11. Eliav, *Rings,* p. 165.
12. Ibid.
13. Amos Ettinger, *Blind Jump: The Story of Yeshayahu (Shaike) Dan* (Tel Aviv: Zmora Bitan, 1986), p. 35.
14. Harel, *Soviet,* p. 66; Ettinger, *Jump,* p. 352.
15. Ettinger, *Jump,* p. 356; and Eliav, *Rings,* pp. 166–70.
16. Zak, *Dialogue,* pp. 301–2; Harel, *Soviet,* p. 22.
17. Eliav, *Rings,* pp. 166–70.
18. *Ha'aretz,* May 29, 1987; *Yediot Aharonot,* January 22, 1988; and Reuters news agency, December 28, 1988.
19. El-Ad, *Decline,* p. 31.
20. Ibid., pp. 267–8.
21. *Hadashot,* November 14, 1986; *Yediot Aharonot,* February 4, 1990.
22. Ibid.
23. Harel, *Security and Democracy,* pp. 270–3; *Jerusalem Post* magazine, January 20, 1989.
24. *Monitin* [Israeli magazine], May 1987.
25. Reuters news agency, "Israeli Who Captured Eichmann," April 6, 1989.
26. Schiff and Haber, *Israel, Army, and Defense,* pp. 36–7; Dennis Eisenberg, Uri Dan, and Eli Landau, *The Mossad: Inside Stories* (New York: New American Library, 1978), pp. 177–98 and 212–27; Steven, *Spymasters,* pp. 130–9.
27. Peter Mann and Uri Dan, *Eichmann in My Hands* (Tel Aviv: Massada Publishers, 1987), p. 164.
28. Reuters news agency, "Israeli Who Captured Eichmann," April 6, 1989.
29. *Monitin,* August 1986.
30. Yigal Mossensohn, interviewed by the authors, December 6, 1988.
31. Ibid.
32. Steven, *Spymasters,* pp. 141–51; Eisenberg, Dan, and Landau, *Mossad,* pp. 36–53.
33. *Matara* [Israeli magazine], September 1989; *The Jewish Week* [New York], "Nazi Said to Have Aided Israeli Spy Unit," September 29, 1989.
34. One of the journalists concerned, Samuel Segev, interviewed by the authors, October 21, 1988; Bar-Zohar, *Isser Harel,* p. 240.

6: Amit Reshapes the Mossad

1. Eitan Haber, *War Will Break Out Today: Memoirs of Brigadier General Israel Lior, Aide-de-Camp to Prime Ministers Levi Eshkol and Golda Meir* (Tel Aviv: Edanim/Yediot Aharonot, 1988), p. 62.
2. Ibid., p. 62.
3. Steven, *Spymasters,* pp. 158, 180, and 186–7; Yair Kotler, *Joe Returns to the Limelight* (Tel Aviv: Modan, 1988), p. 40.
4. Kotler, *Joe Returns,* p. 61; Haber, *Lior,* p. 62; and *Yediot Aharonot,* October 16, 1987.
5. Kotler, *Joe Returns,* pp. 66–8; Harel, in *Yediot Aharonot,* October 16, 1987.
6. Kotler, *Joe Returns,* p. 61; Steven, *Spymasters,* pp. 186–7.
7. A long-time Mossad operative, who wished to remain anonymous, interviewed by the authors, 1988.
8. Yitzhak Shamir, in an interview with Melman, September 10, 1987.
9. Kotler, *Joe Returns,* p. 45.

10. Steven, *Spymasters,* pp. 188–93; Melman, *C.I.A. Report.*
11. *Hadashot,* July 23, 1987.
12. *Ha'ir,* September 2, 1988.
13. *Yediot Aharonot,* May 3, 1987.
14. *Ha'ir,* September 2, 1988.
15. Ibid.
16. Melman, *C.I.A. Report,* pp. 41–56; Walter Laqueur, *A World of Secrets: The Use and Limits of Intelligence* (New York: Basic Books, 1985), p. 220.
17. Steven, *Spymasters,* pp. 188–93.
18. Bar-Zohar, *Isser Harel,* pp. 184–9
19. Eisenberg, Dan, and Landau, *Mossad,* pp. 51–65.
20. Ibid., pp. 60–1.
21. Ibid., p. 61; Steven, *Spymasters,* pp. 214–20.
22. Samuel Segev, *Alone in Damascus: The Life and Death of Eli Cohen* (Jerusalem: Keter, 1986), p. 60.
23. Ibid., p. 23; Steven, *Spymasters,* pp. 202–4.
24. Wolfgang Lotz, *The Champagne Spy* (New York: St. Martin's Press, 1972), p. 14. Other information and quotations in this chapter are from pp. 17, 19, 21, 26, 83, 106, 111, 115–7, 157.
25. This claim appears in E. H. Cookridge, *Gehlen: Spy of the Century* (New York: Random House, 1971), as quoted in Steven, *Spymasters,* p. 171.
26. Segev, *Alone in Damascus,* p. 14.
27. Ibid.; *Ha'aretz,* July 14 and 21, 1972, and March 8, 1974.
28. Bloch and Fitzgerald, *British,* pp. 159–60.

7: The Road to War

1. Tadmor, *Silent Warriors,* pp. 119–23.
2. Copeland, *Game Player,* pp. 180–2.
3. "Frontline" documentary, Public Broadcasting Service (PBS), May 16, 1989.
4. Laqueur, *Intelligence,* p. 22; Melman, *C.I.A. Report,* pp. 46, 56, and 58; Bloch and Fitzgerald, *British,* pp. 162–3.
5. *Yediot Aharonot,* January 2, 9, and 16, 1987; *Ma'ariv,* October 24, 1986.
6. Melman, *C.I.A. Report; Ma'ariv* and the *Observer,* March 15, 1988.
7. Steven, *Spymasters,* pp. 240–52; also *Monitin* quoting *Time,* December 29, 1975.
8. *Monitin,* June 1987.
9. *Yediot Aharonot,* October 16 and 19, 1987.
10. Ibid.
11. James Bamford, *The Puzzle Palace* (Boston: Houghton Mifflin, 1987), pp. 284–92.

8: Shin Bet Has Its Day

1. Ehud Yaari, *Fatah* (Tel Aviv: Levin-Epstein Books, 1970), pp. 101–2.
2. Ibid., pp. 90–1; David Ronen, *The Year of the Shabak* (Tel Aviv, 1989).
3. Haber, *Lior,* pp. 130–1.
4. *Ma'ariv,* December 4, 1987; *Hadashot,* June 19, 1987; numerous interviews with practitioners of the counterespionage art who prefer anonymity.
5. Ibid., and *Ma'ariv,* April 7, 1988.
6. Haber, *Lior,* pp. 130–1.

7. Shlomo Gazit, *The Stick and the Carrot: The Israeli Administration in Judea and Samaria* (Tel Aviv: Zmora Bitan, 1985), p. 107.
8. Ibid., pp. 133, 223, 284.
9. Melman, *C.I.A. Report,* p. 93, quoting a CIA report on the Israeli intelligence community, dated 1976 and published by the Iranian militants who seized the U.S. embassy in Teheran in 1979.
10. Ibid.
11. Ibid.
12. Yaari, *Fatah,* pp. 91–103.
13. *Yediot Aharonot* devoted an investigative issue in April 1988 to Israel's occupation of the territories; see also David Grossman, *The Yellow Wind* (Jerusalem: Keter, 1987) [Hebrew edition]; see also *Koteret Rashit,* "The Swiss Scenery," April 29, 1987.
14. *Hadashot,* November 6, 1987.
15. *Hadashot,* June 19, 1987.
16. Yossi Melman and Dan Raviv, "Expelling Palestinians," in *Washington Post,* "Outlook" section, February 7, 1988.
17. Haber, *Lior,* p. 324.
18. *Ma'ariv,* February 2, 1989.
19. Haber, *Lior,* pp. 328–30.
20. Steven, *Spymasters,* pp. 304–5; also Haber and Schiff, *Israel, Army, and Defense,* p. 195.
21. Haber, *Lior,* pp. 343–4; Haber and Schiff, *Israel, Army, and Defense,* p. 74.
22. *International Herald Tribune* and *Washington Post,* April 22, 1988; see also *Hadashot,* December 2, 1988.
23. Haber and Schiff, *Israel, Army, and Defense,* pp. 322–3; *Daily Express* [London], "Israel Stole Seven Tons of Secrets," January 3, 1970.
24. Advertisement which appeared several times in early 1988 in *Yediot Aharonot.*
25. *Ma'ariv,* September 23, 1987, and February 5, 1988.
26. *Hadashot,* November 6, 1987.
27. Steven, *Spymasters,* pp. 309–10.
28. Yoel Marcus was the first journalist to expose the activities of "Committee X," in *Ha'aretz,* June 10, 1986.
29. Operational details can be found in David B. Tinnin with Dag Christensen, *The Hit Team* (London: Futura Books, 1977).
30. *Monitin,* February 1988.
31. Michael Bar-Zohar and Eitan Haber, *The Quest for the Red Prince* (London: Weidenfeld and Nicolson, 1983), pp. 215–21; Steven, *Spymasters,* pp. 339–52; David Ignatius in *Wall Street Journal,* February 10, 1983.
32. *Ma'ariv,* April 19, 1987; Steve Posner, *Israel Undercover: Secret Warfare and Hidden Diplomacy in the Middle East* (Syracuse, N.Y.: Syracuse University Press, 1987), pp. 20–78.

9: The Secret Weapon

1. Golan, *Road to Peace,* p. 73.
2. *Ha'aretz,* January 5, 1978, quoting *Newsweek.*
3. Ibid., and *Washington Post,* June 5, 1986.
4. *Washington Post,* December 5, 1987.
5. United Press International, June 14, 1986.

6. Pringle and Spiegelman, *Nuclear Barons,* p. 297. The complete story was published in Elaine Davenport, Paul Eddy, and Peter Gillman, *The Plumbat Affair* (London: Andre Deutsch, 1978). Also see *Ha'aretz,* June 26, 1978.
7. *Ha'aretz,* January 5, 1978.
8. Melman, *C.I.A. Report,* p. 52.
9. *Ha'aretz,* April 17 and May 22, 1987.
10. Israeli Defense Ministry memorandum on Weizman-Turfanian meeting in Tel Aviv, dated July 18, 1977, marked "Top Secret" but published by the Islamic militants who seized the U.S. embassy in Teheran in 1979.
11. *Ma'ariv,* September 20, 1988; also Perlmutter, Handel, and Bar-Joseph, *Two Minutes over Baghdad,* p. 46.
12. Steven, *Spymasters,* pp. 210–20; Eisenberg, Dan, and Landau, *Mossad,* pp. 177–98, 212–27.
13. The history of Lakam, published here for the first time, was related to the authors by sources who demanded anonymity.

10: The Surprises of War and Peace

1. *Ha'ir,* October 2, 1987; Haber and Schiff, *Israel, Army, and Defense,* p. 219.
2. Bamford, *Puzzle Palace.*
3. Melman, *C.I.A. Report,* pp. 69–75.
4. Richard Nixon, *RN: The Memoirs of Richard Nixon,* vol. 2 (New York: Warner Books, 1978), p. 475.
5. Sadat, quoted in Marvin Kalb and Bernard Kalb, *Kissinger* (New York: Dell Publishing, 1975), p. 514.
6. Haber, *Lior,* p. 20; also Yoel Ben-Porat in *Al Hamishmar,* September 20, 1988. Ben-Porat was in charge of an Aman review panel that investigated "the Yom Kippur surprise" and traded accusations with Zvi Zamir in *Monitin* magazine, September and December 1988; Zamir threatened to sue Ben-Porat and the magazine.
7. Dayan told Israeli newspaper editors on October 8, 1973; also Perlmutter, *Two Minutes,* pp. 43–9.
8. *Koteret Rashit,* November 16, 1988.
9. Perlmutter, *Two Minutes,* pp. 43–51.
10. *Davar,* weekly supplement, December 7, 1987.
11. Classified CIA report on Israel's intelligence community, published by the Islamic militants who seized the U.S. embassy in Teheran in 1979.
12. Melman, *C.I.A. Report,* pp. 101–4.
13. Melman and Raviv, *Behind the Uprising.*
14. Bob Woodward, *Veil: The Secret Wars of the CIA 1981–1987* (New York: Simon and Schuster, 1987), p. 381; earlier revealed by Woodward's *Washington Post* colleague Don Oberdorfer.
15. Woodward, *Veil,* p. 308; and Steven, *Spymasters,* p. 240.
16. Haber and Schiff, *Israel, Army, and Defense,* p. 203.
17. See William Stevenson, *90 Minutes at Entebbe* (New York: Bantam Books, 1976).
18. Melman, *C.I.A. Report,* p. 57.
19. Davenport et al., *Plumbat Affair,* pp. 178–9.
20. Stevenson, *90 Minutes at Entebbe;* Bloch and Fitzgerald, *British,* pp. 128–9, 159–160; *Ha'aretz,* April 3, 1981; *Davar,* May 28 and 29, 1978.
21. Kol Israel radio report, June 8, 1983.

22. Ali told the tale to Israeli official Dan Pattir, who later told *Ma'ariv*, November 22, 1987.
23. Moshe Dayan, *Breakthrough: A Personal Account of the Egypt-Israel Peace Negotiations* (New York: Alfred A. Knopf, 1981), pp. 43–4, 52.
24. Major General Shlomo Gazit, in *Ma'ariv*, January 7, 1983.
25. Ze'ev Schiff, *A History of the Israeli Army* (New York: Macmillan, 1985), p. 204.
26. Ehud Yaari, in *Monitin*, September 1986.

11: For the Good of the Jews

1. Tudor Parfitt, *Operation Moses* (New York: Stein and Day, 1985), serialized by *Yediot Aharonot*, October 25, 1985.
2. Ibid.; Yehiel Kadishai, interviewed by the authors, October 31, 1988.
3. Ettinger, *Jump*, pp. 378, 390.
4. *Ha'ir*, October 23, 1987.
5. *Ha'aretz*, May 4, 1981.
6. *Ha'aretz*, January 11, 1988; and Ilya Dzhirkvelov, *Secret Servant: My Life with the KGB and the Soviet Elite* (London: Collins, 1987), pp. 244–9.
7. Pincher, *Traitors*, p. 98; *Ha'aretz*, December 1, 1982.
8. *Ma'ariv*, November 4, 1988.
9. Ibid.; *Ha'aretz*, January 11, 1988.
10. *Al Hamishmar*, May 15, 1988; *Yediot Aharonot*, February 26 and May 15, 1988; *Davar*, December 6, 1988; *CB Weapons Today* (Stockholm: Stockholm International Peace Research Institute, 1973), vol. 2:242.
11. Ettinger, *Jump*, p. 13.
12. Ibid., p. 386; Harel, *Soviet*, pp. 24–5.
13. *Ma'ariv*, October 19, 1987; Ettinger, *Jump*, p. 386.
14. *Ha'aretz*, November 18, 1988.
15. Kadishai, interviewed by the authors.
16. *Koteret Rashit*, October 30, 1985; *Yediot Aharonot*, October 25 and November 2, 1985, serializing Parfitt, *Moses*.
17. *Koteret Rashit*, October 30, 1985; *Ma'ariv*, November 3, 1988.

12: The Age of Adventurism

1. *Ma'ariv*, May 13, 1988, report by Shin Bet operative Noam Federman.
2. Ariel Sharon, *Warrior: The Autobiography of Ariel Sharon* (New York: Simon and Schuster, 1989), p. 84.
3. Haber and Schiff, *Israel, Army, and Defense*, pp. 462, 521–3; Sharon, *Warrior*, pp. 84–91.
4. Sharon, *Warrior*, pp. 260–2.
5. Shlomo Nakdimon, *Tammuz in Flames* (Jerusalem: Edanim/Yediot Aharonot, 1986), pp. 38–47; also Perlmutter, *Two Minutes*, pp. 58–60.
6. Nakdimon, *Tammuz*, p. 88; Perlmutter, *Two Minutes*, pp. 69–70.
7. Perlmutter, *Two Minutes*, pp. 69–70; *Yediot Aharonot*, October 16, 1987.
8. Nakdimon, *Tammuz*, pp. 83, 100.
9. Quoted by various cabinet ministers, anonymously, to Israeli journalists in 1980.
10. *Washington Post*, "Outlook" section, May 31, 1987.

11. Avraham Tamir, interviewed by the authors, November 28, 1988.
12. *Ha'aretz,* June 18, 1981.
13. *Ma'ariv,* June 22, 1981.
14. Nakdimon, *Tammuz,* pp. 294–5.
15. Speech by Ariel Sharon on November 7, 1981, at the Jaffe Center for Strategic Studies at the University of Tel Aviv.
16. *Davar,* April 22, 1984.
17. Sharon, *Warrior,* p. 416. Additional details were disclosed by separate sources who took part in the secret contacts but insisted on anonymity.
18. The Mossad's crushing of the Sudan-Iran project was revealed to author Raviv by confidential sources.
19. Woodward, *Veil,* pp. 204–12.
20. Shimon Shiffer, *Snow Ball: The Story Behind the Lebanon War* (Jerusalem: Edanim/Yediot Aharonot, 1984).
21. Sharon, *Warrior,* p. 443.
22. Thomas Friedman, *From Beirut to Jerusalem* (New York: Harper and Row, 1989), p. 139.
23. Sharon, *Warrior,* pp. 444, 449.
24. Ibid., pp. 452–4.
25. Ibid., p. 455.
26. Ibid., p. 499.
27. Ibid., p. 502.
28. *Ha'aretz,* August 14, 1983, October 10, 1983, January 25, 1983; based on reports in the "Foreign Report" of the *Economist.*
29. Various Israeli newspaper accounts, February 15 to 25, 1983.

13: Killings and Coverups

1. *Hadashot,* September 23, 1987.
2. Alex Libak, interviewed by the authors, November 13, 1988.
3. *Koteret Rashit,* May 28, 1986
4. Ibid.
5. Ibid.
6. Karp Commission Report, published by Government of Israel, December 30, 1987.
7. *Washington Post,* April 12, 1987.
8. *Hadashot,* September 23, 1987.
9. *Yediot Aharonot,* May 29, 1987.
10. *Yediot Aharonot,* June 2, 1987.
11. *Yediot Aharonot,* May 29, 1987.
12. *Hadashot,* November 4, 1988.
13. *Yediot Aharonot,* November 11, 1987.
14. *Koteret Rashit,* December 2, 1987.
15. Landau Commission Report, published by the Government of Israel, December 1, 1987.

14: A Spy in America

1. *Washington Post,* November 24, 1985.
2. *New York Times,* November 27, 1985; and *Washington Post,* November 30, 1985.

3. *U.S. News and World Report,* June 1, 1987.
4. *Washington Post,* October 30, 1986; *Ha'aretz, Davar,* and *Al-Hamishmar,* November 2, 1986.
5. Wolf Blitzer, *Territory of Lies* (New York: Harper and Row, 1989), pp. 90–1.
6. Ibid., pp. 96, 130–1.
7. *U.S. News and World Report,* June 1, 1987.
8. Blitzer, *Territory of Lies,* p. 169.
9. *Washington Post,* November 23, 1985.
10. *U.S. News and World Report,* June 1, 1987.
11. *Washington Post,* June 7, 1986.
12. Blitzer, *Territory of Lies,* pp. 142–4.
13. *Los Angeles Times,* November 27, 1985.
14. CIA, *Israel: Foreign Intelligence* ["Secret"], p. 9.
15. *New York Times,* March 5, 1987.
16. *Time,* March 16, 1987.
17. *Washington Post* and *New York Times,* December 21, 1985.
18. *Hadashot,* March 15, 1987.
19. *Los Angeles Times,* March 7, 1987.
20. *Christian Science Monitor* and *Los Angeles Times,* March 4, 1987.
21. *Los Angeles Times,* March 7, 1987.
22. A former Director of Central Intelligence, who preferred not to be named, interviewed by the authors, April 14, 1988.

15: The Chaos of Irangate

1. Stephen Green, *Living by the Sword: America and Israel in the Middle East, 1968–1987* (London: Faber and Faber, 1988), p. 218.
2. Haber and Schiff, *Israel, Army, Defense,* p. 502.
3. BBC Television, "Panorama," February 1, 1982.
4. Kimche, interviewed in *Yediot Aharonot,* January 2, 1987.
5. The authors have read Ghorbanifar's secret study written for the Mossad.
6. *Davar,* December 12, 1986.
7. *New York Times,* December 3, 1988; *Washington Post,* December 2 and 3, 1988.
8. The sequence of events of Irangate was related to the authors by separate sources who took part in the events and even shared some relevant documents, but insisted on anonymity.

16: Business at All Costs

1. *Christian Science Monitor,* December 27, 1982.
2. CBS Evening News, February 20, 1980.
3. NBC Nightly News, October 25, 1989; *New York Times,* October 27, 1989.
4. *The Military Balance 1981/82* (London: International Institute of Strategic Studies, 1982).
5. Aaron Klieman, *Israel's Global Reach: Arms Sales as Diplomacy* (McLean, Virginia: Pergamon-Brassey's, 1985), pp. 2–7.
6. Yossi Melman and Dan Raviv, "Israel's Other Arms Deal," *Washington Post,* "Outlook" section, November 30, 1986.
7. *Los Angeles Times,* August 4, 1988.

8. *Christian Science Monitor,* April 24, 1986.
9. Harari appeared on Israeli television on January 6, 1990.
Ha'ir, June 5, 1987; *Ma'ariv,* January 22, 1988.
10. *Yediot Aharonot,* May 20, 1988.
11. Jonathan Marshall, Peter Dale Scott, and Jane Hunter, *The Iran-Contra Connection* (Boston: South End Press, 1987), pp. 115–20.
12. Ibid., pp. 92–105.
13. Yair Klein, interviewed on Israeli television, August 25, 1989.
14. The London *Sunday Telegraph,* July 8, 1984; Dan Raviv, in the *Glasgow Herald,* July 12, 1984.
15. *Ma'ariv,* April 25, 1988.
16. *Yediot Aharonot,* August 5, 1988, and March 3, 1989.

17: The Nuclear Traitor

1. Vanunu told his tale to *Sunday Times* [London], October 5, 1986.
2. *Hadashot* and *Yediot Aharonot,* November 3, 1986.
3. Ibid.
4. Reverend John McKnight, interviewed by the authors, December 16, 1986.
5. *Sunday Times,* October 5, 1986.
6. *Sunday Mirror* [London], September 29, 1986.
7. *Sunday Times,* November 16, 1986.
8. Ibid., and authors' interviews with members of *Sunday Times* reporting team.
9. Ibid.
10. *Sunday Times,* November 16, 1986.
11. *Jerusalem Post,* November 9, 1986.
12. *Jerusalem Post,* August 9, 1987.
13. *Yediot Aharonot,* March 28, 1988.
14. *Sunday Times,* February 21, 1988.
15. Haber and Schiff, *Israel, Army, Defense,* p. 416; London *Daily Telegraph,* June 16, 1988.
16. London *Daily Star,* August 18, 1987; *Sunday Telegraph,* May 8 and July 24, 1988; *Daily Telegraph* and *Independent,* June 16, 1988; *Daily Mail,* June 17, 1988; *Guardian,* June 18, 1988.
17. *Ma'ariv,* February 23, 1988.
18. The *Economist,* September 24, 1988.

18: The Death of the Informers

1. *Jerusalem Post,* February 26, 1988; *Los Angeles Times,* February 27, 1988; *Washington Post,* March 1, 1988.
2. *New York Times,* February 17, 1988.
3. *Washington Post,* April 17, 1988.
4. *Sunday Times,* April 24, 1988.
5. Ibid.
6. Yossi Melman, *The Master Terrorist: The True Story Behind Abu Nidal* (London: Sidgwick and Jackson, 1987), pp. 142–3, 170–4.
7. Reuters news agency, November 5 and 7, 1988.

8. Retired general Ariel Sharon, in charge of that operation, revealed the details in a *New York Times* interview, reprinted in *Ma'ariv,* November 10, 1988.
9. Reuters, August 24 and September 7, 1989.

19: A World Without Trust

1. Amir Oren in *Davar,* April 1, 1988.
2. "Role of the Israeli Military Censor," *Jane's Defence Weekly,* August 26, 1989, pp. 348–9.
3. *Ma'ariv,* March 4, 1988; *Yediot Aharonot* and *Ma'ariv,* February 24, 1989.
4. The journalist was David Halevy, writing in the *Washington Star.*
5. The network was ABC, and the censor had no proof that its news correspondent in Israel was behind the disclosure.
6. *Jane's Defence Weekly,* August 26, 1989, p. 349.
7. CIA, *Israel: Foreign Intelligence* ["Secret"], p. 9.
8. Avi Pazner, Prime Minister Shamir's spokesman, interviewed by the authors, September 22, 1988.
9. The Israeli version of the Pollard affair was recounted in the *New York Times,* November 29, 1985; the major participants in the leak were interviewed by the authors.
10. Glenn Frankel of the *Washington Post* and Martin Fletcher of NBC News temporarily lost their Israeli government-granted press credentials in 1988 for reporting that Israel killed Abu Jihad in Tunisia. Similar action was taken later that year against Paul Taylor and Steve Weizman of Reuters, for reporting rumors of Israeli death squads in the West Bank; in 1980, against one of the authors, Dan Raviv of CBS News, for reporting on Israel–South Africa nuclear development; and, in 1970, against CBS Radio newsman Tony Hatch, when Israeli officials were especially angry that he reported on a commando raid into Egypt while it was still in progress.
11. *Ha'aretz,* September 1, 1982.
12. *Ha'aretz,* December 31, 1989; *Yediot Aharonot,* January 5, 1990.

20: Into the Future

1. *Washington Post,* September 20, 1988; and *Time,* August 29, 1988. Strategic analysts Seth Carus, Paul Rogers, Aaron Karp, Martin Nevias, and Captain John Moore contributed background to the discussion that follows.
2. BBC Television, "Panorama," September 11, 1989.
3. CIA, *Israel: Foreign Intelligence* ["Secret"], p. 40.
4. Archie Roosevelt, *For Lust of Knowing: Memoirs of an Intelligence Officer* (London: Weidenfeld and Nicolson, 1987), p. 468; and Nigel West, *Games of Intelligence* (London: Weidenfeld and Nicolson, 1989), pp. 171, 176–7, 180.
5. Reuters Information Services, "Shamir Accused of Lying on P.L.O. Report," March 22, 1989.
6. *Davar,* February 9, 1989, citing New York's *Village Voice.*

BIBLIOGRAPHY

Books in English

Adams, James. *Secret Armies: The Full Story of SAS, Delta Force and Spetsnaz.* London: Hutchinson, 1987.

Bahbah, Bishara. *Israel and Latin America: The Military Connection.* New York: St. Martin's Press, 1986.

Bar-Zohar, Michael, and Eitan Haber. *The Quest for the Red Prince.* London: Weidenfeld and Nicolson, 1983.

Barnaby, Frank. *The Invisible Bomb: The Nuclear Arms Race in the Middle East.* London: I. B. Tauris, 1989.

Beit-Hallahmi, Benjamin. *The Israeli Connection: Who Israel Arms and Why.* New York: Pantheon, 1987.

Blitzer, Wolf. *Territory of Lies.* New York: Harper and Row, 1989.

Bloch, Jonathan, and Patrick Fitzgerald. *British Intelligence and Covert Action.* London: Junction, 1983.

Breecher, Michael. *Decisions in Israel's Foreign Policy.* London: Oxford University Press, 1974.

———. *The Foreign Policy System of Israel.* London: Oxford University Press, 1972.

Cookridge, E. H. *Gehlen: Spy of the Century.* New York: Random House, 1971.

Copeland, Miles. *The Game Player.* London: Aurum, 1989.

Davenport, Elaine, Paul Eddy, and Peter Gillman. *The Plumbat Affair.* London: Andre Deutsch, 1978.

Dayan, Moshe. *Breakthrough: A Personal Account of the Egypt-Israel Peace Negotiations.* New York: Alfred A. Knopf, 1981.

Deacon, Richard (Donald McCormick) *"C": A Biography of Sir Maurice Oldfield, Head of MI6.* London: Futura, 1985.

———. *The Israeli Secret Service.* London: Sphere, 1979.

———. *Spyclopedia.* London: Macdonald, 1988.

Deacon, Richard, with Nigel West. *Spy!* London: Grafton, 1988.

Dzhirkvelov, Ilya. *Secret Servant: My Life with the KGB and the Soviet Elite.* London: Collins, 1987.

Eisenberg, Dennis, Eli Landau, and Menahem Portugali. *Operation Uranium Ship.* Tel Aviv: Steimatzky's, 1978.

Eisenberg, Dennis, Uri Dan, and Eli Landau. *The Mossad, Israel's Secret Intelligence Service: Inside Stories.* New York: New American Library, 1978.

El-Ad, Avri. *Decline of Honor.* Chicago: Regency, 1976.

Elkins, Michael. *Forged in Fury.* London: Corgi, 1982.

Friedman, Thomas J. *From Beirut to Jerusalem.* New York: Harper and Row, 1989.

Gabriel, Richard A. *Operation Peace for Galilee: The Israeli-PLO War in Lebanon.* New York: Hill and Wang, 1984.

Golan, Aviezer, and Danny Pinkas. *Shula, Code Name the Pearl.* New York: Delacorte Press, 1980.

Golan, Matti. *The Road to Peace: A Biography of Shimon Peres.* New York: Warner Books, 1989.

Green, Stephen. *Living by the Sword: America and Israel in the Middle East, 1968–1987.* London: Faber and Faber, 1988.

———. *Taking Sides: America's Secret Relations with a Militant Israel.* New York: William Morrow, 1984.

Haber, Eitan, Ze'ev Schiff, and Ehud Yaari. *The Year of the Dove.* New York: Bantam, 1979.

Hart, Alan. *Arafat: Terrorist or Peacemaker?* London: Sidgwick and Jackson, 1984.

Henderson, Bernard R. *Pollard: The Spy's Story.* New York: Alpha, 1988.

International Institute of Strategic Studies (IISS). *The Military Balance 1981/82.* London: IISS, 1982.

Jonas, George. *Vengeance: The True Story of a Counter-terrorist Mission.* London: Collins, 1984.

Kalb, Marvin, and Bernard Kalb. *Kissinger.* New York: Dell, 1975.

Kessler, Ronald. *Khashoggi: The Rise and Fall of the World's Richest Man.* London: Corgi, 1987.

Kissinger, Henry. *Years of Upheaval.* Boston: Little, Brown, 1982.

Klieman, Aaron S. *Israel's Global Reach: Arms Sales as Diplomacy.* McLean, Virginia: Pergamon Brassey/International Defence, 1985.

Knightley, Philip. *The Second Oldest Profession: The Spy as Bureaucrat, Patriot, Fantasist and Whore.* London: Pan Books, 1987.

Laqueur, Walter. *A World of Secrets: The Use and Limits of Intelligence.* New York: Basic Books, 1985.

le Carré, John (David J. M. Cornwell). *The Little Drummer Girl.* London: Hodder and Stoughton, 1983.

Lotz, Wolfgang. *The Champagne Spy.* New York: St. Martin's Press, 1972.

Marshall, Jonathan, Peter Dale Scott, and Jane Hunter. *The Iran-Contra Connection: Secret Teams and Covert Operations in the Reagan Era.* Boston: South End Press, 1987.

Martin, David C. *Wilderness of Mirrors.* New York: Harper and Row, 1980.

Martin, David C., and John Walcott. *Best Laid Plans: The Inside Story of America's War Against Terrorism.* New York: Harper and Row, 1988.

Melman, Yossi. *The Master Terrorist: The True Story Behind Abu Nidal.* London: Sidgwick and Jackson, 1987.

Melman, Yossi, and Dan Raviv. *Behind the Uprising: Israelis, Jordanians and Palestinians.* Westport, Connecticut: Greenwood, 1989.

Ninio, Marcelle. *Operation Susannah.* New York: Harper and Row, 1978.

Nixon, Richard M. *RN: The Memoirs of Richard Nixon.* New York: Warner Books, 1978.

Parfitt, Tudor. *Operation Moses: The Untold Story of the Secret Exodus of the Falasha Jews from Ethiopia.* New York: Stein and Day, 1985.

Perlmutter, Amos, Michael Handel, and Uri Bar-Joseph. *Two Minutes over Baghdad.* London: Vallentine Mitchell, 1982.

Pincher, Chapman. *Traitors: Labyrinths of Treason.* London: Sidgwick and Jackson, 1987.
Posner, Steve. *Israel Undercover: Secret Warfare and Hidden Diplomacy in the Middle East.* Syracuse, New York: Syracuse University Press, 1987.
President's Special Review Board. *The Tower Commission Report.* New York: Bantam and Times Books, 1987.
Pringle, Peter, and James Spiegelman. *The Nuclear Barons: The Inside Story of How They Created Our Nuclear Nightmare.* London: Michael Joseph, 1982.
Randal, Jonathan C. *The Tragedy of Lebanon.* London: Chatto and Windus, 1984.
Ranelagh, John. *The Agency: The Rise and Decline of the CIA.* London: Weidenfeld and Nicolson, 1986.
Roosevelt, Archie. *For Lust of Knowing: Memoirs of an Intelligence Officer.* London: Weidenfeld and Nicolson, 1987.
Sachar, Howard M. *A History of Israel.* New York: Alfred A. Knopf, 1985.
Schiff, Ze'ev. *A History of the Israeli Army: 1874 to the Present.* New York: Macmillan, 1985.
Segev, Samuel *The Iranian Triangle: The Untold Story of Israel's Role in the Iran-Contra Affair.* New York: Free Press, 1988.
Sharon, Ariel. *Warrior: The Autobiography of Ariel Sharon.* New York: Simon and Schuster, 1989.
Sterling, Claire. *The Terror Network.* New York: Berkley, 1982.
Steven, Stewart. *The Spymasters of Israel.* New York: Ballantine Books, 1980.
Stevenson, William. *90 Minutes at Entebbe.* New York: Bantam, 1976.
Tadmor, Joshua. *The Silent Warriors.* New York: Macmillan, 1970.
Tinnin, David B., with Dag Christensen. *Hit Team.* London: Futura, 1976.
Toronska, Teresa. *Oni [Them].* London: An-Eks, 1985.
Turner, Stansfield. *Secrecy and Democracy: The CIA in Transition.* London: Sidgwick and Jackson, 1986.
West, Nigel. *Games of Intelligence.* London: Weidenfeld and Nicolson, 1989.
Woodward, Bob. *Veil: The Secret Wars of the CIA, 1981–1987.* New York: Simon and Schuster, 1987.
Wright, Peter. *Spycatcher: The Candid Autobiography of a Senior Intelligence Officer.* New York: Viking-Penguin, 1987.

Books in Hebrew

Bar-Zohar, Michael. *Bridge over the Mediterranean: Israeli-French Relations, 1947–1963.* Tel Aviv: Am Hasefer, 1965.
———. *Isser Harel and Israel's Security Services.* Jerusalem: Weidenfeld and Nicolson, 1970.
Beer, Israel. *Israel's Security: Yesterday, Today, Tomorrow.* Tel Aviv: Amikam, 1966.
Eliav, Aryeh (Lova). *Rings of Faith.* Tel Aviv: Am-Oved, 1983.
Eshed, Hagai. *One-Man Mossad: Reuven Shiloah, Father of Israeli Intelligence.* Jerusalem: Edanim/Yediot Aharonot, 1988.
Ettinger, Amos. *Blind Jump: The Story of Yeshayahu (Shaike) Dan.* Tel Aviv: Zmora Bitan, 1986.
Freundlich, Yehoshua, ed. *Documents on the Foreign Policy of Israel,* Vol. 5: *1950.* Jerusalem: State of Israel Archives, 1988.

Gazit, Shlomo. *The Stick and the Carrot: The Israeli Administration in Judea and Samaria.* Tel Aviv: Zmora Bitan, 1985.

Goren, Dina. *Secrecy, Security and the Freedom of the Press.* Jerusalem: Magnes/Hebrew University Press, 1976.

Golan, Matti. *Peres.* Tel Aviv: Schocken, 1982.

Grossman, David. *The Yellow Wind.* Jerusalem: Keter, 1987.

Haber, Eitan. *Today War Will Break Out: The Reminiscences of Brigadier General Israel Lior, Aide-de-Camp to Prime Ministers Levi Eshkol and Golda Meir.* Jerusalem: Edanim/Yediot Aharonot, 1988.

Harel, Isser. *Security and Democracy.* Jerusalem: Edanim/Yediot Aharonot, 1989.

———. *Soviet Espionage: Communism in Israel.* Jerusalem: Edanim/Yediot Aharonot, 1987.

Hillel, Shlomo. *Operation Babylon.* Jerusalem: Edanim/Yediot Aharonot, 1985.

Kenan, Amos. *Your Land, Your Country.* Jerusalem: Edanim/Yediot Aharonot, 1981.

Kotler, Yair. *Joe Returns to the Limelight.* Tel Aviv: Modan, 1988.

Mann, Peter, and Uri Dan. *Eichmann in My Hands.* Tel Aviv: Massada, 1987.

Melman, Yossi. *The CIA Report on the Israeli Intelligence Community.* Tel Aviv: Erez/Zmora Bitan Modan, 1982.

———. *A Profile of a Terrorist Organisation.* Tel Aviv: Hadar, 1984.

Nakdimon, Shlomo. *Tammuz in Flames.* Jerusalem: Edanim/Yediot Aharonot, 1986.

Ronen, David. *The Year of Shabak.* Tel Aviv: Ministry of Defense, 1989.

Schiff, Ze'ev, and Eitan Haber, eds. *Israel, Army and Defence: A Dictionary.* Tel Aviv: Zmora Bitan Modan, 1976.

Segev, Samuel. *Alone in Damascus: The Life and Death of Eli Cohen.* Tel Aviv: Keter, 1986.

———. *The Iranian Triangle: The Secret Relations Between Israel-Iran-U.S.A.* Tel Aviv: Ma'ariv Books, 1981.

———. *The Iranian Triangle.* Jerusalem: Domino Press, 1988.

Segev, Tom. *1949: The First Israelis.* Jerusalem: Domino Press, 1984.

Shiffer, Shimon. *Snow Ball: The Story Behind the Lebanon War.* Jerusalem: Edanim/Yediot Aharonot, 1984.

Yaari, Ehud. *Fatah.* Tel Aviv: A. Levin Epstein, 1970.

Zak, Moshe. *Israel and the Soviet Union: A Forty-Year Dialogue.* Tel Aviv: Ma'ariv Book Guild, 1988.

Zvi, Ofer, and Avi Kober. *Intelligence and National Security.* Tel Aviv: Maarachot/Ministry of Defense, 1987.

INDEX

DATE DUE			
SEP 2 9 2011			